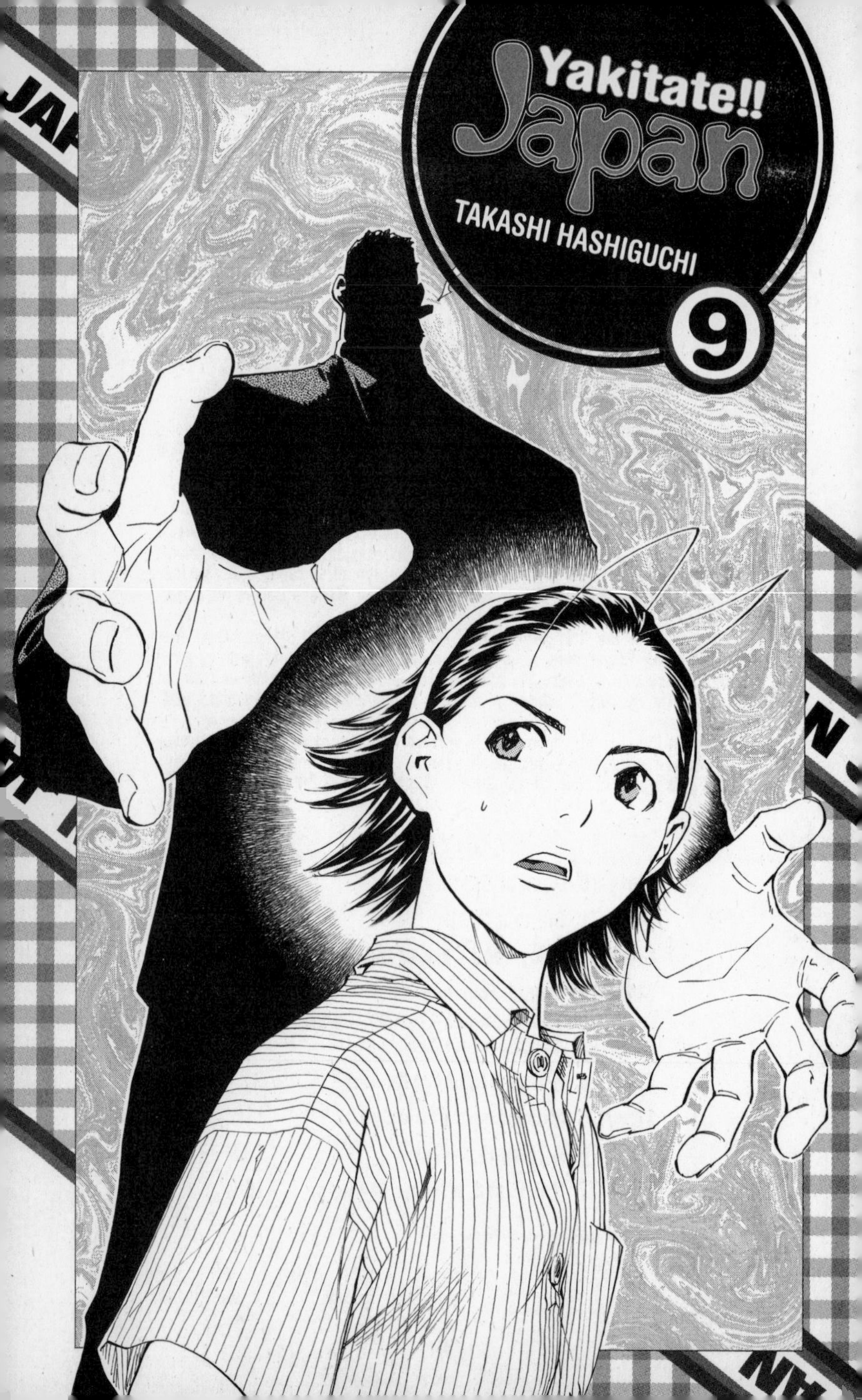

Yakitate!! Japan
TAKASHI HASHIGUCHI
9

JAPAN JAPAN JAPAN JAPAN

# YAKITATE!! JAPAN 9

## VIZ Media Edition

### ★The Story Thus Far★

Kazuma Azuma and his teammates aim to win the Monaco Cup Championship and obtain ten billion yen to prevent their bakery Pantasia from being taken over.

In the exhibition before the actual competition, Team Pantasia's "ten billion-yen Rodin" scheme results in the gambling odds increasing in their favor. However, as a penalty for insulting the dignity of the tournament, they're forced to start the preliminaries with a two-point deduction—which is really bad considering the highest score that can be achieved in the Monaco Cup is ten points.

As they enter the first preliminary already at a marked disadvantage, their challenging assignment is to make bread using only flour and eggs. In this difficult task where the mere act of adding flavor seems like an impossibility, Kazuma's Castella Ja-pan sufficiently impresses the judge.

Then, in the second preliminary, Suwabara works hard so that he isn't overshadowed by Azuma's virtuosity. He bakes a bread that contains 34 ingredients and gets a perfect score. Team Japan brilliantly passes the preliminaries!!

### CONTENTS



Research Assistance/Bakery Consultant:
Koichi Uchimura.

JAPAN JAPAN JAPAN JAPAN

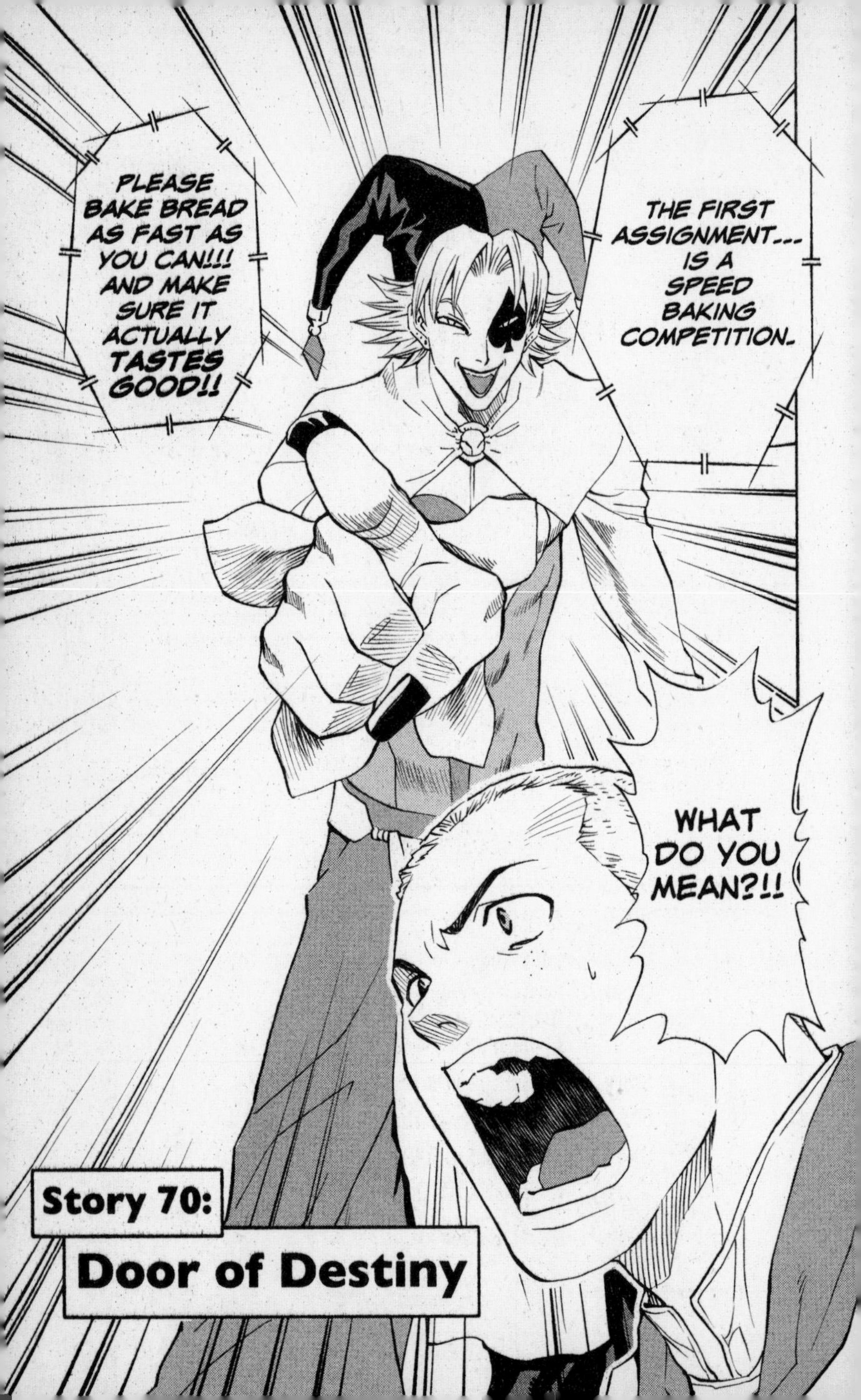
THE FIRST ASSIGNMENT... IS A SPEED BAKING COMPETITION.
PLEASE BAKE BREAD AS FAST AS YOU CAN!!! AND MAKE SURE IT ACTUALLY TASTES GOOD!!
WHAT DO YOU MEAN?!!
Story 70:
Door of Destiny

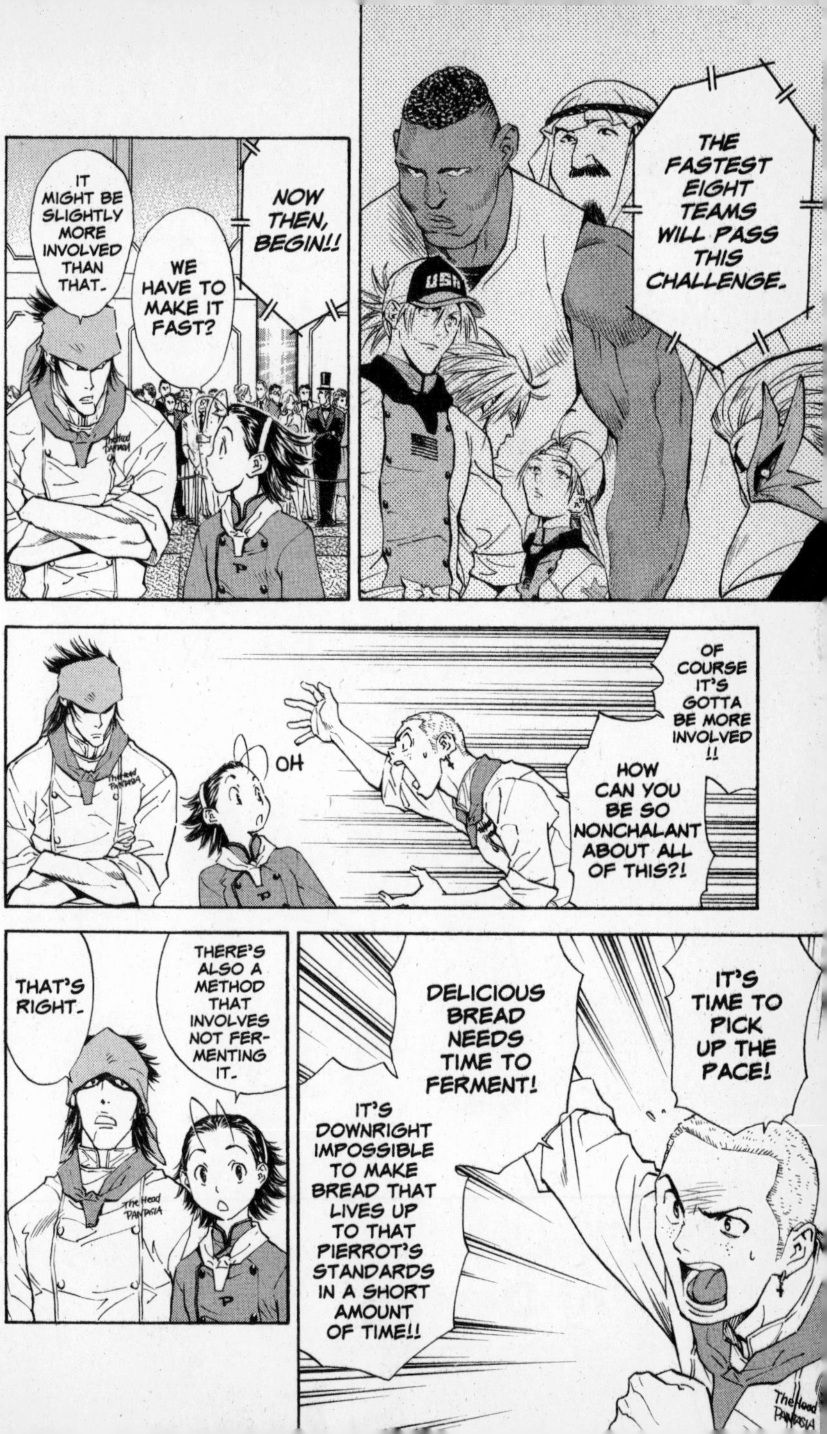
THE FASTEST EIGHT TEAMS WILL PASS THIS CHALLENGE.
NOW THEN, BEGIN!!
WE HAVE TO MAKE IT FAST?
IT MIGHT BE SLIGHTLY MORE INVOLVED THAN THAT.
OF COURSE IT'S GOTTA BE MORE INVOLVED!!
HOW CAN YOU BE SO NONCHALANT ABOUT ALL OF THIS?!
OH
IT'S TIME TO PICK UP THE PACE!
DELICIOUS BREAD NEEDS TIME TO FERMENT!
IT'S DOWNRIGHT IMPOSSIBLE TO MAKE BREAD THAT LIVES UP TO THAT PIERROT'S STANDARDS IN A SHORT AMOUNT OF TIME!!
THERE'S ALSO A METHOD THAT INVOLVES NOT FERMENTING IT.
THAT'S RIGHT.

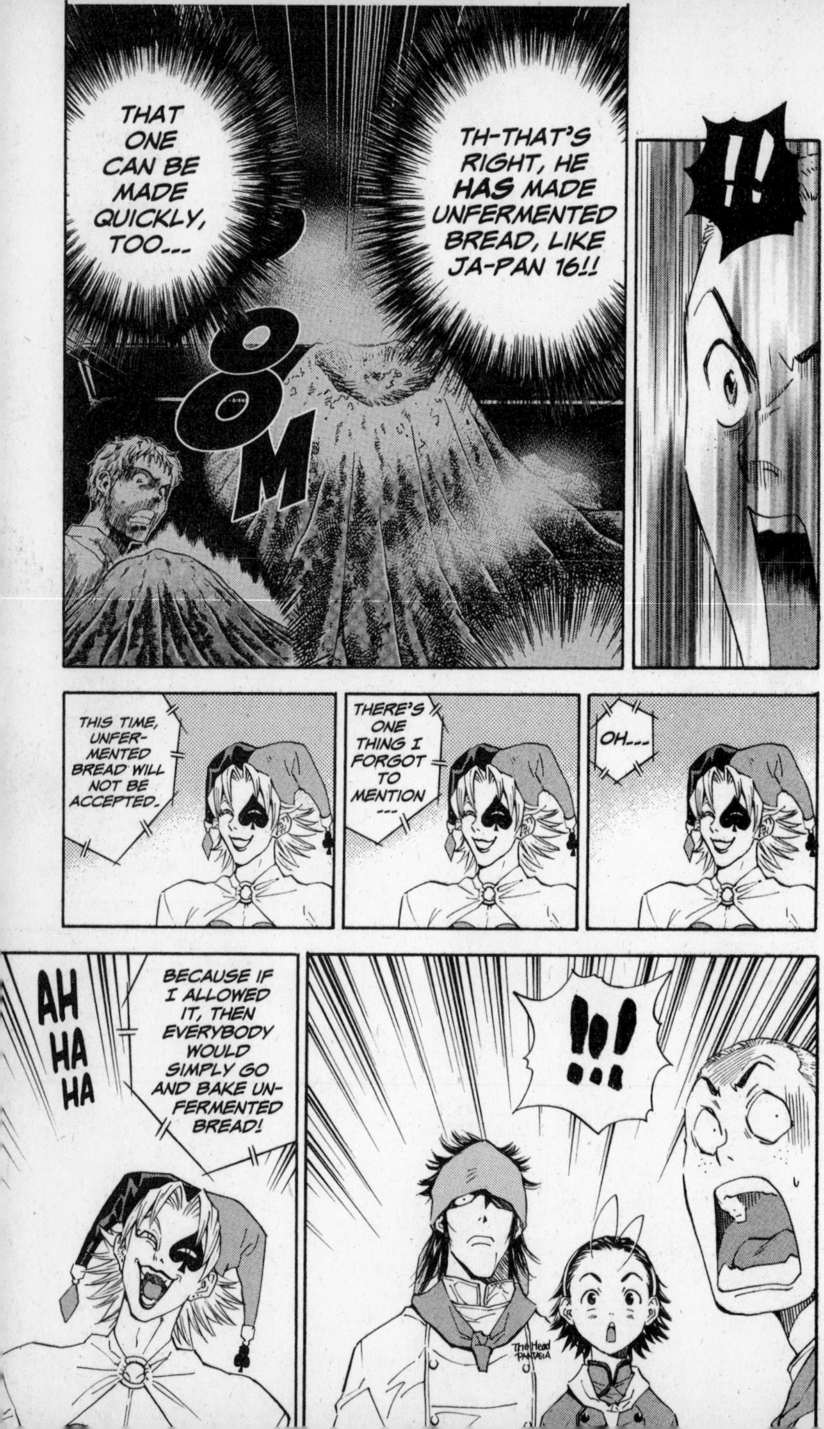
!!
TH-THAT'S RIGHT, HE HAS MADE UNFERMENTED BREAD, LIKE JA-PAN 16!!
THAT ONE CAN BE MADE QUICKLY, TOO...
OOM
OH...
THERE'S ONE THING I FORGOT TO MENTION...
THIS TIME, UNFERMENTED BREAD WILL NOT BE ACCEPTED.
!!
The Head PANTASIA
BECAUSE IF I ALLOWED IT, THEN EVERYBODY WOULD SIMPLY GO AND BAKE UNFERMENTED BREAD!
AH HA HA

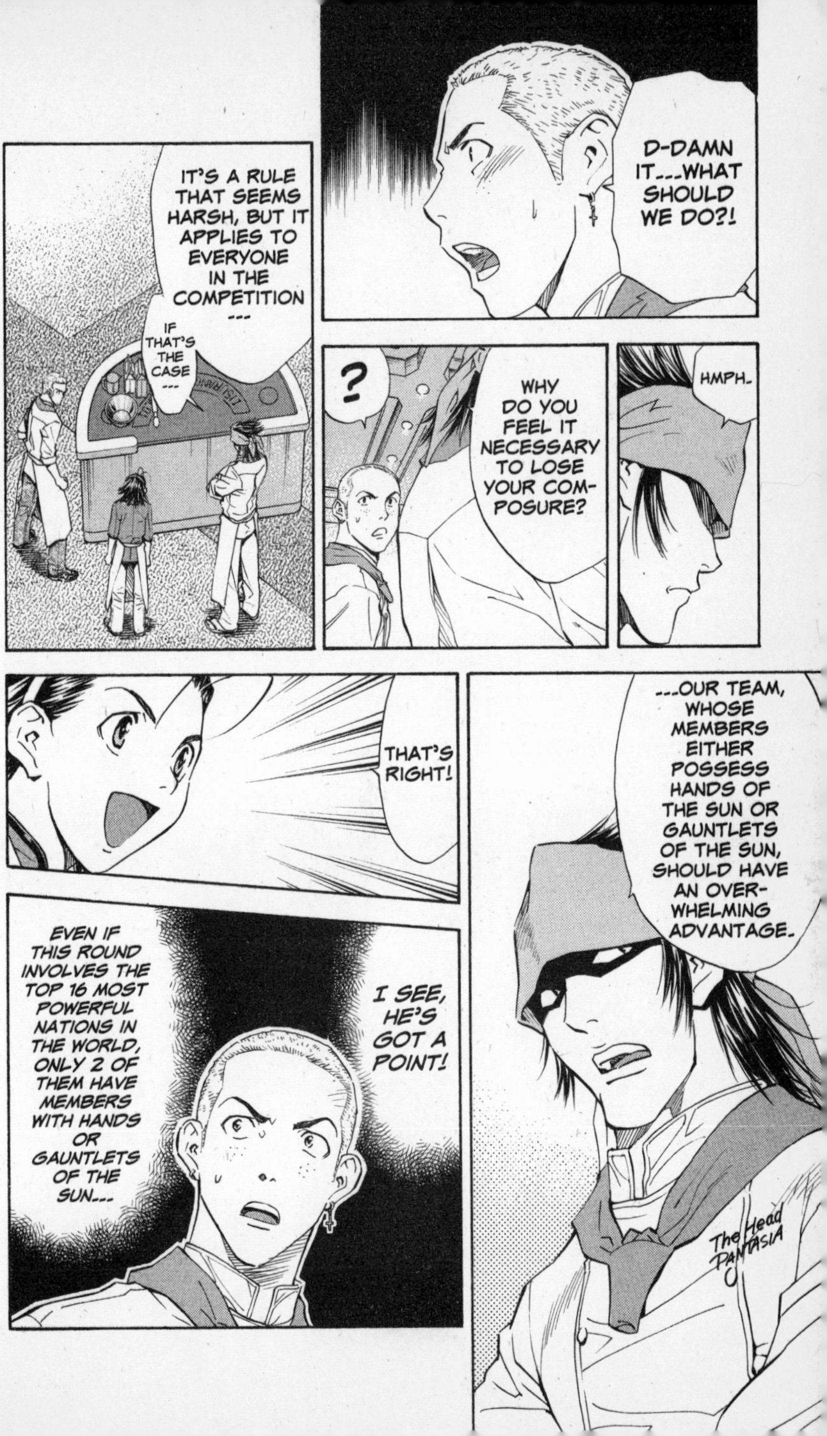
D-DAMN IT...WHAT SHOULD WE DO?!
HMPH.
?
WHY DO YOU FEEL IT NECESSARY TO LOSE YOUR COMPOSURE?
IT'S A RULE THAT SEEMS HARSH, BUT IT APPLIES TO EVERYONE IN THE COMPETITION...
IF THAT'S THE CASE...
...OUR TEAM, WHOSE MEMBERS EITHER POSSESS HANDS OF THE SUN OR GAUNTLETS OF THE SUN, SHOULD HAVE AN OVERWHELMING ADVANTAGE.
The Head PANTASIA
THAT'S RIGHT!
I SEE, HE'S GOT A POINT!
EVEN IF THIS ROUND INVOLVES THE TOP 16 MOST POWERFUL NATIONS IN THE WORLD, ONLY 2 OF THEM HAVE MEMBERS WITH HANDS OR GAUNTLETS OF THE SUN...

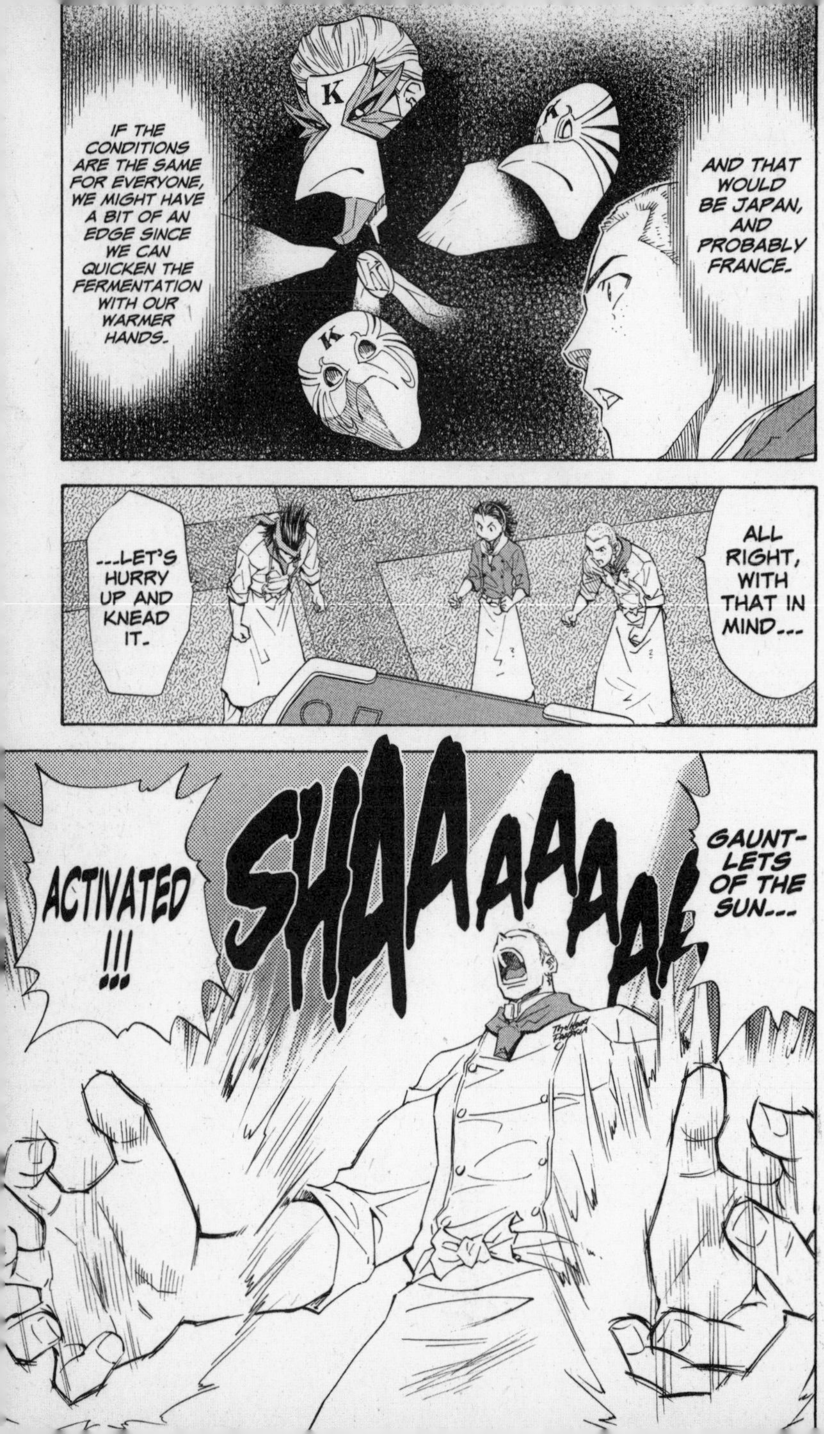
AND THAT WOULD BE JAPAN, AND PROBABLY FRANCE.
IF THE CONDITIONS ARE THE SAME FOR EVERYONE, WE MIGHT HAVE A BIT OF AN EDGE SINCE WE CAN QUICKEN THE FERMENTATION WITH OUR WARMER HANDS.
ALL RIGHT, WITH THAT IN MIND...
...LET'S HURRY UP AND KNEAD IT.
GAUNT-LETS OF THE SUN...
SHAAAAAAA
ACTIVATED!!!

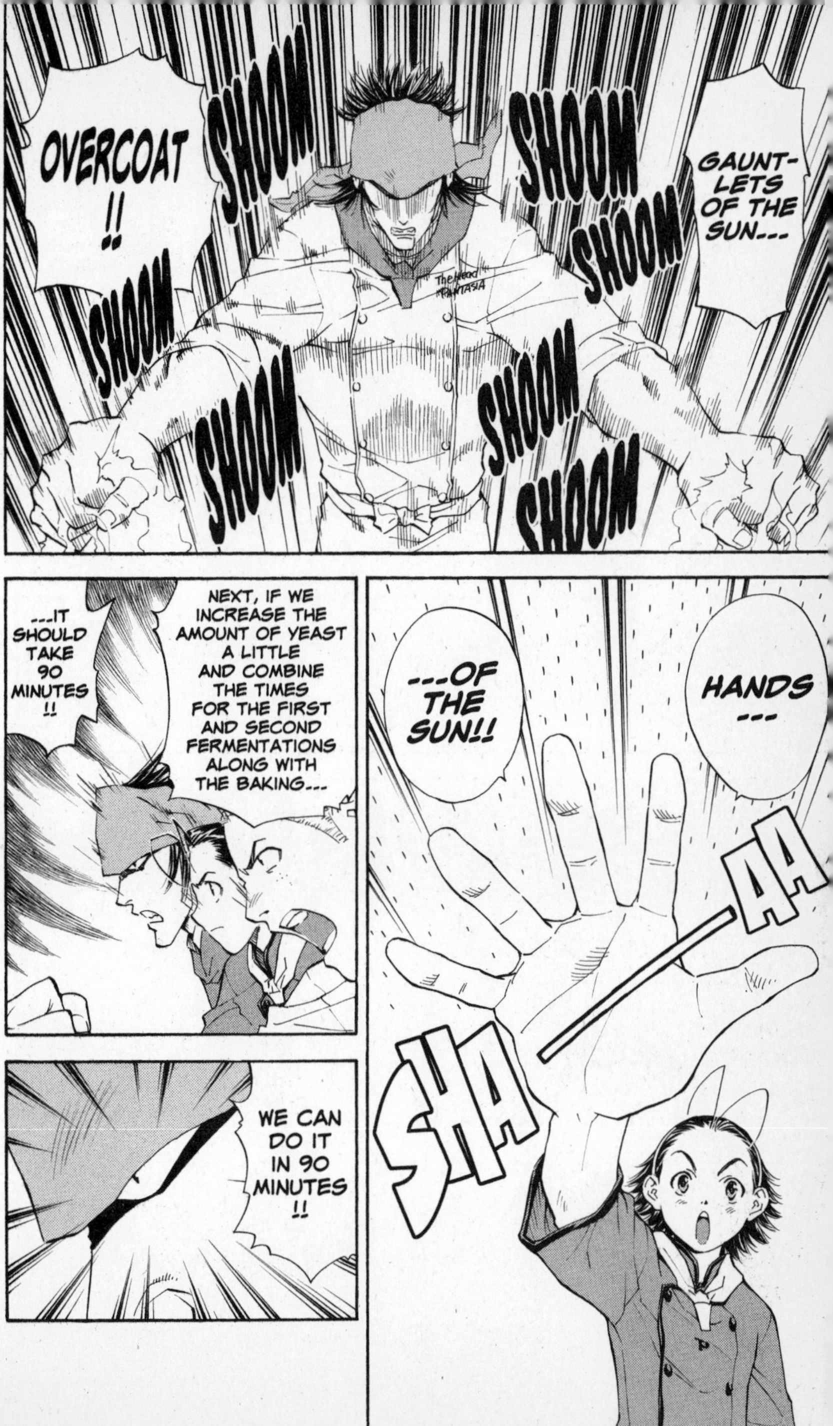
GAUNT-LETS OF THE SUN...
SHOOM SHOOM
SHOOM
SHOOM SHOOM
SHOOM
SHOOM
SHOOM
OVERCOAT !!
HANDS ---
---OF THE SUN!!
SHAAA
NEXT, IF WE INCREASE THE AMOUNT OF YEAST A LITTLE AND COMBINE THE TIMES FOR THE FIRST AND SECOND FERMENTATIONS ALONG WITH THE BAKING...
...IT SHOULD TAKE 90 MINUTES !!
WE CAN DO IT IN 90 MINUTES !!

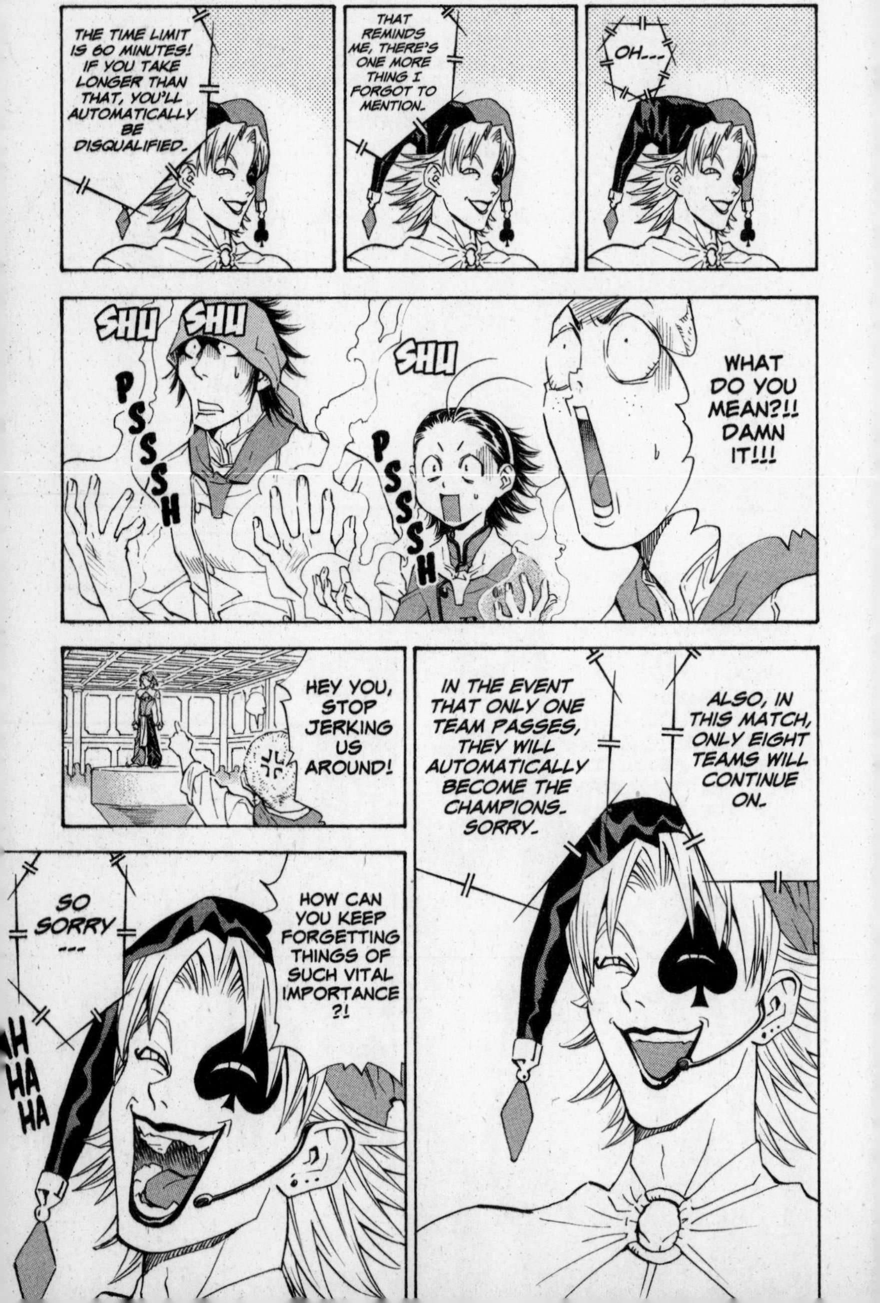
OH...
THAT REMINDS ME, THERE'S ONE MORE THING I FORGOT TO MENTION.
THE TIME LIMIT IS 60 MINUTES! IF YOU TAKE LONGER THAN THAT, YOU'LL AUTOMATICALLY BE DISQUALIFIED.
WHAT DO YOU MEAN?!! DAMN IT!!!
SHU
SHU SHU
PSSSH
PSSSSH
ALSO, IN THIS MATCH, ONLY EIGHT TEAMS WILL CONTINUE ON.
IN THE EVENT THAT ONLY ONE TEAM PASSES, THEY WILL AUTOMATICALLY BECOME THE CHAMPIONS. SORRY.
HEY YOU, STOP JERKING US AROUND!
HOW CAN YOU KEEP FORGETTING THINGS OF SUCH VITAL IMPORTANCE?!
SO SORRY...
HA HA

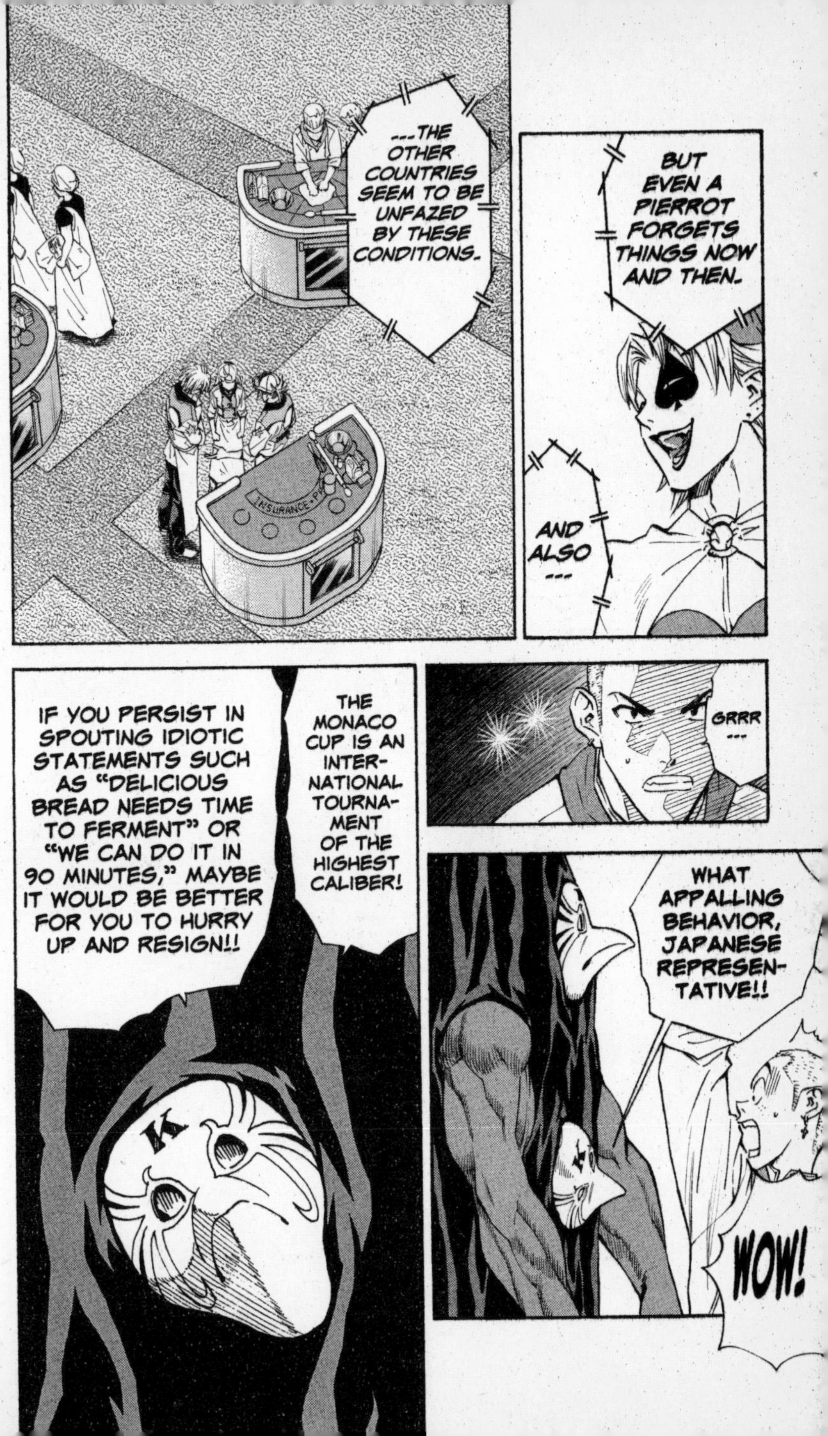
BUT EVEN A PIERROT FORGETS THINGS NOW AND THEN.
AND ALSO---
---THE OTHER COUNTRIES SEEM TO BE UNFAZED BY THESE CONDITIONS.
INSURANCE
GRRR---
WHAT APPALLING BEHAVIOR, JAPANESE REPRESENTATIVE!!
WOW!
THE MONACO CUP IS AN INTERNATIONAL TOURNAMENT OF THE HIGHEST CALIBER!
IF YOU PERSIST IN SPOUTING IDIOTIC STATEMENTS SUCH AS "DELICIOUS BREAD NEEDS TIME TO FERMENT" OR "WE CAN DO IT IN 90 MINUTES," MAYBE IT WOULD BE BETTER FOR YOU TO HURRY UP AND RESIGN!!

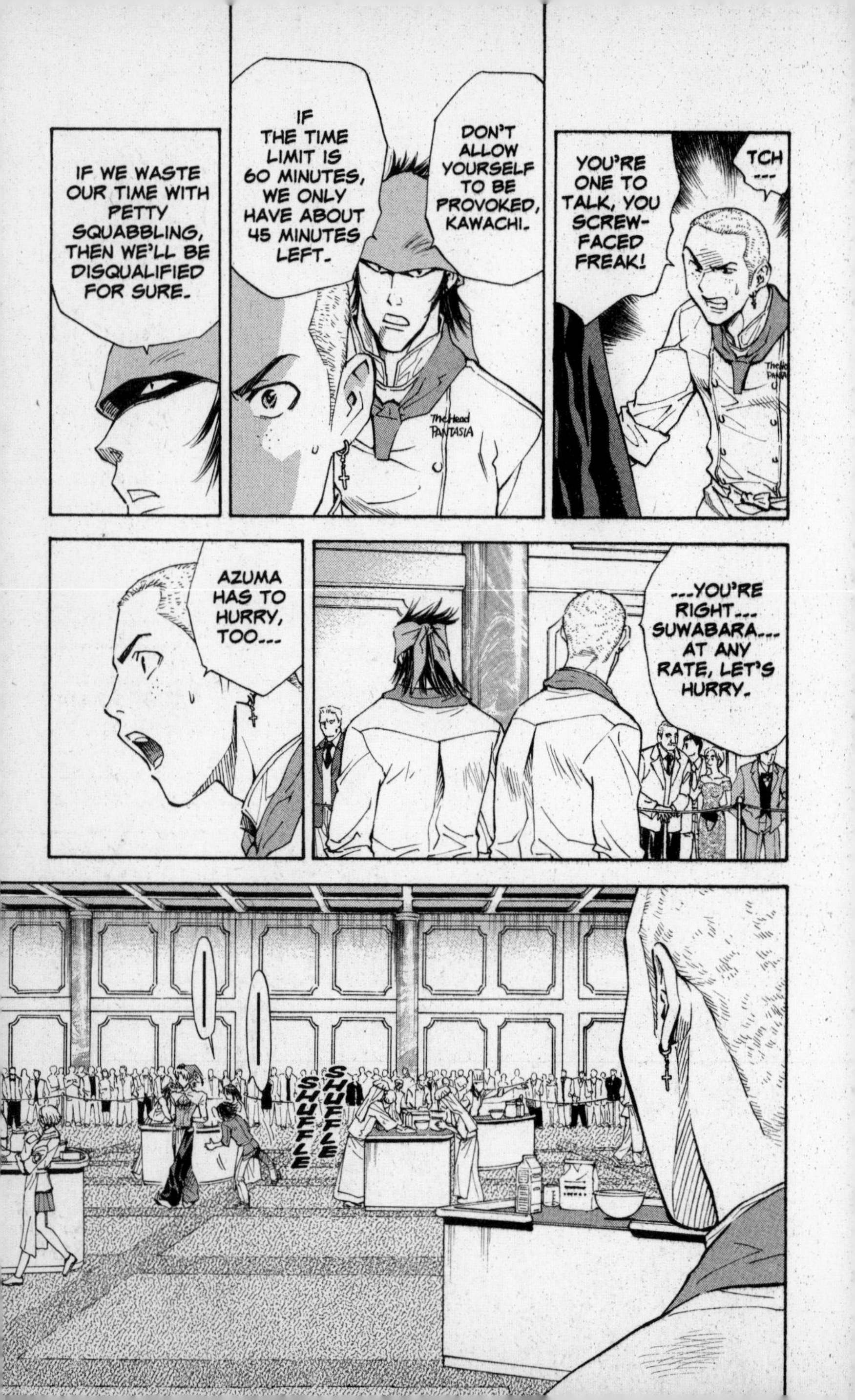
TCH ...
YOU'RE ONE TO TALK, YOU SCREW-FACED FREAK!
DON'T ALLOW YOURSELF TO BE PROVOKED, KAWACHI.
IF THE TIME LIMIT IS 60 MINUTES, WE ONLY HAVE ABOUT 45 MINUTES LEFT.
IF WE WASTE OUR TIME WITH PETTY SQUABBLING, THEN WE'LL BE DISQUALIFIED FOR SURE.
...YOU'RE RIGHT... SUWABARA... AT ANY RATE, LET'S HURRY.
AZUMA HAS TO HURRY, TOO...
SHUFFLE
SHUFFLE

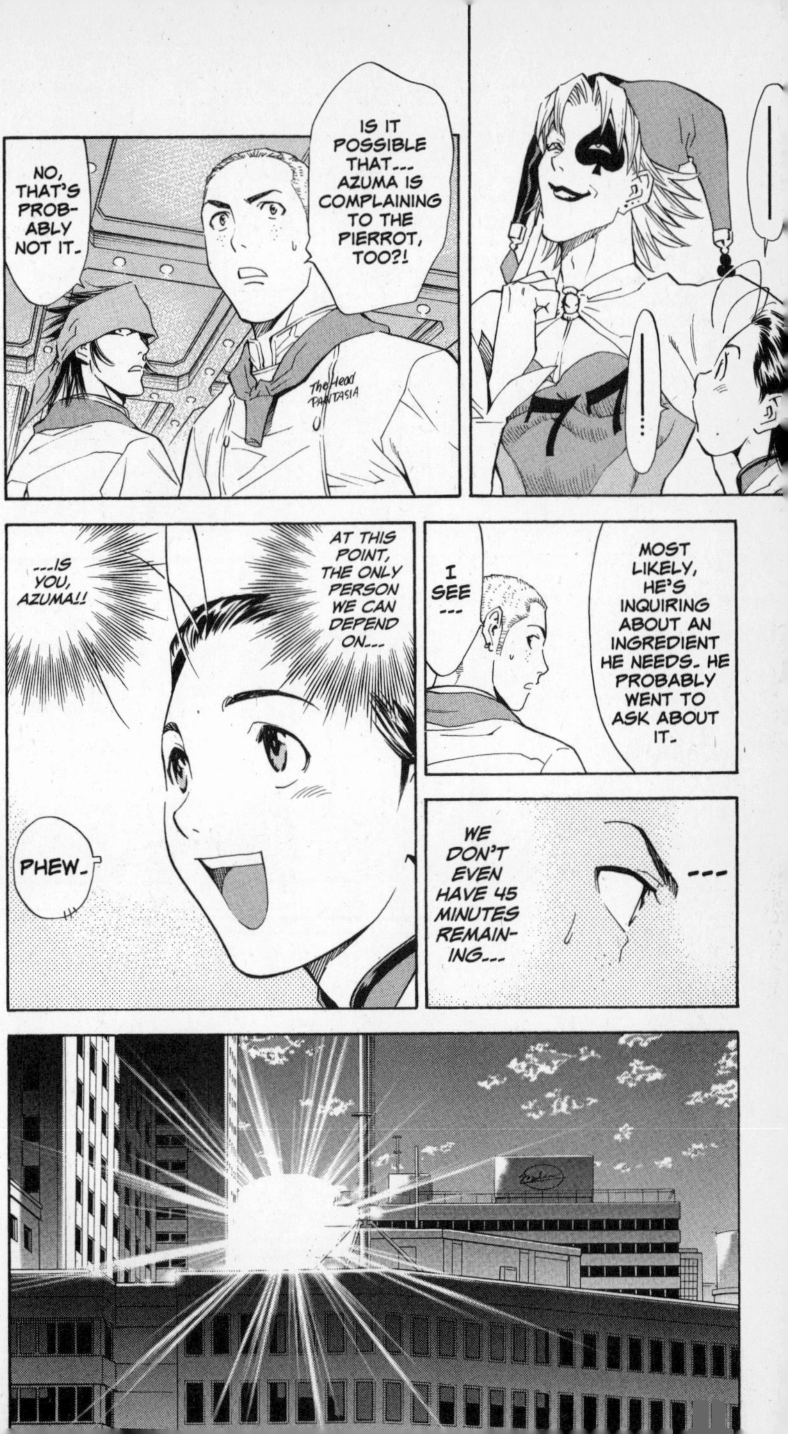
!
!...
IS IT POSSIBLE THAT... AZUMA IS COMPLAINING TO THE PIERROT, TOO?!
NO, THAT'S PROBABLY NOT IT.
MOST LIKELY, HE'S INQUIRING ABOUT AN INGREDIENT HE NEEDS. HE PROBABLY WENT TO ASK ABOUT IT.
I SEE...
...
WE DON'T EVEN HAVE 45 MINUTES REMAINING...
AT THIS POINT, THE ONLY PERSON WE CAN DEPEND ON...
...IS YOU, AZUMA!!
PHEW.

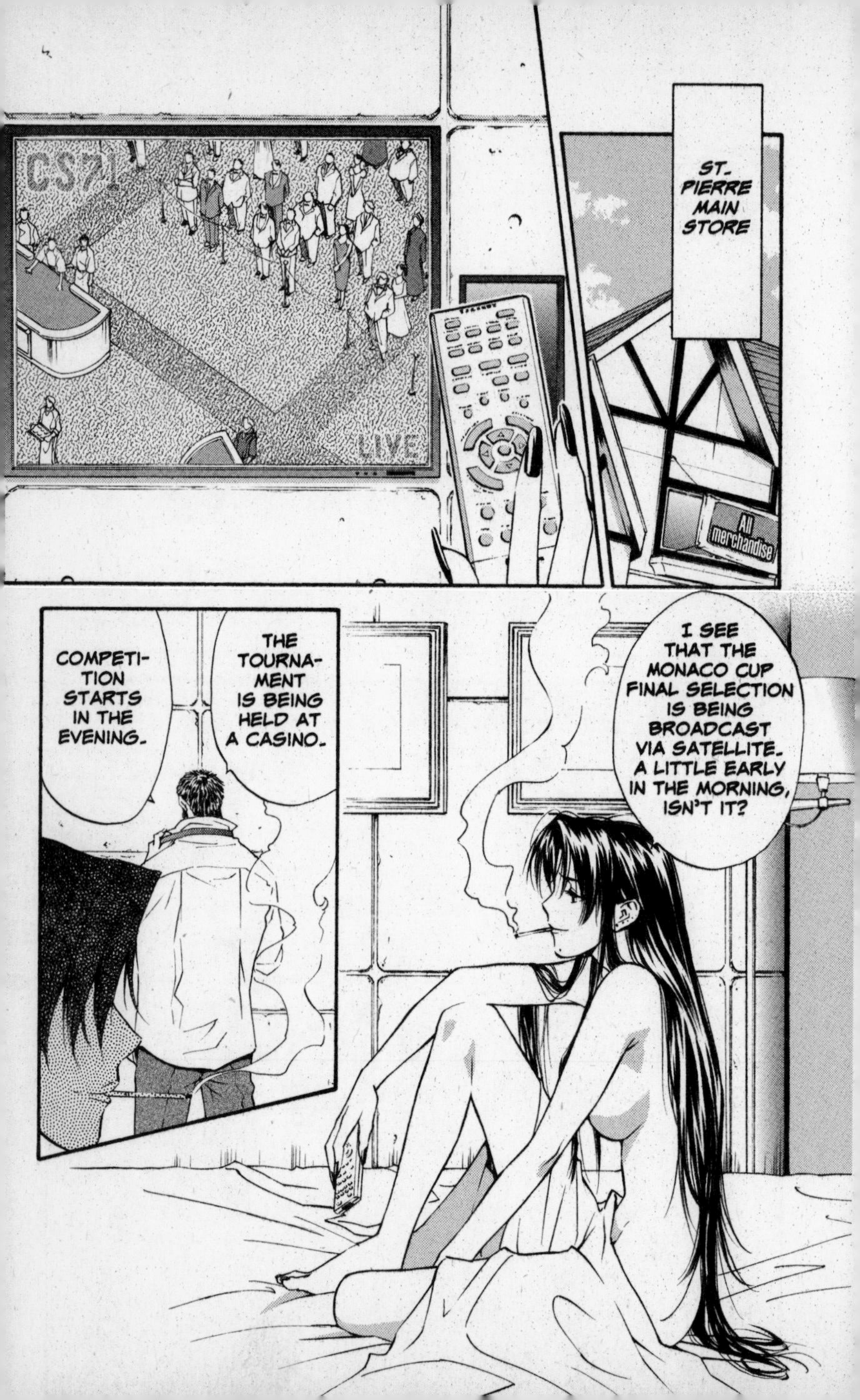
ST. PIERRE MAIN STORE
All merchandise
CS71
LIVE
I SEE THAT THE MONACO CUP FINAL SELECTION IS BEING BROADCAST VIA SATELLITE. A LITTLE EARLY IN THE MORNING, ISN'T IT?
THE TOURNAMENT IS BEING HELD AT A CASINO.
COMPETITION STARTS IN THE EVENING.

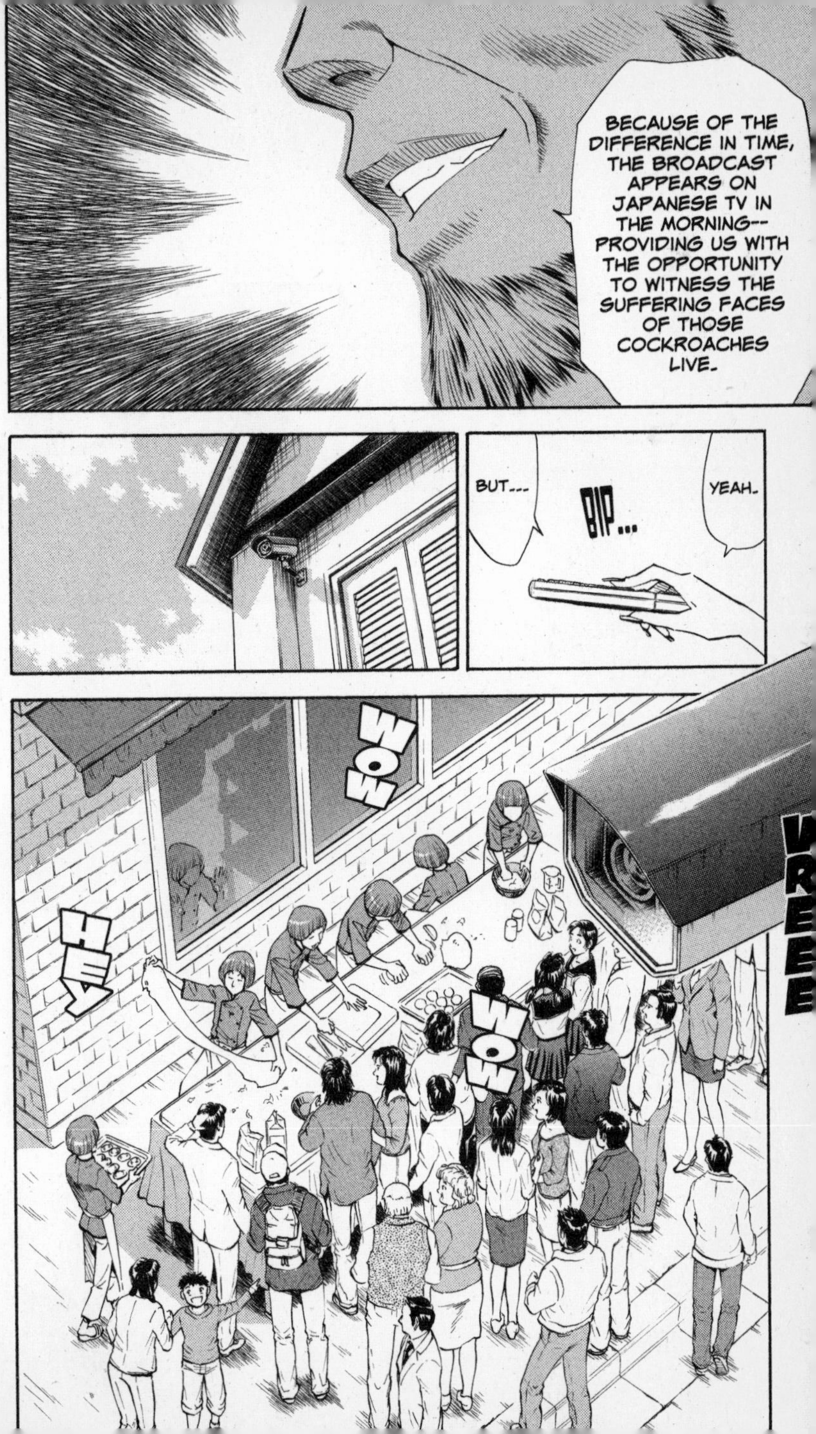
BECAUSE OF THE DIFFERENCE IN TIME, THE BROADCAST APPEARS ON JAPANESE TV IN THE MORNING-- PROVIDING US WITH THE OPPORTUNITY TO WITNESS THE SUFFERING FACES OF THOSE COCKROACHES LIVE.
YEAH.
BIP...
BUT...
WREEE
WOW
WOW
HEY

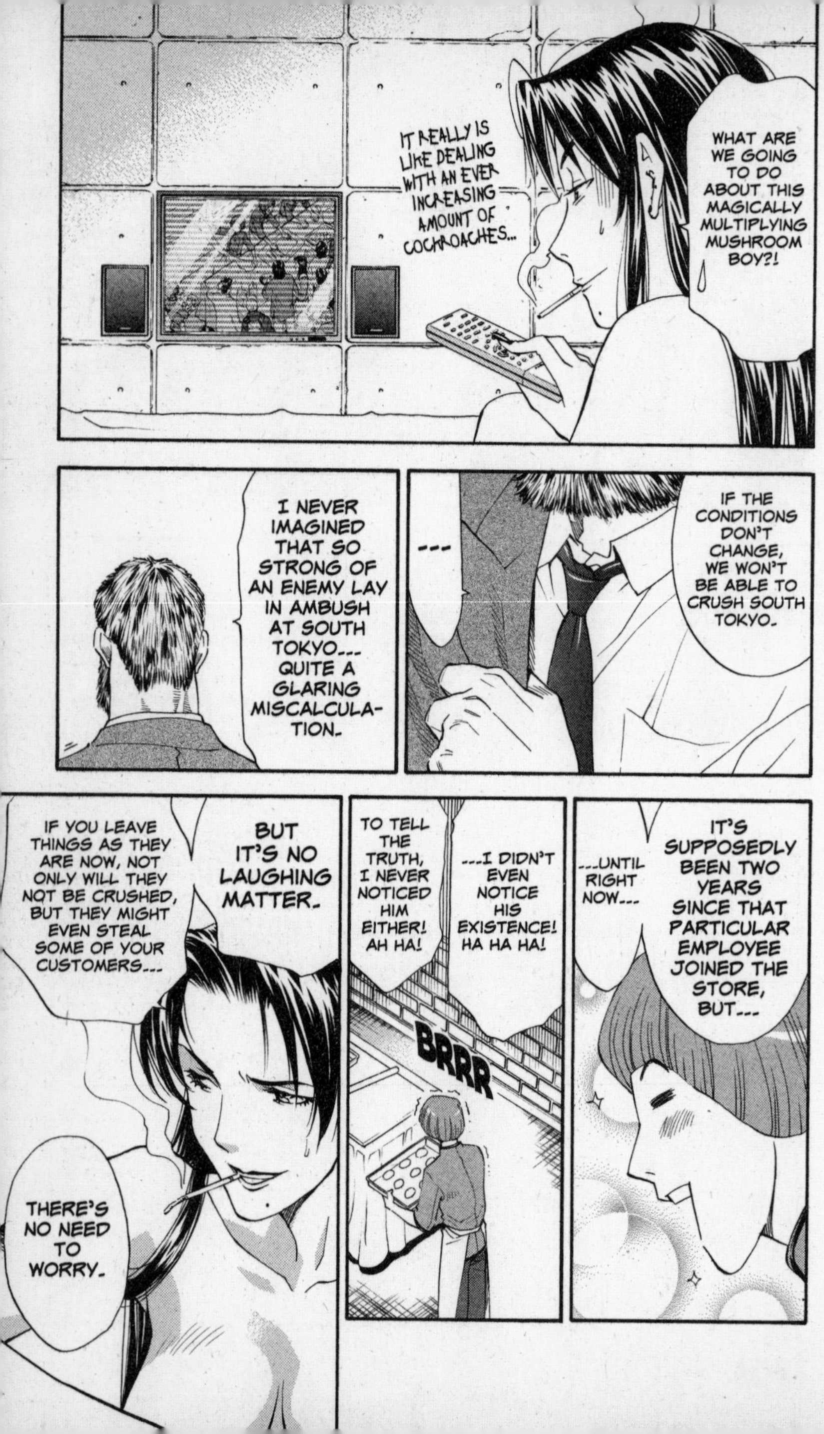
WHAT ARE WE GOING TO DO ABOUT THIS MAGICALLY MULTIPLYING MUSHROOM BOY?!
IT REALLY IS LIKE DEALING WITH AN EVER INCREASING AMOUNT OF COCKROACHES...
IF THE CONDITIONS DON'T CHANGE, WE WON'T BE ABLE TO CRUSH SOUTH TOKYO.
...
I NEVER IMAGINED THAT SO STRONG OF AN ENEMY LAY IN AMBUSH AT SOUTH TOKYO... QUITE A GLARING MISCALCULATION.
IT'S SUPPOSEDLY BEEN TWO YEARS SINCE THAT PARTICULAR EMPLOYEE JOINED THE STORE, BUT...
...UNTIL RIGHT NOW...
...I DIDN'T EVEN NOTICE HIS EXISTENCE! HA HA HA!
TO TELL THE TRUTH, I NEVER NOTICED HIM EITHER! AH HA!
BRRR
BUT IT'S NO LAUGHING MATTER.
IF YOU LEAVE THINGS AS THEY ARE NOW, NOT ONLY WILL THEY NOT BE CRUSHED, BUT THEY MIGHT EVEN STEAL SOME OF YOUR CUSTOMERS...
THERE'S NO NEED TO WORRY.

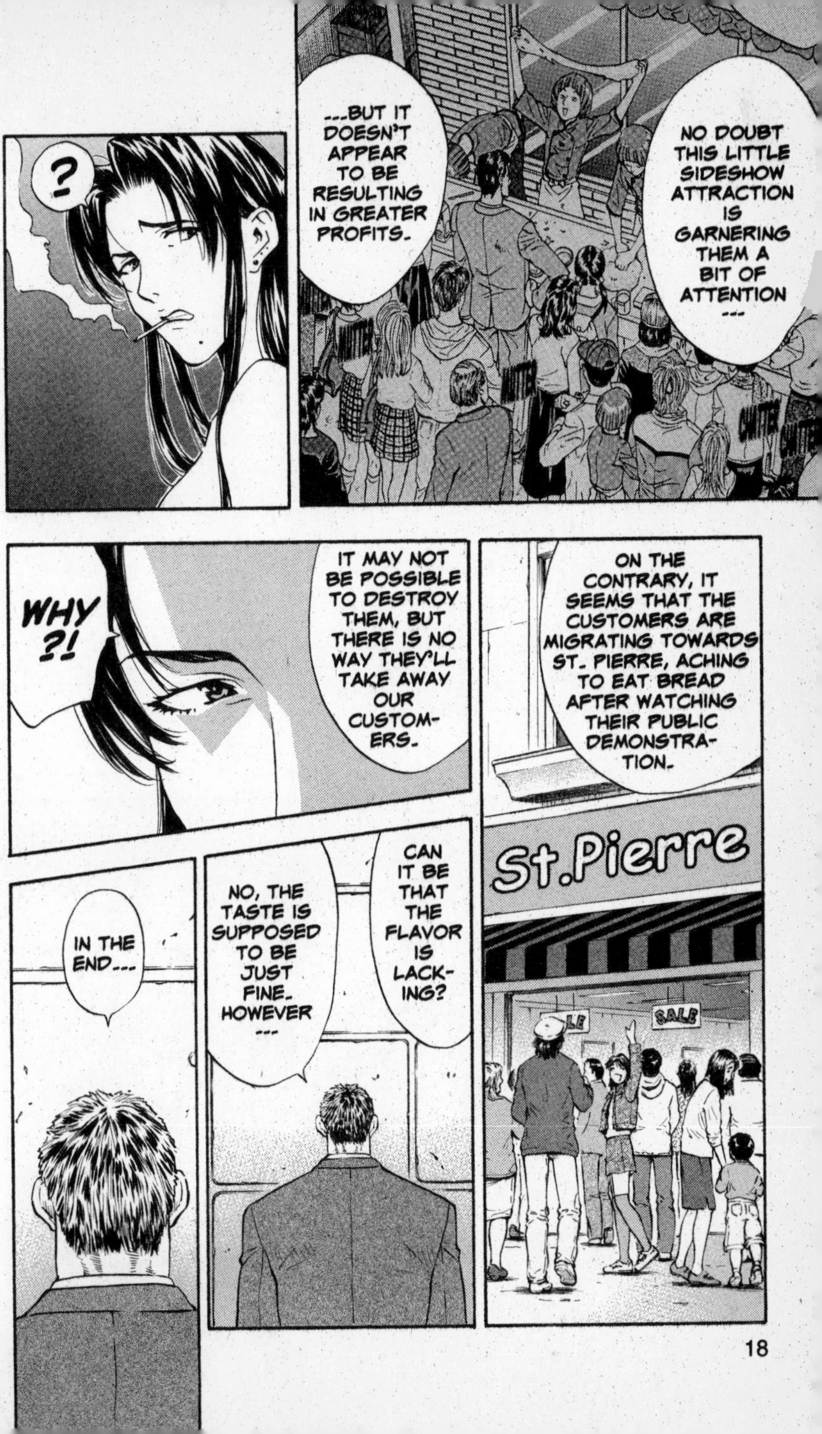
NO DOUBT THIS LITTLE SIDESHOW ATTRACTION IS GARNERING THEM A BIT OF ATTENTION...
...BUT IT DOESN'T APPEAR TO BE RESULTING IN GREATER PROFITS.
?
ON THE CONTRARY, IT SEEMS THAT THE CUSTOMERS ARE MIGRATING TOWARDS ST. PIERRE, ACHING TO EAT BREAD AFTER WATCHING THEIR PUBLIC DEMONSTRATION.
St.Pierre
SALE
IT MAY NOT BE POSSIBLE TO DESTROY THEM, BUT THERE IS NO WAY THEY'LL TAKE AWAY OUR CUSTOMERS.
WHY?!
CAN IT BE THAT THE FLAVOR IS LACKING?
NO, THE TASTE IS SUPPOSED TO BE JUST FINE. HOWEVER...
IN THE END...

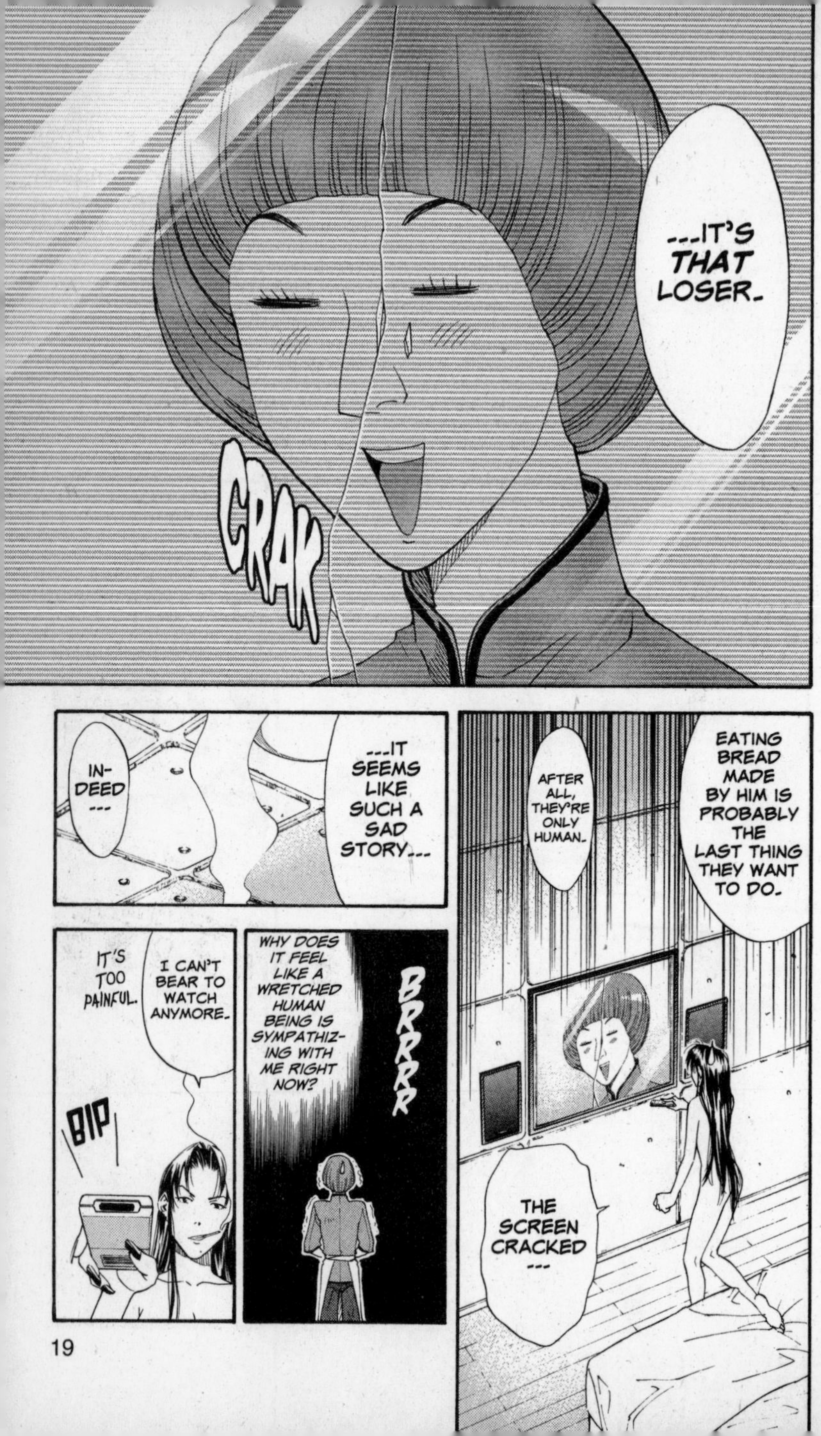
---IT'S THAT LOSER.
CRAK
EATING BREAD MADE BY HIM IS PROBABLY THE LAST THING THEY WANT TO DO.
AFTER ALL, THEY'RE ONLY HUMAN.
THE SCREEN CRACKED---
---IT SEEMS LIKE SUCH A SAD STORY...
IN-DEED---
WHY DOES IT FEEL LIKE A WRETCHED HUMAN BEING IS SYMPATHIZING WITH ME RIGHT NOW?
BRRRR
I CAN'T BEAR TO WATCH ANYMORE.
IT'S TOO PAINFUL.
BIP

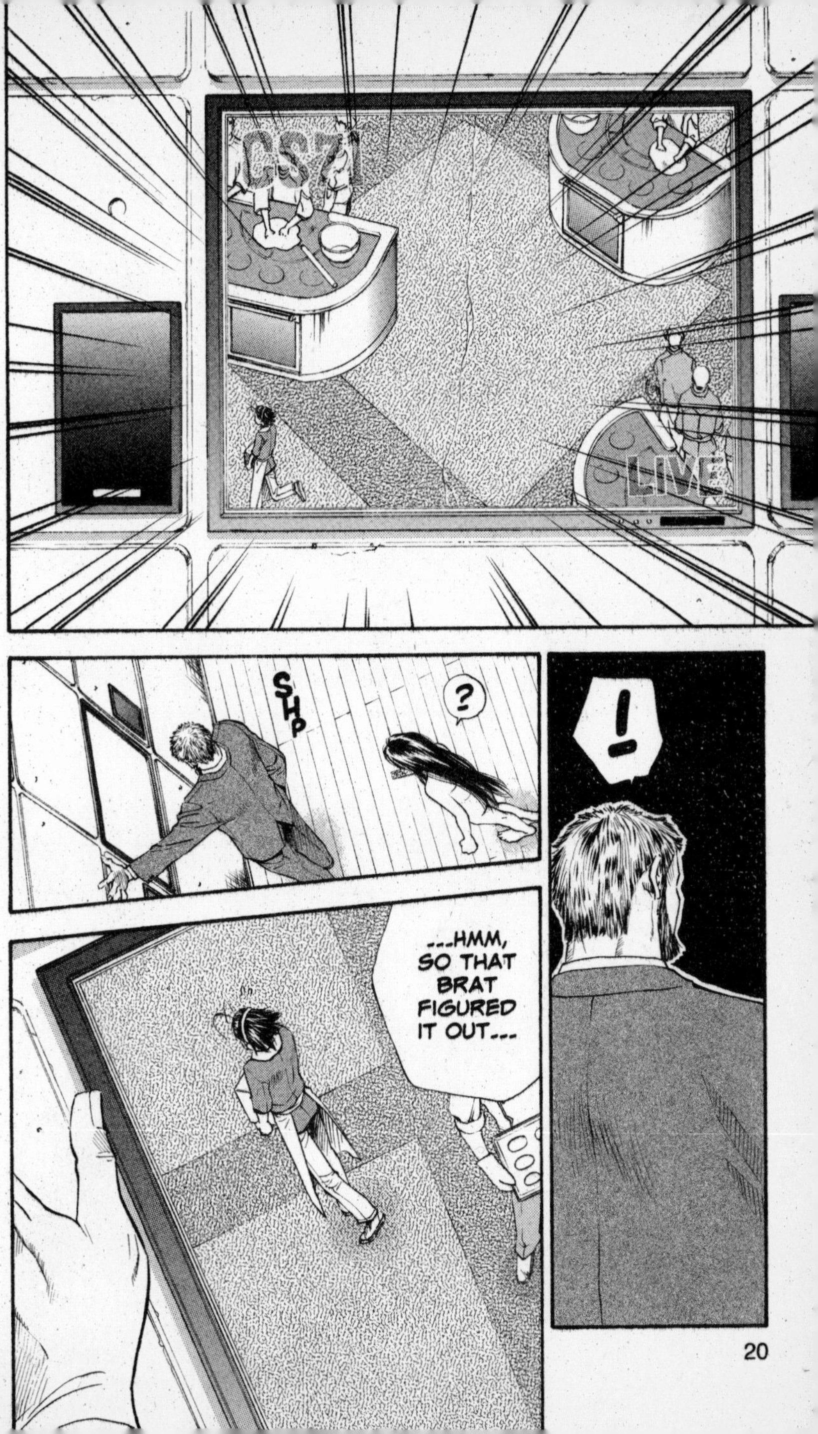
CS7
LIVE
!
SHP
?
...HMM, SO THAT BRAT FIGURED IT OUT...

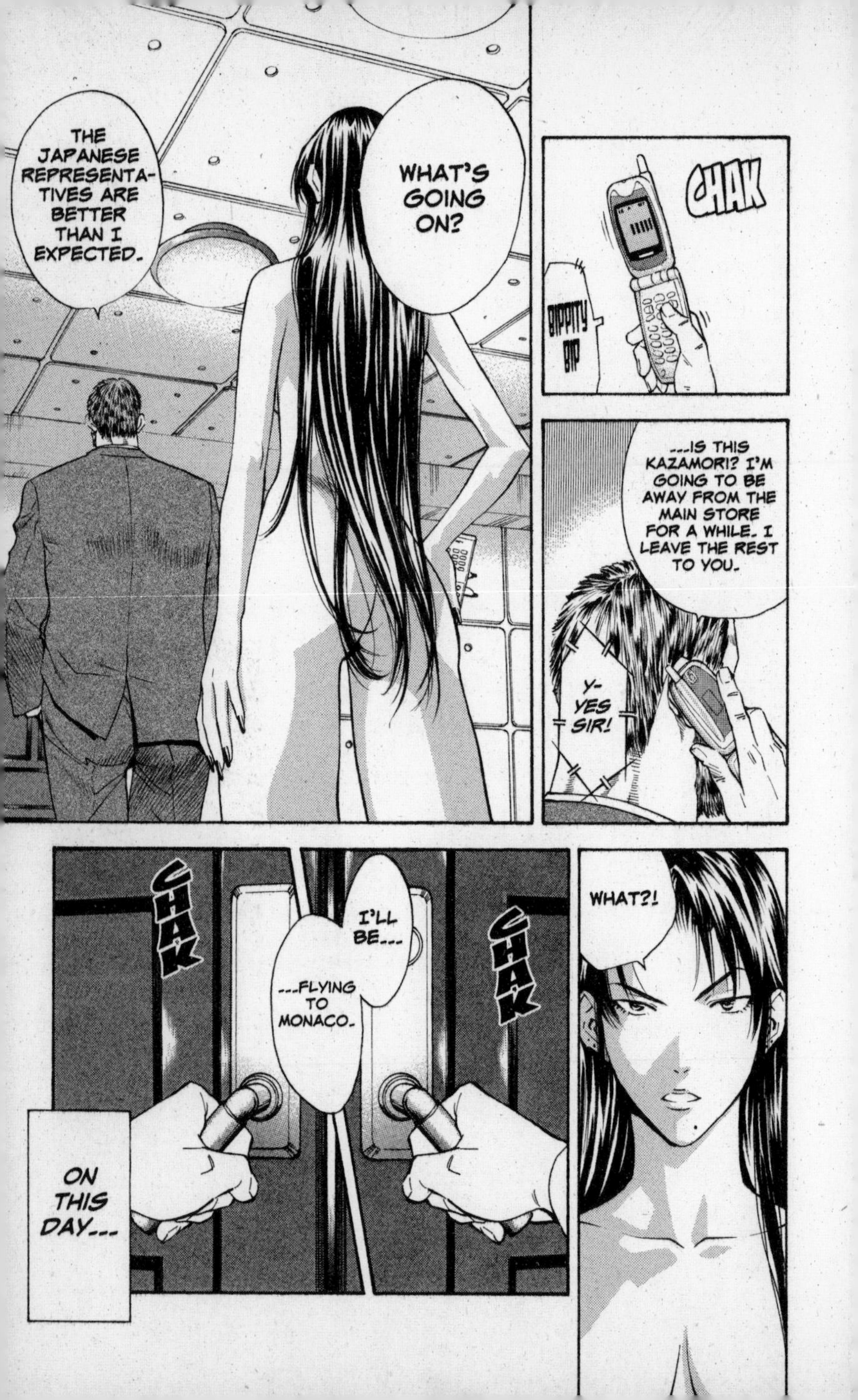

CHAK
BIPPITY BIP
...IS THIS KAZAMORI? I'M GOING TO BE AWAY FROM THE MAIN STORE FOR A WHILE. I LEAVE THE REST TO YOU.
Y-YES SIR!
WHAT'S GOING ON?
THE JAPANESE REPRESENTATIVES ARE BETTER THAN I EXPECTED.
WHAT?!
CHAK
I'LL BE...
...FLYING TO MONACO.
CHAK
ON THIS DAY...

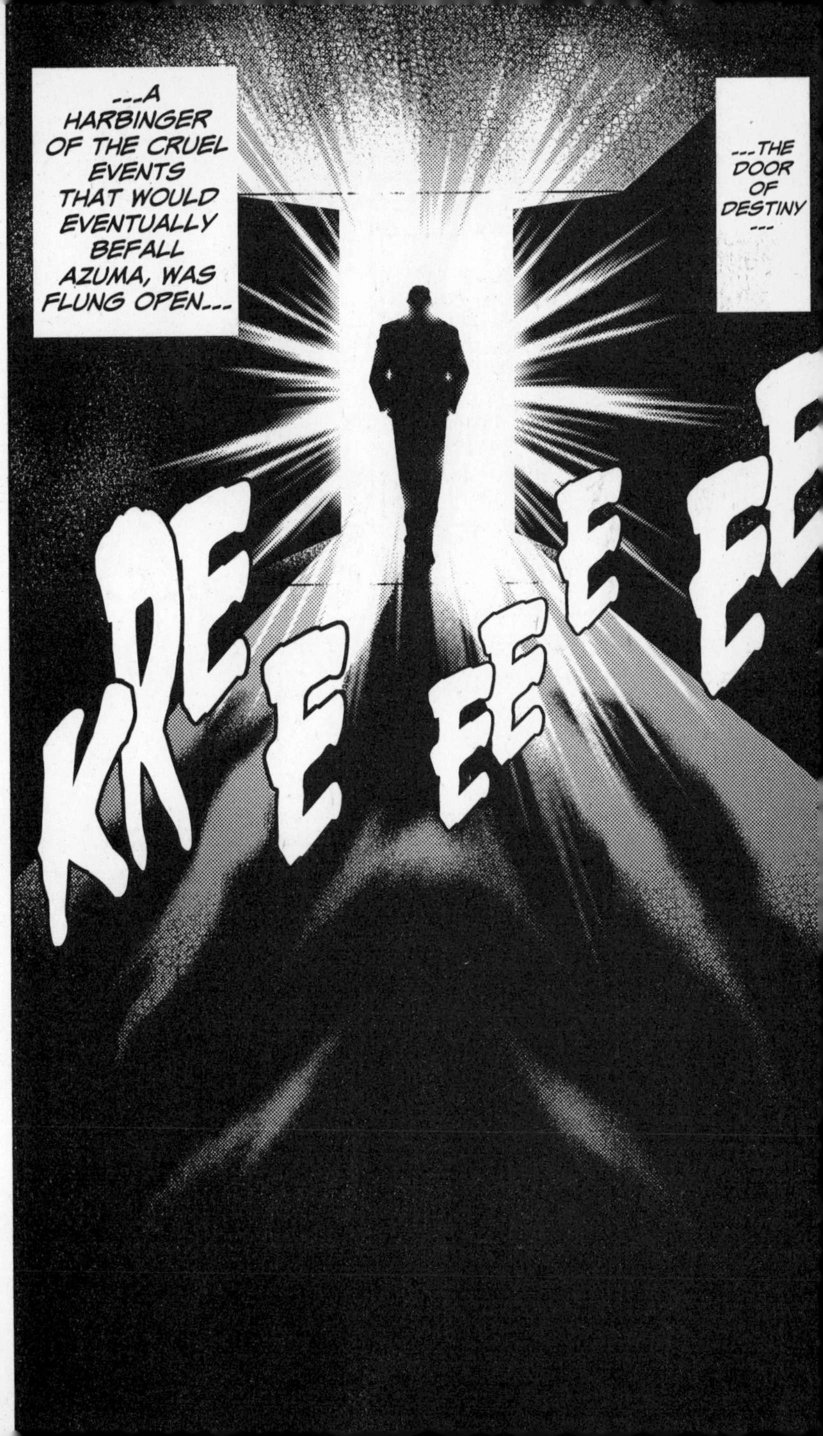
---THE DOOR OF DESTINY ---
---A HARBINGER OF THE CRUEL EVENTS THAT WOULD EVENTUALLY BEFALL AZUMA, WAS FLUNG OPEN---
KREEEEEEEEEE

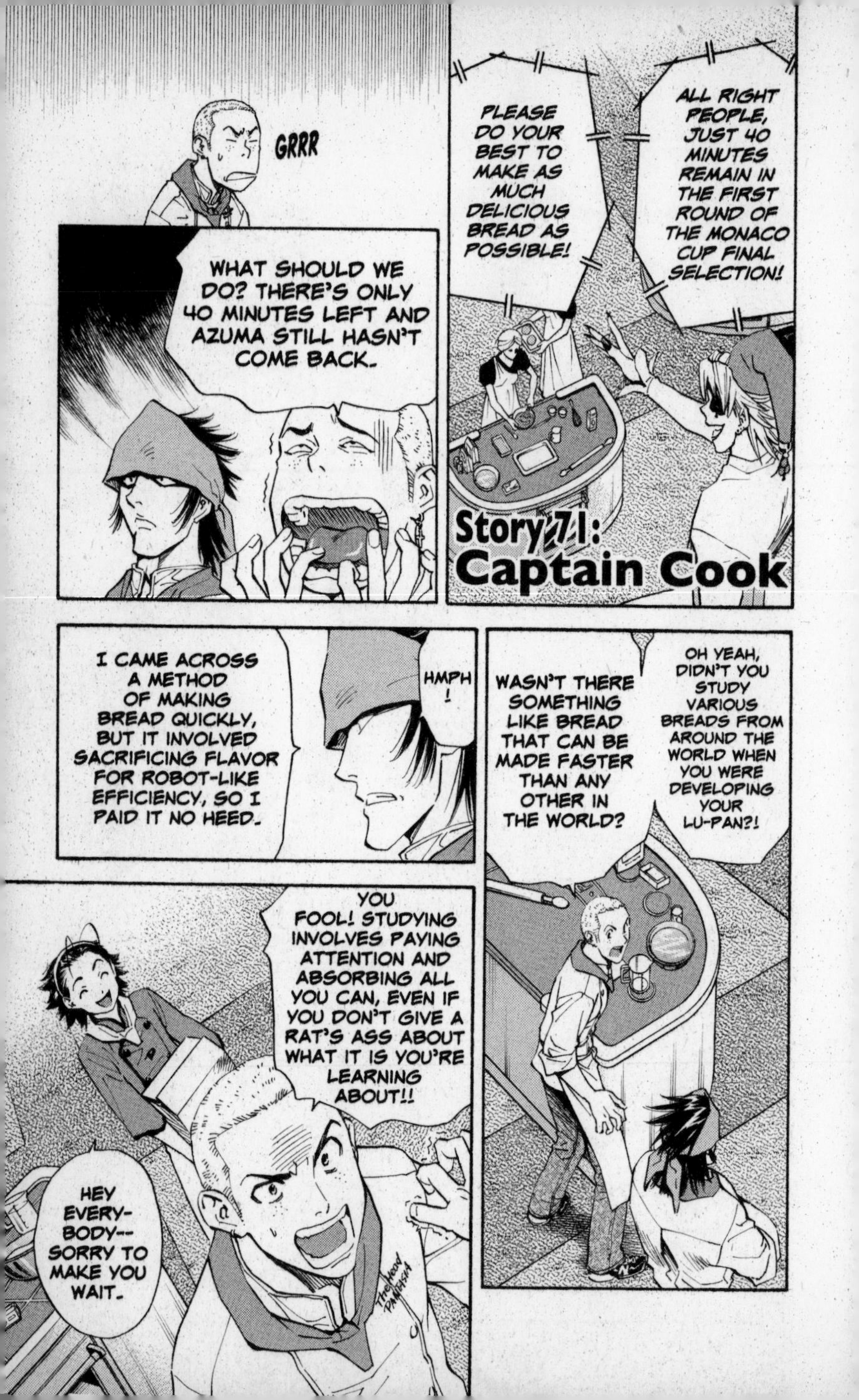
ALL RIGHT PEOPLE, JUST 40 MINUTES REMAIN IN THE FIRST ROUND OF THE MONACO CUP FINAL SELECTION!
PLEASE DO YOUR BEST TO MAKE AS MUCH DELICIOUS BREAD AS POSSIBLE!
Story 71: Captain Cook
GRRR
WHAT SHOULD WE DO? THERE'S ONLY 40 MINUTES LEFT AND AZUMA STILL HASN'T COME BACK.
OH YEAH, DIDN'T YOU STUDY VARIOUS BREADS FROM AROUND THE WORLD WHEN YOU WERE DEVELOPING YOUR LU-PAN?!
WASN'T THERE SOMETHING LIKE BREAD THAT CAN BE MADE FASTER THAN ANY OTHER IN THE WORLD?
HMPH!
I CAME ACROSS A METHOD OF MAKING BREAD QUICKLY, BUT IT INVOLVED SACRIFICING FLAVOR FOR ROBOT-LIKE EFFICIENCY, SO I PAID IT NO HEED.
YOU FOOL! STUDYING INVOLVES PAYING ATTENTION AND ABSORBING ALL YOU CAN, EVEN IF YOU DON'T GIVE A RAT'S ASS ABOUT WHAT IT IS YOU'RE LEARNING ABOUT!!
HEY EVERY-BODY-- SORRY TO MAKE YOU WAIT.
The Head PANTASIA

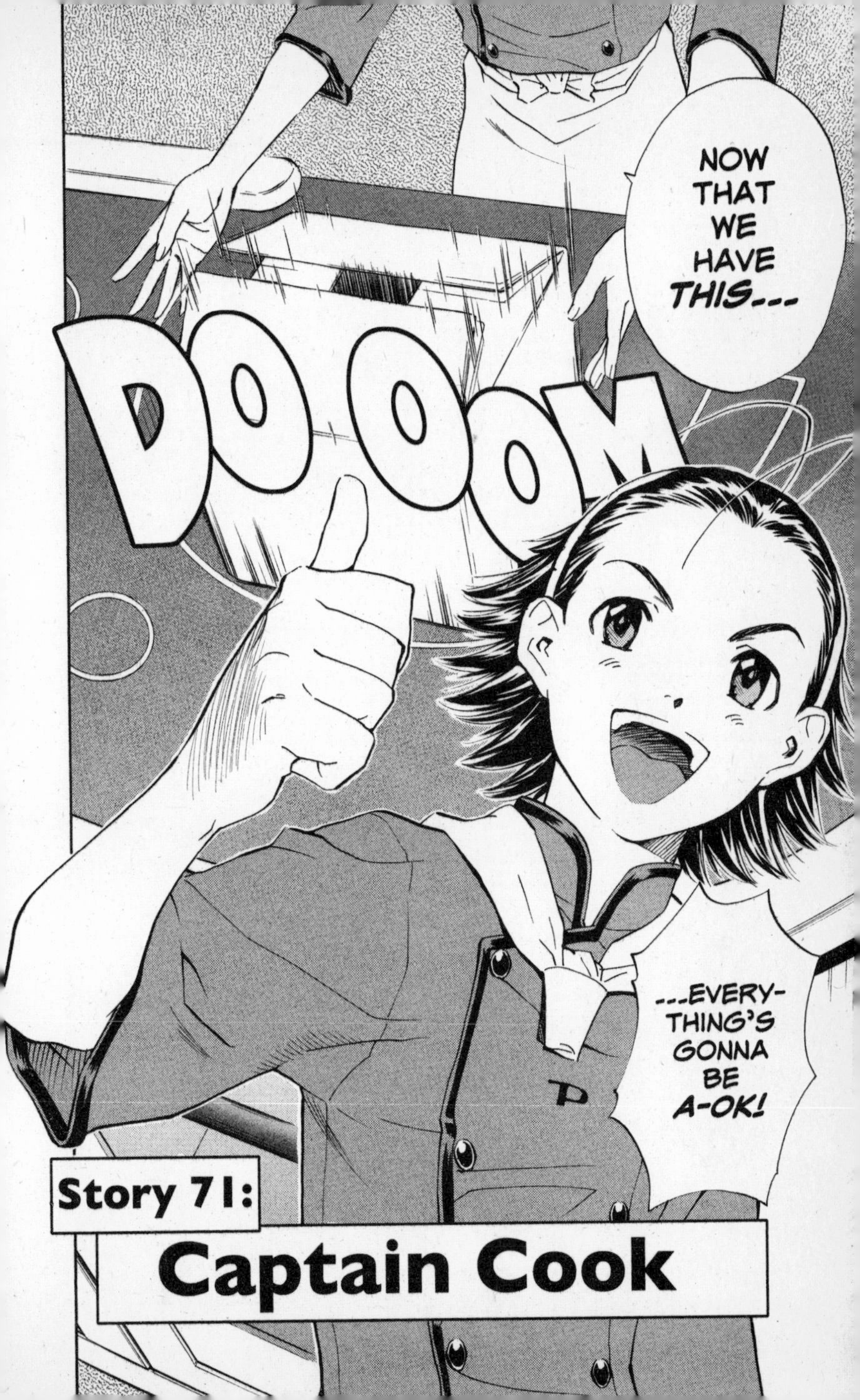
NOW THAT WE HAVE THIS...
DO-OOM
...EVERYTHING'S GONNA BE A-OK!
Story 71:
Captain Cook

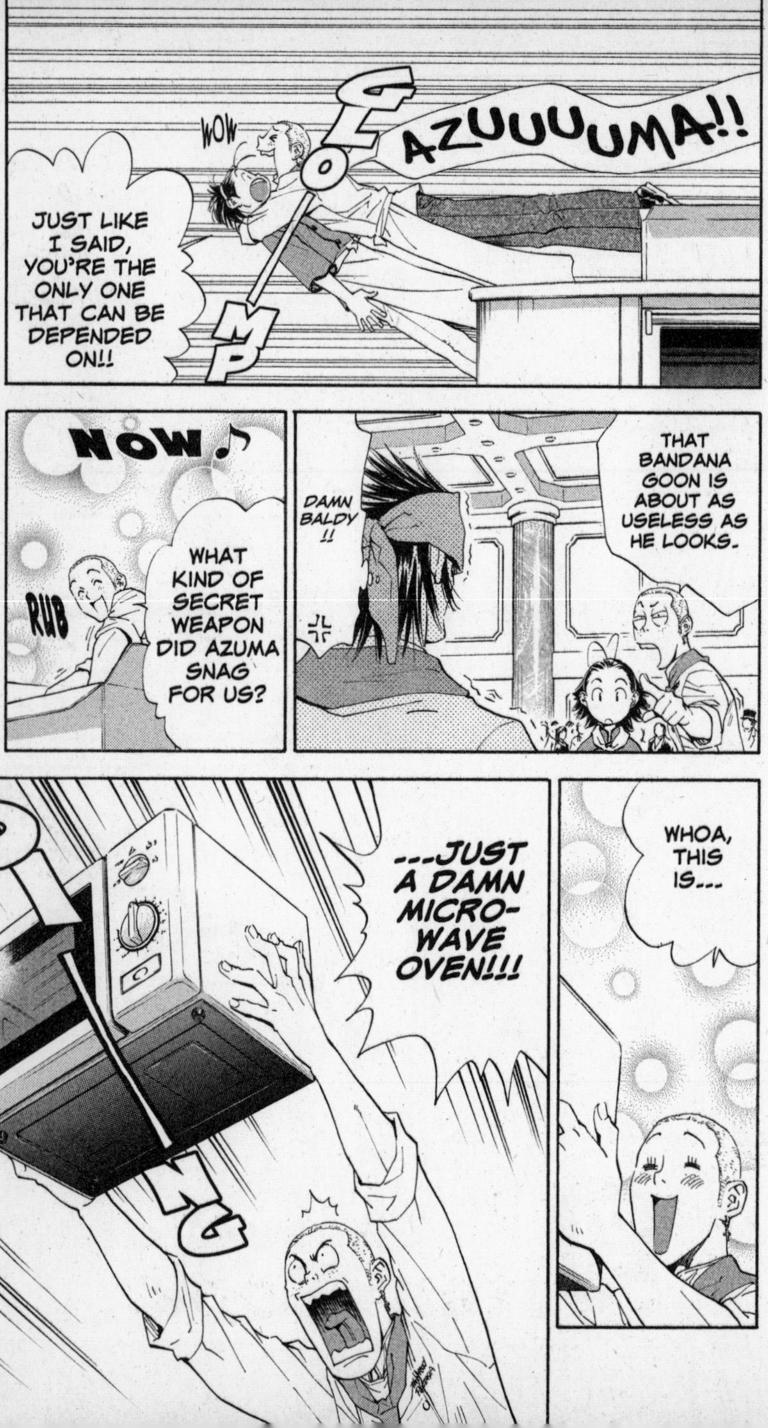
AZUUUUMA!!
GLOMP
WOW
JUST LIKE I SAID, YOU'RE THE ONLY ONE THAT CAN BE DEPENDED ON!!
THAT BANDANA GOON IS ABOUT AS USELESS AS HE LOOKS.
DAMN BALDY!!
NOW♪
WHAT KIND OF SECRET WEAPON DID AZUMA SNAG FOR US?
RUB
WHOA, THIS IS...
...JUST A DAMN MICRO-WAVE OVEN!!!
DING

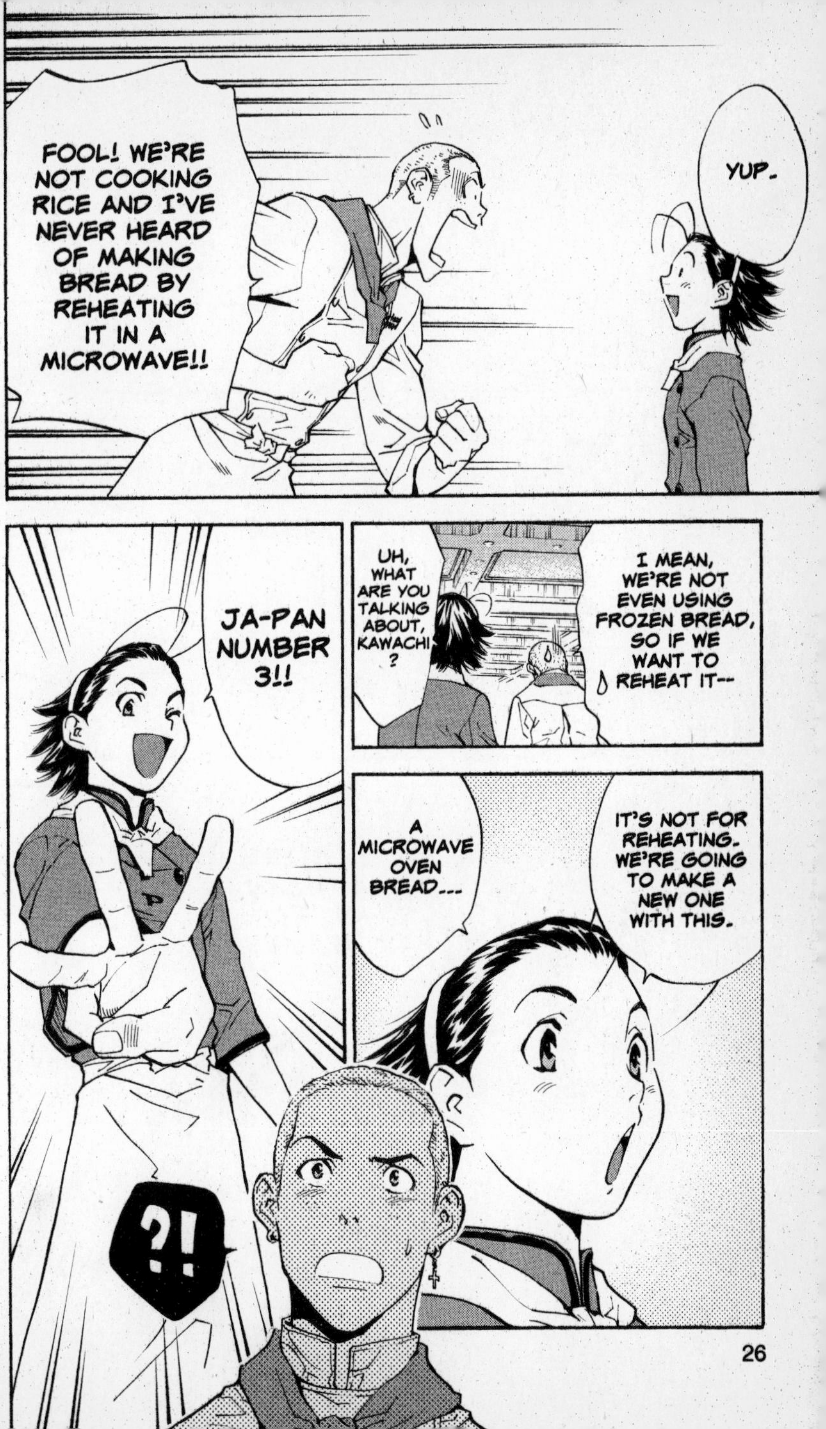
YUP.
FOOL! WE'RE NOT COOKING RICE AND I'VE NEVER HEARD OF MAKING BREAD BY REHEATING IT IN A MICROWAVE!!
I MEAN, WE'RE NOT EVEN USING FROZEN BREAD, SO IF WE WANT TO REHEAT IT--
UH, WHAT ARE YOU TALKING ABOUT, KAWACHI?
IT'S NOT FOR REHEATING. WE'RE GOING TO MAKE A NEW ONE WITH THIS.
A MICROWAVE OVEN BREAD...
JA-PAN NUMBER 3!!
?!

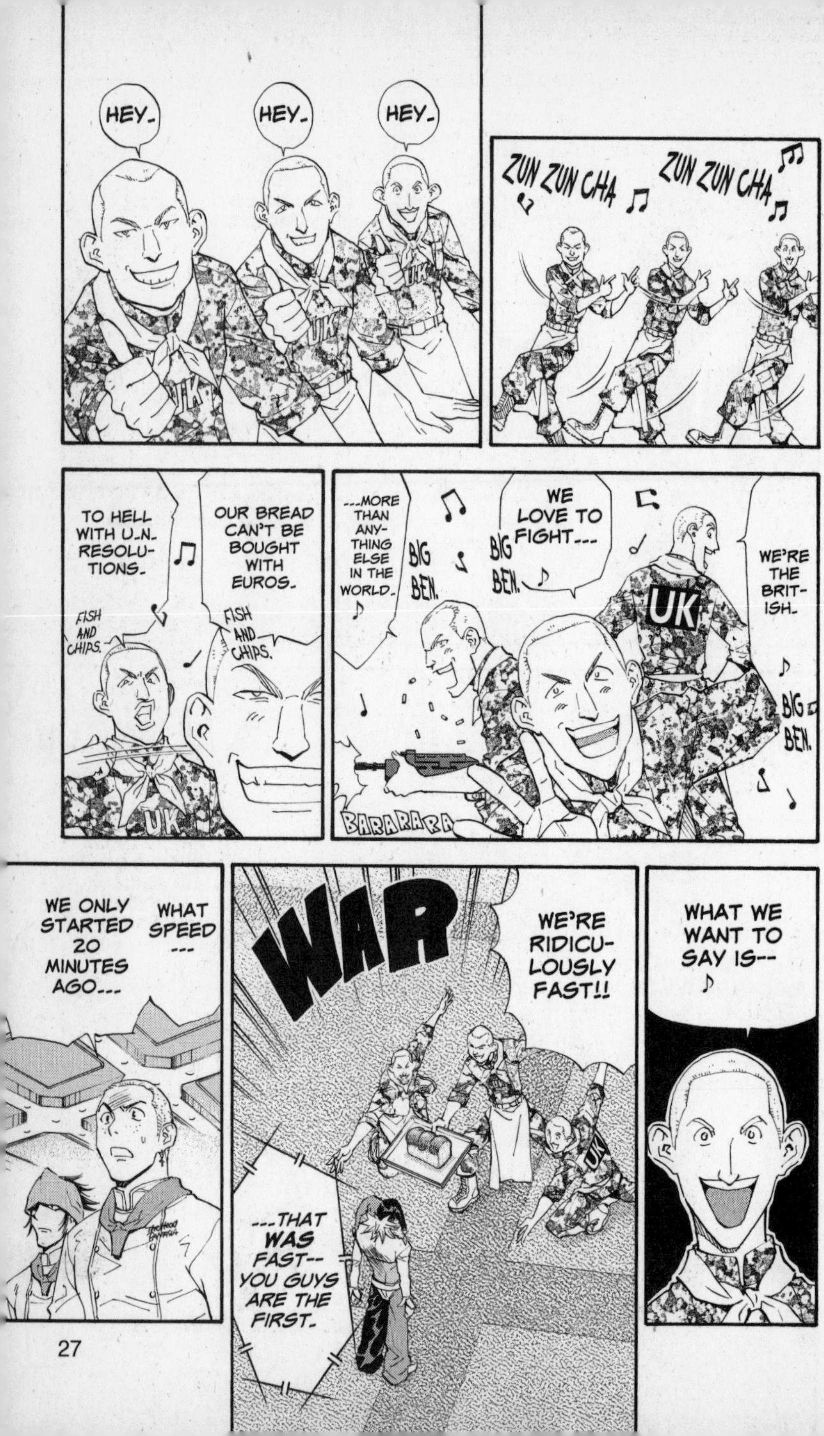
ZUN ZUN CHA
ZUN ZUN CHA
HEY.
HEY.
HEY.
WE'RE THE BRITISH.
WE LOVE TO FIGHT---
BIG BEN.
BIG BEN.
---MORE THAN ANYTHING ELSE IN THE WORLD.
BIG BEN.
BARARARA
OUR BREAD CAN'T BE BOUGHT WITH EUROS.
FISH AND CHIPS.
TO HELL WITH U.N. RESOLUTIONS.
FISH AND CHIPS.
WHAT WE WANT TO SAY IS--
WE'RE RIDICULOUSLY FAST!!
WAR
---THAT WAS FAST-- YOU GUYS ARE THE FIRST.
WHAT SPEED---
WE ONLY STARTED 20 MINUTES AGO---

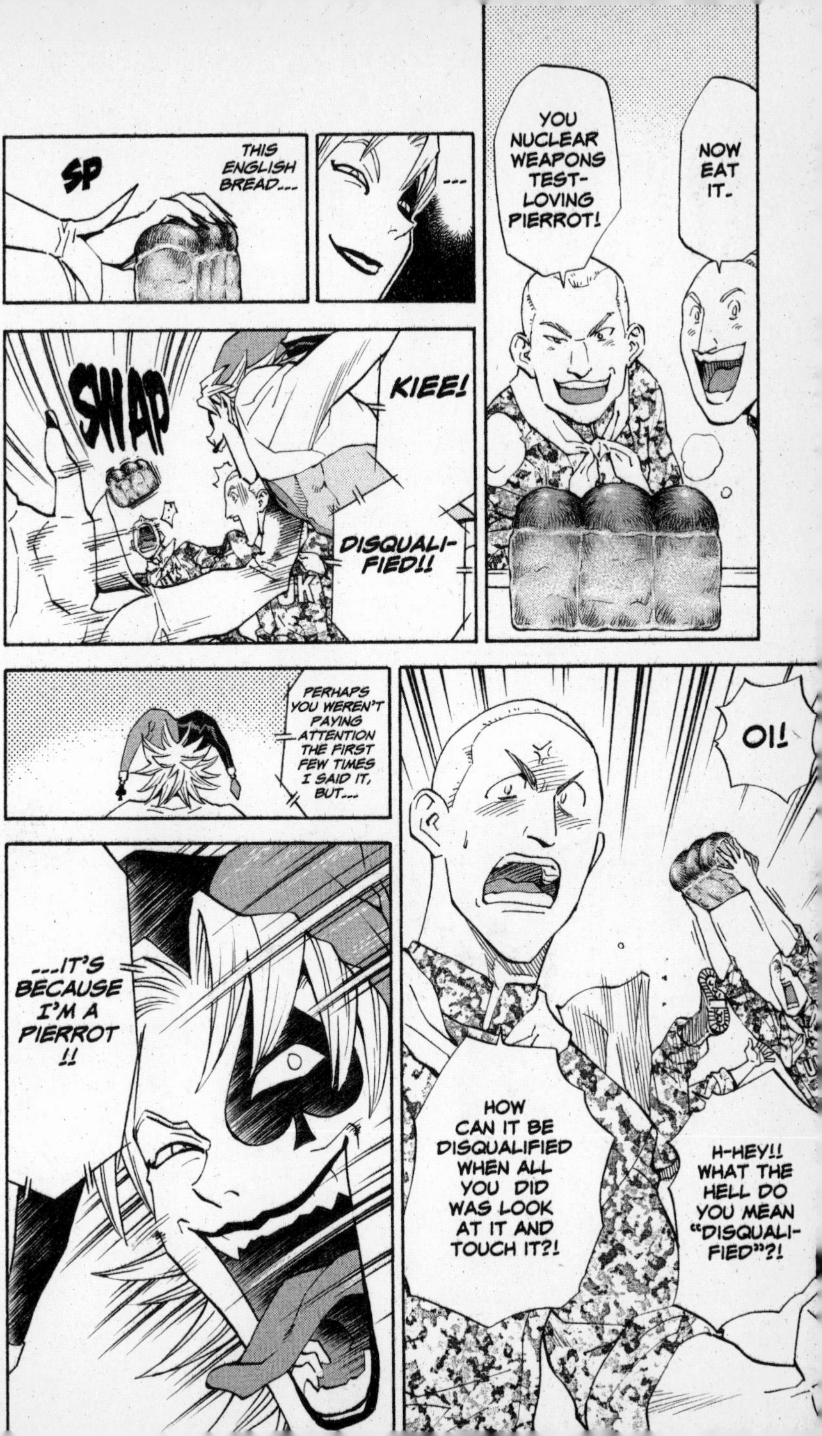
NOW EAT IT.
YOU NUCLEAR WEAPONS TEST-LOVING PIERROT!
...
THIS ENGLISH BREAD...
SP
KIEE!
DISQUALIFIED!!
SWAP
OI!
H-HEY!! WHAT THE HELL DO YOU MEAN "DISQUALIFIED"?!
HOW CAN IT BE DISQUALIFIED WHEN ALL YOU DID WAS LOOK AT IT AND TOUCH IT?!
PERHAPS YOU WEREN'T PAYING ATTENTION THE FIRST FEW TIMES I SAID IT, BUT...
...IT'S BECAUSE I'M A PIERROT!!

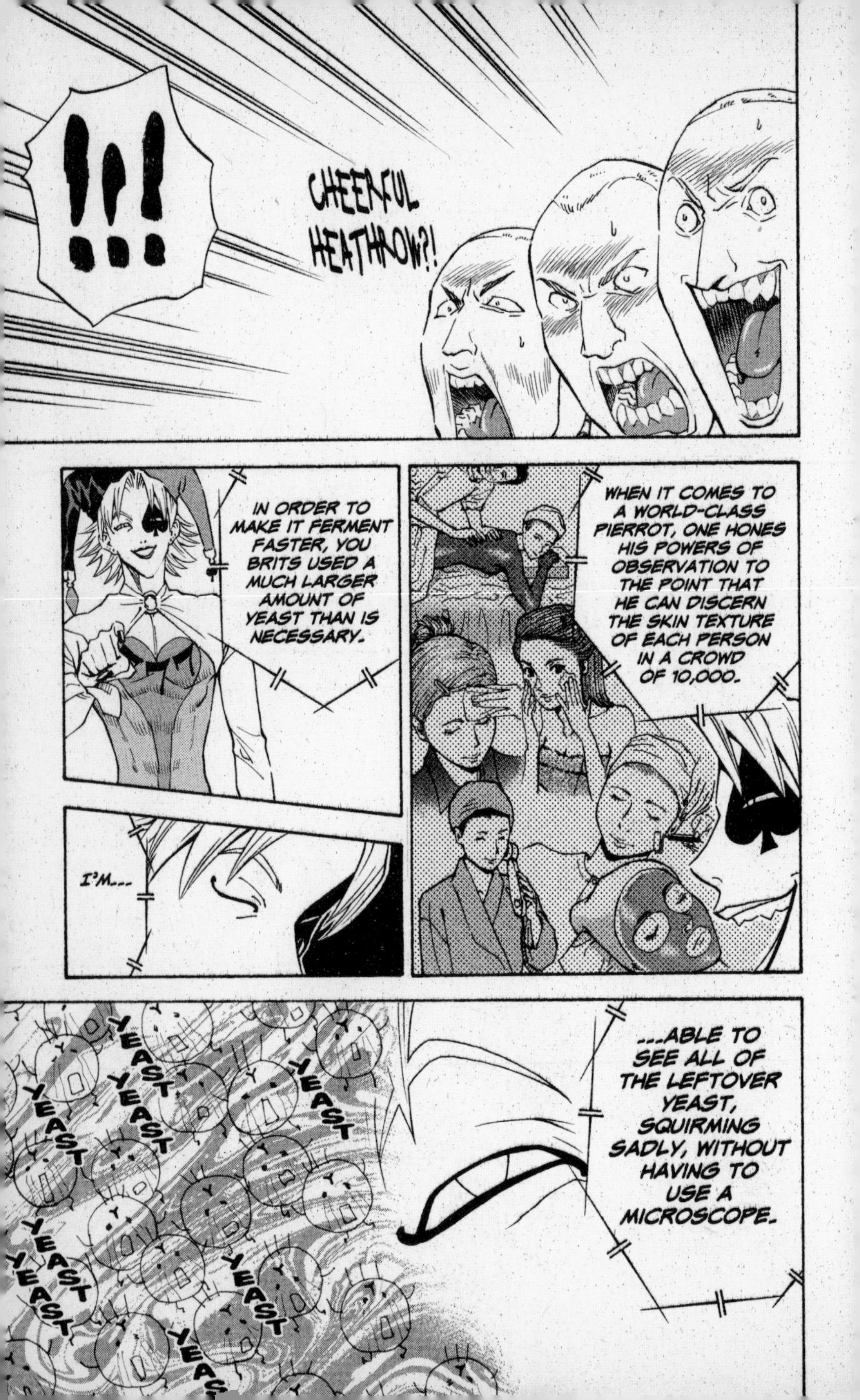
CHEERFUL HEATHROW?!
!?!
...
WHEN IT COMES TO A WORLD-CLASS PIERROT, ONE HONES HIS POWERS OF OBSERVATION TO THE POINT THAT HE CAN DISCERN THE SKIN TEXTURE OF EACH PERSON IN A CROWD OF 10,000.
IN ORDER TO MAKE IT FERMENT FASTER, YOU BRITS USED A MUCH LARGER AMOUNT OF YEAST THAN IS NECESSARY.
I'M...
...ABLE TO SEE ALL OF THE LEFTOVER YEAST, SQUIRMING SADLY, WITHOUT HAVING TO USE A MICROSCOPE.
YEAST
YEAST
YEAST
YEAST
YEAST
YEAST
YEAST
YEAST

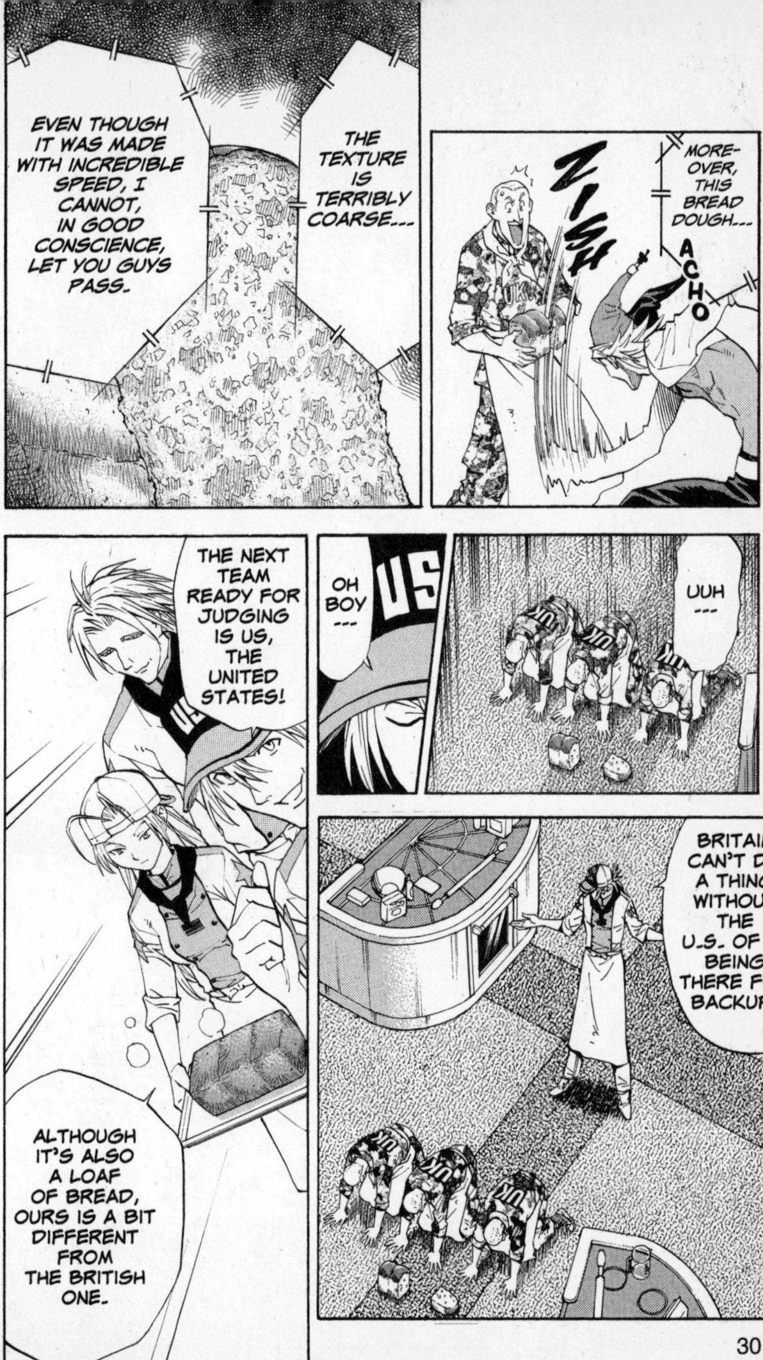
ZISH
MORE-OVER, THIS BREAD DOUGH...
ACHO
THE TEXTURE IS TERRIBLY COARSE...
EVEN THOUGH IT WAS MADE WITH INCREDIBLE SPEED, I CANNOT, IN GOOD CONSCIENCE, LET YOU GUYS PASS.
UUH ...
OH BOY ...
BRITAIN CAN'T DO A THING WITHOUT THE U.S. OF A. BEING THERE FOR BACKUP.
THE NEXT TEAM READY FOR JUDGING IS US, THE UNITED STATES!
ALTHOUGH IT'S ALSO A LOAF OF BREAD, OURS IS A BIT DIFFERENT FROM THE BRITISH ONE.

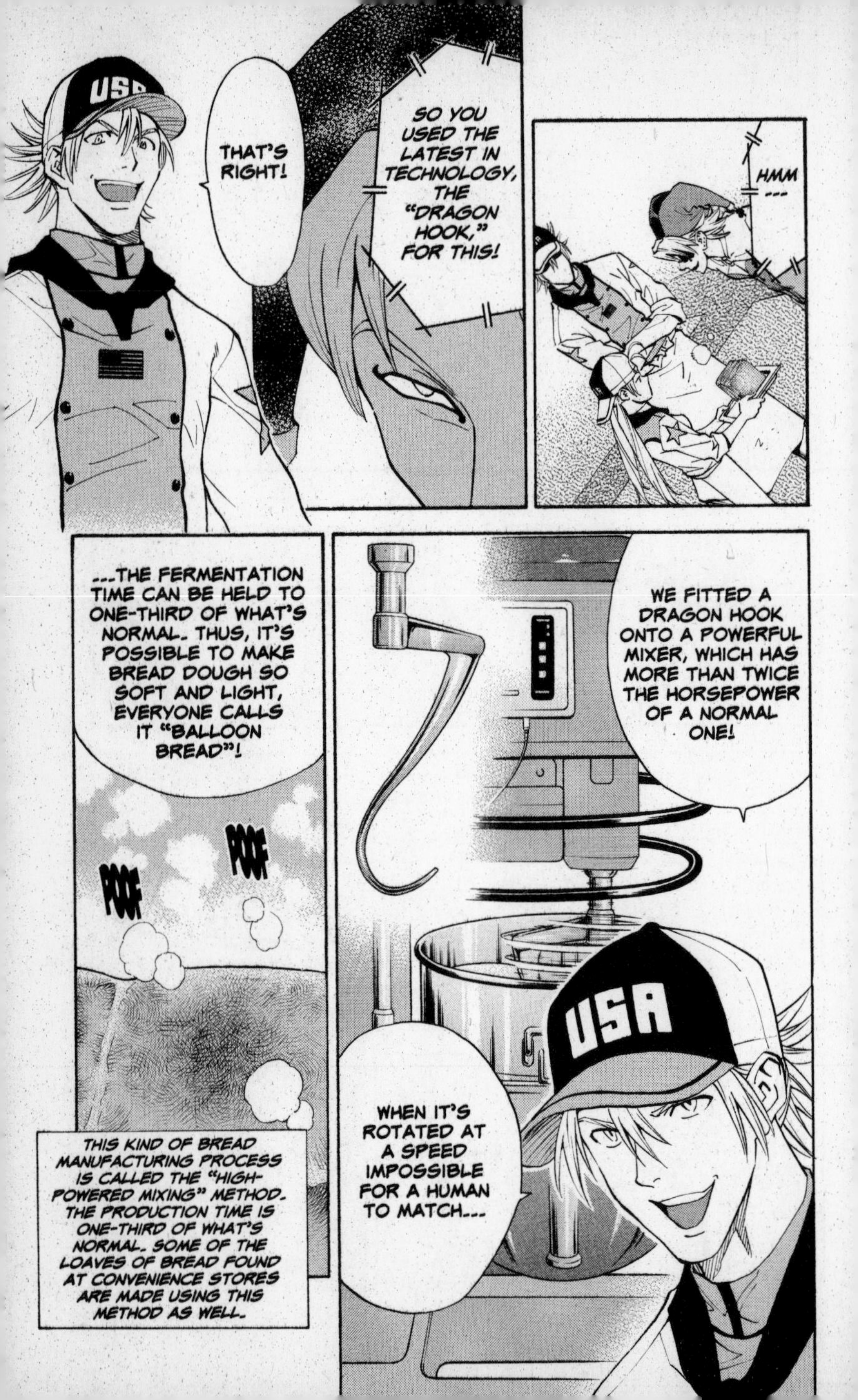
HMM ---
SO YOU USED THE LATEST IN TECHNOLOGY, THE "DRAGON HOOK," FOR THIS!
THAT'S RIGHT!
WE FITTED A DRAGON HOOK ONTO A POWERFUL MIXER, WHICH HAS MORE THAN TWICE THE HORSEPOWER OF A NORMAL ONE!
WHEN IT'S ROTATED AT A SPEED IMPOSSIBLE FOR A HUMAN TO MATCH...
...THE FERMENTATION TIME CAN BE HELD TO ONE-THIRD OF WHAT'S NORMAL. THUS, IT'S POSSIBLE TO MAKE BREAD DOUGH SO SOFT AND LIGHT, EVERYONE CALLS IT "BALLOON BREAD"!
POOF
POOF
THIS KIND OF BREAD MANUFACTURING PROCESS IS CALLED THE "HIGH-POWERED MIXING" METHOD. THE PRODUCTION TIME IS ONE-THIRD OF WHAT'S NORMAL. SOME OF THE LOAVES OF BREAD FOUND AT CONVENIENCE STORES ARE MADE USING THIS METHOD AS WELL.

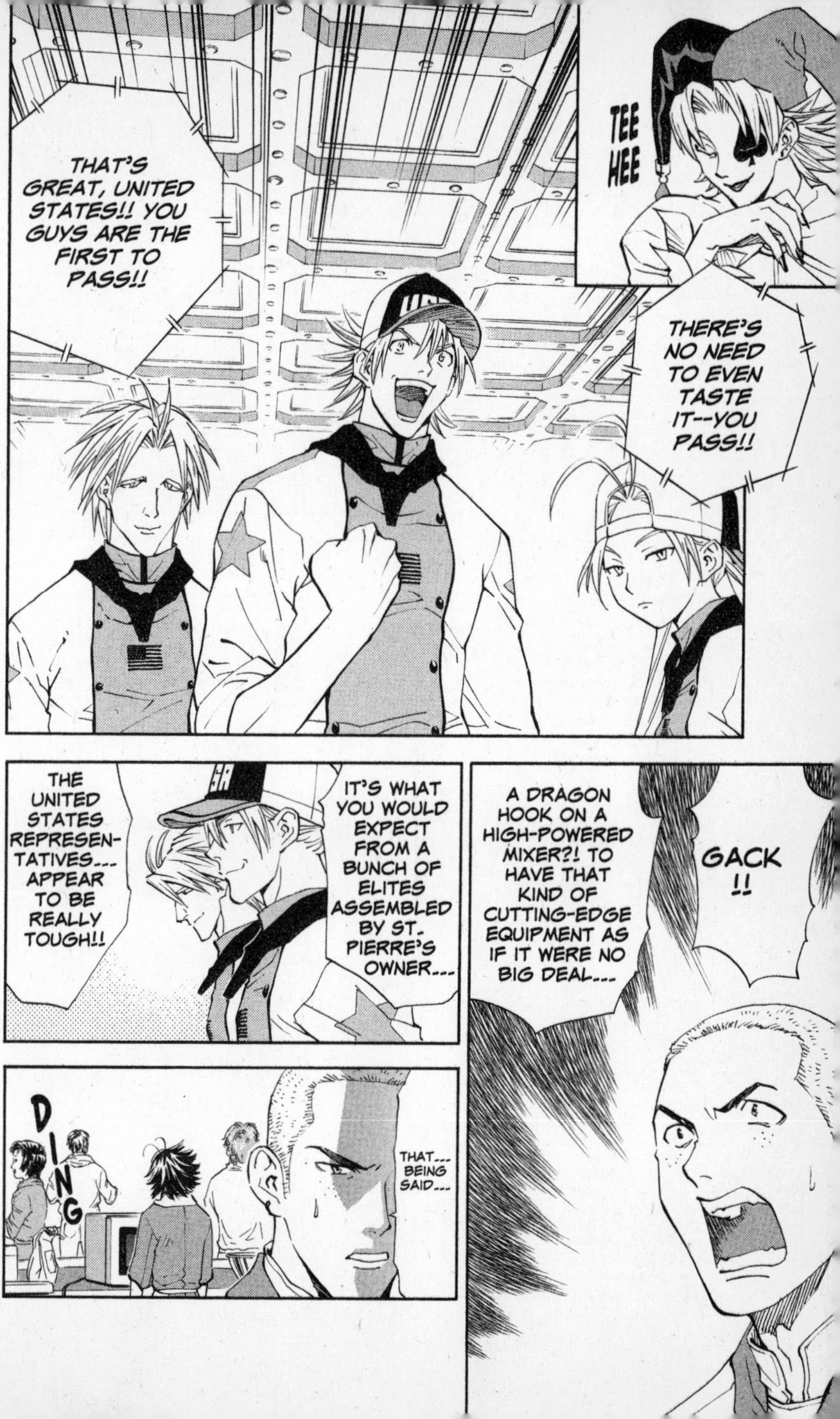
TEE HEE
THAT'S GREAT, UNITED STATES!! YOU GUYS ARE THE FIRST TO PASS!!
THERE'S NO NEED TO EVEN TASTE IT--YOU PASS!!
GACK !!
A DRAGON HOOK ON A HIGH-POWERED MIXER?! TO HAVE THAT KIND OF CUTTING-EDGE EQUIPMENT AS IF IT WERE NO BIG DEAL...
IT'S WHAT YOU WOULD EXPECT FROM A BUNCH OF ELITES ASSEMBLED BY ST. PIERRE'S OWNER...
THE UNITED STATES REPRESEN-TATIVES... APPEAR TO BE REALLY TOUGH!!
THAT... BEING SAID...
DING

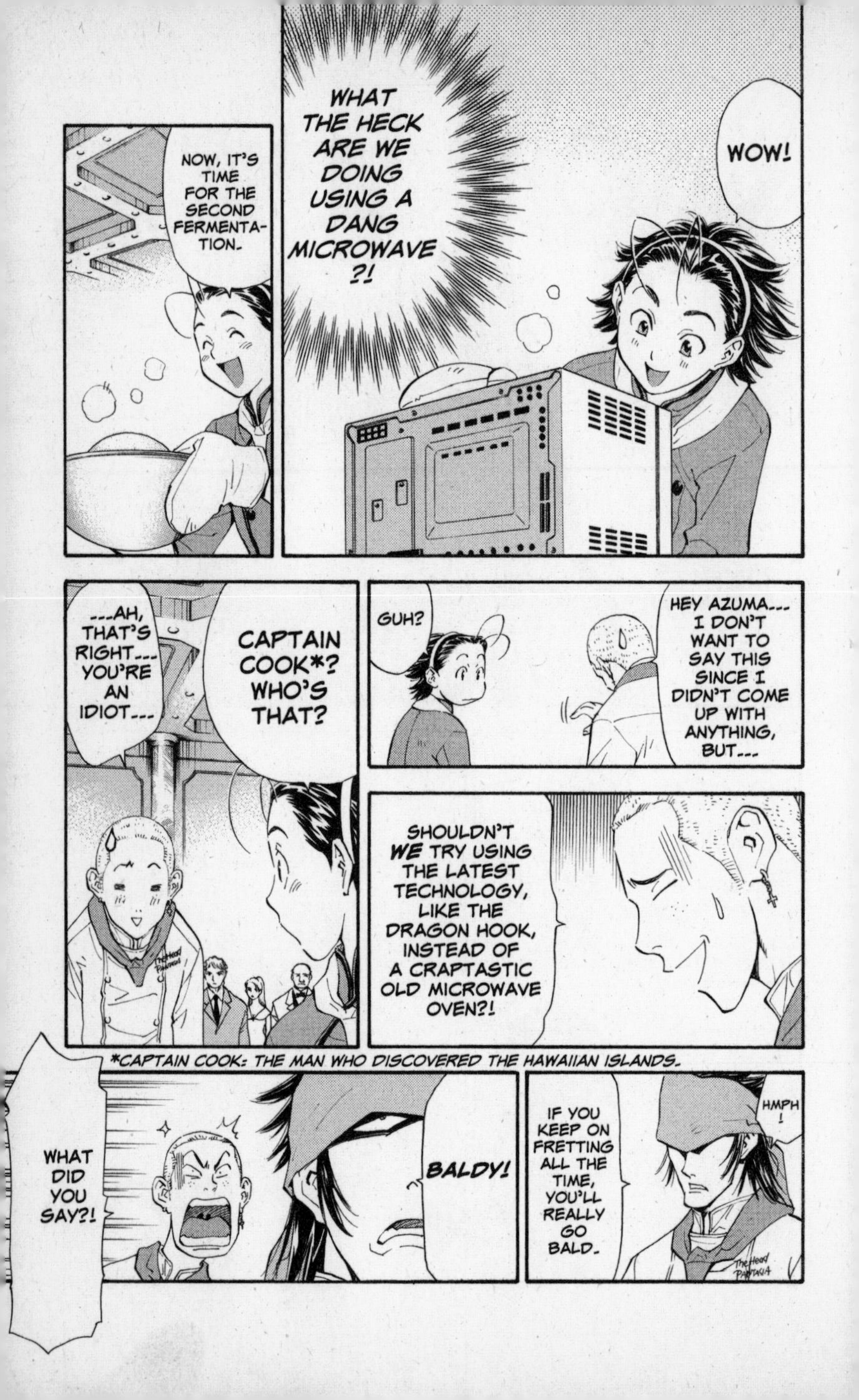
WOW!
WHAT THE HECK ARE WE DOING USING A DANG MICROWAVE ?!
NOW, IT'S TIME FOR THE SECOND FERMENTA-TION.
HEY AZUMA... I DON'T WANT TO SAY THIS SINCE I DIDN'T COME UP WITH ANYTHING, BUT...
GUH?
SHOULDN'T WE TRY USING THE LATEST TECHNOLOGY, LIKE THE DRAGON HOOK, INSTEAD OF A CRAPTASTIC OLD MICROWAVE OVEN?!
CAPTAIN COOK*? WHO'S THAT?
...AH, THAT'S RIGHT... YOU'RE AN IDIOT...
*CAPTAIN COOK: THE MAN WHO DISCOVERED THE HAWAIIAN ISLANDS.
HMPH!
IF YOU KEEP ON FRETTING ALL THE TIME, YOU'LL REALLY GO BALD.
BALDY!
WHAT DID YOU SAY?!

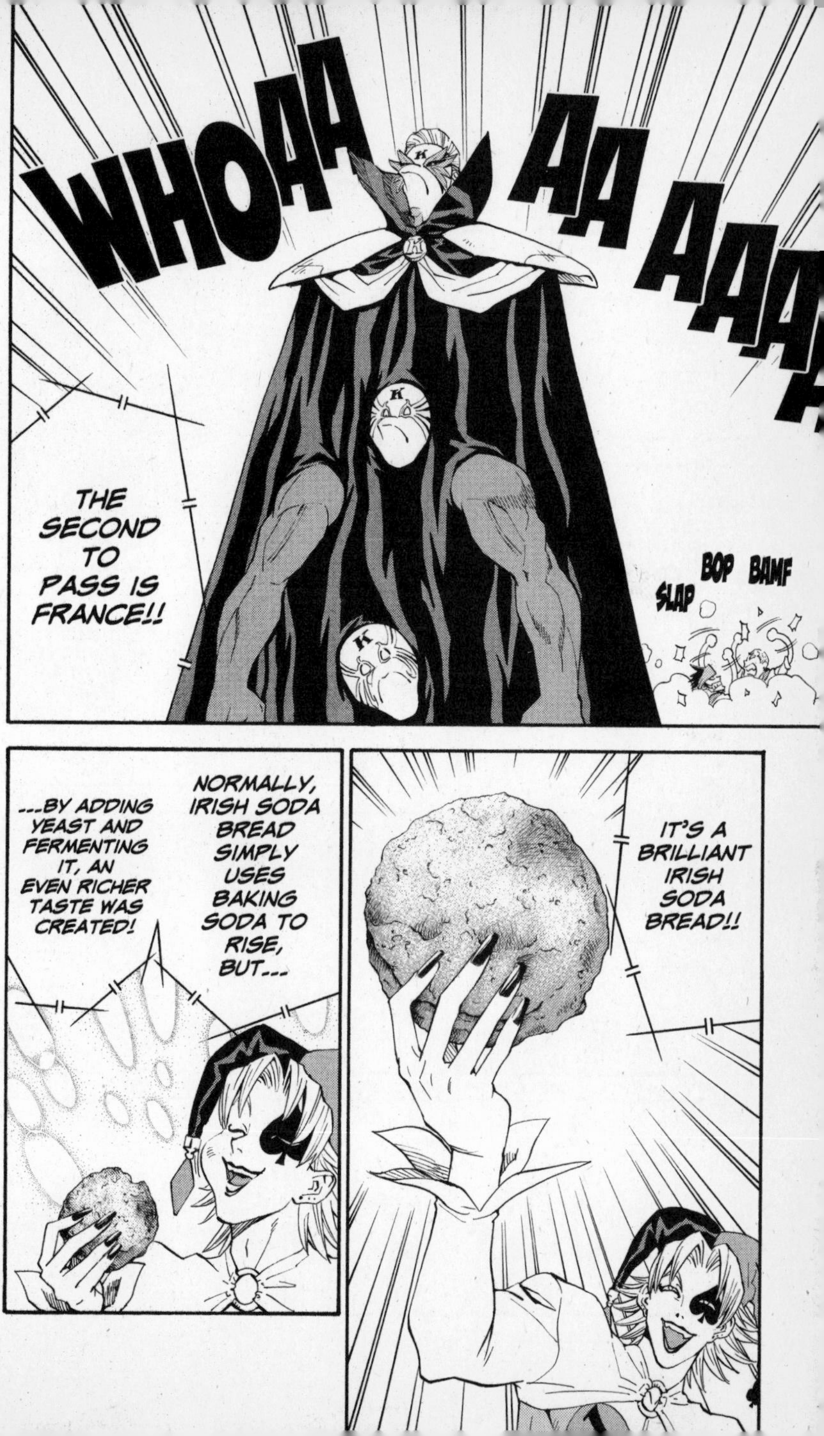
WHOAA AA AAAA
BAMF BOP SLAP
THE SECOND TO PASS IS FRANCE!!
IT'S A BRILLIANT IRISH SODA BREAD!!
NORMALLY, IRISH SODA BREAD SIMPLY USES BAKING SODA TO RISE, BUT...
...BY ADDING YEAST AND FERMENTING IT, AN EVEN RICHER TASTE WAS CREATED!

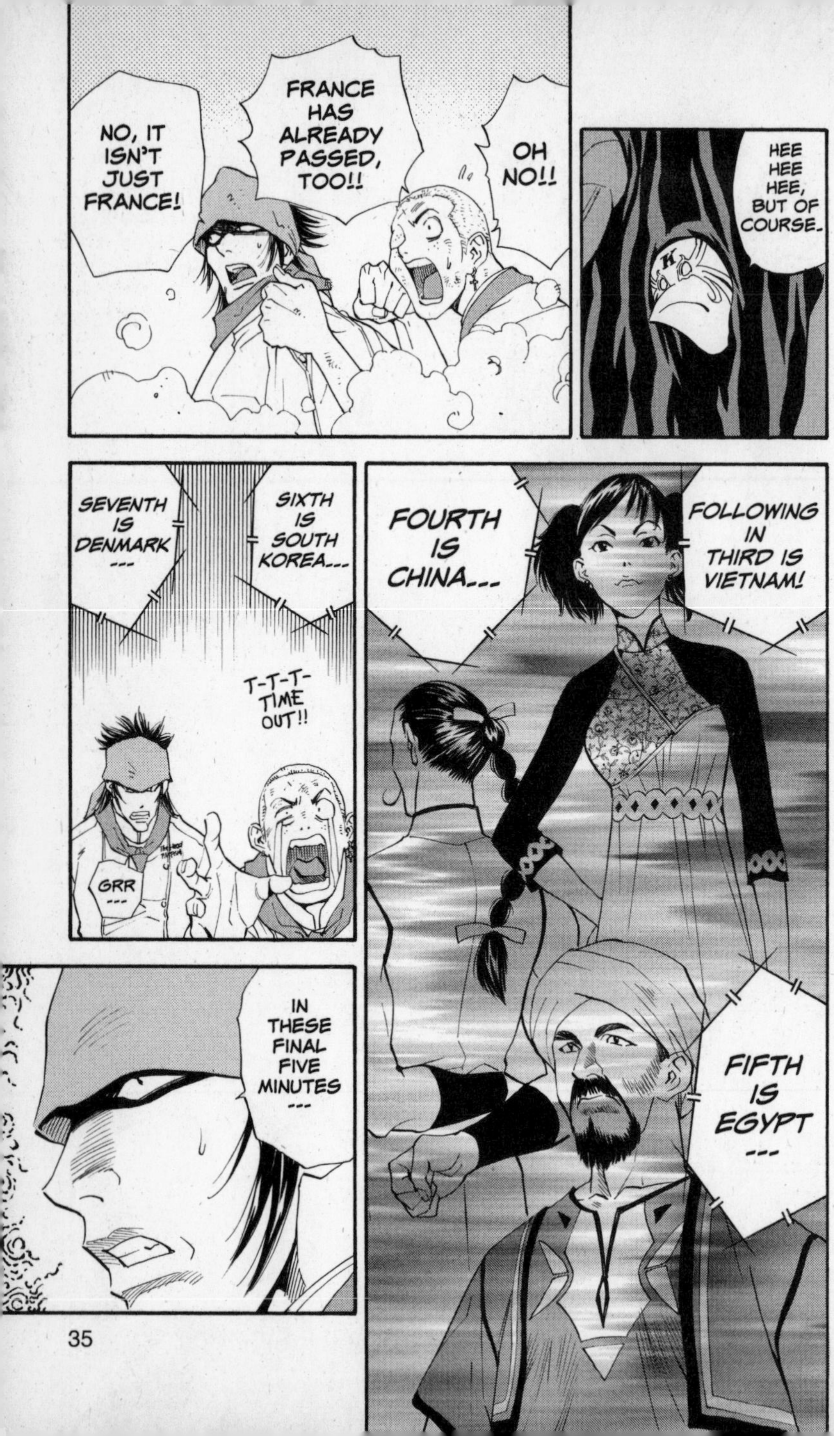
HEE HEE HEE, BUT OF COURSE...
OH NO!!
FRANCE HAS ALREADY PASSED, TOO!!
NO, IT ISN'T JUST FRANCE!
FOLLOWING IN THIRD IS VIETNAM!
FOURTH IS CHINA...
FIFTH IS EGYPT ...
SIXTH IS SOUTH KOREA...
SEVENTH IS DENMARK ...
T-T-T-TIME OUT!!
GRR ...
IN THESE FINAL FIVE MINUTES ...

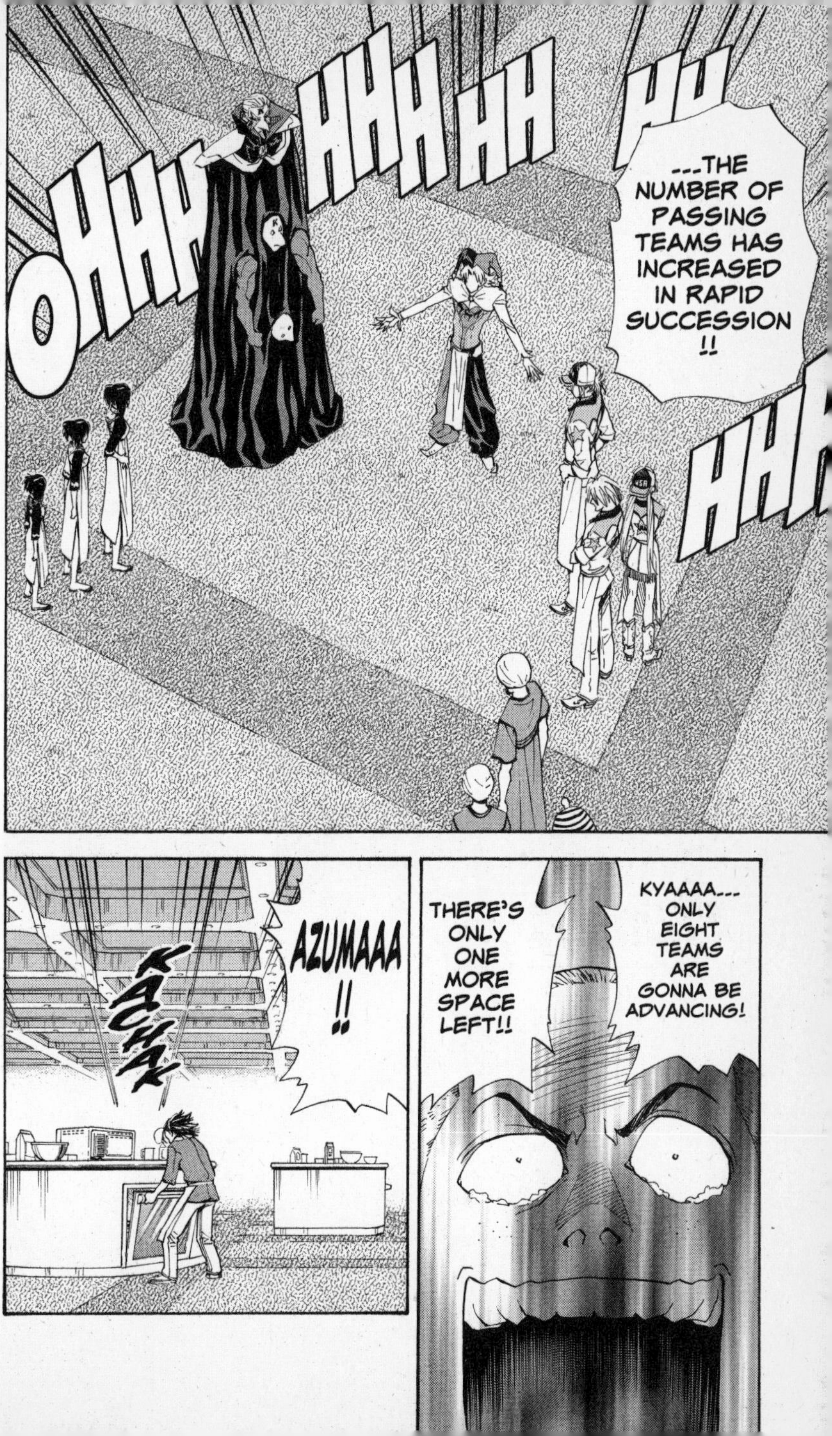

OHHHHHHHHHHHHU
---THE NUMBER OF PASSING TEAMS HAS INCREASED IN RAPID SUCCESSION !!
HHH
KYAAAA... ONLY EIGHT TEAMS ARE GONNA BE ADVANCING!
THERE'S ONLY ONE MORE SPACE LEFT!!
AZUMAAA !!
KACHAK

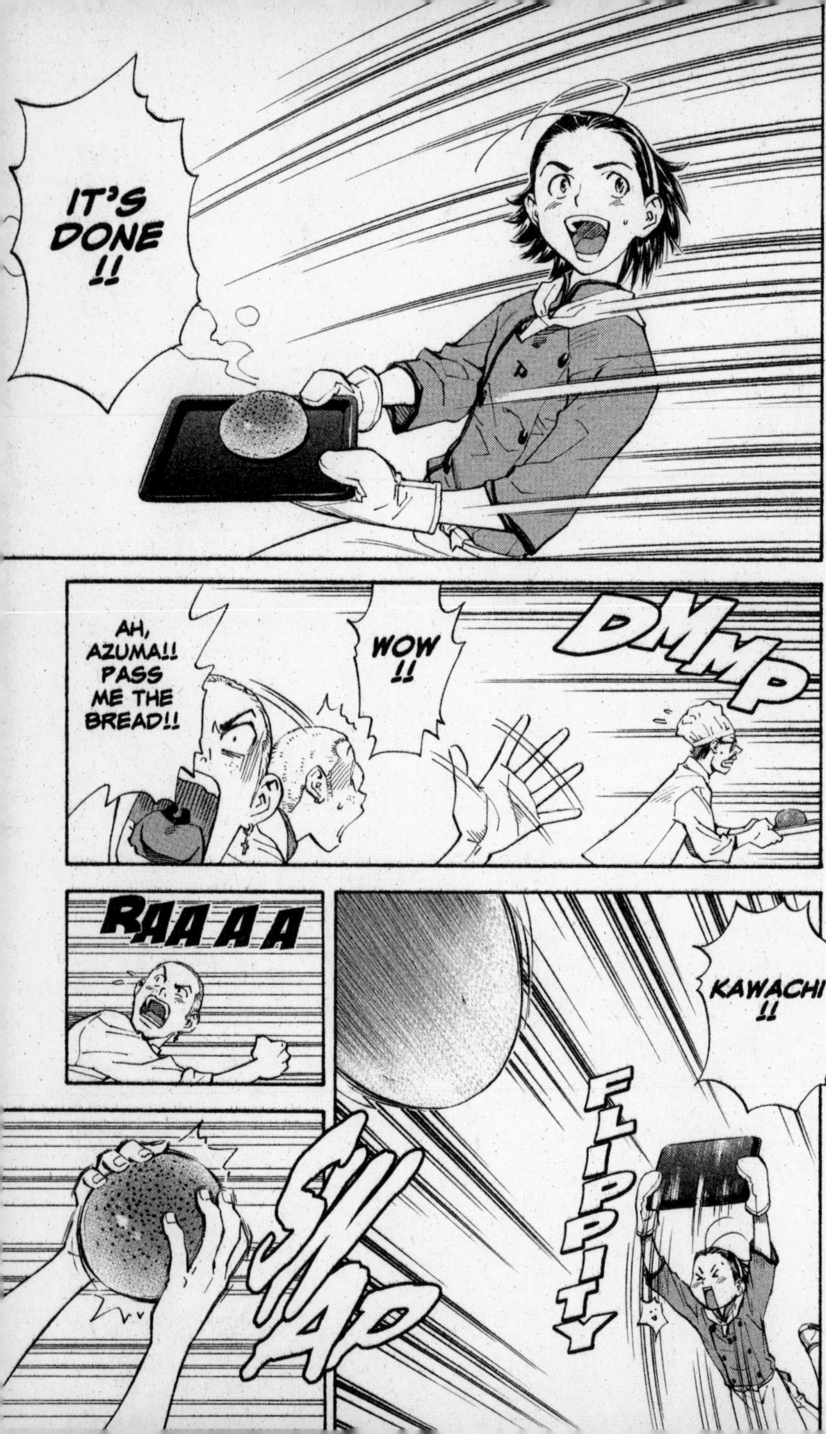
IT'S DONE !!
DMMP
WOW !!
AH, AZUMA!! PASS ME THE BREAD!!
KAWACHI !!
FLIPPITY
RAAAA
SHAP

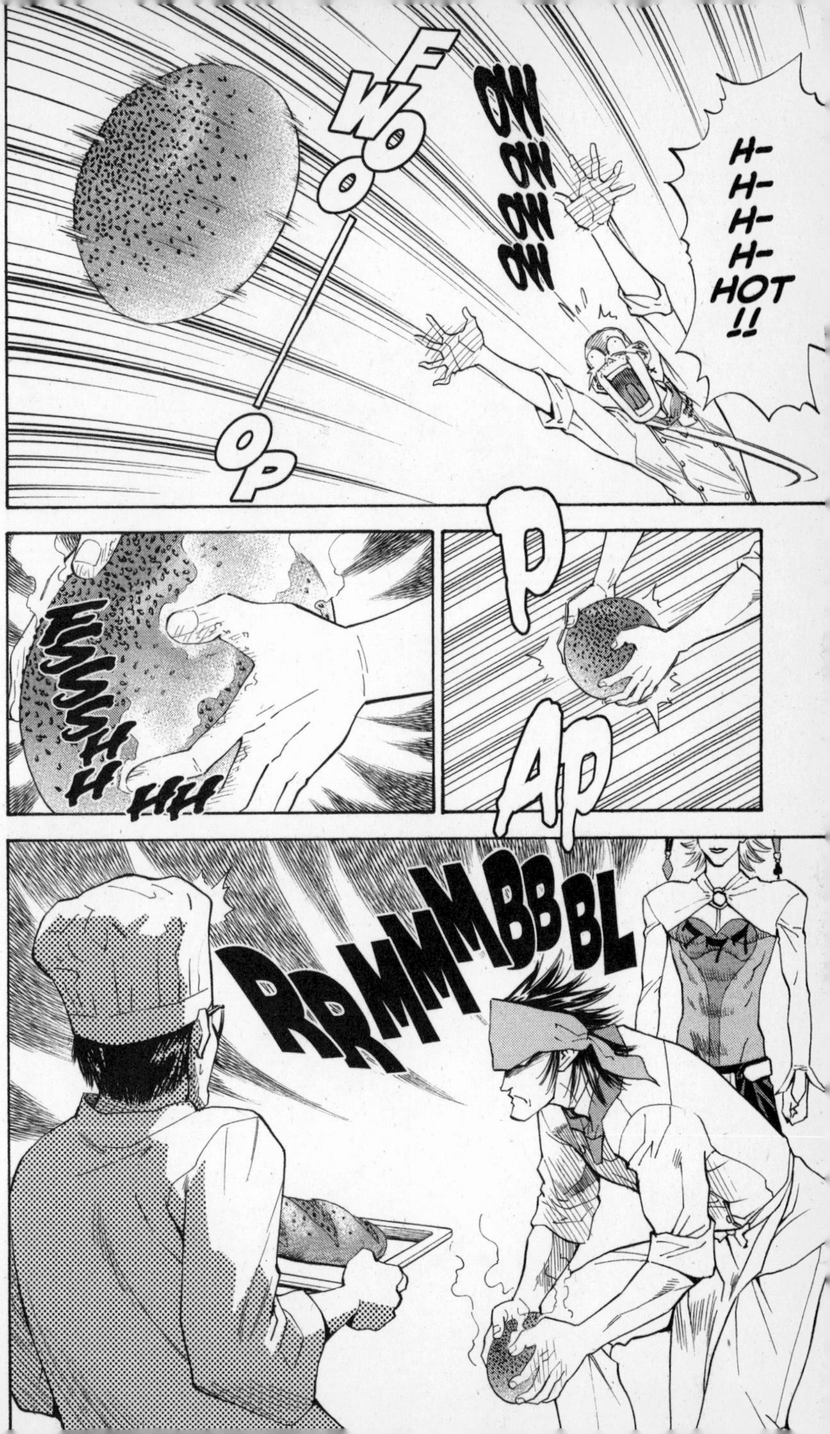
H-
H-
H-
H-
HOT
!!
OW OW OW OW
FWOOO—OP
P
AP
FSSSSHHHHH
RRMMMBBBL

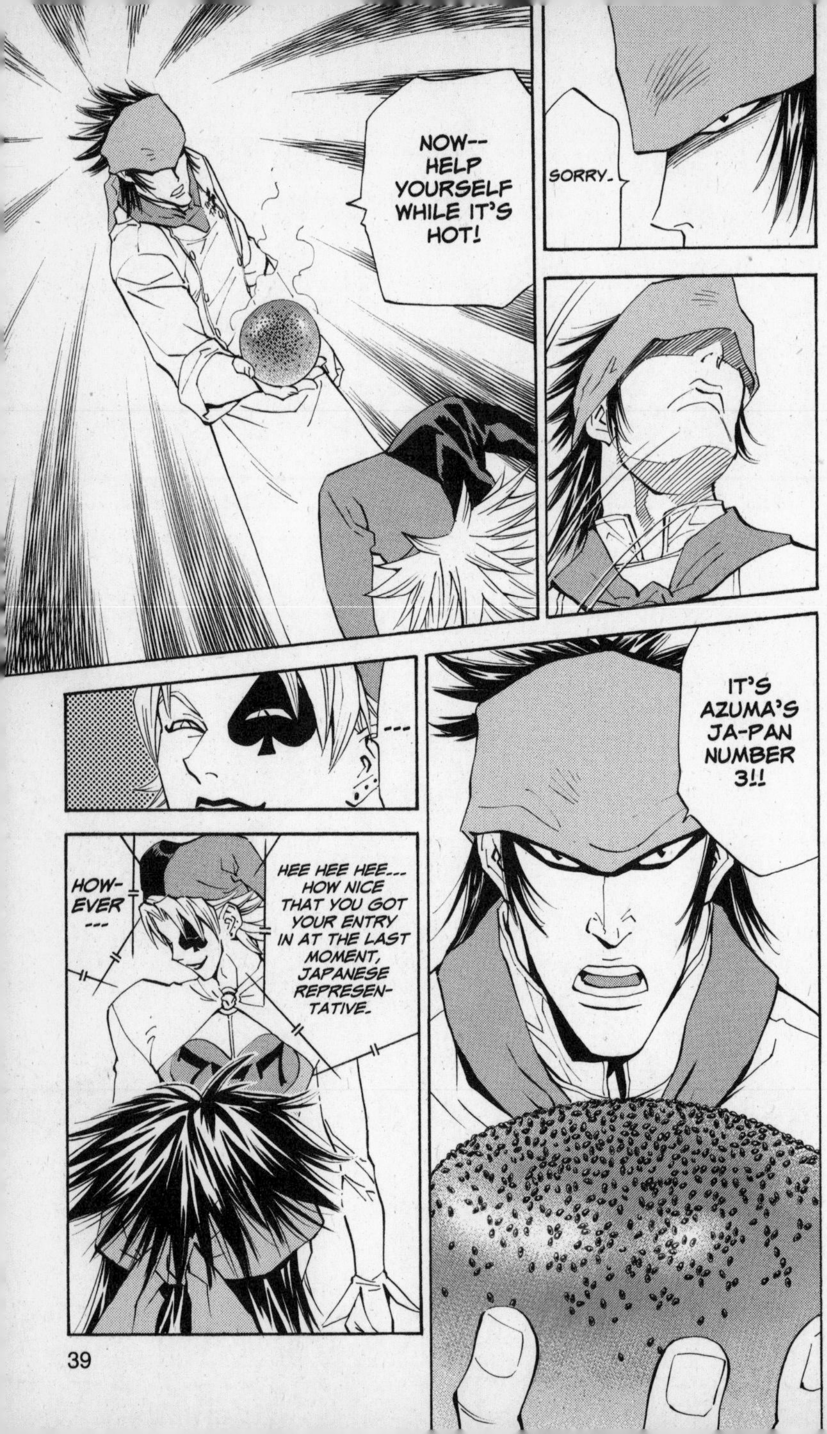
SORRY.
NOW-- HELP YOURSELF WHILE IT'S HOT!
IT'S AZUMA'S JA-PAN NUMBER 3!!
---
HEE HEE HEE... HOW NICE THAT YOU GOT YOUR ENTRY IN AT THE LAST MOMENT, JAPANESE REPRESEN-TATIVE.
HOW-EVER ---

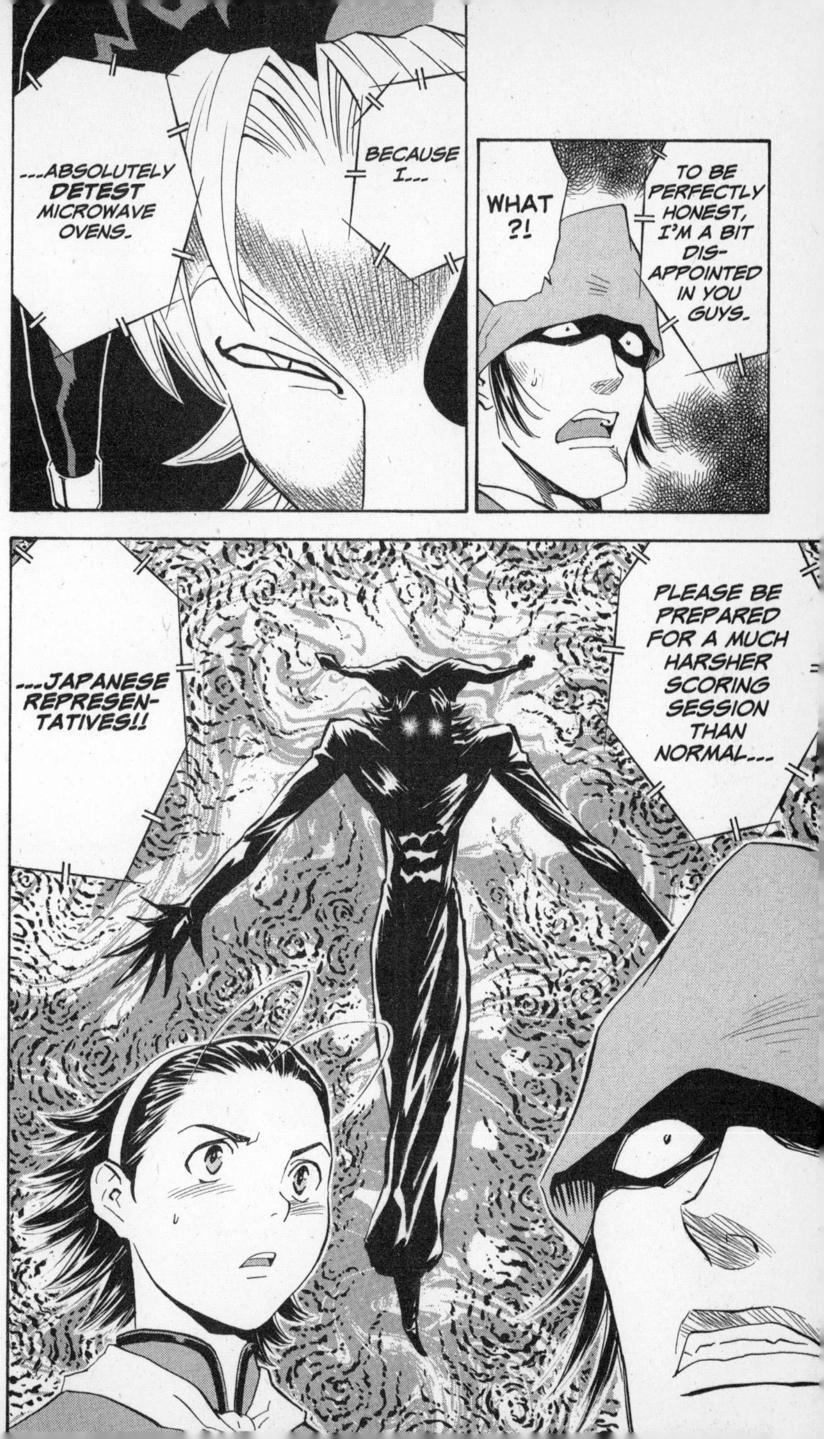
TO BE PERFECTLY HONEST, I'M A BIT DIS-APPOINTED IN YOU GUYS.
WHAT ?!
BECAUSE I...
...ABSOLUTELY DETEST MICROWAVE OVENS.
PLEASE BE PREPARED FOR A MUCH HARSHER SCORING SESSION THAN NORMAL...
...JAPANESE REPRESEN-TATIVES!!

# Story 72: Take Good Care of the Electrons

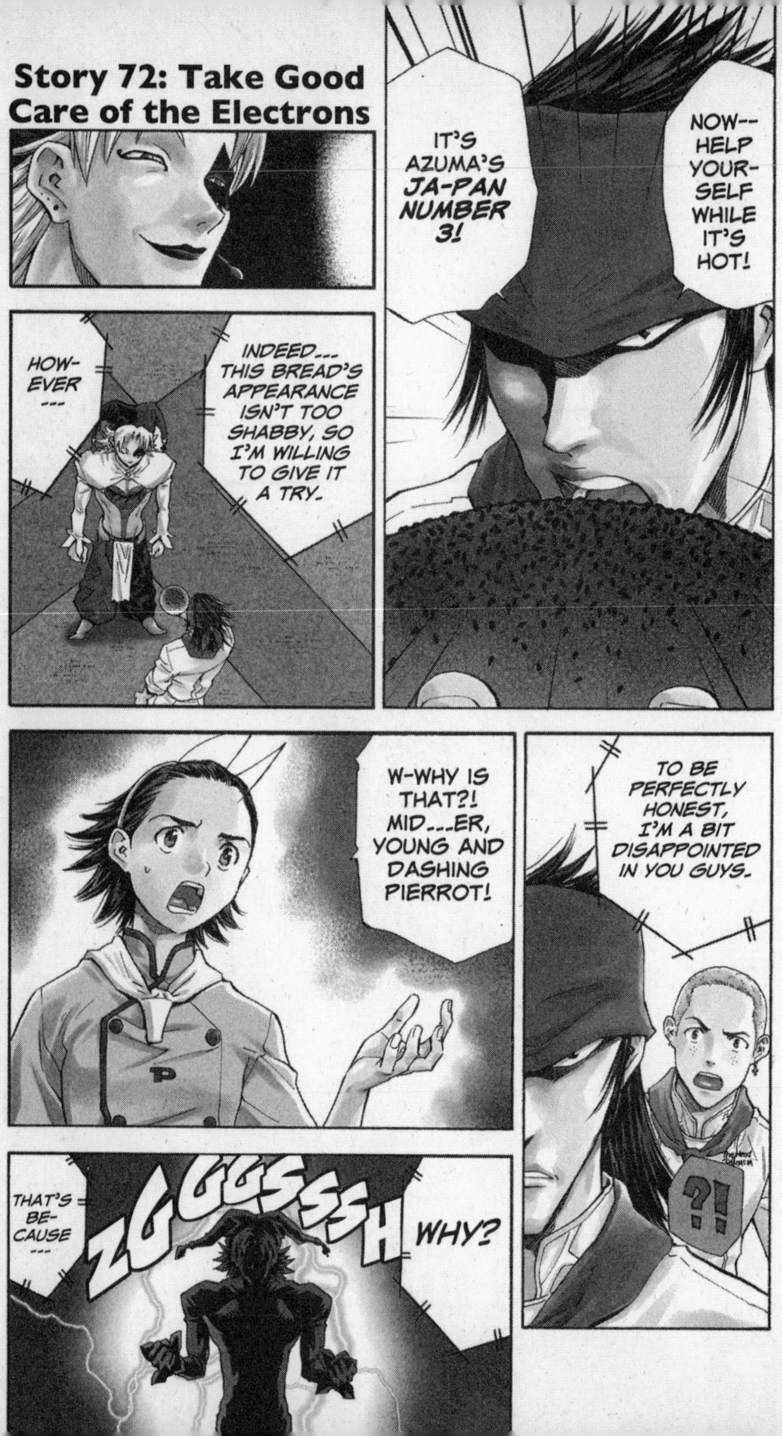
NOW--HELP YOURSELF WHILE IT'S HOT!
IT'S AZUMA'S JA-PAN NUMBER 3!
INDEED... THIS BREAD'S APPEARANCE ISN'T TOO SHABBY, SO I'M WILLING TO GIVE IT A TRY.
HOWEVER---
TO BE PERFECTLY HONEST, I'M A BIT DISAPPOINTED IN YOU GUYS.
?!
W-WHY IS THAT?! MID...ER, YOUNG AND DASHING PIERROT!
WHY?
ZGGSSSH
THAT'S BECAUSE---

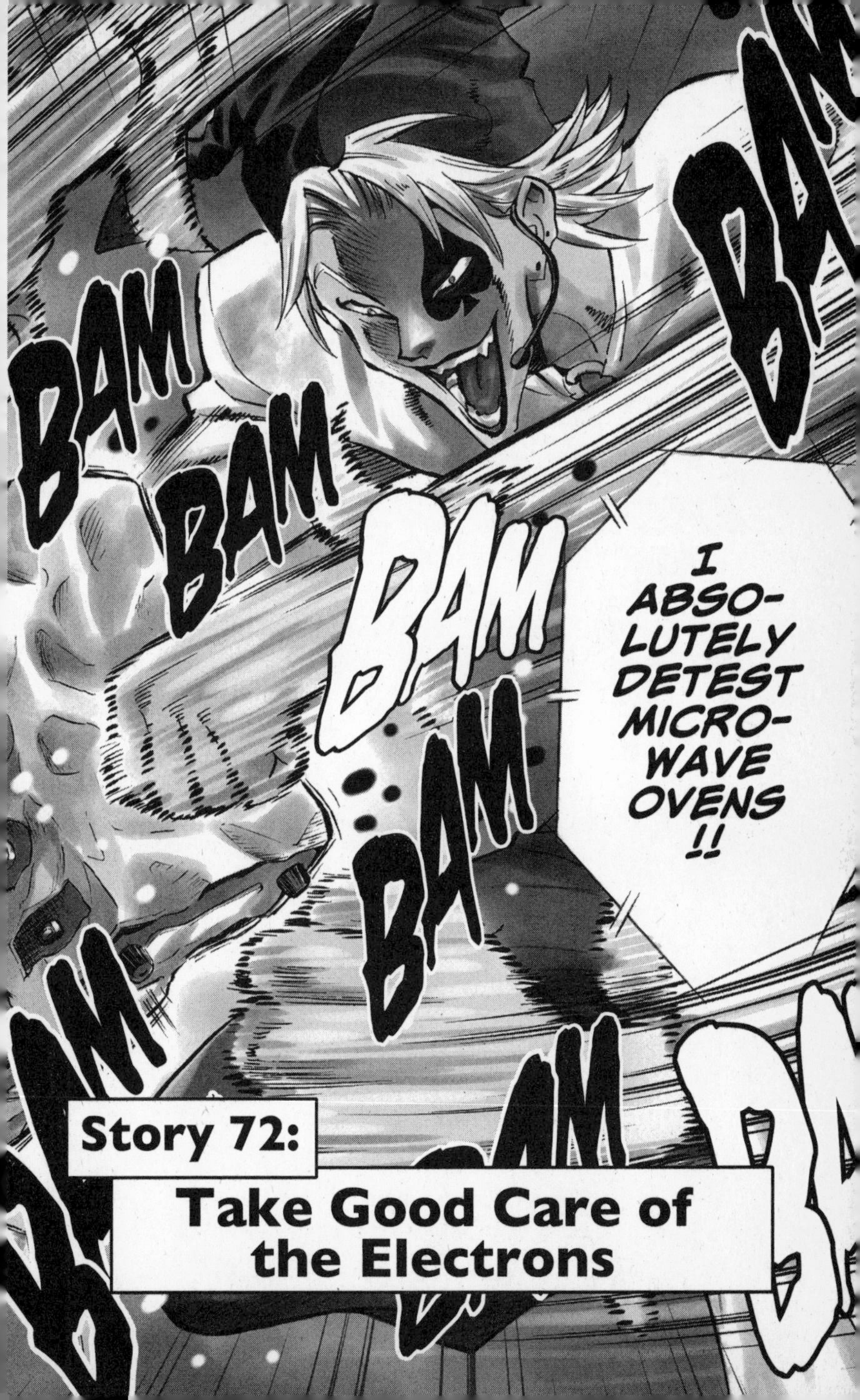
BAM
BAM
BAM
BAM
BAM
I ABSO-LUTELY DETEST MICRO-WAVE OVENS !!
BAM
BAM
Story 72:
Take Good Care of the Electrons

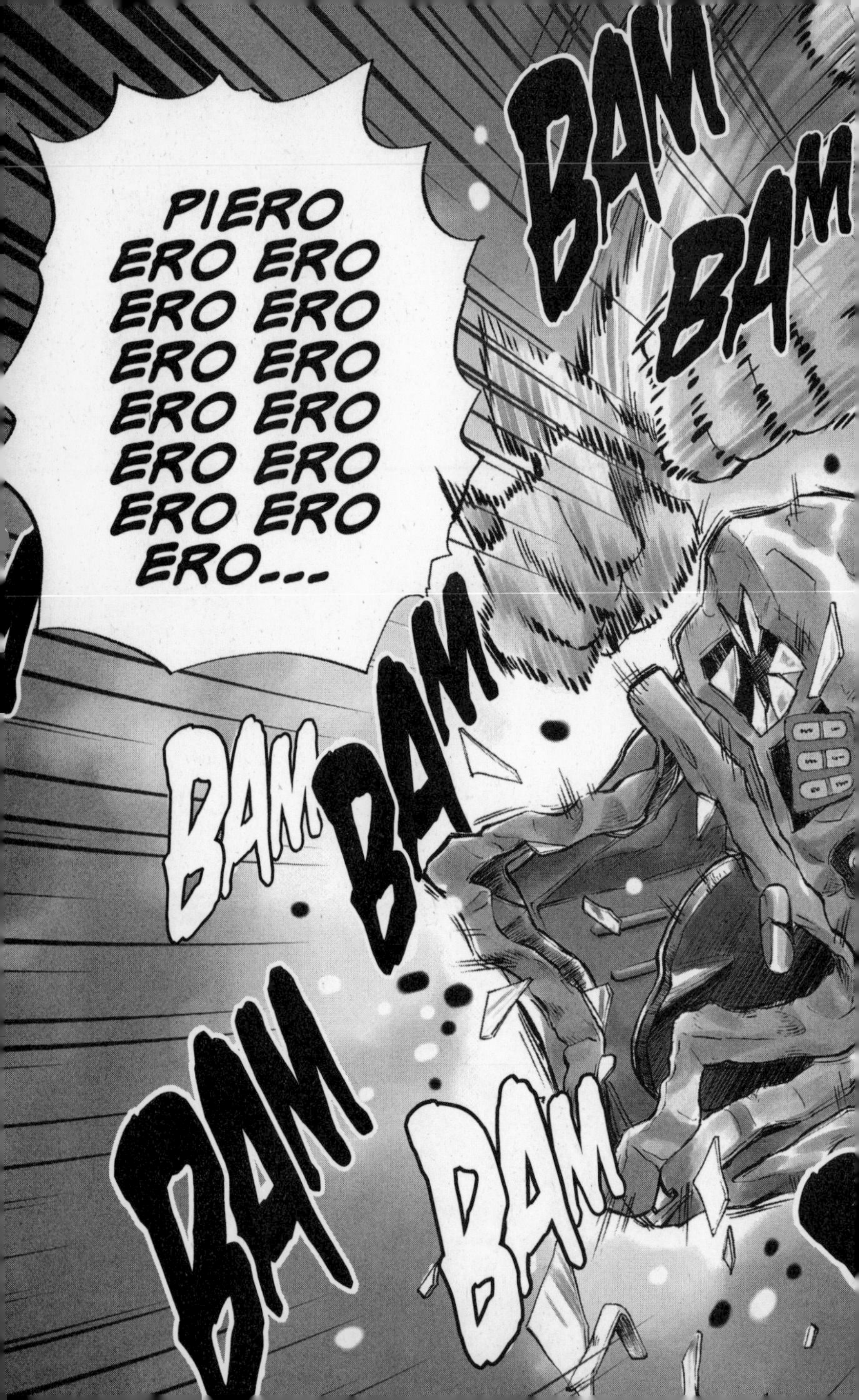
BAM
BAM
PIERO ERO ERO ERO ERO ERO ERO ERO ERO ERO ERO ERO ERO ERO...
BAM
BAM
BAM
BAM

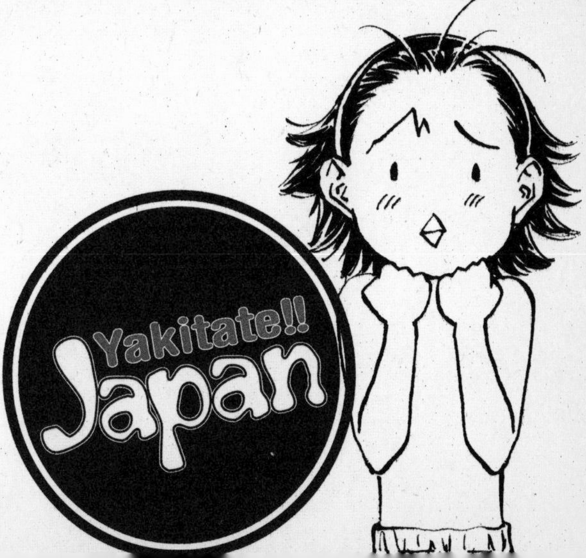
Yakitate!! Japan

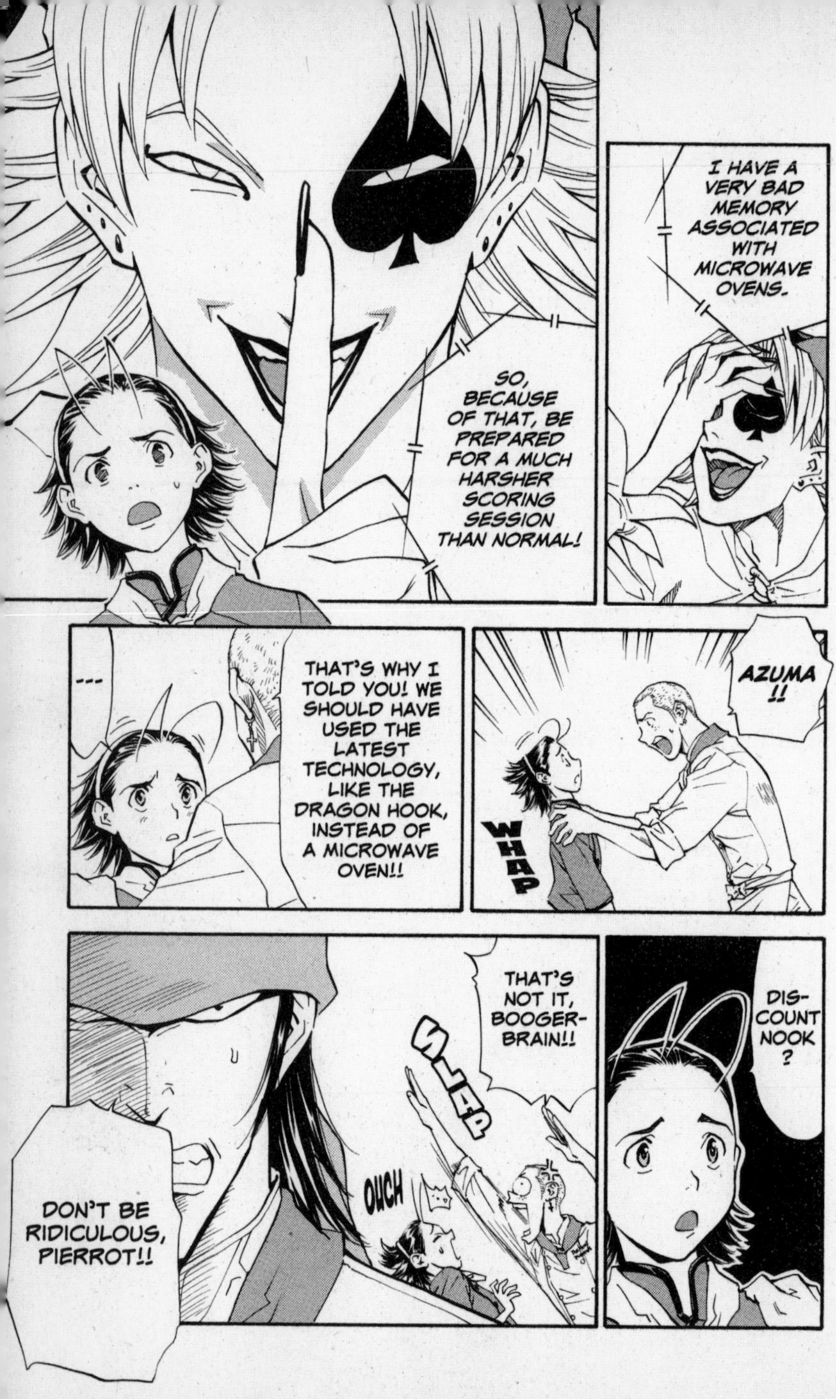
I HAVE A VERY BAD MEMORY ASSOCIATED WITH MICROWAVE OVENS.
SO, BECAUSE OF THAT, BE PREPARED FOR A MUCH HARSHER SCORING SESSION THAN NORMAL!
AZUMA!!
WHAP
THAT'S WHY I TOLD YOU! WE SHOULD HAVE USED THE LATEST TECHNOLOGY, LIKE THE DRAGON HOOK, INSTEAD OF A MICROWAVE OVEN!!
...
DIS-COUNT NOOK?
THAT'S NOT IT, BOOGER-BRAIN!!
SLAP
OUCH
DON'T BE RIDICULOUS, PIERROT!!

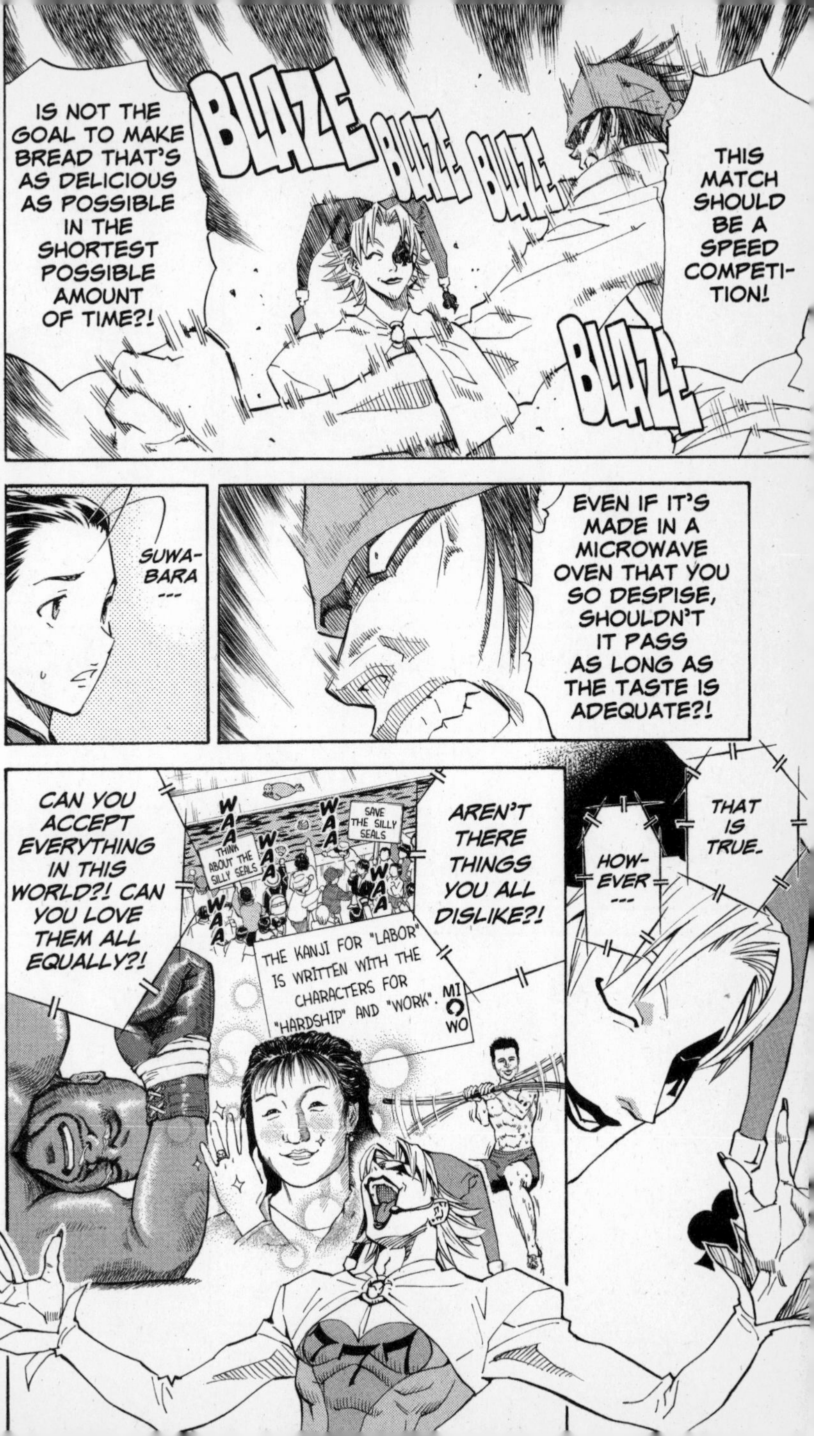
THIS MATCH SHOULD BE A SPEED COMPETITION!
BLAZE BLAZE BLAZE BLAZE
IS NOT THE GOAL TO MAKE BREAD THAT'S AS DELICIOUS AS POSSIBLE IN THE SHORTEST POSSIBLE AMOUNT OF TIME?!
BLAZE
EVEN IF IT'S MADE IN A MICROWAVE OVEN THAT YOU SO DESPISE, SHOULDN'T IT PASS AS LONG AS THE TASTE IS ADEQUATE?!
SUWA-BARA ---
THAT IS TRUE.
HOW-EVER ---
AREN'T THERE THINGS YOU ALL DISLIKE?!
SAVE THE SILLY SEALS
WAA WAA WAA WAA WAA
THINK ABOUT THE SILLY SEALS
CAN YOU ACCEPT EVERYTHING IN THIS WORLD?! CAN YOU LOVE THEM ALL EQUALLY?!
THE KANJI FOR "LABOR" IS WRITTEN WITH THE CHARACTERS FOR "HARDSHIP" AND "WORK".
MI WO

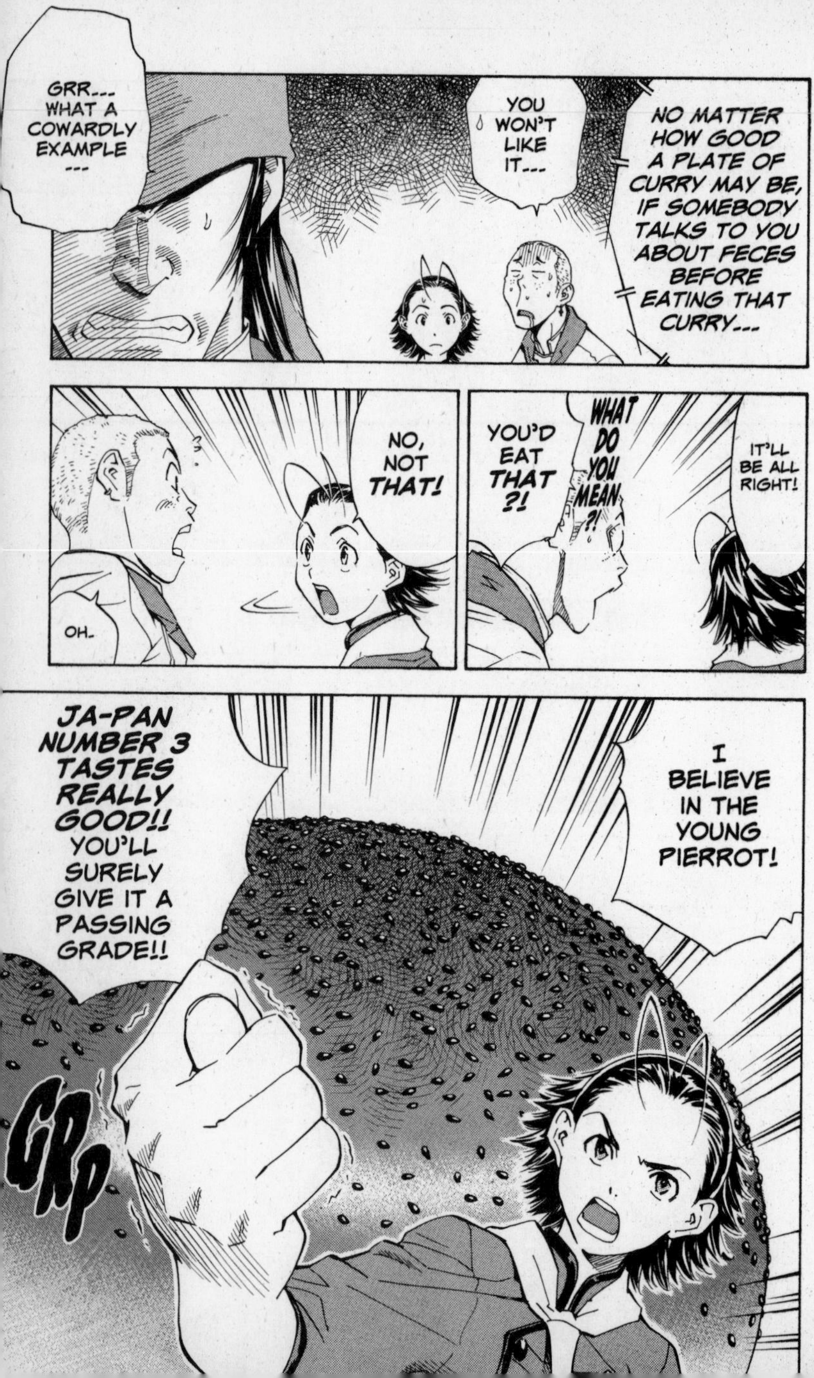
NO MATTER HOW GOOD A PLATE OF CURRY MAY BE, IF SOMEBODY TALKS TO YOU ABOUT FECES BEFORE EATING THAT CURRY...
YOU WON'T LIKE IT...
GRR... WHAT A COWARDLY EXAMPLE...
IT'LL BE ALL RIGHT!
WHAT DO YOU MEAN?!
YOU'D EAT THAT?!
NO, NOT THAT!
OH.
I BELIEVE IN THE YOUNG PIERROT!
JA-PAN NUMBER 3 TASTES REALLY GOOD!! YOU'LL SURELY GIVE IT A PASSING GRADE!!
GRP

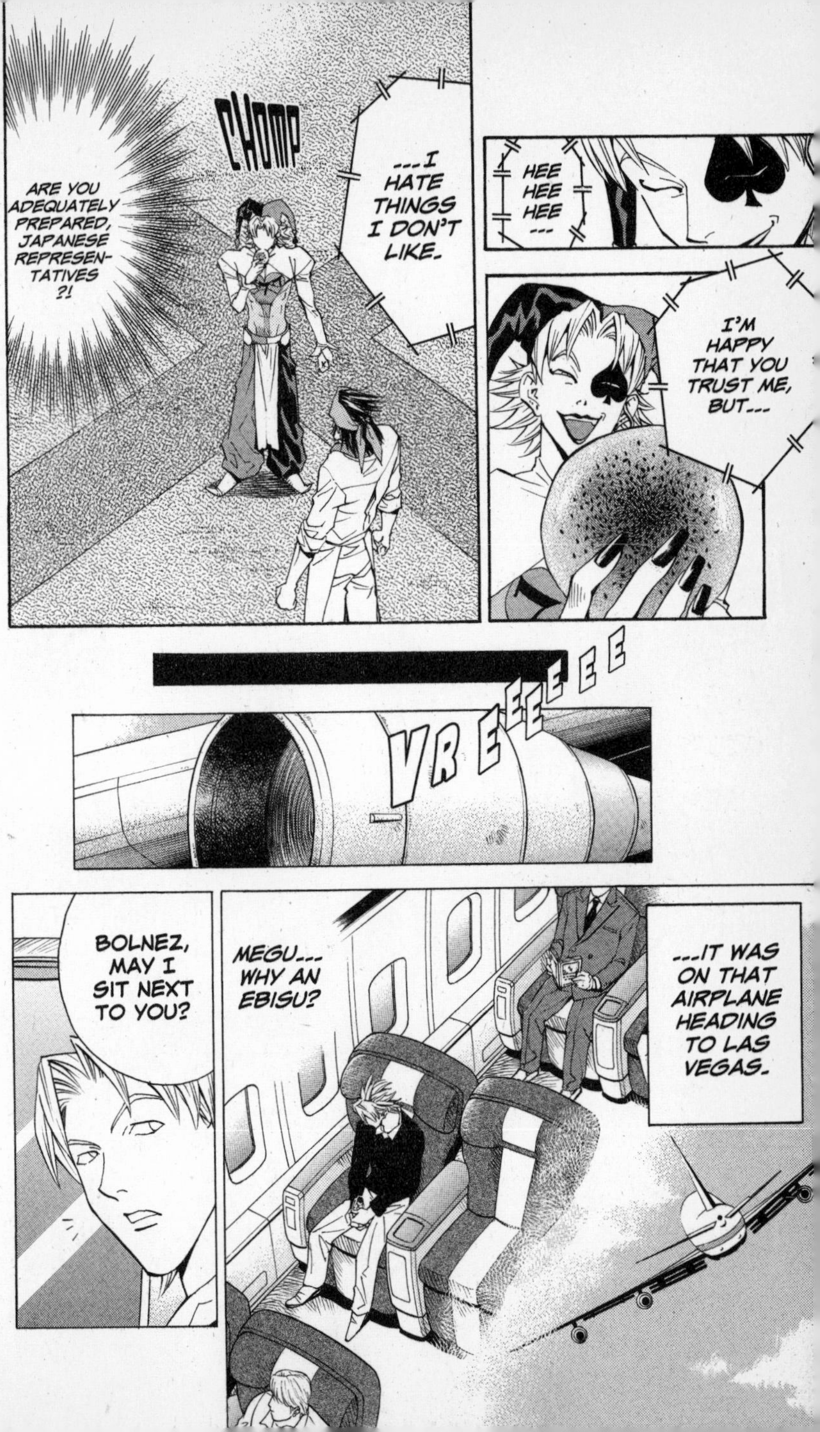
HEE HEE HEE ---
I'M HAPPY THAT YOU TRUST ME, BUT---
---I HATE THINGS I DON'T LIKE.
CHOMP
ARE YOU ADEQUATELY PREPARED, JAPANESE REPRESEN-TATIVES ?!
VREEEEEEE
---IT WAS ON THAT AIRPLANE HEADING TO LAS VEGAS.
MEGU--- WHY AN EBISU?
BOLNEZ, MAY I SIT NEXT TO YOU?

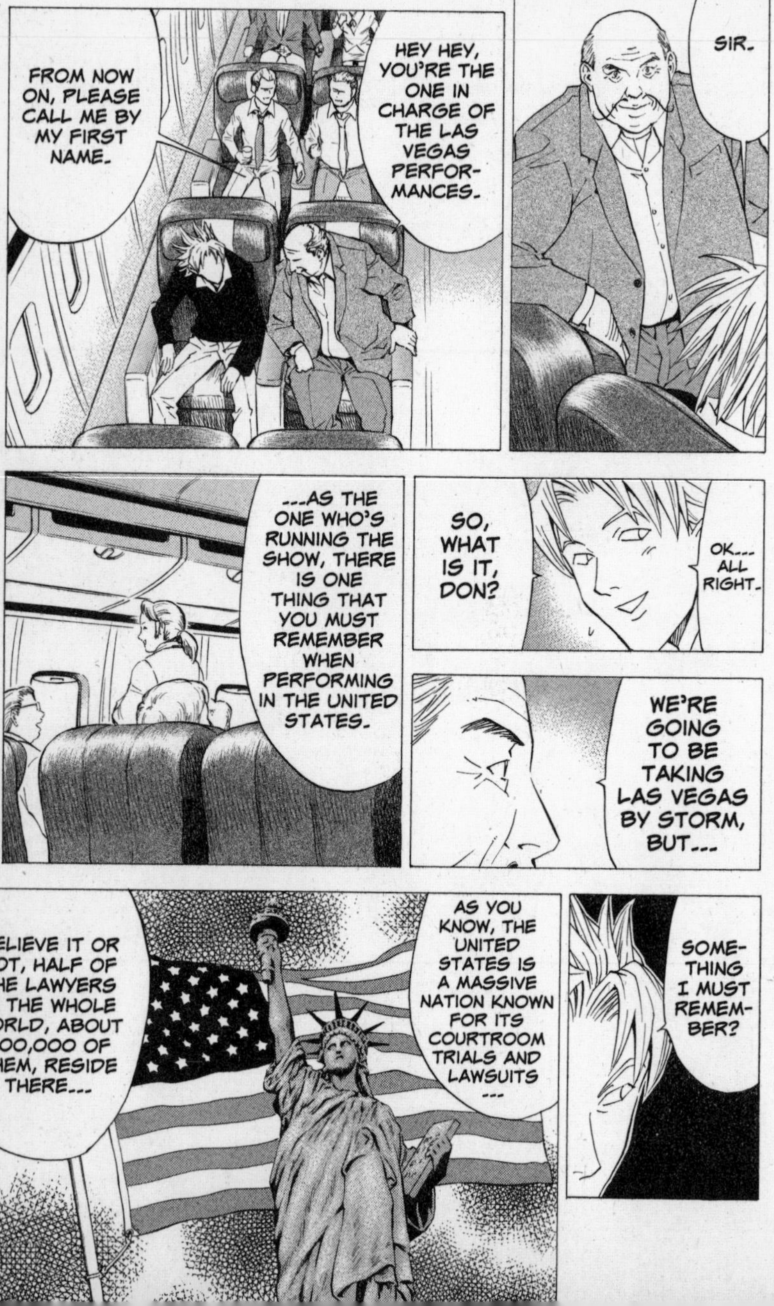
SIR.
HEY HEY, YOU'RE THE ONE IN CHARGE OF THE LAS VEGAS PERFOR-MANCES.
FROM NOW ON, PLEASE CALL ME BY MY FIRST NAME.
OK... ALL RIGHT.
SO, WHAT IS IT, DON?
WE'RE GOING TO BE TAKING LAS VEGAS BY STORM, BUT...
...AS THE ONE WHO'S RUNNING THE SHOW, THERE IS ONE THING THAT YOU MUST REMEMBER WHEN PERFORMING IN THE UNITED STATES.
SOME-THING I MUST REMEM-BER?
AS YOU KNOW, THE UNITED STATES IS A MASSIVE NATION KNOWN FOR ITS COURTROOM TRIALS AND LAWSUITS ...
BELIEVE IT OR NOT, HALF OF THE LAWYERS IN THE WHOLE WORLD, ABOUT 900,000 OF THEM, RESIDE THERE...

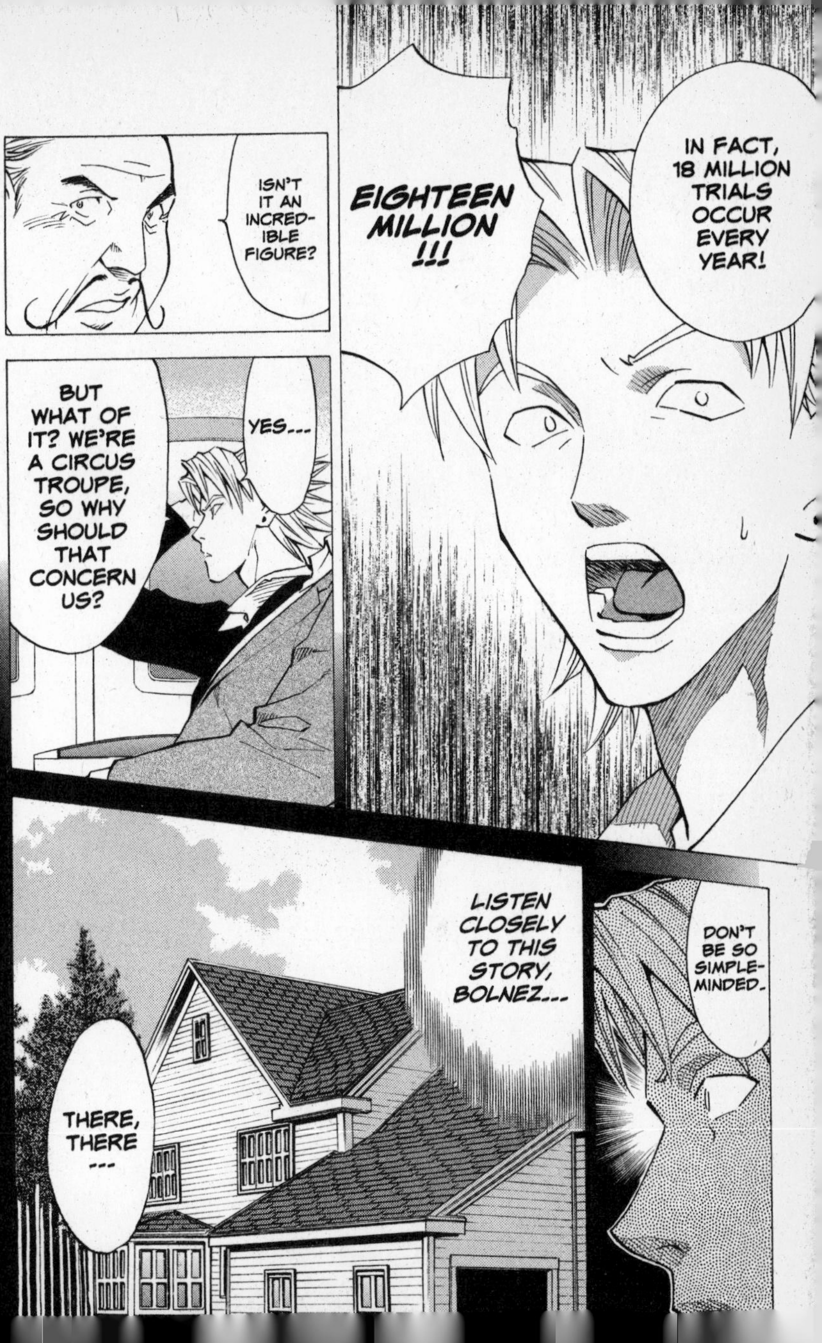
IN FACT, 18 MILLION TRIALS OCCUR EVERY YEAR!
EIGHTEEN MILLION!!!
ISN'T IT AN INCREDIBLE FIGURE?
YES...
BUT WHAT OF IT? WE'RE A CIRCUS TROUPE, SO WHY SHOULD THAT CONCERN US?
DON'T BE SO SIMPLE-MINDED.
LISTEN CLOSELY TO THIS STORY, BOLNEZ...
THERE, THERE...

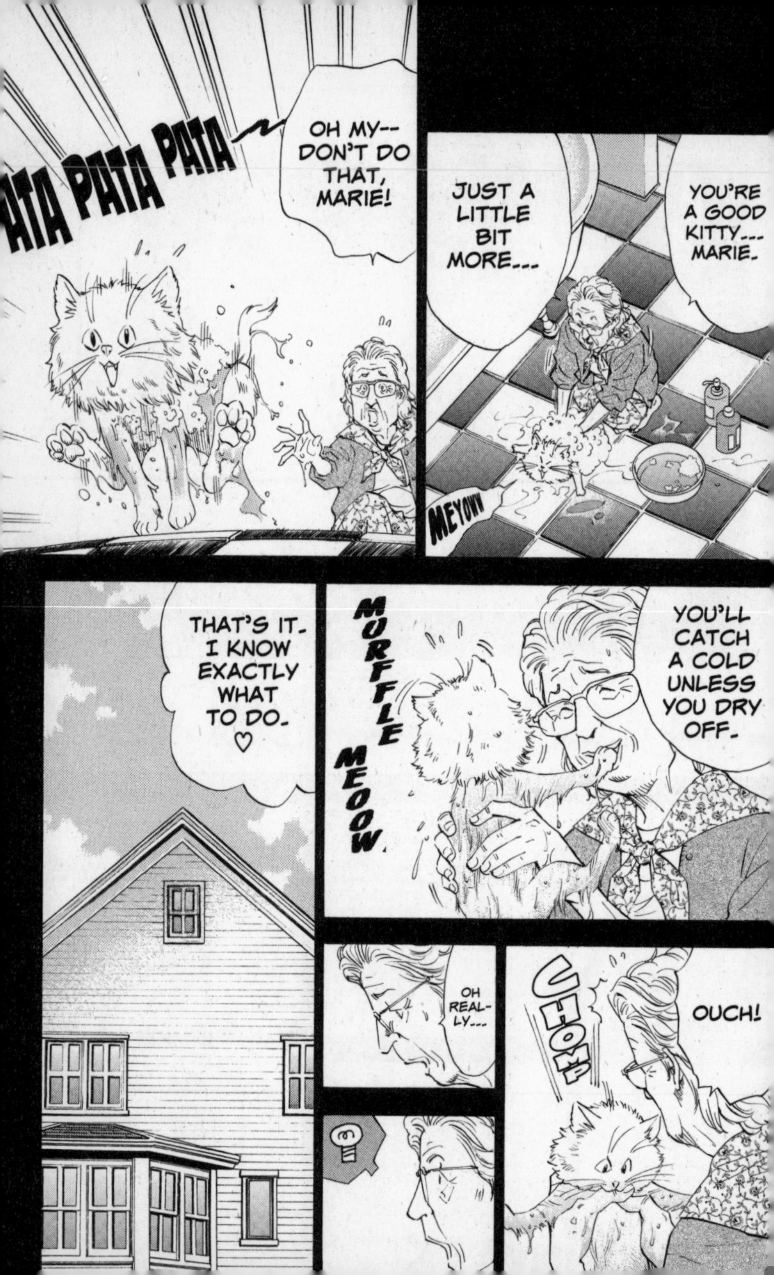
YOU'RE A GOOD KITTY... MARIE.
JUST A LITTLE BIT MORE...
MEYOWW
OH MY-- DON'T DO THAT, MARIE!
PATA PATA PATA
YOU'LL CATCH A COLD UNLESS YOU DRY OFF.
MURFFLE
MEOOW
OUCH!
CHOMP
OH REAL-LY...
THAT'S IT. I KNOW EXACTLY WHAT TO DO. ♡

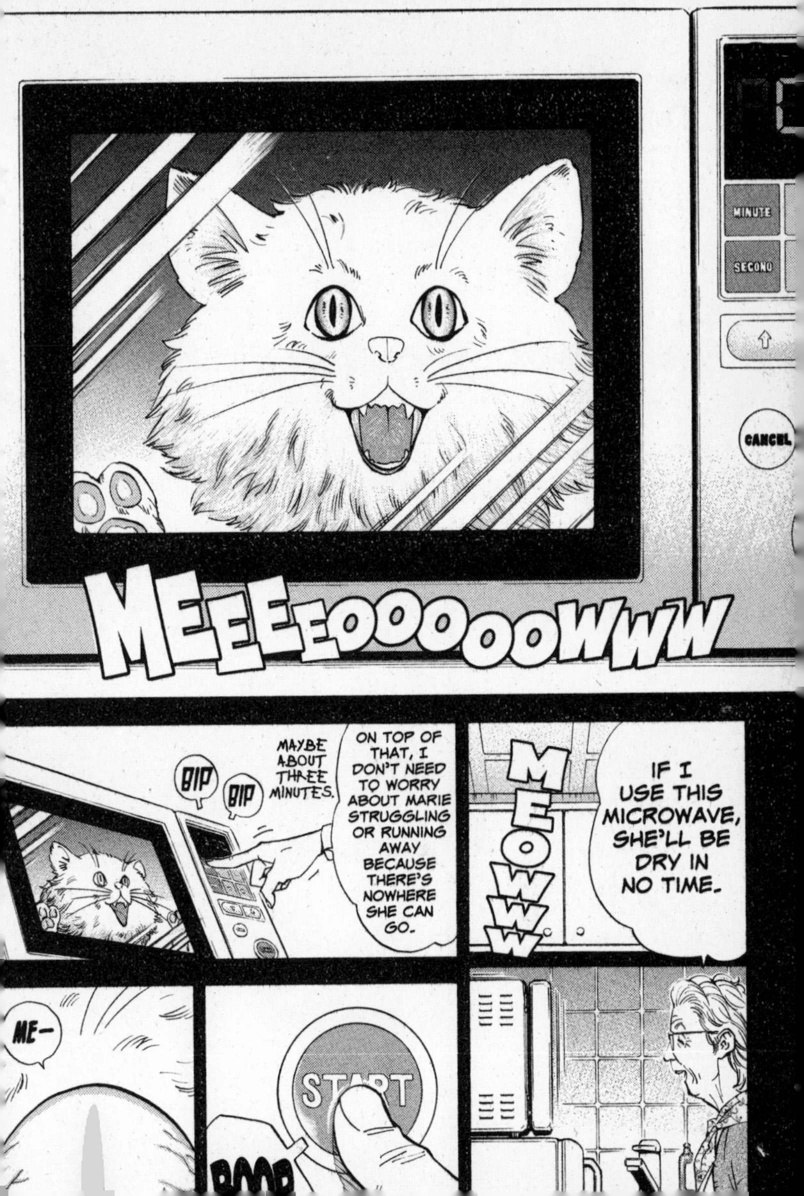
MINUTE
SECOND
CANCEL
MEEEEOOOOOWWW
MEOWWW
IF I USE THIS MICROWAVE, SHE'LL BE DRY IN NO TIME.
ON TOP OF THAT, I DON'T NEED TO WORRY ABOUT MARIE STRUGGLING OR RUNNING AWAY BECAUSE THERE'S NOWHERE SHE CAN GO.
MAYBE ABOUT THREE MINUTES.
BIP
BIP
START
ME-

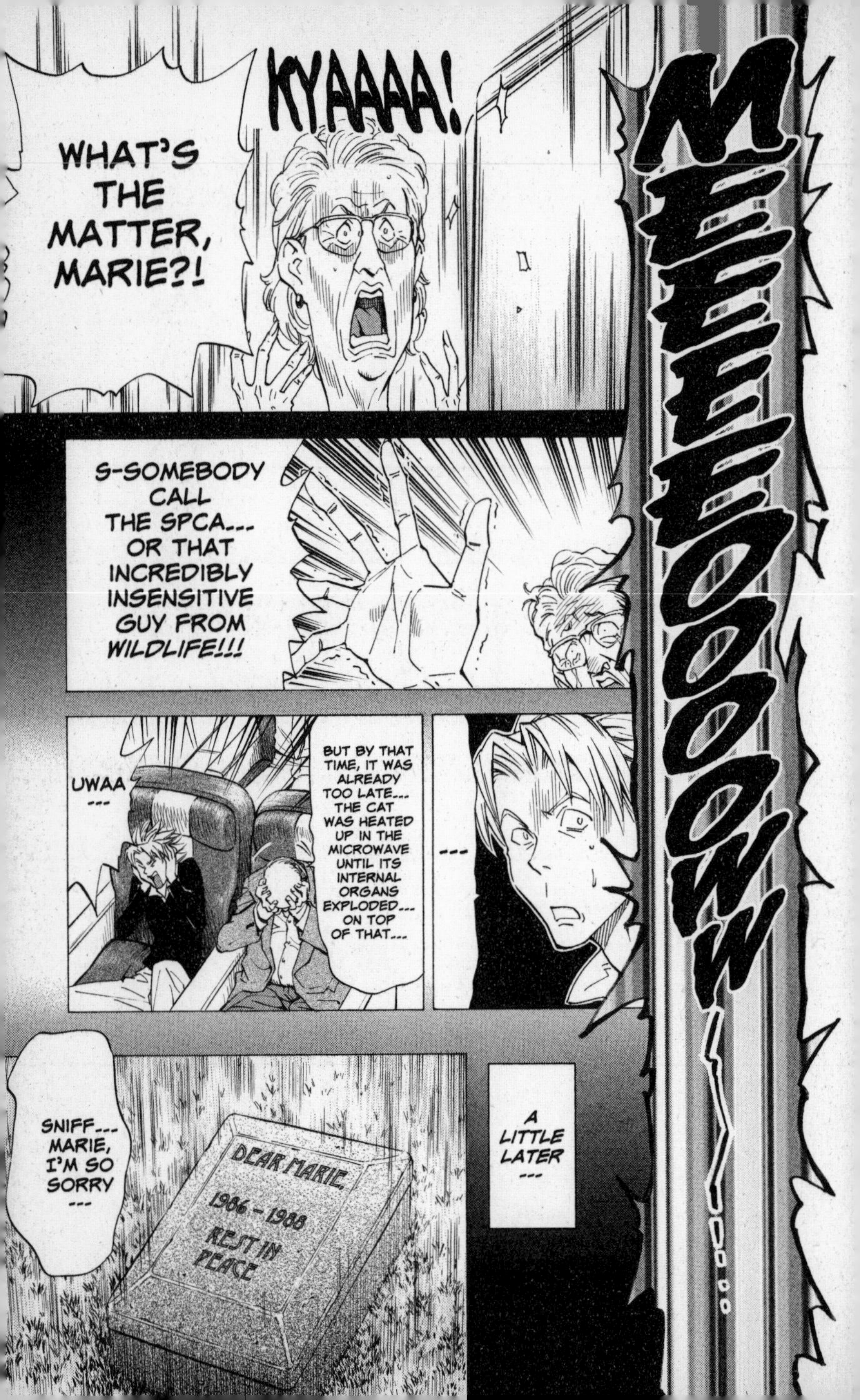
MEEEEEOOOOW...
KYAAAA!
WHAT'S THE MATTER, MARIE?!
S-SOMEBODY CALL THE SPCA... OR THAT INCREDIBLY INSENSITIVE GUY FROM WILDLIFE!!!
...
BUT BY THAT TIME, IT WAS ALREADY TOO LATE... THE CAT WAS HEATED UP IN THE MICROWAVE UNTIL ITS INTERNAL ORGANS EXPLODED... ON TOP OF THAT...
UWAA...
A LITTLE LATER...
DEAR MARIE
1986 – 1988
REST IN PEACE
SNIFF... MARIE, I'M SO SORRY...

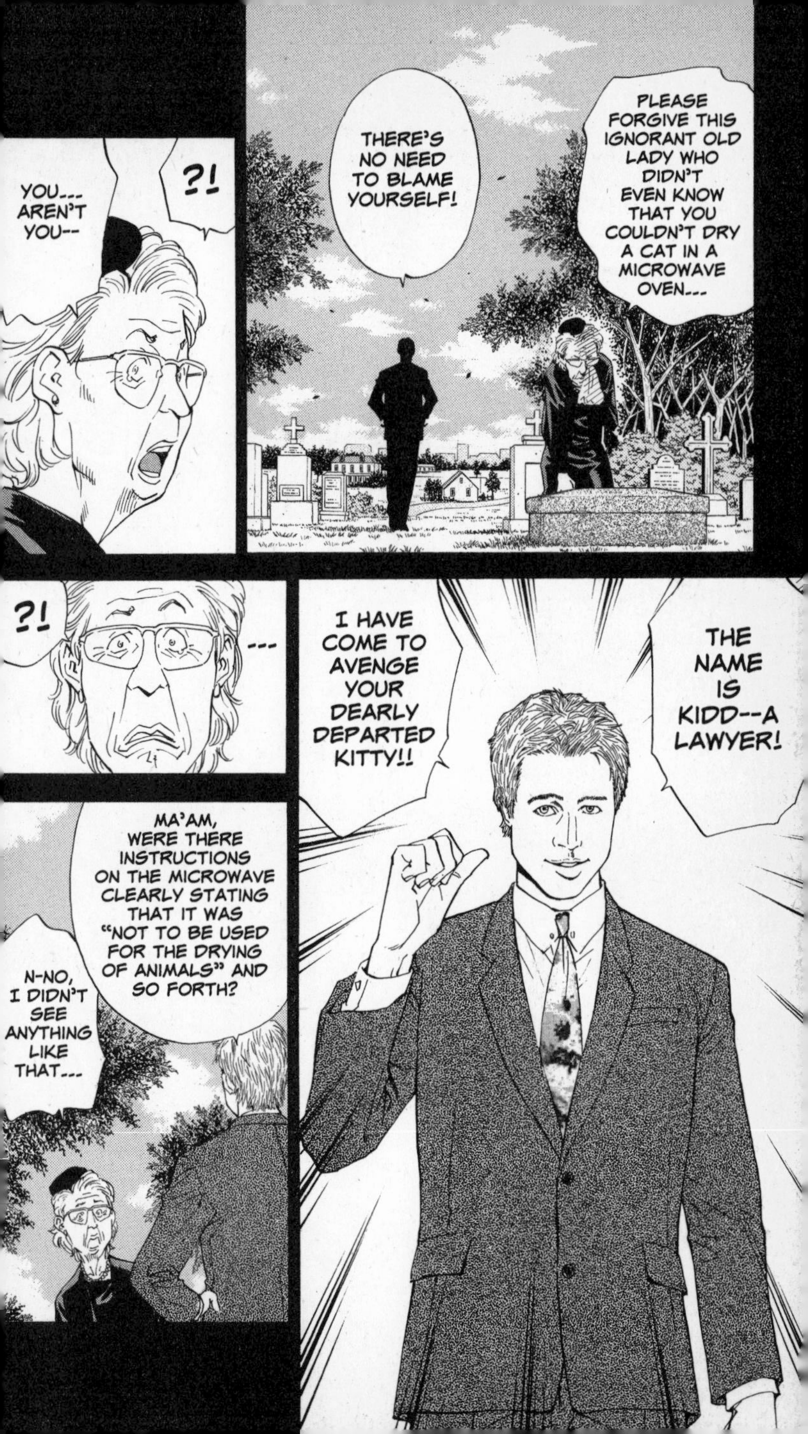
PLEASE FORGIVE THIS IGNORANT OLD LADY WHO DIDN'T EVEN KNOW THAT YOU COULDN'T DRY A CAT IN A MICROWAVE OVEN...
THERE'S NO NEED TO BLAME YOURSELF!
?!
YOU... AREN'T YOU--
THE NAME IS KIDD--A LAWYER!
I HAVE COME TO AVENGE YOUR DEARLY DEPARTED KITTY!!
?!
...
MA'AM, WERE THERE INSTRUCTIONS ON THE MICROWAVE CLEARLY STATING THAT IT WAS "NOT TO BE USED FOR THE DRYING OF ANIMALS" AND SO FORTH?
N-NO, I DIDN'T SEE ANYTHING LIKE THAT...

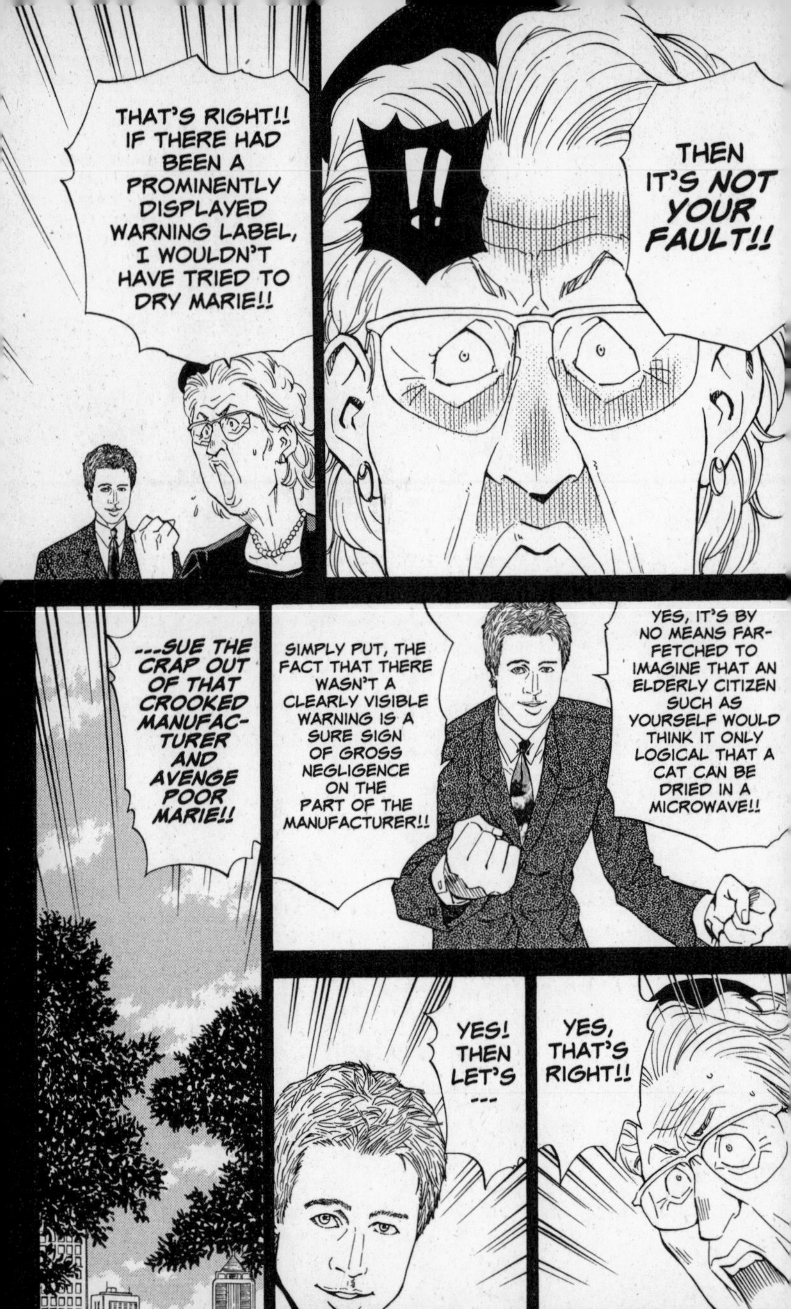
THEN IT'S *NOT YOUR FAULT!!*
!!
THAT'S RIGHT!! IF THERE HAD BEEN A PROMINENTLY DISPLAYED WARNING LABEL, I WOULDN'T HAVE TRIED TO DRY MARIE!!
YES, IT'S BY NO MEANS FAR-FETCHED TO IMAGINE THAT AN ELDERLY CITIZEN SUCH AS YOURSELF WOULD THINK IT ONLY LOGICAL THAT A CAT CAN BE DRIED IN A MICROWAVE!!
SIMPLY PUT, THE FACT THAT THERE WASN'T A CLEARLY VISIBLE WARNING IS A SURE SIGN OF GROSS NEGLIGENCE ON THE PART OF THE MANUFACTURER!!
YES, THAT'S RIGHT!!
YES! THEN LET'S ---
*---SUE THE CRAP OUT OF THAT CROOKED MANUFAC-TURER AND AVENGE POOR MARIE!!*

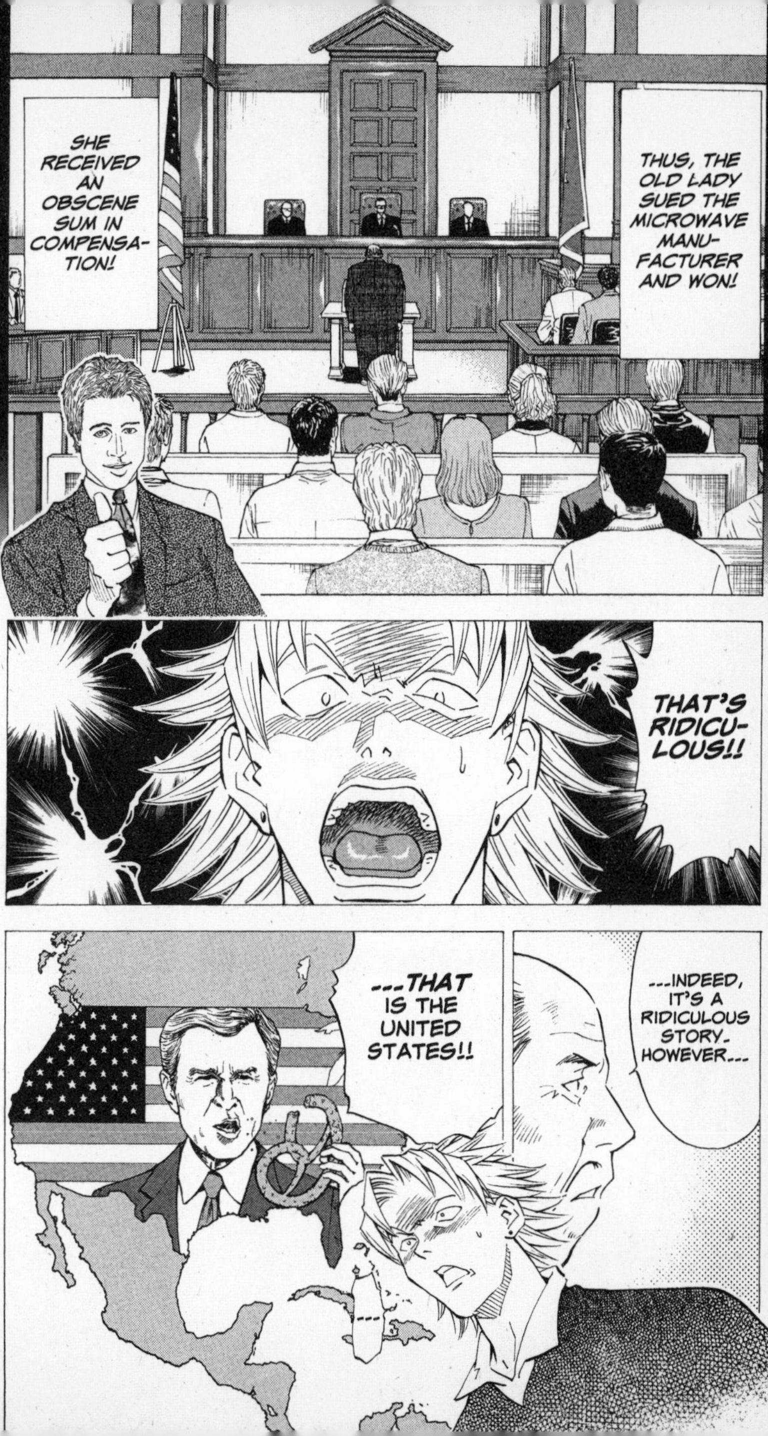
THUS, THE OLD LADY SUED THE MICROWAVE MANU-FACTURER AND WON!
SHE RECEIVED AN OBSCENE SUM IN COMPENSA-TION!
THAT'S RIDICU-LOUS!!
---INDEED, IT'S A RIDICULOUS STORY. HOWEVER---
---THAT IS THE UNITED STATES!!

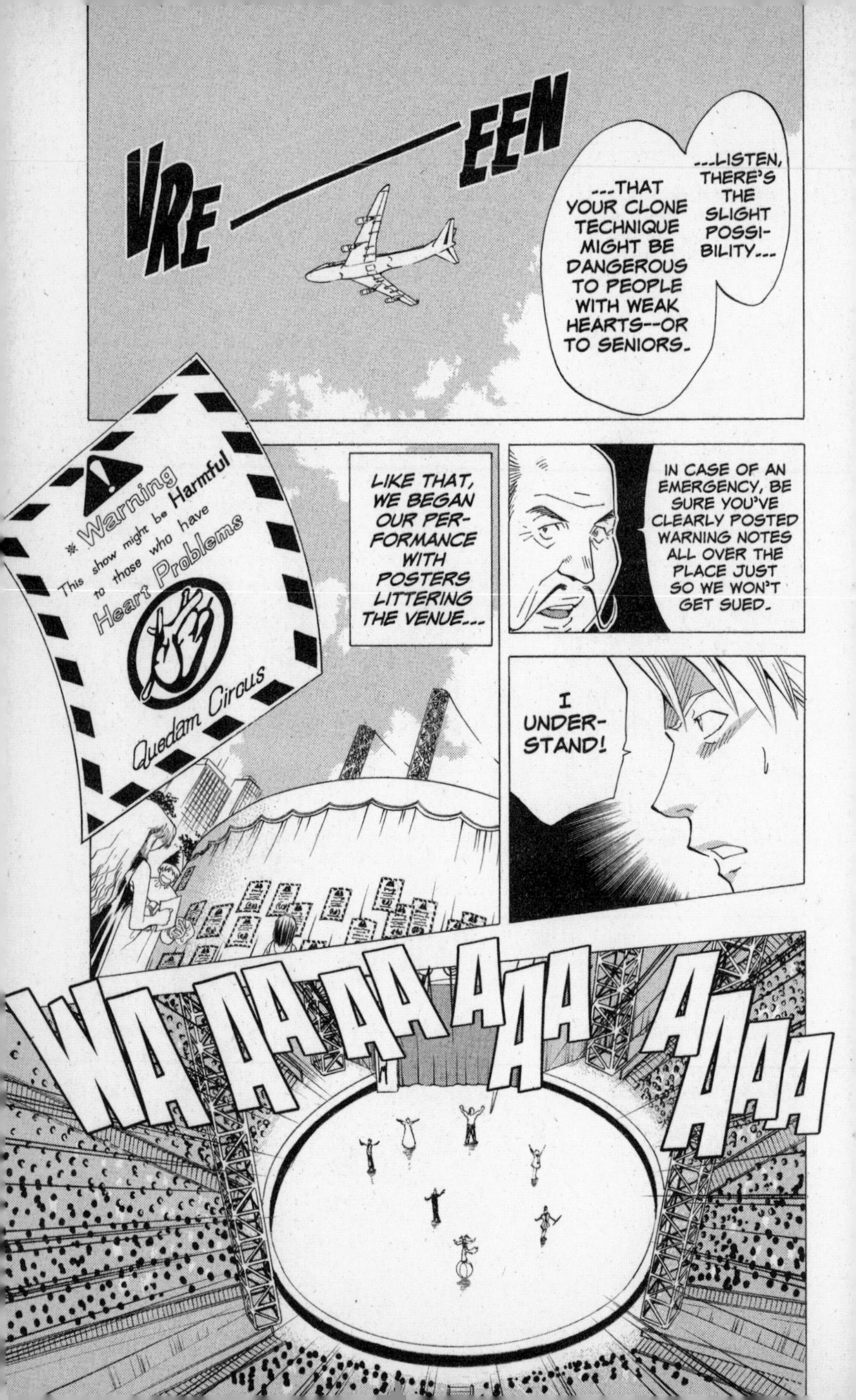
VREEEN
---LISTEN, THERE'S THE SLIGHT POSSIBILITY---
---THAT YOUR CLONE TECHNIQUE MIGHT BE DANGEROUS TO PEOPLE WITH WEAK HEARTS--OR TO SENIORS.
IN CASE OF AN EMERGENCY, BE SURE YOU'VE CLEARLY POSTED WARNING NOTES ALL OVER THE PLACE JUST SO WE WON'T GET SUED.
I UNDERSTAND!
LIKE THAT, WE BEGAN OUR PERFORMANCE WITH POSTERS LITTERING THE VENUE...
※ Warning
This show might be Harmful to those who have Heart Problems
Quedam Circus
WAAAAAAAAAAAA

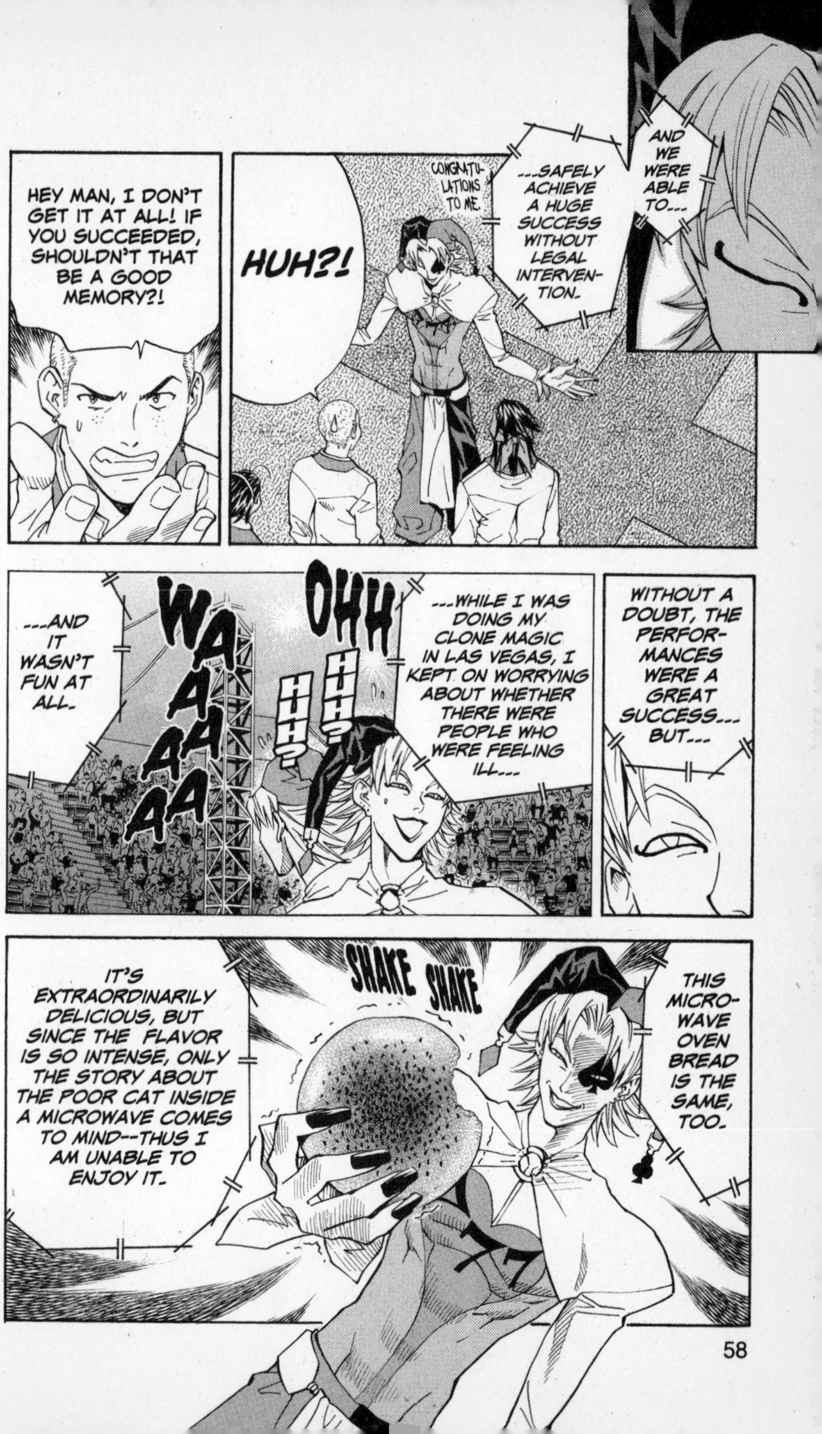
AND WE WERE ABLE TO...
...SAFELY ACHIEVE A HUGE SUCCESS WITHOUT LEGAL INTERVENTION.
CONGRATULATIONS TO ME.
HUH?!
HEY MAN, I DON'T GET IT AT ALL! IF YOU SUCCEEDED, SHOULDN'T THAT BE A GOOD MEMORY?!
WITHOUT A DOUBT, THE PERFORMANCES WERE A GREAT SUCCESS... BUT...
...WHILE I WAS DOING MY CLONE MAGIC IN LAS VEGAS, I KEPT ON WORRYING ABOUT WHETHER THERE WERE PEOPLE WHO WERE FEELING ILL...
OHH
HUH?
HUH?
WAAAAA
...AND IT WASN'T FUN AT ALL.
THIS MICROWAVE OVEN BREAD IS THE SAME, TOO.
SHAKE SHAKE
IT'S EXTRAORDINARILY DELICIOUS, BUT SINCE THE FLAVOR IS SO INTENSE, ONLY THE STORY ABOUT THE POOR CAT INSIDE A MICROWAVE COMES TO MIND--THUS I AM UNABLE TO ENJOY IT.

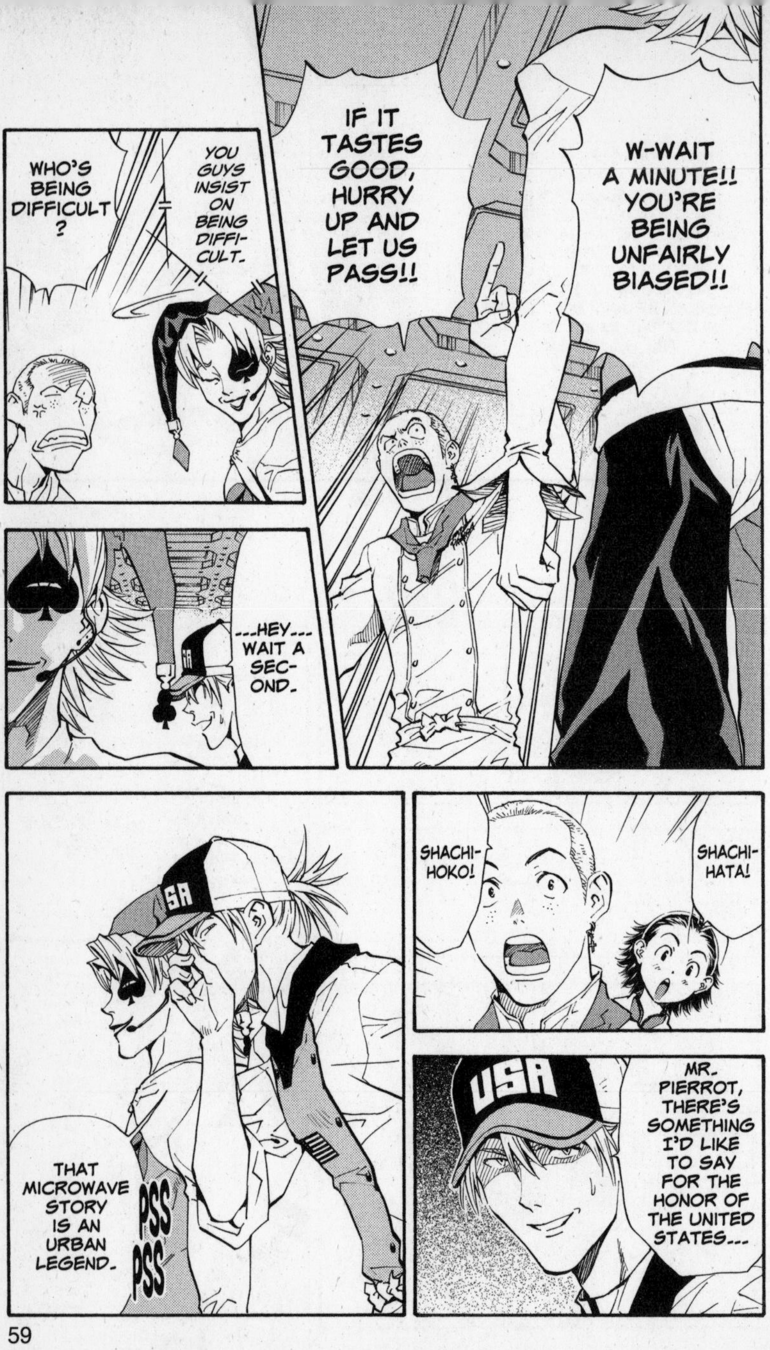
W-WAIT A MINUTE!! YOU'RE BEING UNFAIRLY BIASED!!
IF IT TASTES GOOD, HURRY UP AND LET US PASS!!
YOU GUYS INSIST ON BEING DIFFICULT.
WHO'S BEING DIFFICULT?
...HEY... WAIT A SECOND.
SHACHIHATA!
SHACHIHOKO!
MR. PIERROT, THERE'S SOMETHING I'D LIKE TO SAY FOR THE HONOR OF THE UNITED STATES...
PSS PSS
THAT MICROWAVE STORY IS AN URBAN LEGEND.

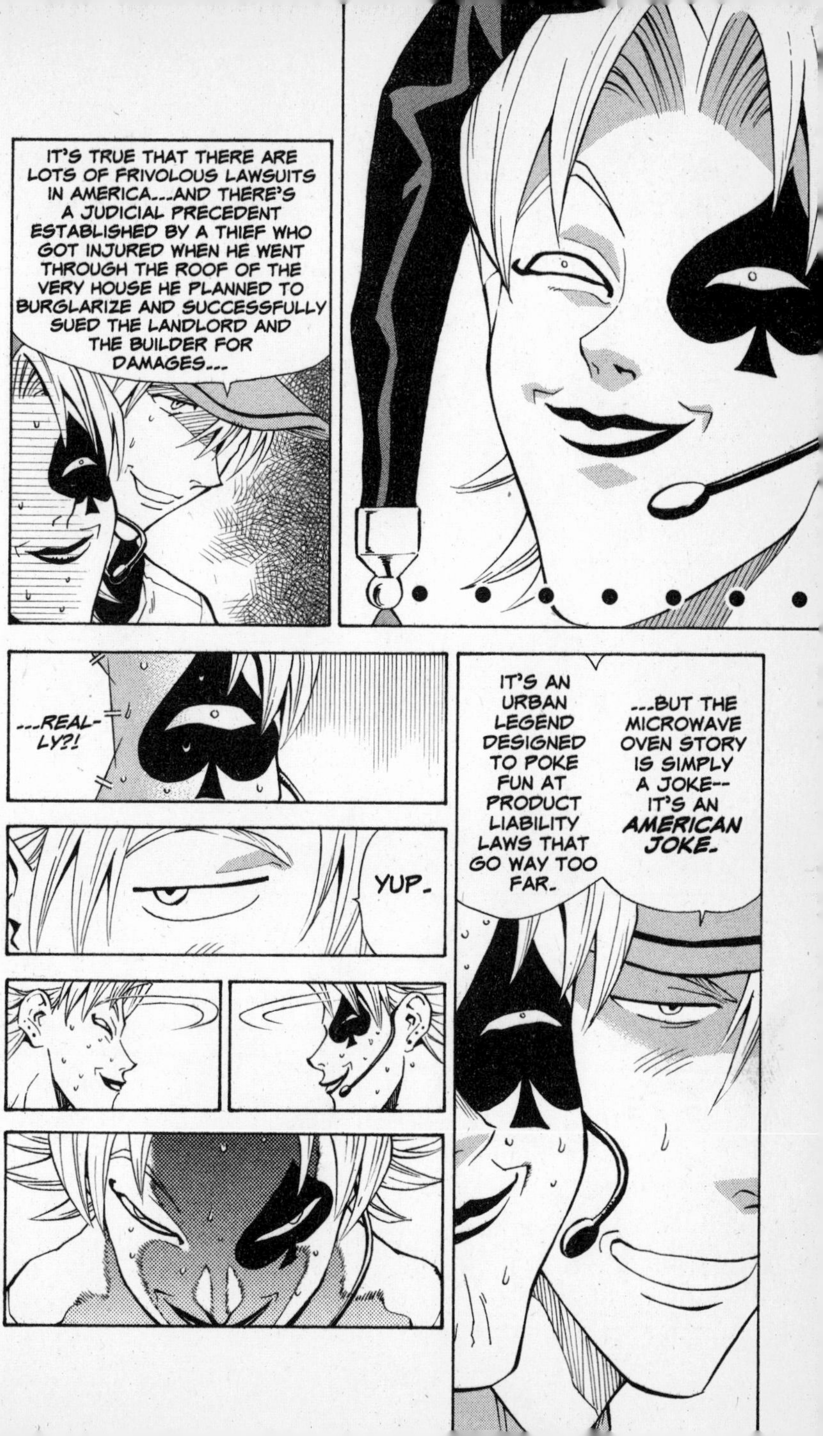
IT'S TRUE THAT THERE ARE LOTS OF FRIVOLOUS LAWSUITS IN AMERICA...AND THERE'S A JUDICIAL PRECEDENT ESTABLISHED BY A THIEF WHO GOT INJURED WHEN HE WENT THROUGH THE ROOF OF THE VERY HOUSE HE PLANNED TO BURGLARIZE AND SUCCESSFULLY SUED THE LANDLORD AND THE BUILDER FOR DAMAGES...
...BUT THE MICROWAVE OVEN STORY IS SIMPLY A JOKE-- IT'S AN *AMERICAN JOKE.*
IT'S AN URBAN LEGEND DESIGNED TO POKE FUN AT PRODUCT LIABILITY LAWS THAT GO WAY TOO FAR.
...REAL-LY?!
YUP.

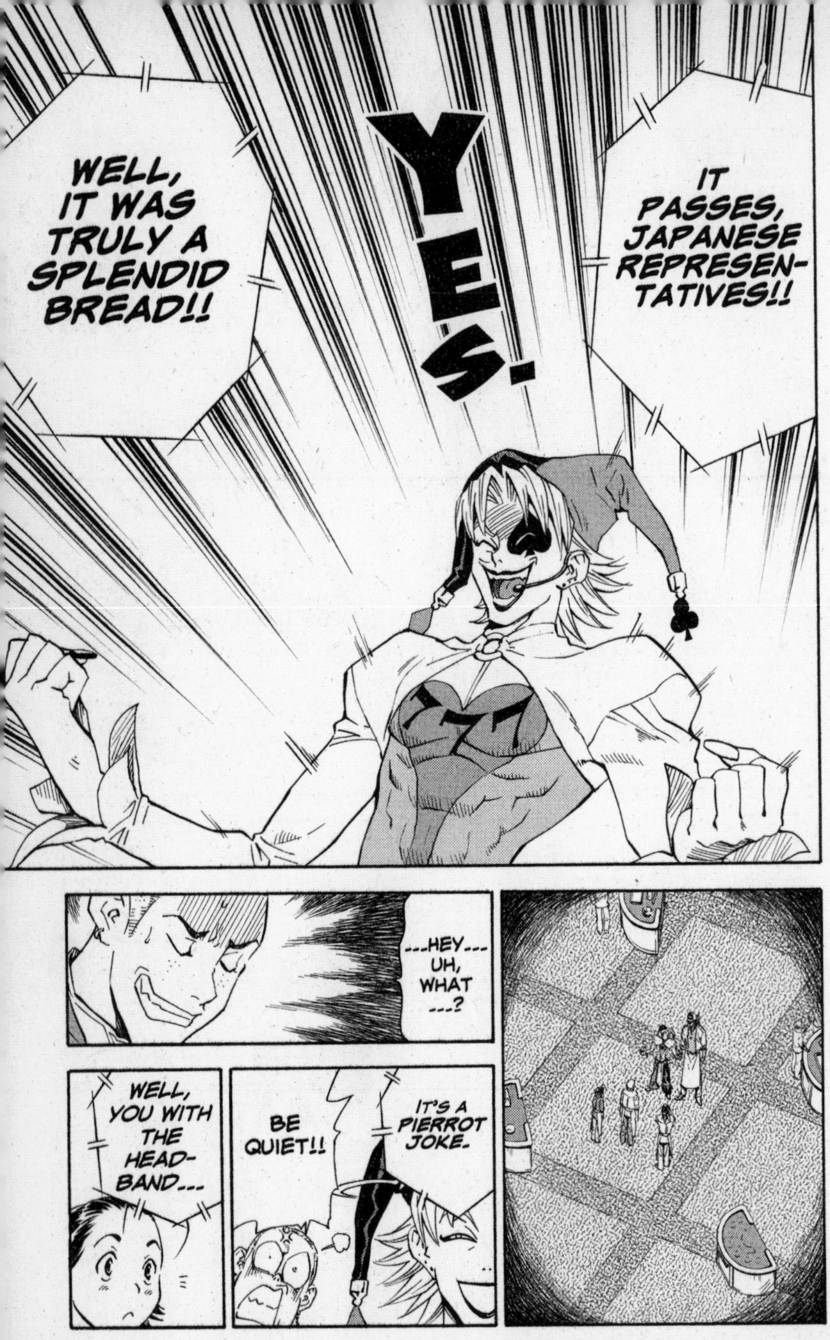
YES!
IT PASSES, JAPANESE REPRESENTATIVES!!
WELL, IT WAS TRULY A SPLENDID BREAD!!
---HEY--- UH, WHAT ---?
IT'S A PIERROT JOKE.
BE QUIET!!
WELL, YOU WITH THE HEAD-BAND---

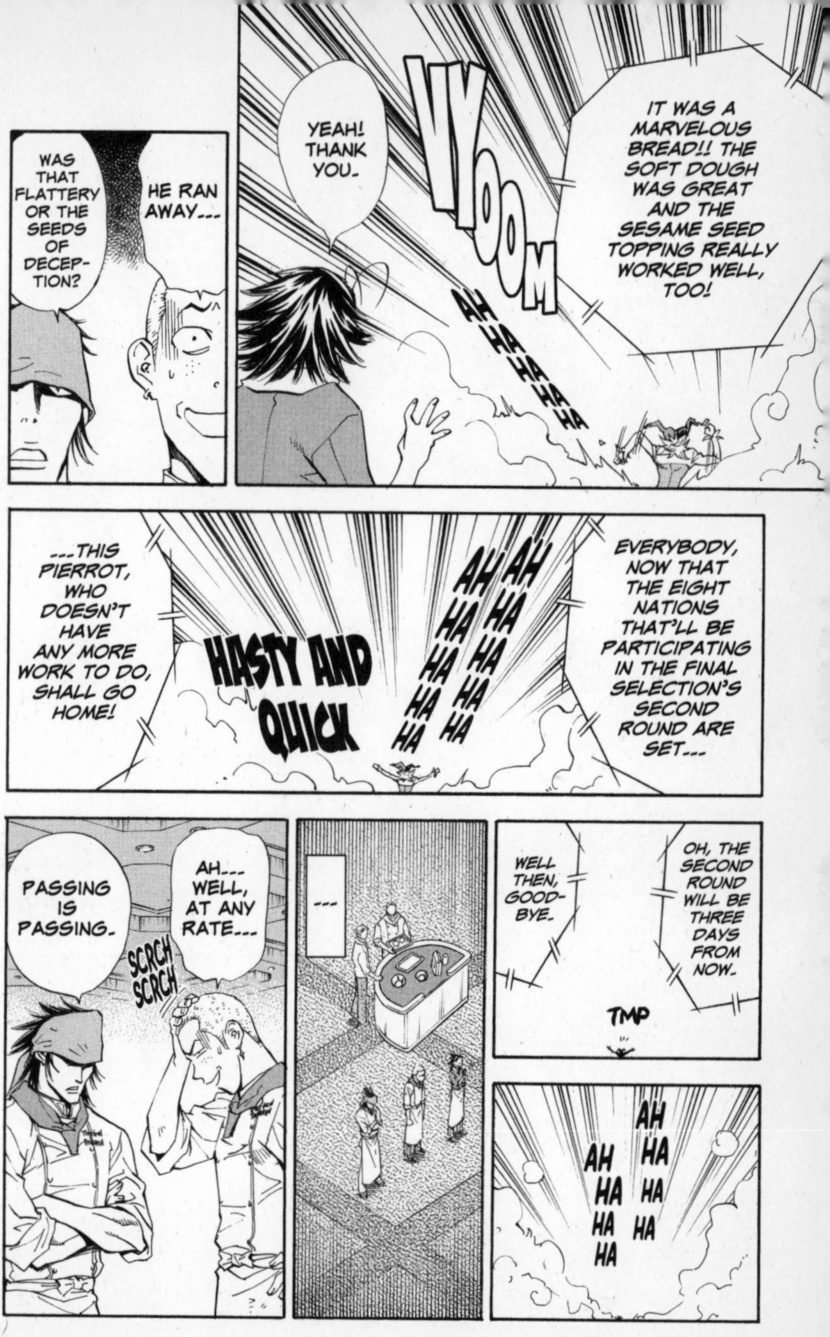
IT WAS A MARVELOUS BREAD!! THE SOFT DOUGH WAS GREAT AND THE SESAME SEED TOPPING REALLY WORKED WELL, TOO!
VYOOM
YEAH! THANK YOU.
AHAHAHAHAHA
HE RAN AWAY...
WAS THAT FLATTERY OR THE SEEDS OF DECEPTION?
EVERYBODY, NOW THAT THE EIGHT NATIONS THAT'LL BE PARTICIPATING IN THE FINAL SELECTION'S SECOND ROUND ARE SET...
AH HA HA HA HA HA
AH HA HA HA HA HA
HASTY AND QUICK
...THIS PIERROT, WHO DOESN'T HAVE ANY MORE WORK TO DO, SHALL GO HOME!
OH, THE SECOND ROUND WILL BE THREE DAYS FROM NOW.
WELL THEN, GOOD-BYE.
TMP
AH HA HA HA
AH HA HA HA HA
...
AH... WELL, AT ANY RATE...
SCRCH SCRCH
PASSING IS PASSING.

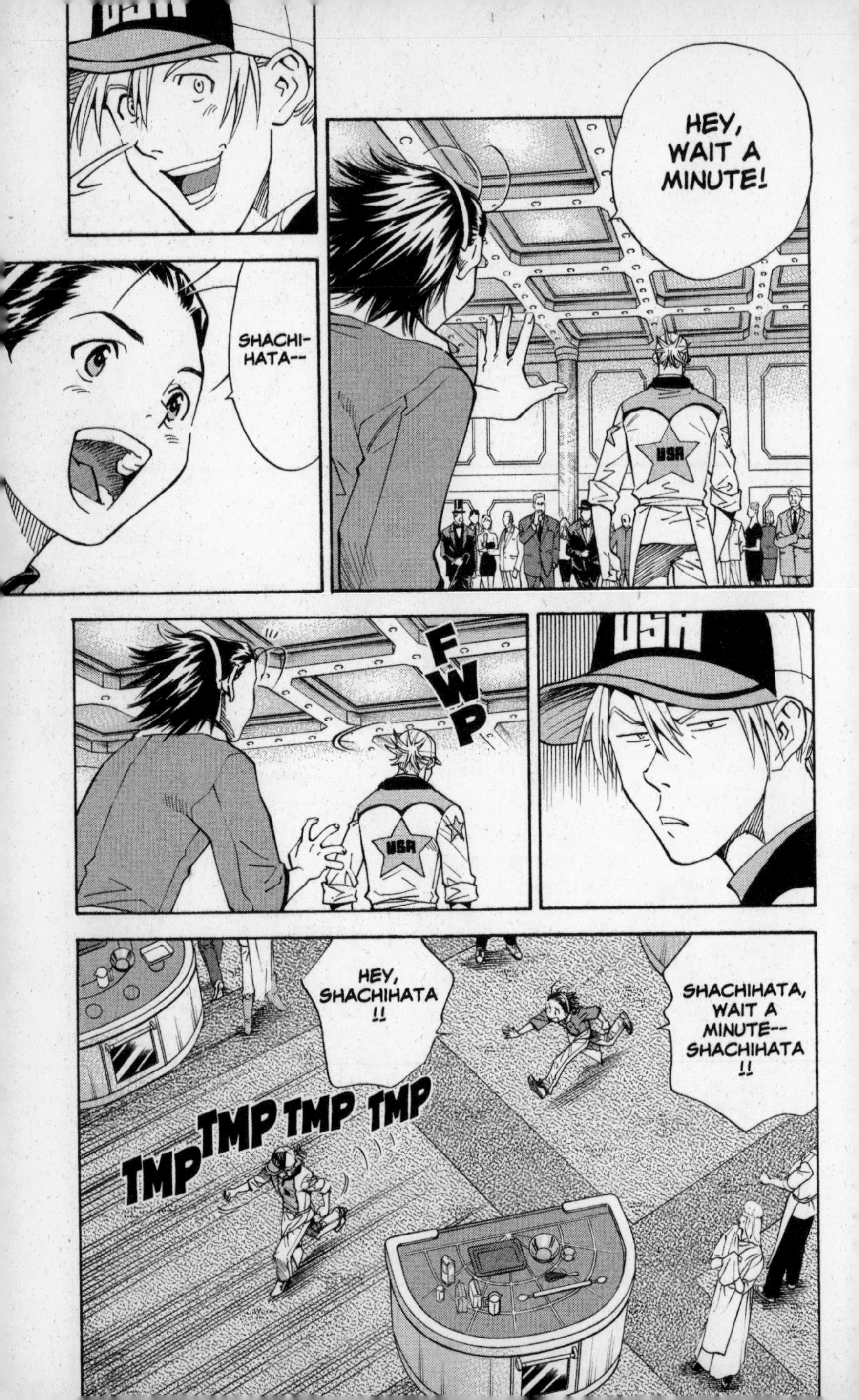
HEY, WAIT A MINUTE!
SHACHI-HATA--
FWP
SHACHIHATA, WAIT A MINUTE-- SHACHIHATA!!
HEY, SHACHIHATA!!
TMP TMP TMP TMP

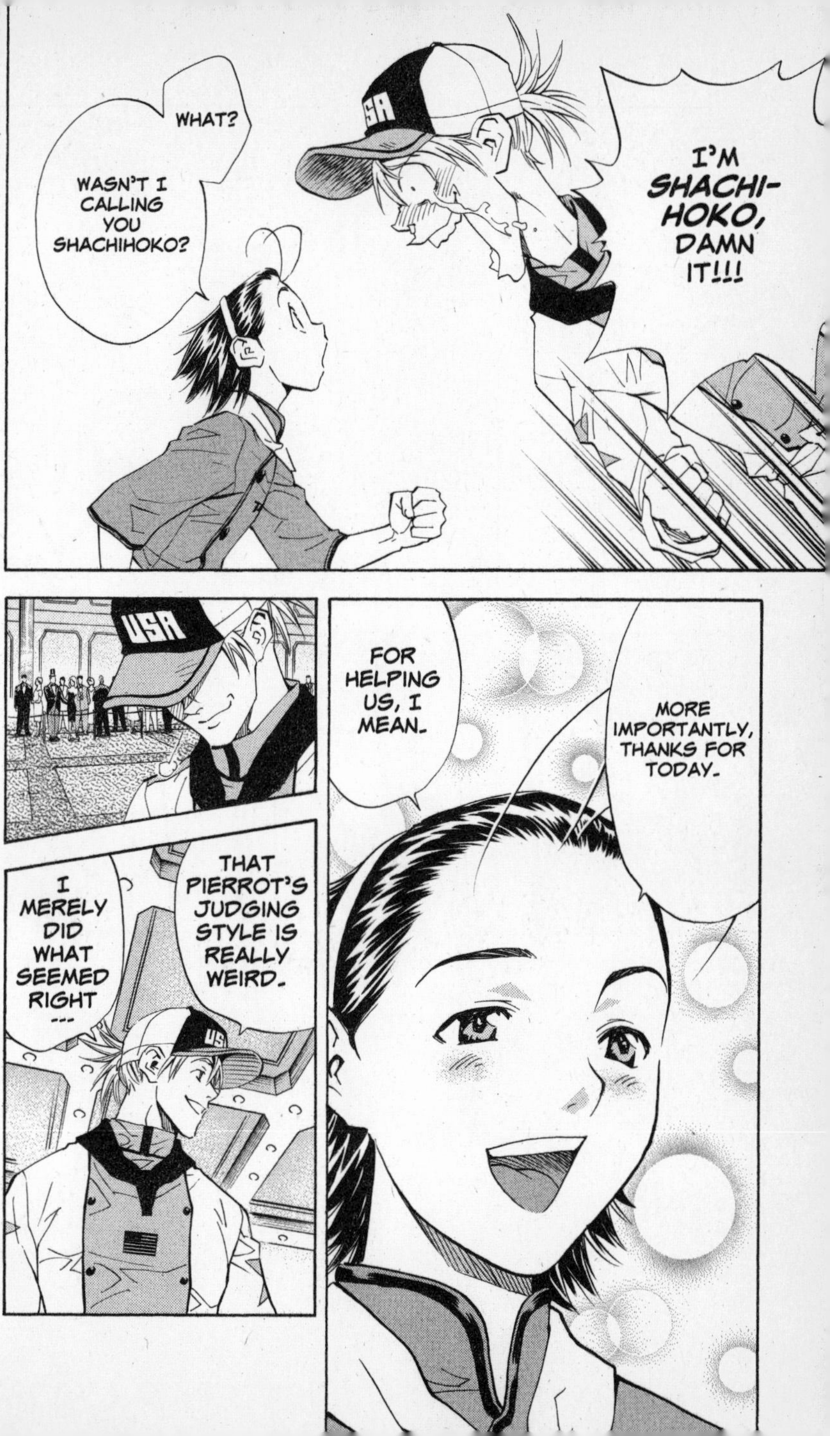
I'M SHACHI-HOKO, DAMN IT!!!
WHAT?
WASN'T I CALLING YOU SHACHIHOKO?
MORE IMPORTANTLY, THANKS FOR TODAY.
FOR HELPING US, I MEAN.
THAT PIERROT'S JUDGING STYLE IS REALLY WEIRD.
I MERELY DID WHAT SEEMED RIGHT ---

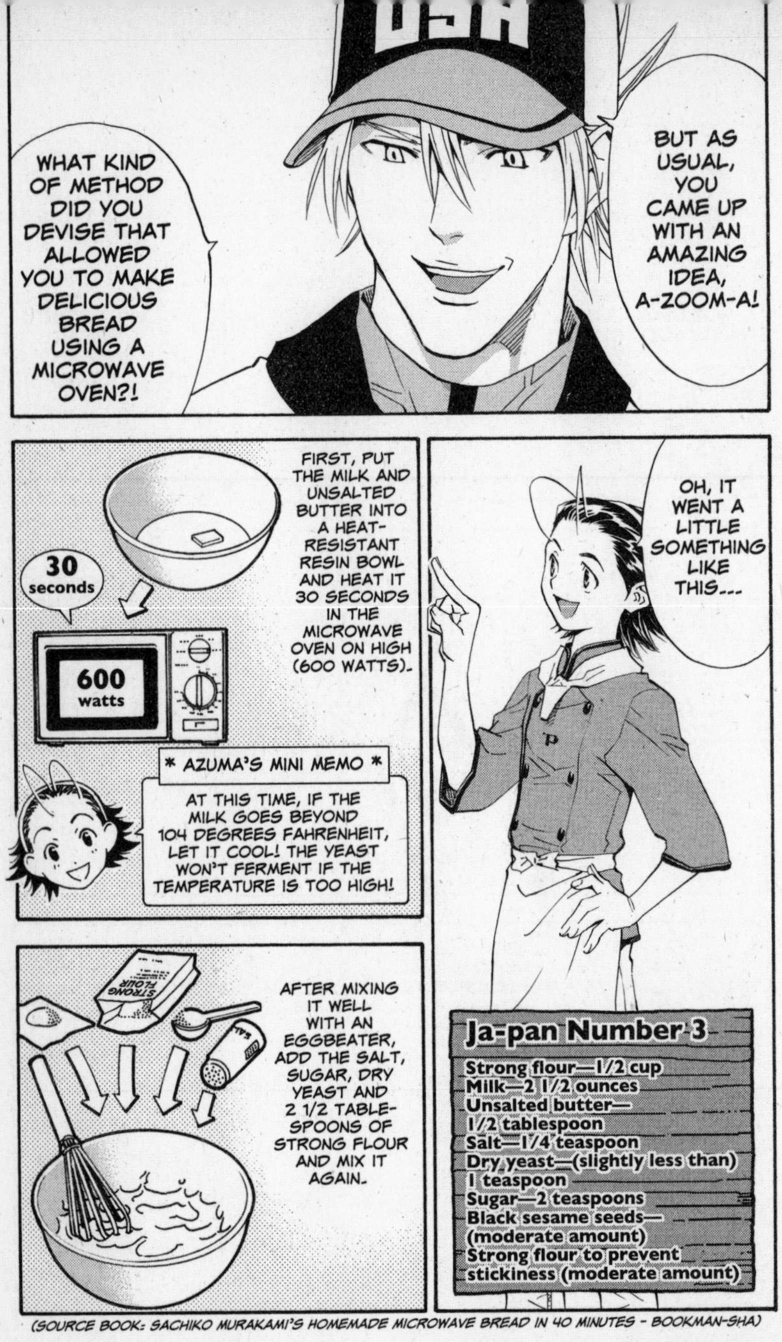
BUT AS USUAL, YOU CAME UP WITH AN AMAZING IDEA, A-ZOOM-A!
WHAT KIND OF METHOD DID YOU DEVISE THAT ALLOWED YOU TO MAKE DELICIOUS BREAD USING A MICROWAVE OVEN?!
OH, IT WENT A LITTLE SOMETHING LIKE THIS...
Ja-pan Number 3
Strong flour—1/2 cup
Milk—2 1/2 ounces
Unsalted butter—1/2 tablespoon
Salt—1/4 teaspoon
Dry yeast—(slightly less than) 1 teaspoon
Sugar—2 teaspoons
Black sesame seeds—(moderate amount)
Strong flour to prevent stickiness (moderate amount)
FIRST, PUT THE MILK AND UNSALTED BUTTER INTO A HEAT-RESISTANT RESIN BOWL AND HEAT IT 30 SECONDS IN THE MICROWAVE OVEN ON HIGH (600 WATTS).
30 seconds
600 watts
* AZUMA'S MINI MEMO *
AT THIS TIME, IF THE MILK GOES BEYOND 104 DEGREES FAHRENHEIT, LET IT COOL! THE YEAST WON'T FERMENT IF THE TEMPERATURE IS TOO HIGH!
AFTER MIXING IT WELL WITH AN EGGBEATER, ADD THE SALT, SUGAR, DRY YEAST AND 2 1/2 TABLESPOONS OF STRONG FLOUR AND MIX IT AGAIN.
STRONG FLOUR

(SOURCE BOOK: SACHIKO MURAKAMI'S HOMEMADE MICROWAVE BREAD IN 40 MINUTES - BOOKMAN-SHA)

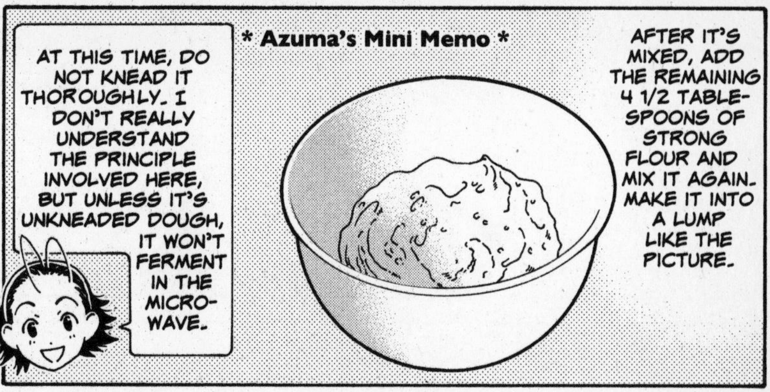
AFTER IT'S MIXED, ADD THE REMAINING 4 1/2 TABLE-SPOONS OF STRONG FLOUR AND MIX IT AGAIN. MAKE IT INTO A LUMP LIKE THE PICTURE.
* Azuma's Mini Memo *
AT THIS TIME, DO NOT KNEAD IT THOROUGHLY. I DON'T REALLY UNDERSTAND THE PRINCIPLE INVOLVED HERE, BUT UNLESS IT'S UNKNEADED DOUGH, IT WON'T FERMENT IN THE MICRO-WAVE.

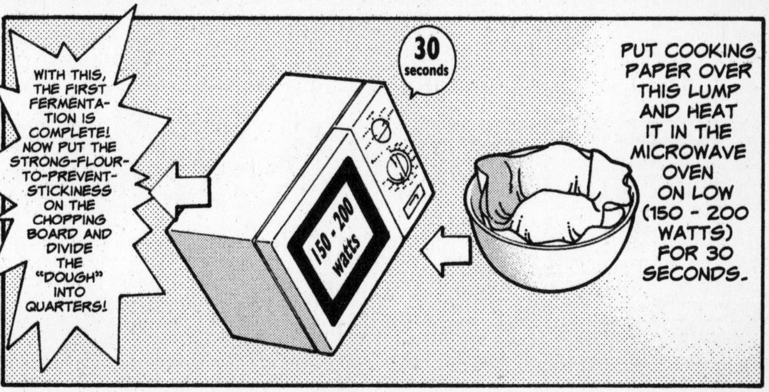
PUT COOKING PAPER OVER THIS LUMP AND HEAT IT IN THE MICROWAVE OVEN ON LOW (150 - 200 WATTS) FOR 30 SECONDS.
30 seconds
150 - 200 watts
WITH THIS, THE FIRST FERMENTA-TION IS COMPLETE! NOW PUT THE STRONG-FLOUR-TO-PREVENT-STICKINESS ON THE CHOPPING BOARD AND DIVIDE THE "DOUGH" INTO QUARTERS!

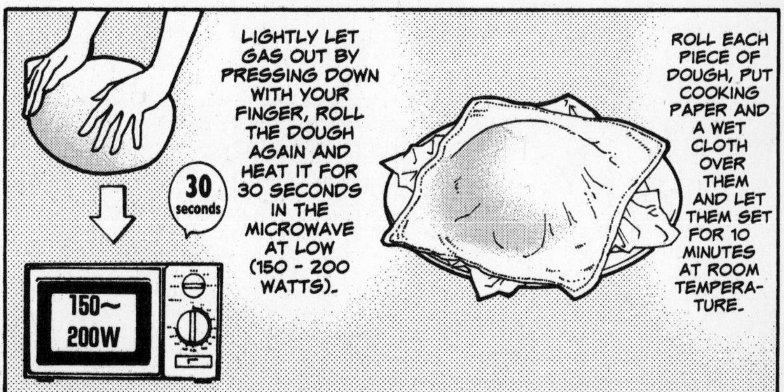
ROLL EACH PIECE OF DOUGH, PUT COOKING PAPER AND A WET CLOTH OVER THEM AND LET THEM SET FOR 10 MINUTES AT ROOM TEMPERA-TURE.
LIGHTLY LET GAS OUT BY PRESSING DOWN WITH YOUR FINGER, ROLL THE DOUGH AGAIN AND HEAT IT FOR 30 SECONDS IN THE MICROWAVE AT LOW (150 - 200 WATTS).
30 seconds
150~ 200W

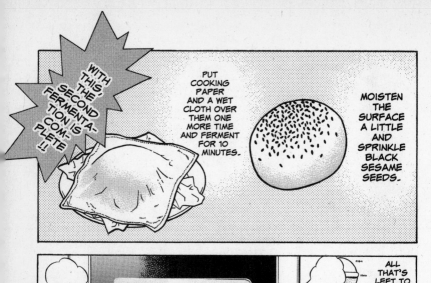

MOISTEN THE SURFACE A LITTLE AND SPRINKLE BLACK SESAME SEEDS.

PUT COOKING PAPER AND A WET CLOTH OVER THEM ONE MORE TIME AND FERMENT FOR 10 MINUTES.

WITH THIS, THE SECOND FERMENTA-TION IS COMPLETE!!

ALL THAT'S LEFT TO DO IS BAKE THE BREAD AT 392 DEGREES FAHRENHEIT FOR ABOUT 10 MINUTES!!

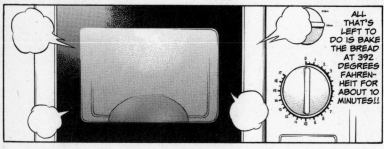

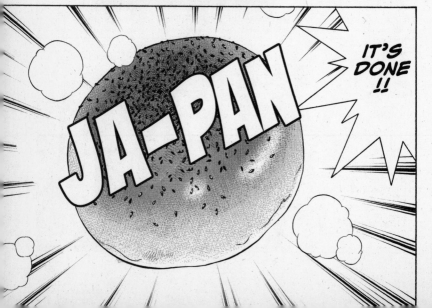

JA-PAN

IT'S DONE!!

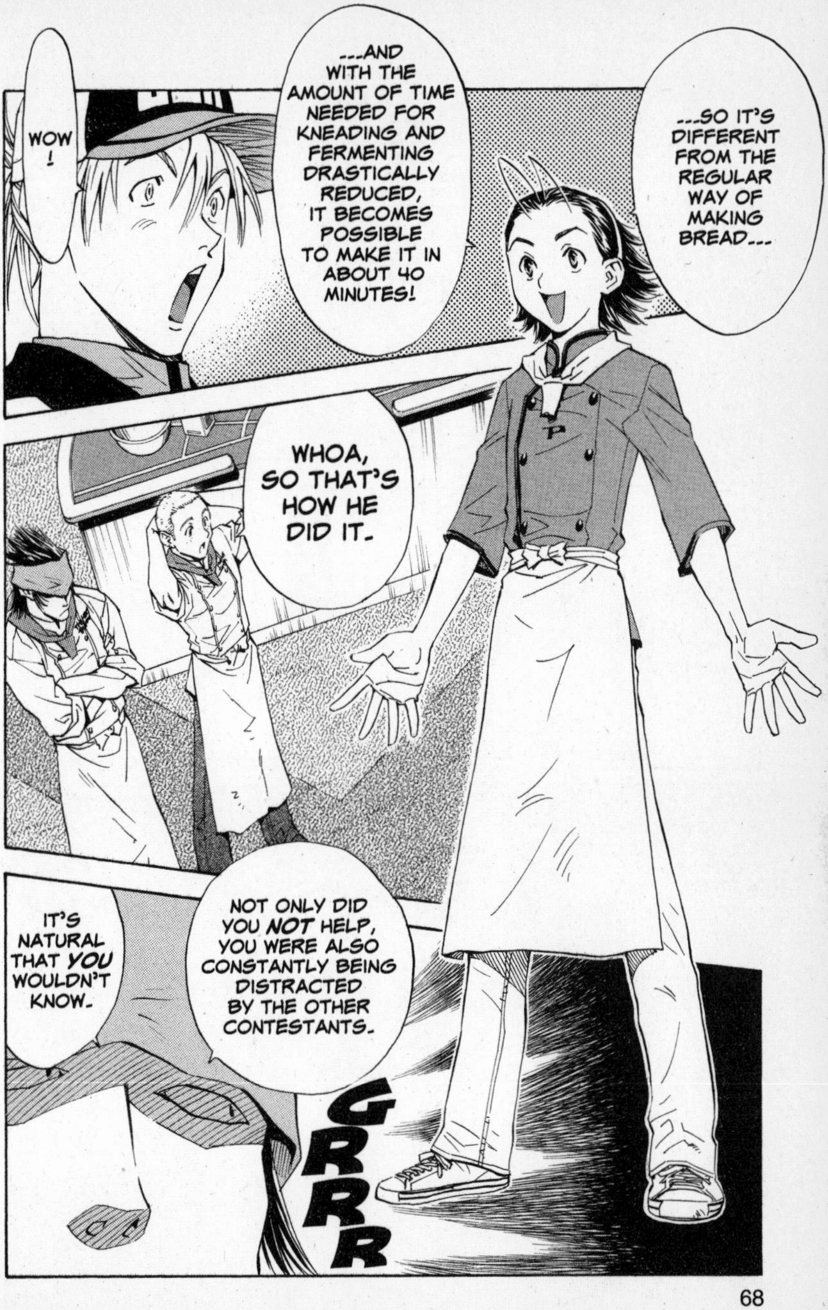
...SO IT'S DIFFERENT FROM THE REGULAR WAY OF MAKING BREAD...
...AND WITH THE AMOUNT OF TIME NEEDED FOR KNEADING AND FERMENTING DRASTICALLY REDUCED, IT BECOMES POSSIBLE TO MAKE IT IN ABOUT 40 MINUTES!
WOW!
WHOA, SO THAT'S HOW HE DID IT.
NOT ONLY DID YOU ***NOT*** HELP, YOU WERE ALSO CONSTANTLY BEING DISTRACTED BY THE OTHER CONTESTANTS.
IT'S NATURAL THAT ***YOU*** WOULDN'T KNOW.
GRRR

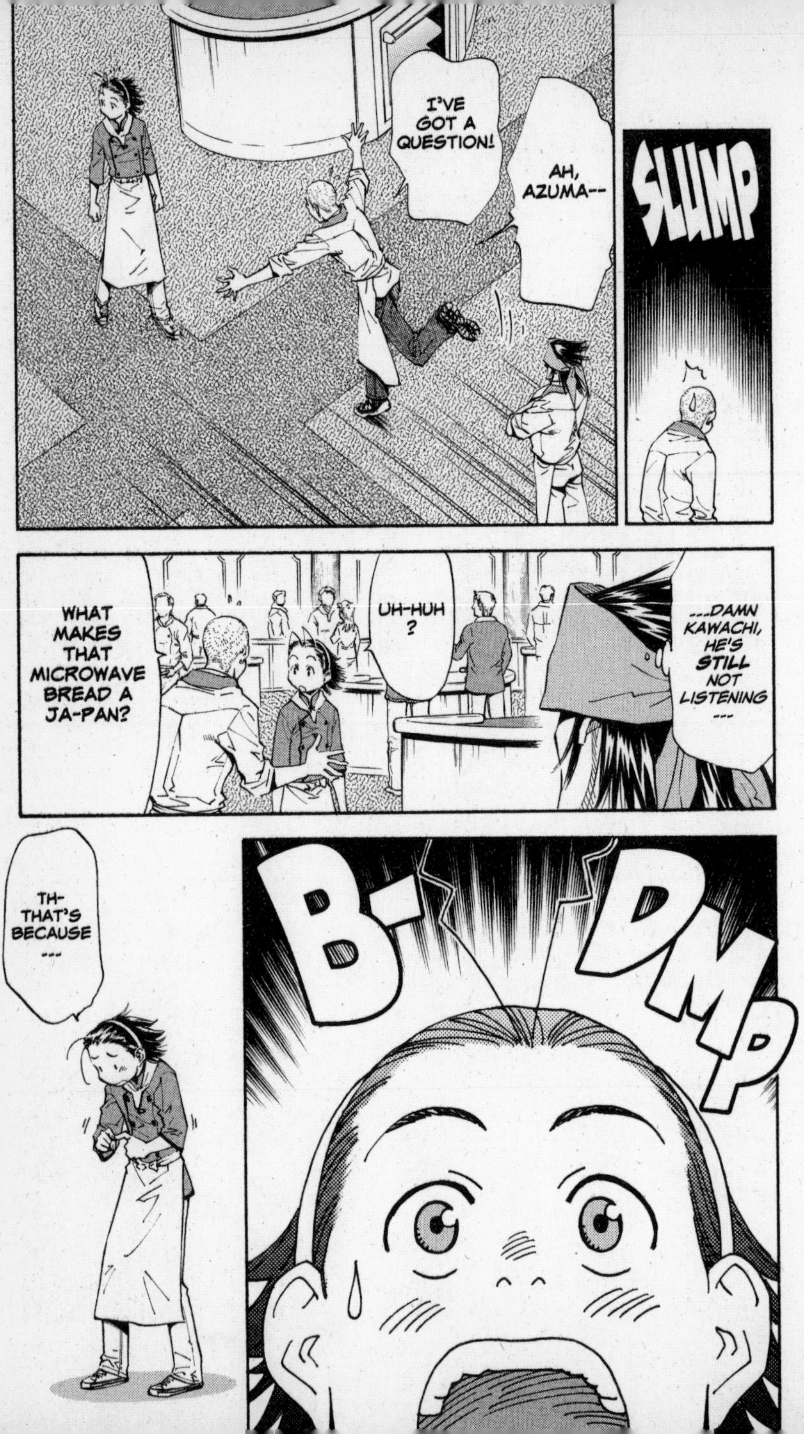
SLUMP
AH, AZUMA--
I'VE GOT A QUESTION!
---DAMN KAWACHI, HE'S STILL NOT LISTENING ---
UH-HUH ?
WHAT MAKES THAT MICROWAVE BREAD A JA-PAN?
B-DMP
TH- THAT'S BECAUSE ---

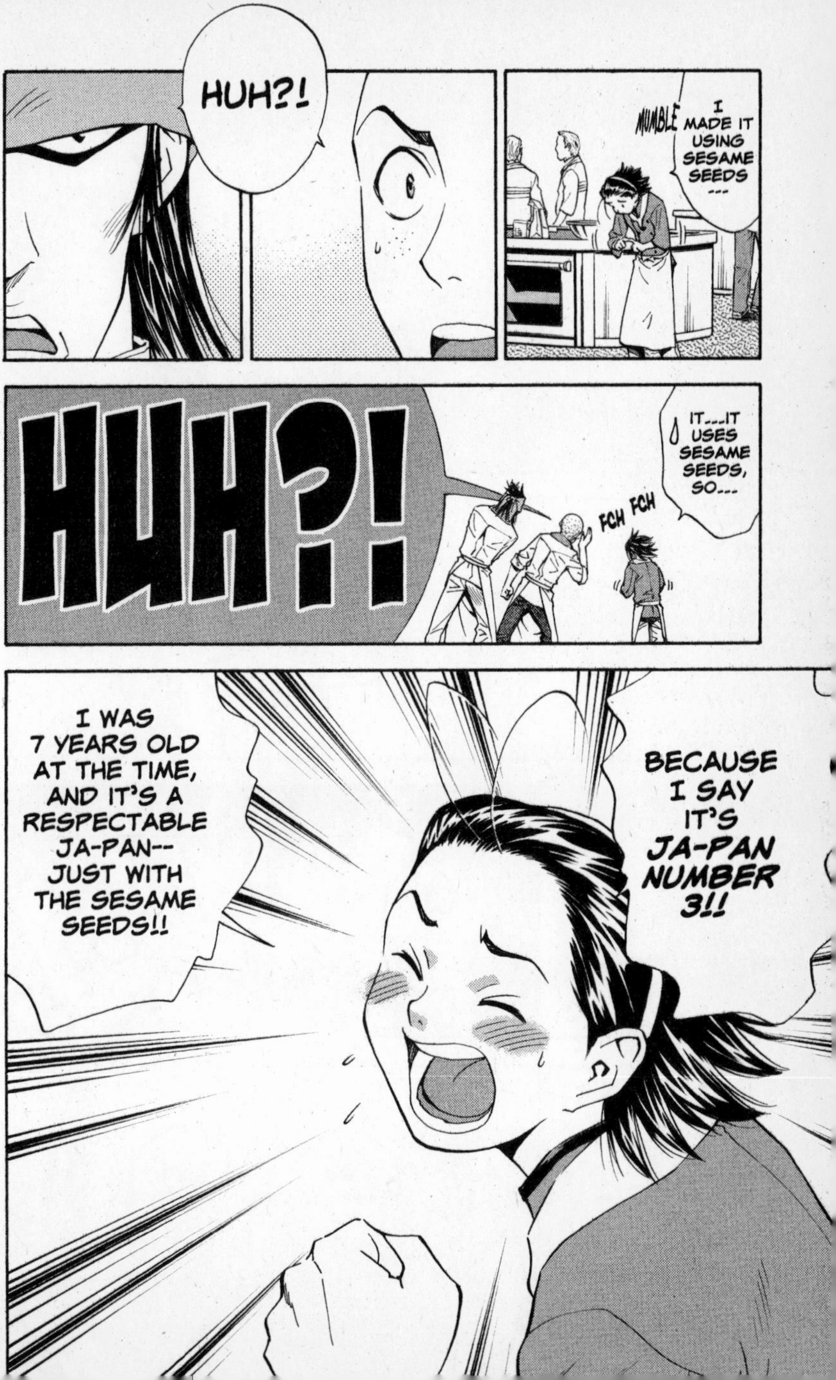
MUMBLE
I MADE IT USING SESAME SEEDS ---
HUH?!
IT---IT USES SESAME SEEDS, SO---
FCH FCH
HUH?!
BECAUSE I SAY IT'S JA-PAN NUMBER 3!!
I WAS 7 YEARS OLD AT THE TIME, AND IT'S A RESPECTABLE JA-PAN-- JUST WITH THE SESAME SEEDS!!

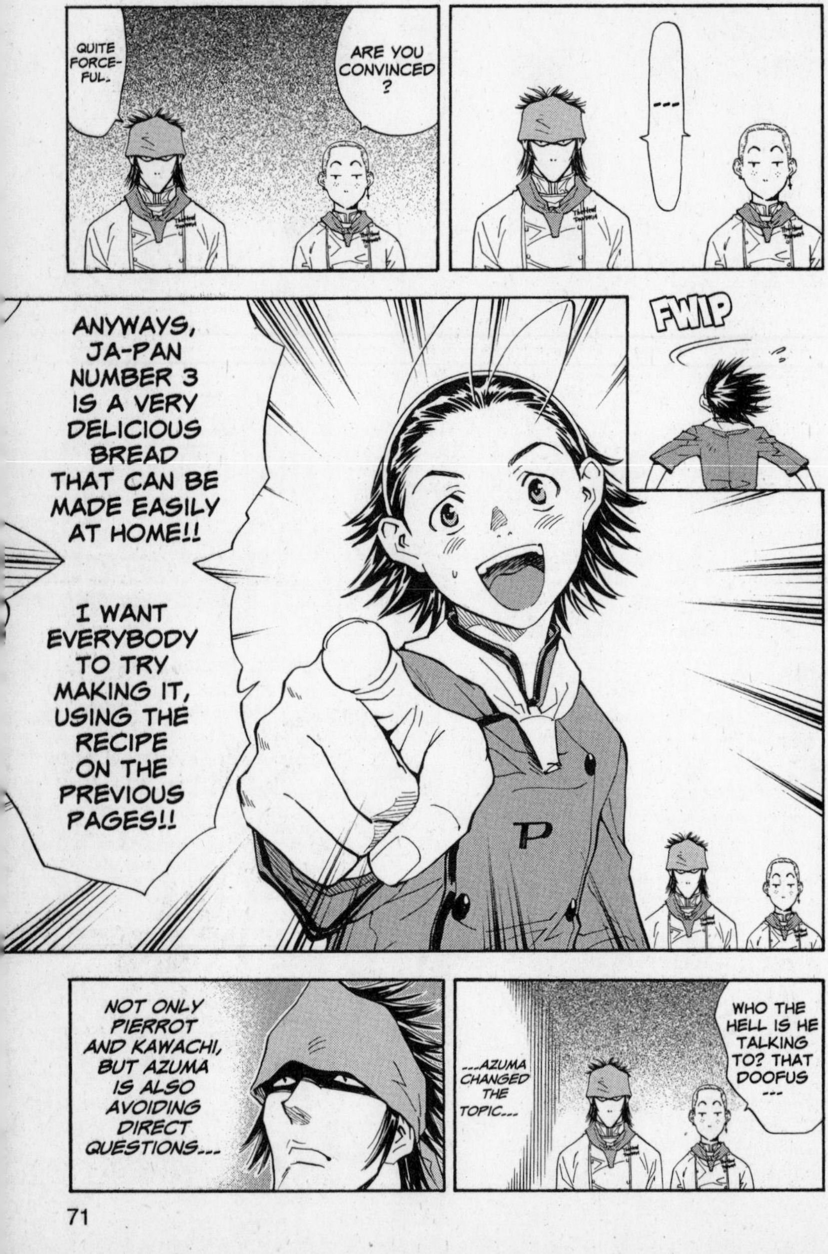
...
ARE YOU CONVINCED?
QUITE FORCE-FUL..
FWIP
ANYWAYS, JA-PAN NUMBER 3 IS A VERY DELICIOUS BREAD THAT CAN BE MADE EASILY AT HOME!!
I WANT EVERYBODY TO TRY MAKING IT, USING THE RECIPE ON THE PREVIOUS PAGES!!
WHO THE HELL IS HE TALKING TO? THAT DOOFUS...
...AZUMA CHANGED THE TOPIC...
NOT ONLY PIERROT AND KAWACHI, BUT AZUMA IS ALSO AVOIDING DIRECT QUESTIONS...

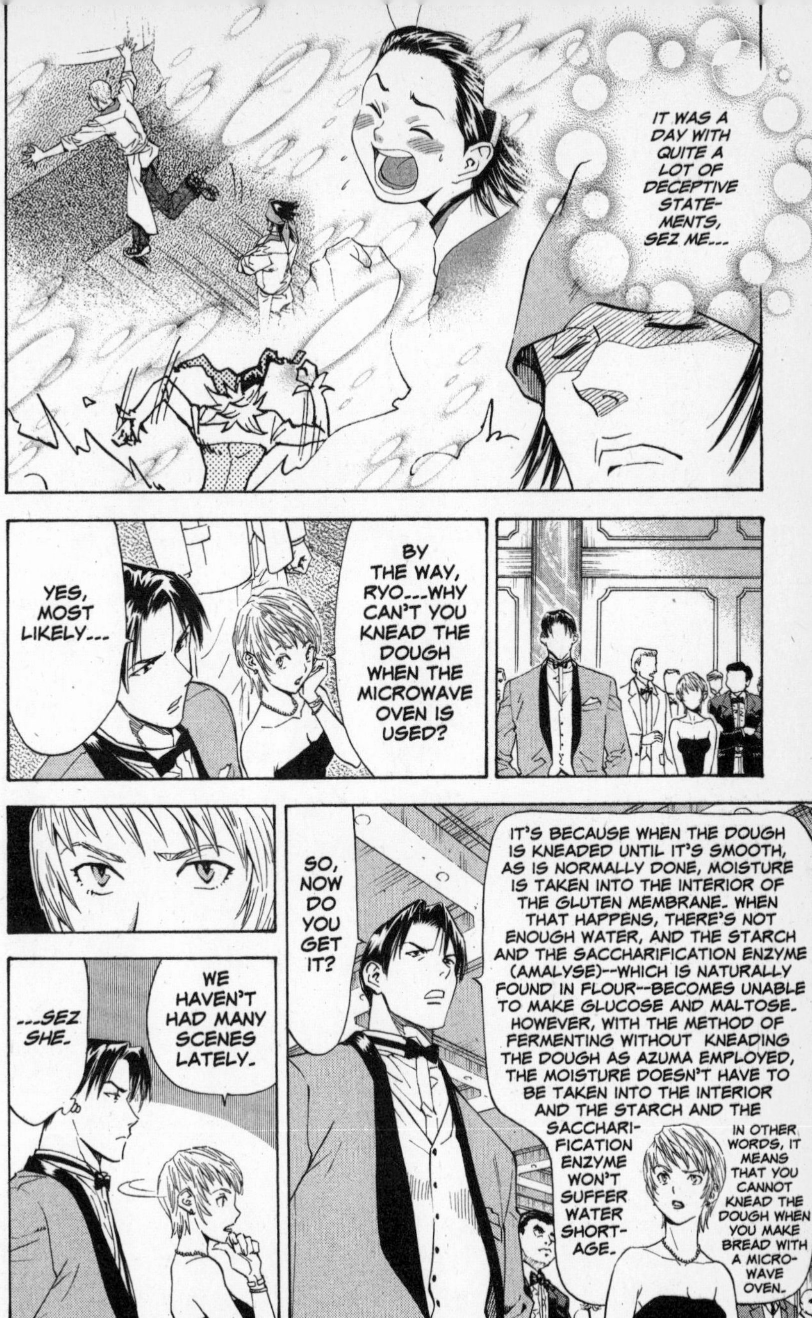
IT WAS A DAY WITH QUITE A LOT OF DECEPTIVE STATEMENTS, SEZ ME...
BY THE WAY, RYO...WHY CAN'T YOU KNEAD THE DOUGH WHEN THE MICROWAVE OVEN IS USED?
YES, MOST LIKELY...
IT'S BECAUSE WHEN THE DOUGH IS KNEADED UNTIL IT'S SMOOTH, AS IS NORMALLY DONE, MOISTURE IS TAKEN INTO THE INTERIOR OF THE GLUTEN MEMBRANE. WHEN THAT HAPPENS, THERE'S NOT ENOUGH WATER, AND THE STARCH AND THE SACCHARIFICATION ENZYME (AMALYSE)--WHICH IS NATURALLY FOUND IN FLOUR--BECOMES UNABLE TO MAKE GLUCOSE AND MALTOSE. HOWEVER, WITH THE METHOD OF FERMENTING WITHOUT KNEADING THE DOUGH AS AZUMA EMPLOYED, THE MOISTURE DOESN'T HAVE TO BE TAKEN INTO THE INTERIOR AND THE STARCH AND THE SACCHARIFICATION ENZYME WON'T SUFFER WATER SHORTAGE.
IN OTHER WORDS, IT MEANS THAT YOU CANNOT KNEAD THE DOUGH WHEN YOU MAKE BREAD WITH A MICROWAVE OVEN.
SO, NOW DO YOU GET IT?
WE HAVEN'T HAD MANY SCENES LATELY.
...SEZ SHE.

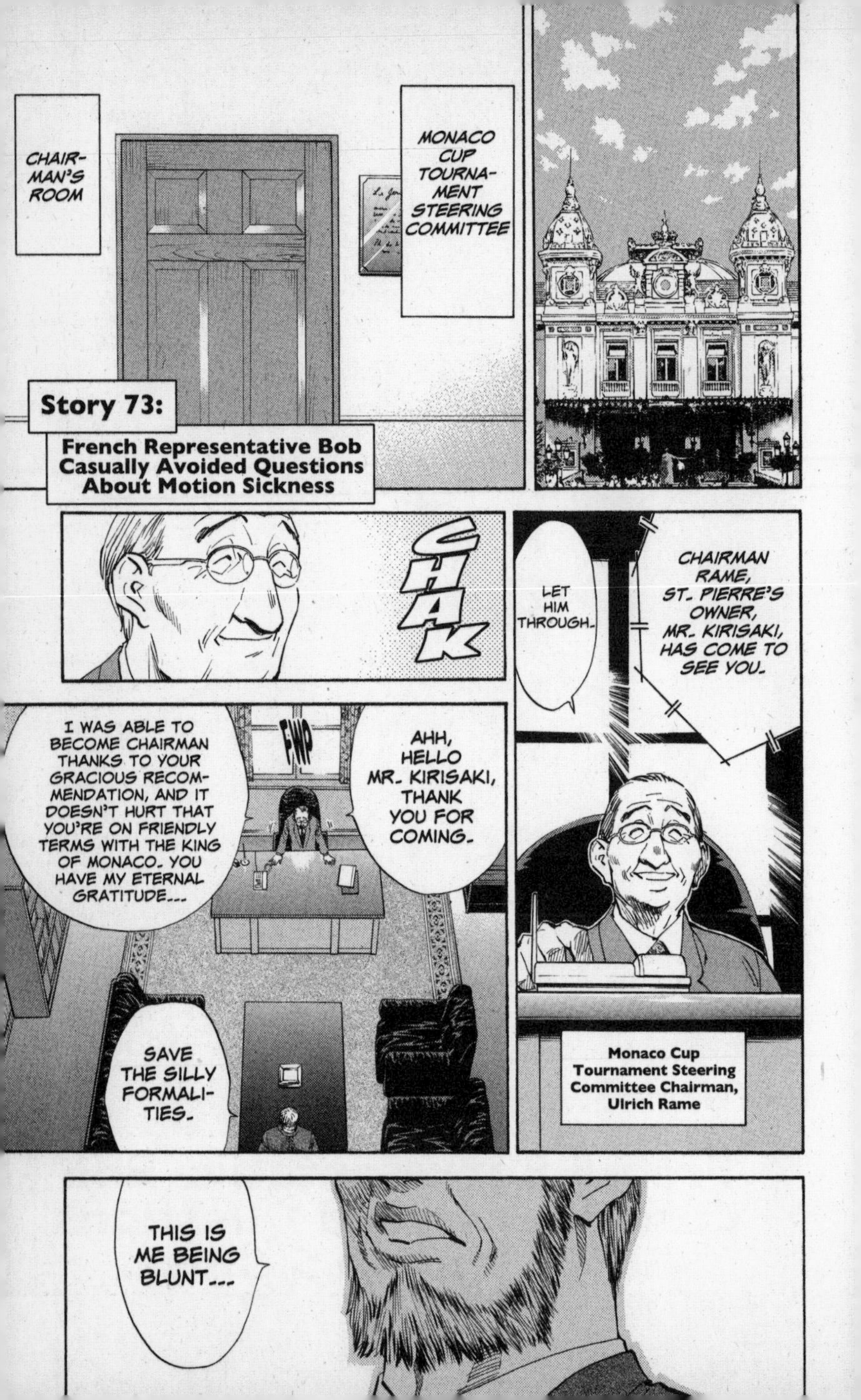
MONACO CUP TOURNAMENT STEERING COMMITTEE
CHAIRMAN'S ROOM
Story 73:
French Representative Bob Casually Avoided Questions About Motion Sickness
CHAIRMAN RAME, ST. PIERRE'S OWNER, MR. KIRISAKI, HAS COME TO SEE YOU.
LET HIM THROUGH.
Monaco Cup Tournament Steering Committee Chairman, Ulrich Rame
CHAK
FWIP
AHH, HELLO MR. KIRISAKI, THANK YOU FOR COMING.
I WAS ABLE TO BECOME CHAIRMAN THANKS TO YOUR GRACIOUS RECOMMENDATION, AND IT DOESN'T HURT THAT YOU'RE ON FRIENDLY TERMS WITH THE KING OF MONACO. YOU HAVE MY ETERNAL GRATITUDE...
SAVE THE SILLY FORMALITIES.
THIS IS ME BEING BLUNT...

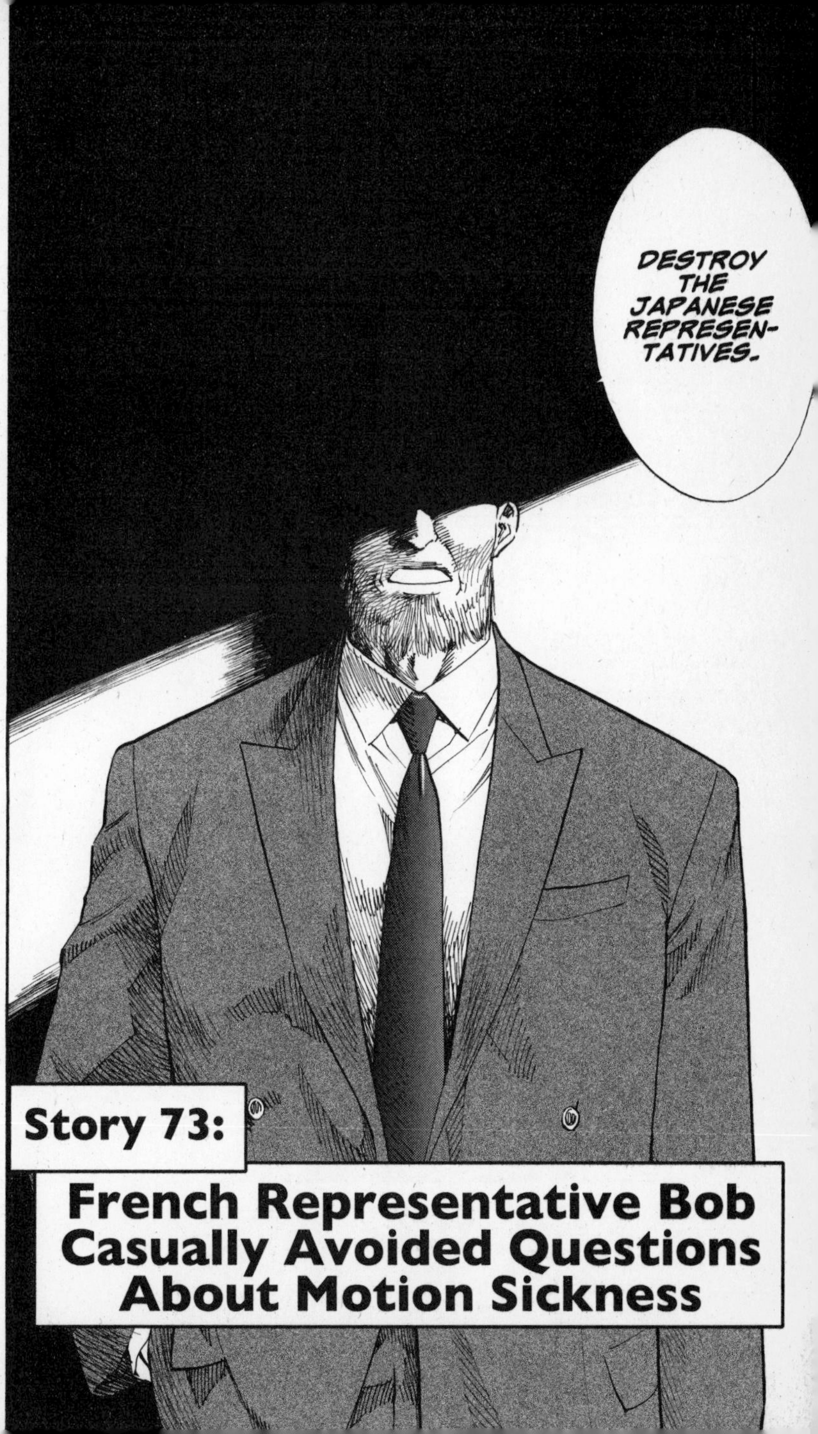
DESTROY THE JAPANESE REPRESEN-TATIVES.

## Story 73:
# French Representative Bob Casually Avoided Questions About Motion Sickness

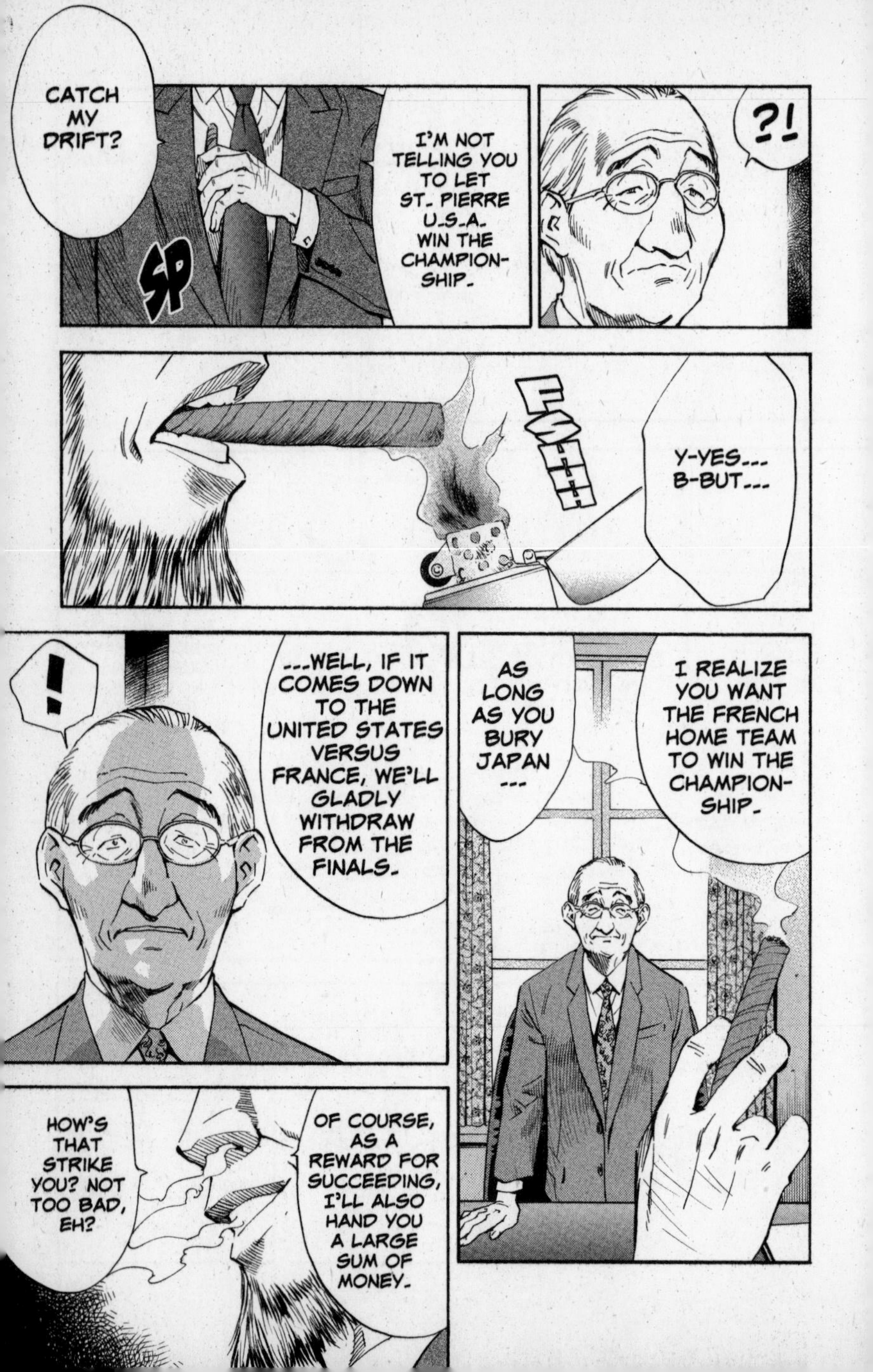
?!
I'M NOT TELLING YOU TO LET ST. PIERRE U.S.A. WIN THE CHAMPION-SHIP.
SP
CATCH MY DRIFT?
Y-YES... B-BUT...
FSHHH
I REALIZE YOU WANT THE FRENCH HOME TEAM TO WIN THE CHAMPION-SHIP.
AS LONG AS YOU BURY JAPAN ---
!
---WELL, IF IT COMES DOWN TO THE UNITED STATES VERSUS FRANCE, WE'LL GLADLY WITHDRAW FROM THE FINALS.
OF COURSE, AS A REWARD FOR SUCCEEDING, I'LL ALSO HAND YOU A LARGE SUM OF MONEY.
HOW'S THAT STRIKE YOU? NOT TOO BAD, EH?

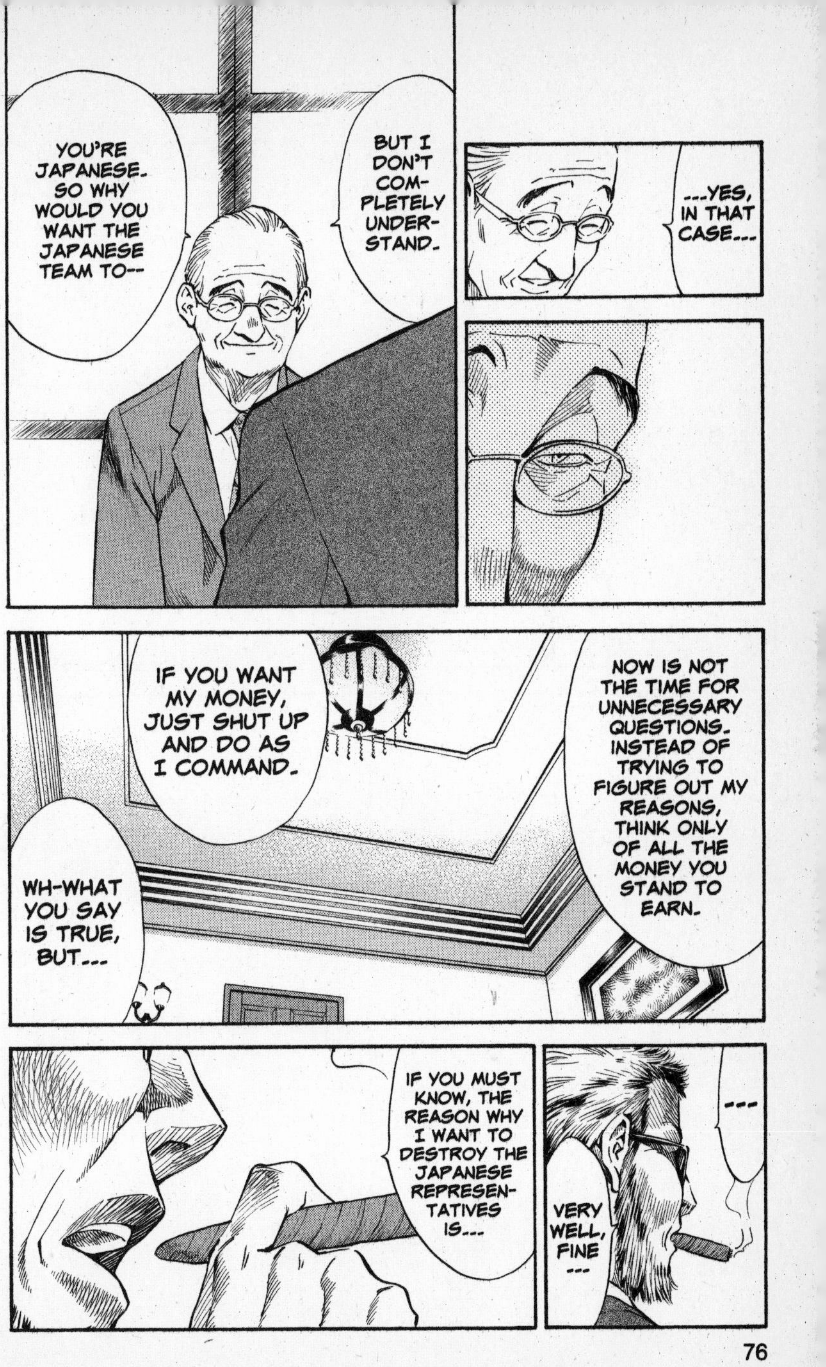
YOU'RE JAPANESE. SO WHY WOULD YOU WANT THE JAPANESE TEAM TO--
BUT I DON'T COMPLETELY UNDERSTAND.
...YES, IN THAT CASE...
WH-WHAT YOU SAY IS TRUE, BUT...
IF YOU WANT MY MONEY, JUST SHUT UP AND DO AS I COMMAND.
NOW IS NOT THE TIME FOR UNNECESSARY QUESTIONS. INSTEAD OF TRYING TO FIGURE OUT MY REASONS, THINK ONLY OF ALL THE MONEY YOU STAND TO EARN.
IF YOU MUST KNOW, THE REASON WHY I WANT TO DESTROY THE JAPANESE REPRESENTATIVES IS...
...
VERY WELL, FINE ...

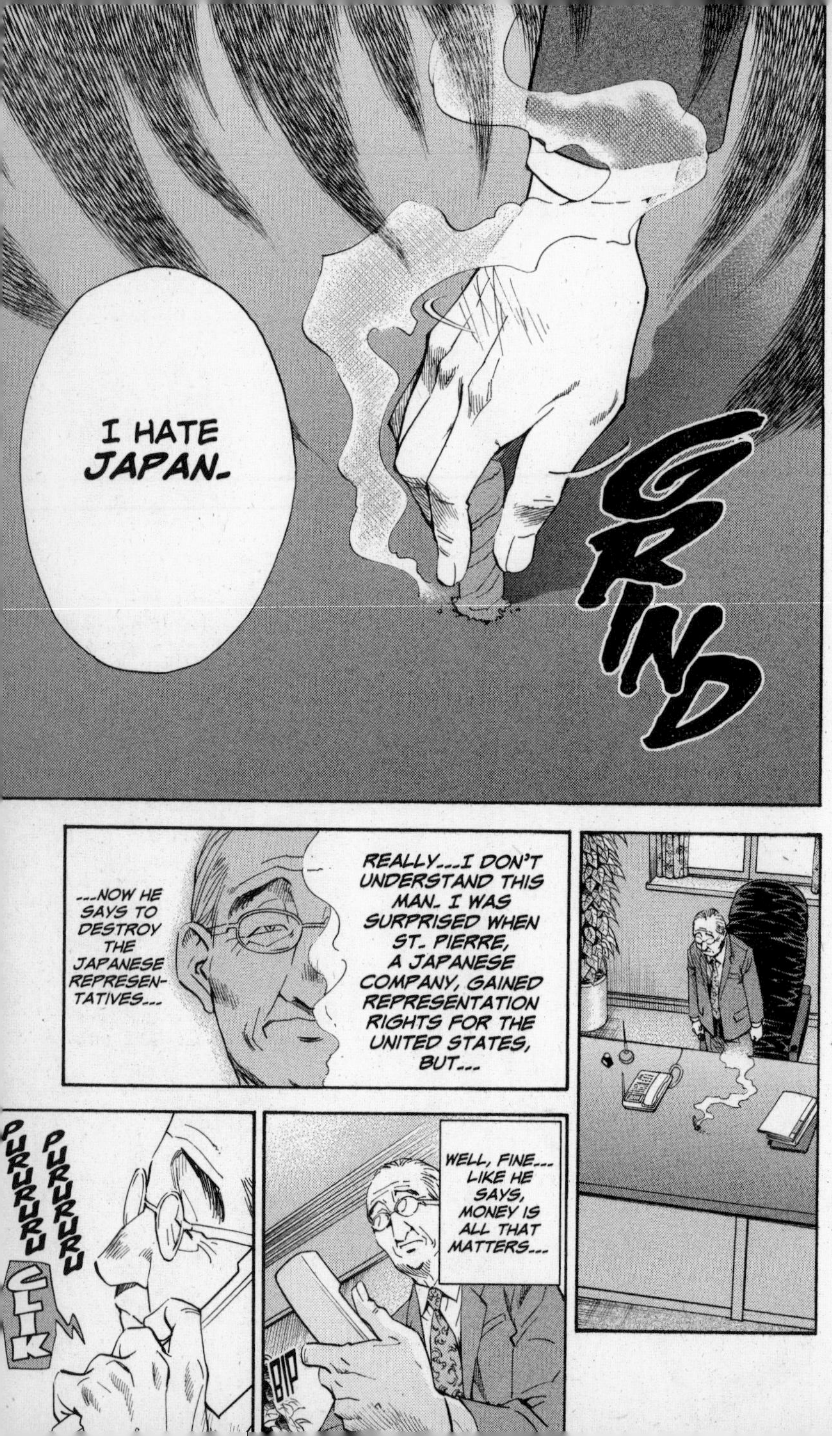
I HATE JAPAN.
GRIND
REALLY... I DON'T UNDERSTAND THIS MAN. I WAS SURPRISED WHEN ST. PIERRE, A JAPANESE COMPANY, GAINED REPRESENTATION RIGHTS FOR THE UNITED STATES, BUT...
...NOW HE SAYS TO DESTROY THE JAPANESE REPRESEN-TATIVES...
WELL, FINE... LIKE HE SAYS, MONEY IS ALL THAT MATTERS...
BIP
PURURURU PURURURU
CLIK

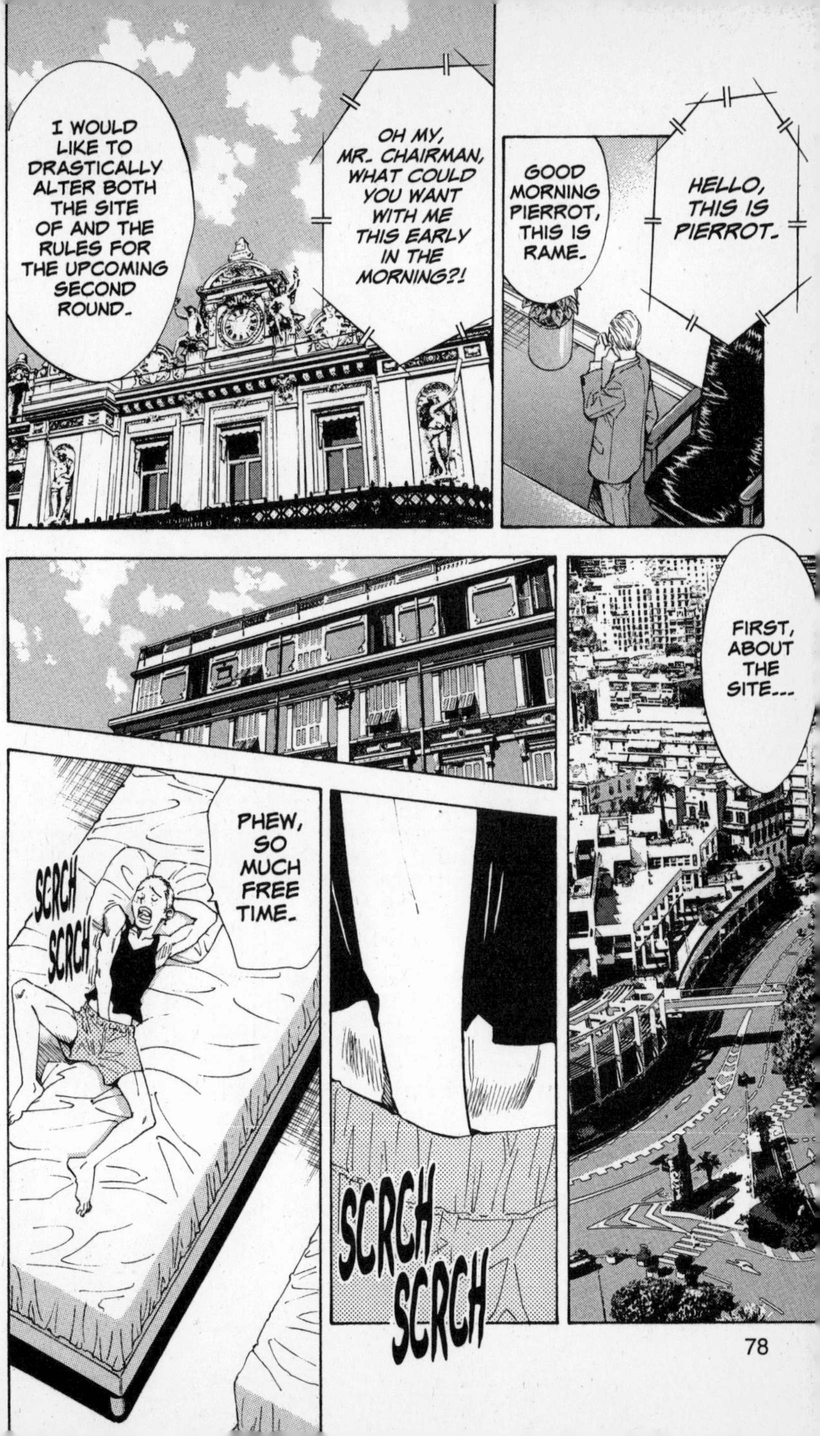
HELLO, THIS IS PIERROT.
GOOD MORNING PIERROT, THIS IS RAME.
OH MY, MR. CHAIRMAN, WHAT COULD YOU WANT WITH ME THIS EARLY IN THE MORNING?!
I WOULD LIKE TO DRASTICALLY ALTER BOTH THE SITE OF AND THE RULES FOR THE UPCOMING SECOND ROUND.
FIRST, ABOUT THE SITE...
SCRCH SCRCH
PHEW, SO MUCH FREE TIME.
SCRCH SCRCH

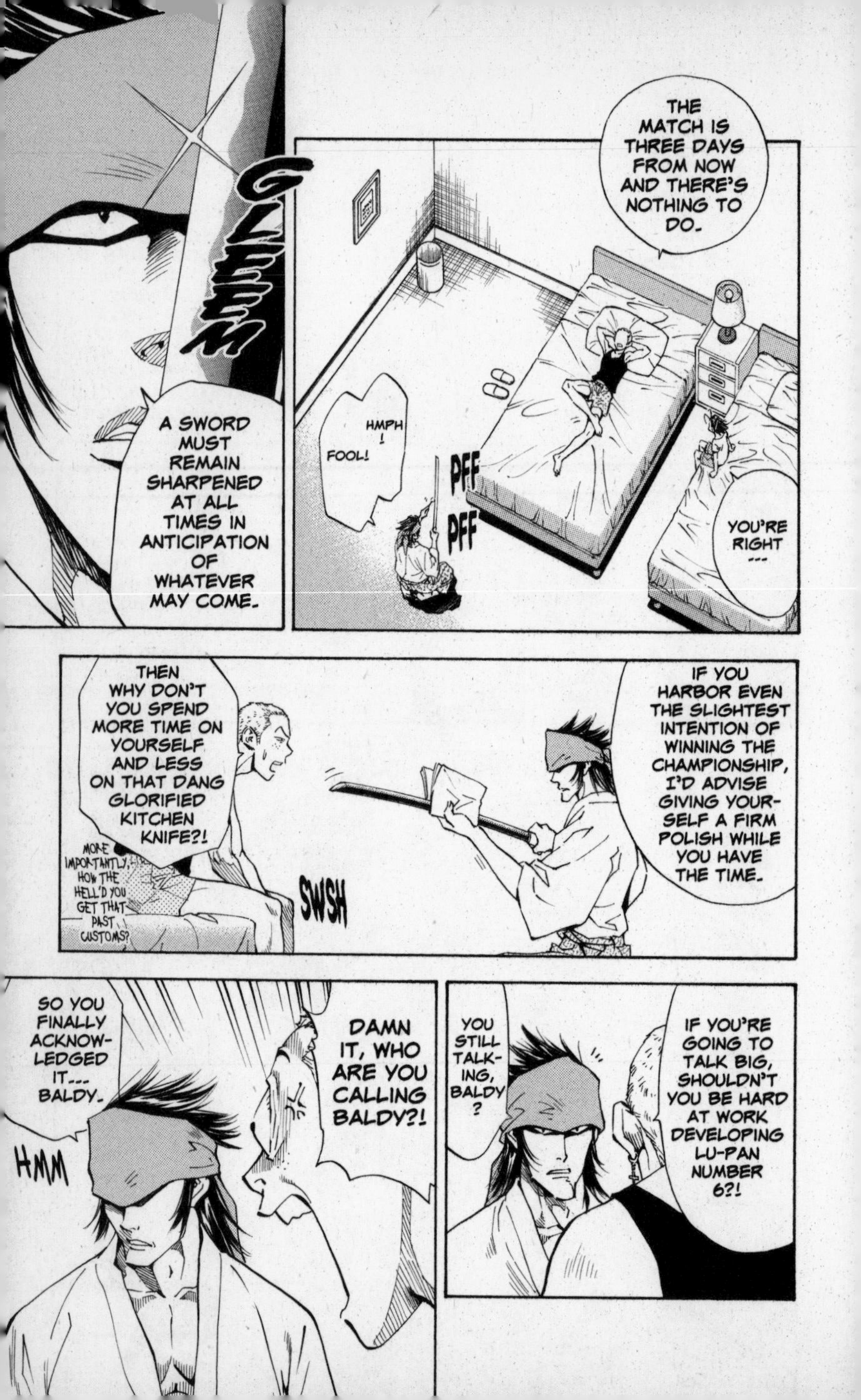
THE MATCH IS THREE DAYS FROM NOW AND THERE'S NOTHING TO DO.
YOU'RE RIGHT...
HMPH! FOOL!
PFF PFF
GLEEEM
A SWORD MUST REMAIN SHARPENED AT ALL TIMES IN ANTICIPATION OF WHATEVER MAY COME.
IF YOU HARBOR EVEN THE SLIGHTEST INTENTION OF WINNING THE CHAMPIONSHIP, I'D ADVISE GIVING YOURSELF A FIRM POLISH WHILE YOU HAVE THE TIME.
SWSH
THEN WHY DON'T YOU SPEND MORE TIME ON YOURSELF AND LESS ON THAT DANG GLORIFIED KITCHEN KNIFE?!
MORE IMPORTANTLY, HOW THE HELL'D YOU GET THAT PAST CUSTOMS?
IF YOU'RE GOING TO TALK BIG, SHOULDN'T YOU BE HARD AT WORK DEVELOPING LU-PAN NUMBER 6?!
YOU STILL TALKING, BALDY?
DAMN IT, WHO ARE YOU CALLING BALDY?!
SO YOU FINALLY ACKNOWLEDGED IT... BALDY.
HMM

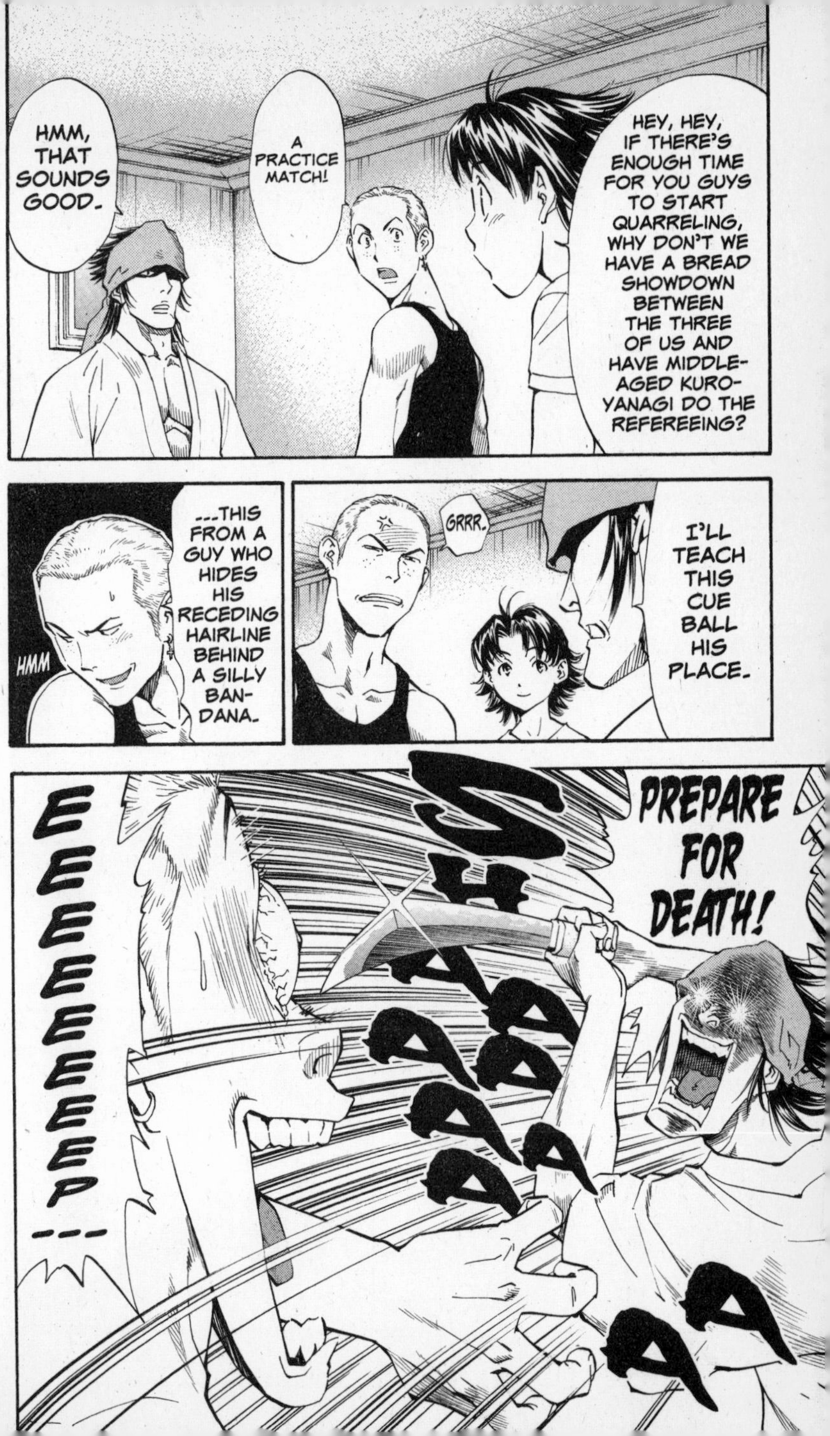

HEY, HEY, IF THERE'S ENOUGH TIME FOR YOU GUYS TO START QUARRELING, WHY DON'T WE HAVE A BREAD SHOWDOWN BETWEEN THE THREE OF US AND HAVE MIDDLE-AGED KURO-YANAGI DO THE REFEREEING?
A PRACTICE MATCH!
HMM, THAT SOUNDS GOOD.
I'LL TEACH THIS CUE BALL HIS PLACE.
GRRR.
...THIS FROM A GUY WHO HIDES HIS RECEDING HAIRLINE BEHIND A SILLY BAN-DANA.
HMM
PREPARE FOR DEATH!
EEEEEEEEEP---

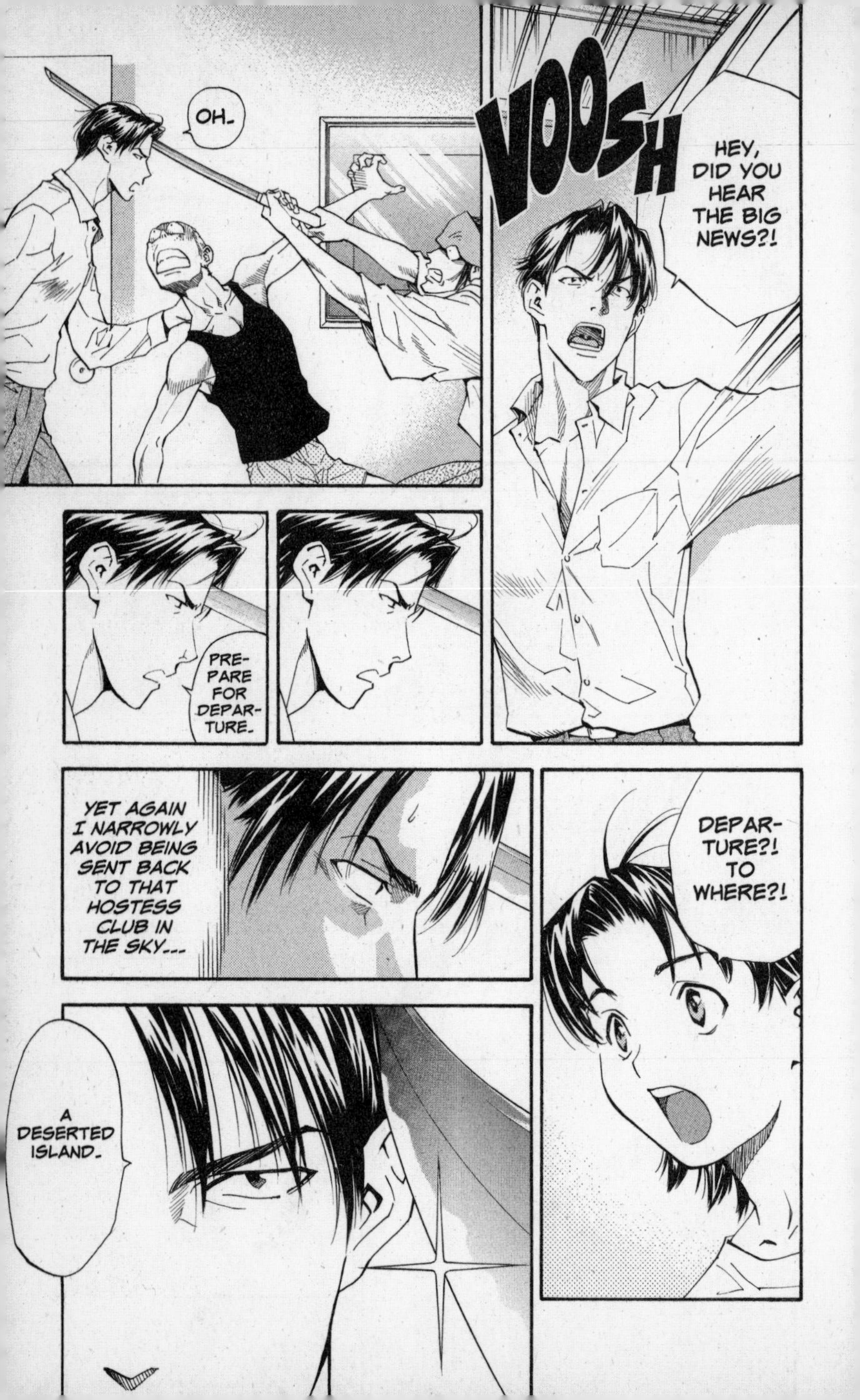
VOOSH
HEY, DID YOU HEAR THE BIG NEWS?!
OH.
PRE-PARE FOR DEPAR-TURE.
DEPAR-TURE?! TO WHERE?!
YET AGAIN I NARROWLY AVOID BEING SENT BACK TO THAT HOSTESS CLUB IN THE SKY...
A DESERTED ISLAND.

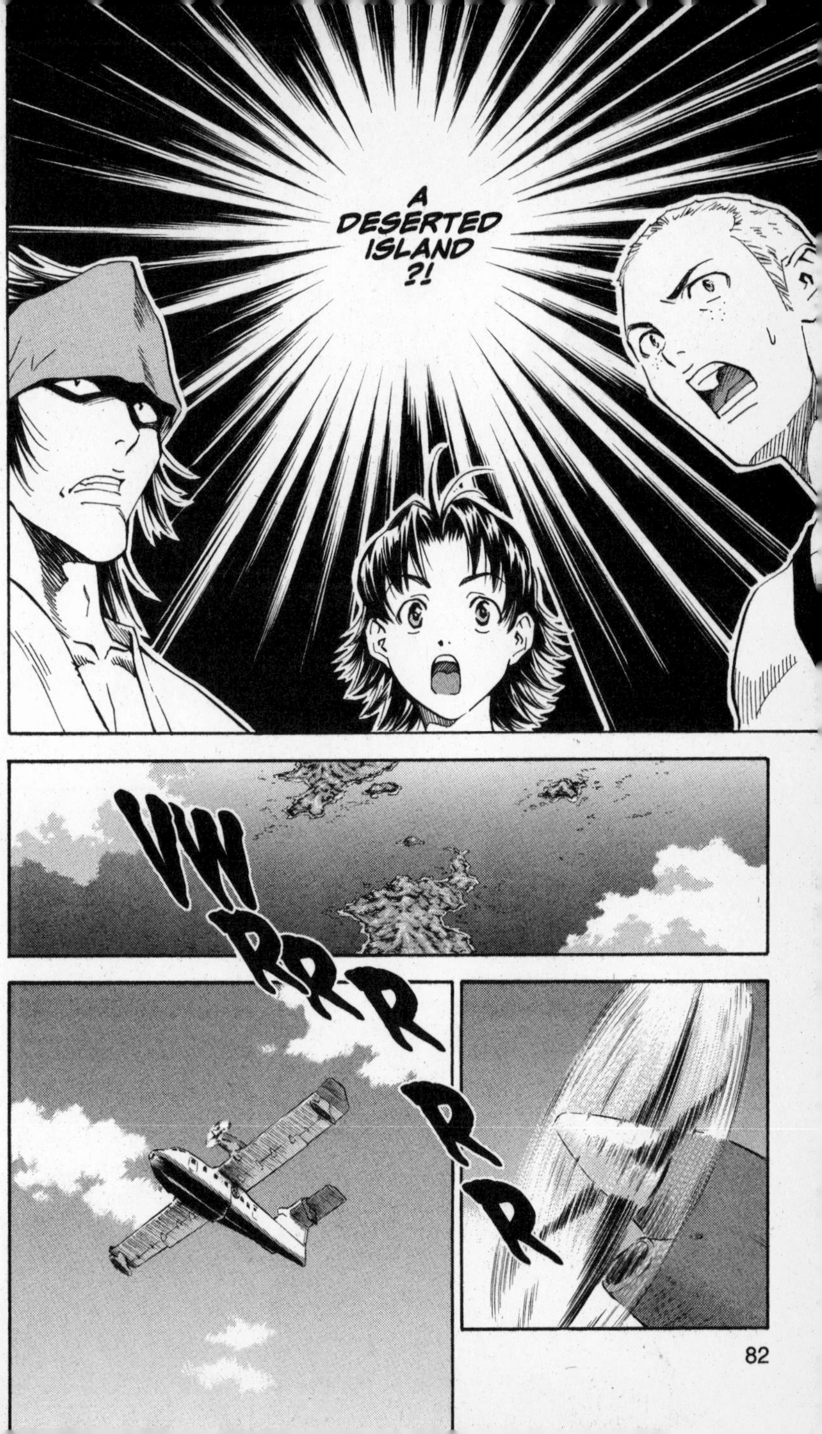
A DESERTED ISLAND ?!
VWRRRRRR

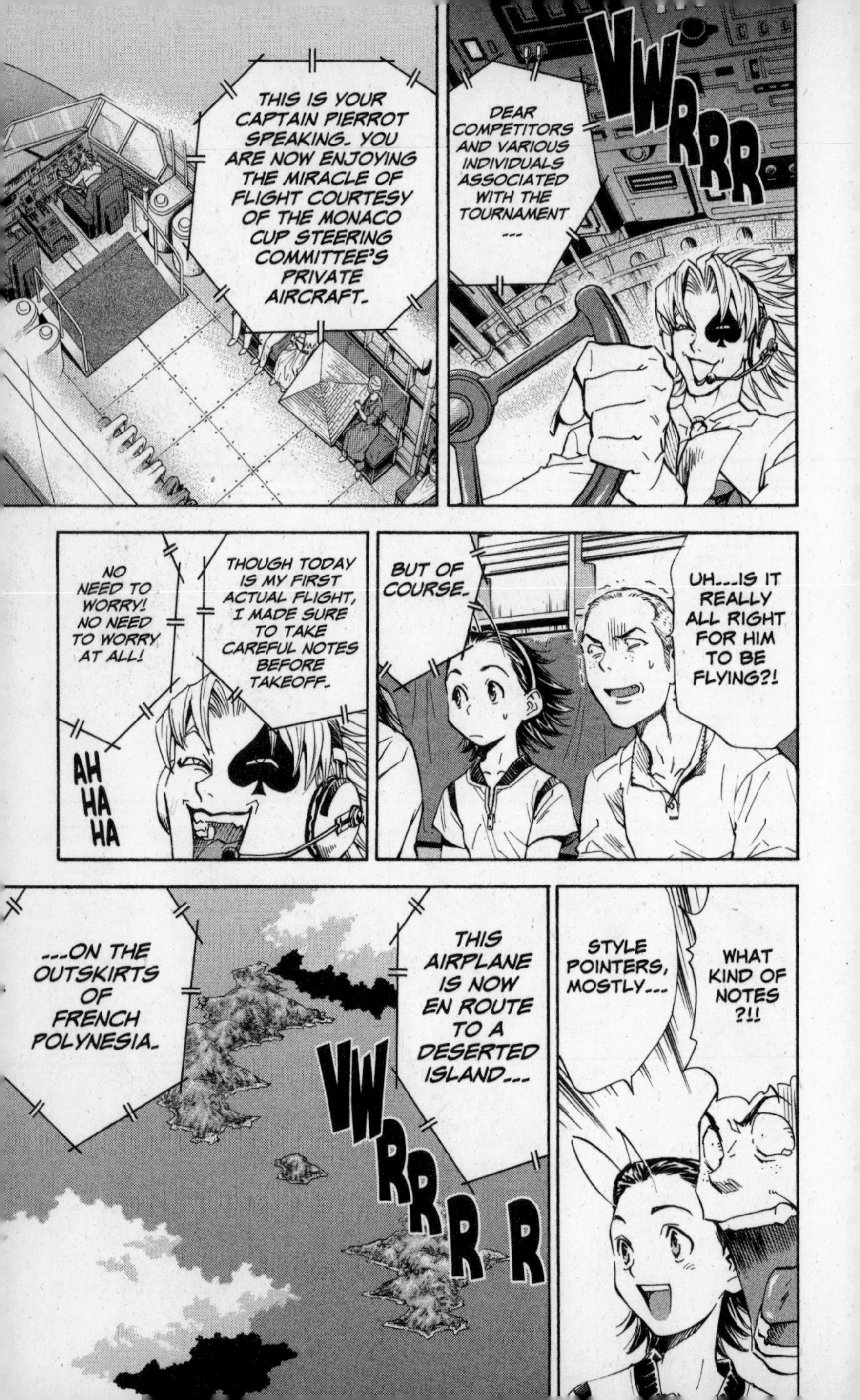
VWRRRR
DEAR COMPETITORS AND VARIOUS INDIVIDUALS ASSOCIATED WITH THE TOURNAMENT ...
THIS IS YOUR CAPTAIN PIERROT SPEAKING. YOU ARE NOW ENJOYING THE MIRACLE OF FLIGHT COURTESY OF THE MONACO CUP STEERING COMMITTEE'S PRIVATE AIRCRAFT.
UH...IS IT REALLY ALL RIGHT FOR HIM TO BE FLYING?!
BUT OF COURSE.
THOUGH TODAY IS MY FIRST ACTUAL FLIGHT, I MADE SURE TO TAKE CAREFUL NOTES BEFORE TAKEOFF.
NO NEED TO WORRY! NO NEED TO WORRY AT ALL!
AH HA HA
WHAT KIND OF NOTES ?!!
STYLE POINTERS, MOSTLY...
THIS AIRPLANE IS NOW EN ROUTE TO A DESERTED ISLAND...
VWRRRR
...ON THE OUTSKIRTS OF FRENCH POLYNESIA.

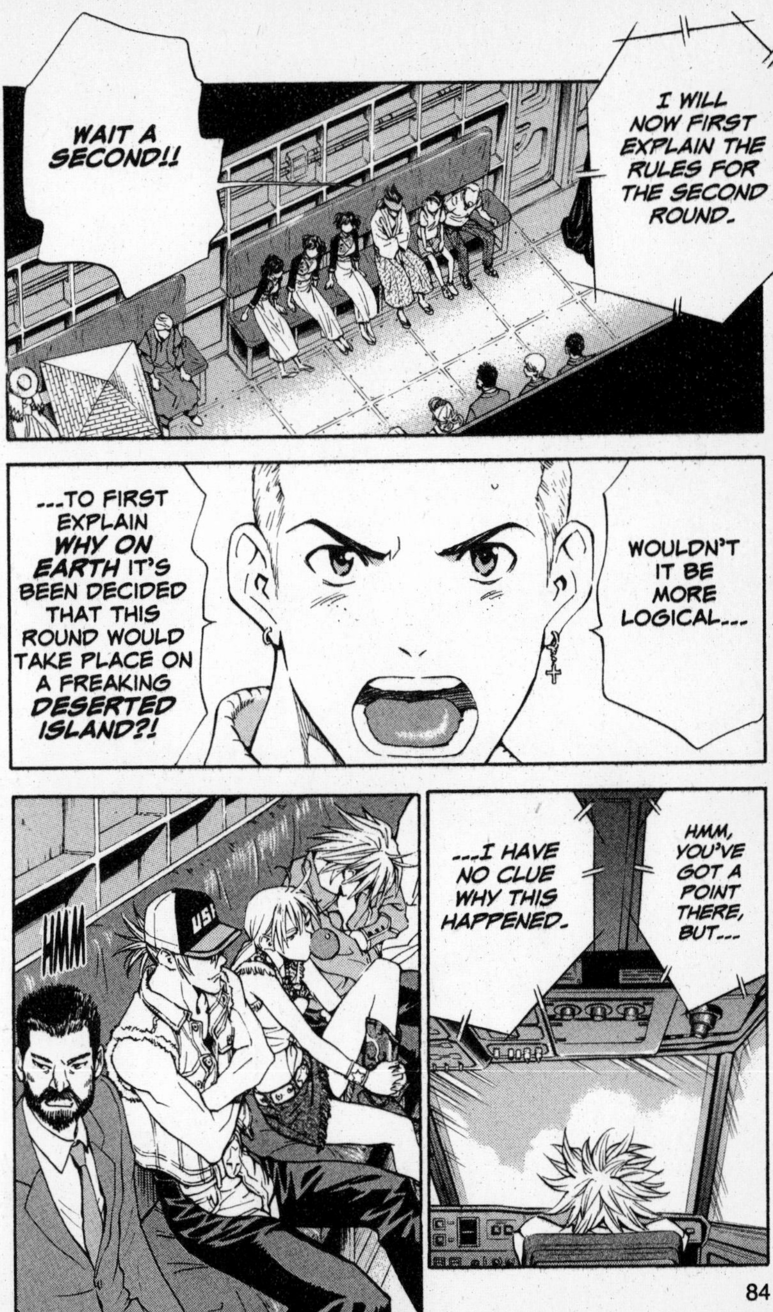
I WILL NOW FIRST EXPLAIN THE RULES FOR THE SECOND ROUND.
WAIT A SECOND!!
WOULDN'T IT BE MORE LOGICAL...
...TO FIRST EXPLAIN WHY ON EARTH IT'S BEEN DECIDED THAT THIS ROUND WOULD TAKE PLACE ON A FREAKING DESERTED ISLAND?!
HMM, YOU'VE GOT A POINT THERE, BUT...
...I HAVE NO CLUE WHY THIS HAPPENED.
HMM

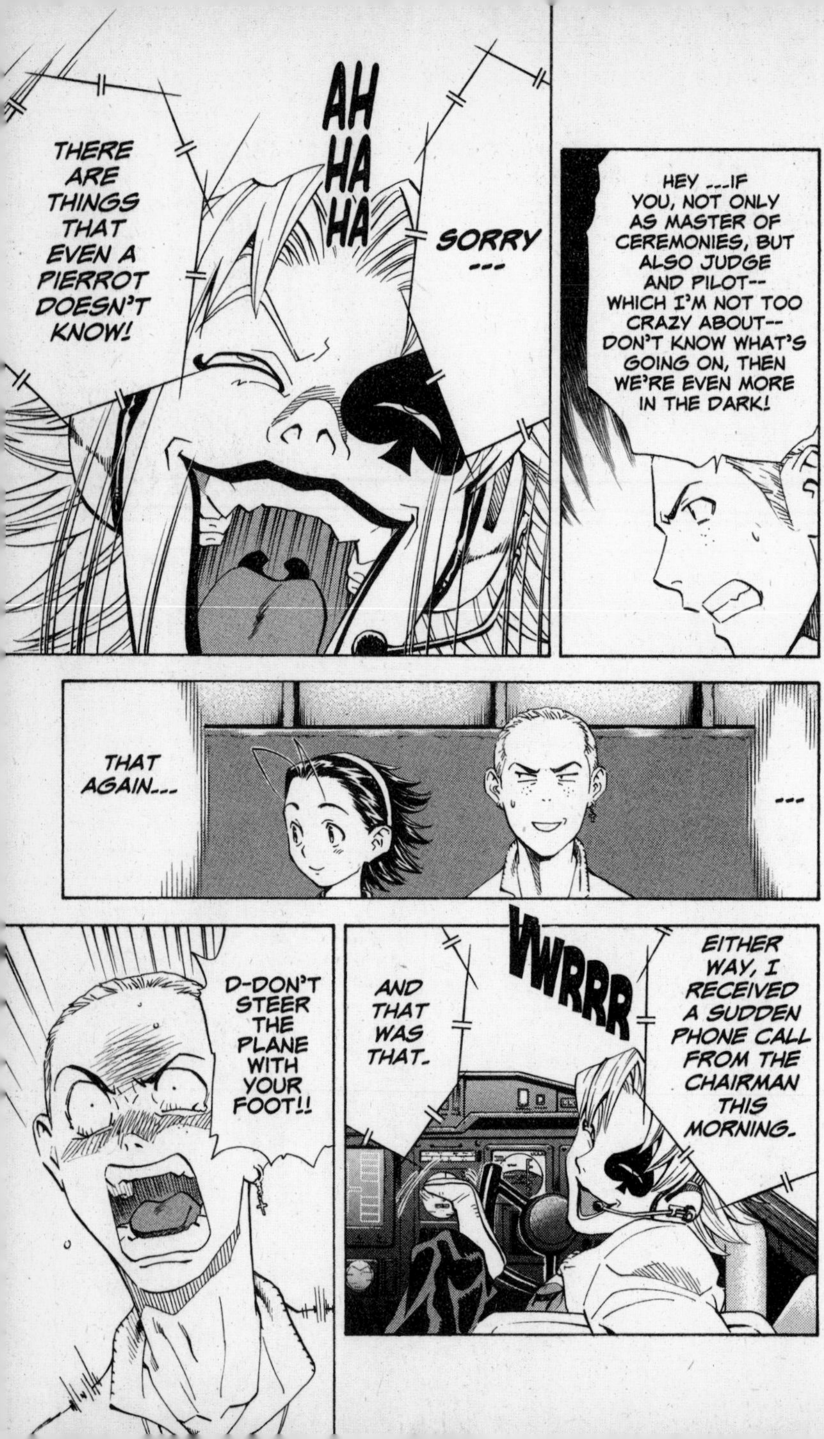
HEY ...IF YOU, NOT ONLY AS MASTER OF CEREMONIES, BUT ALSO JUDGE AND PILOT-- WHICH I'M NOT TOO CRAZY ABOUT-- DON'T KNOW WHAT'S GOING ON, THEN WE'RE EVEN MORE IN THE DARK!
AH HA HA HA
SORRY ...
THERE ARE THINGS THAT EVEN A PIERROT DOESN'T KNOW!
...
THAT AGAIN...
EITHER WAY, I RECEIVED A SUDDEN PHONE CALL FROM THE CHAIRMAN THIS MORNING.
VWRRR
AND THAT WAS THAT.
D-DON'T STEER THE PLANE WITH YOUR FOOT!!

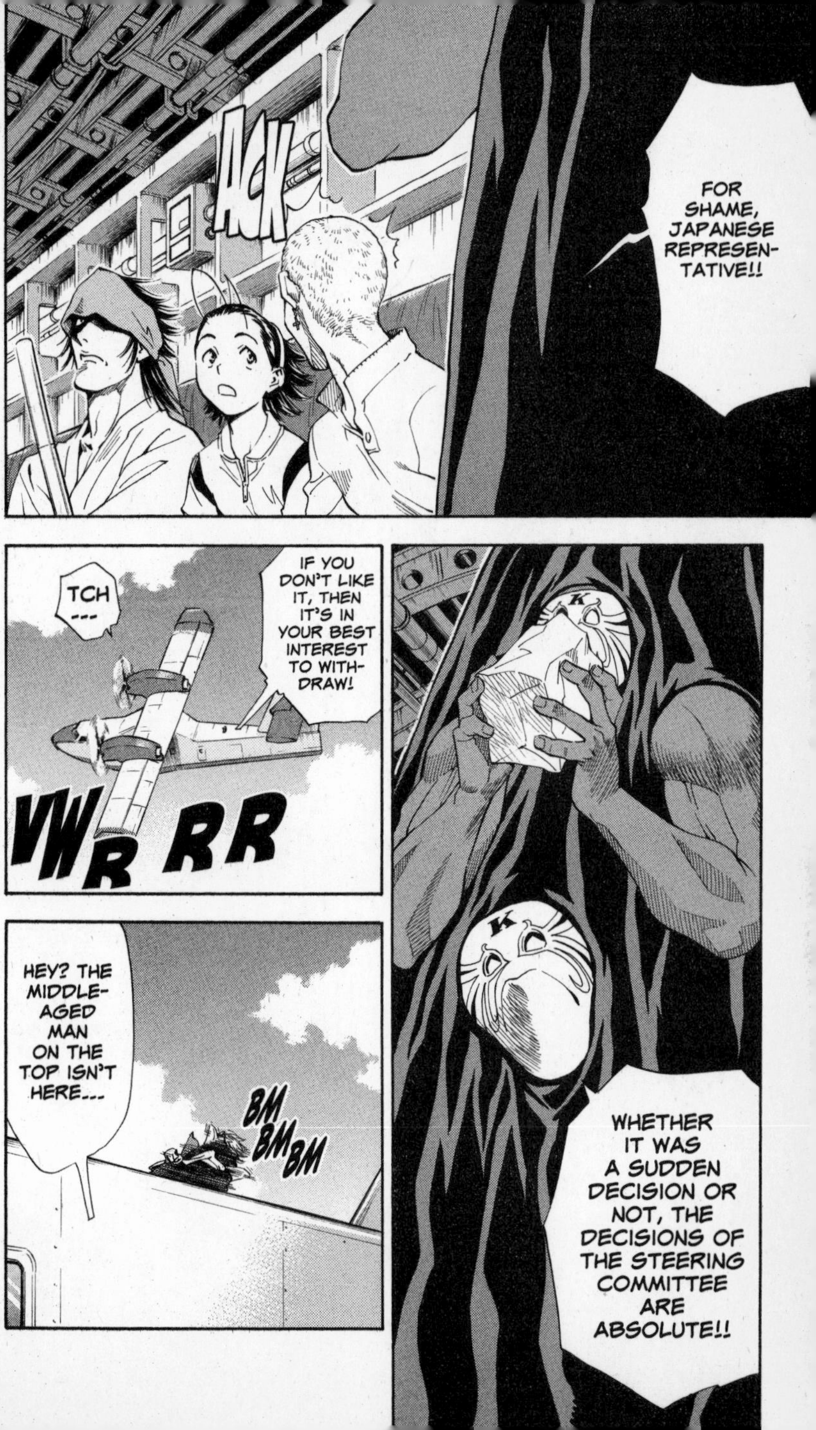
FOR SHAME, JAPANESE REPRESEN-TATIVE!!
ACK
WHETHER IT WAS A SUDDEN DECISION OR NOT, THE DECISIONS OF THE STEERING COMMITTEE ARE ABSOLUTE!!
IF YOU DON'T LIKE IT, THEN IT'S IN YOUR BEST INTEREST TO WITH-DRAW!
TCH ---
VWRRRR
HEY? THE MIDDLE-AGED MAN ON THE TOP ISN'T HERE...
BM BM BM BM

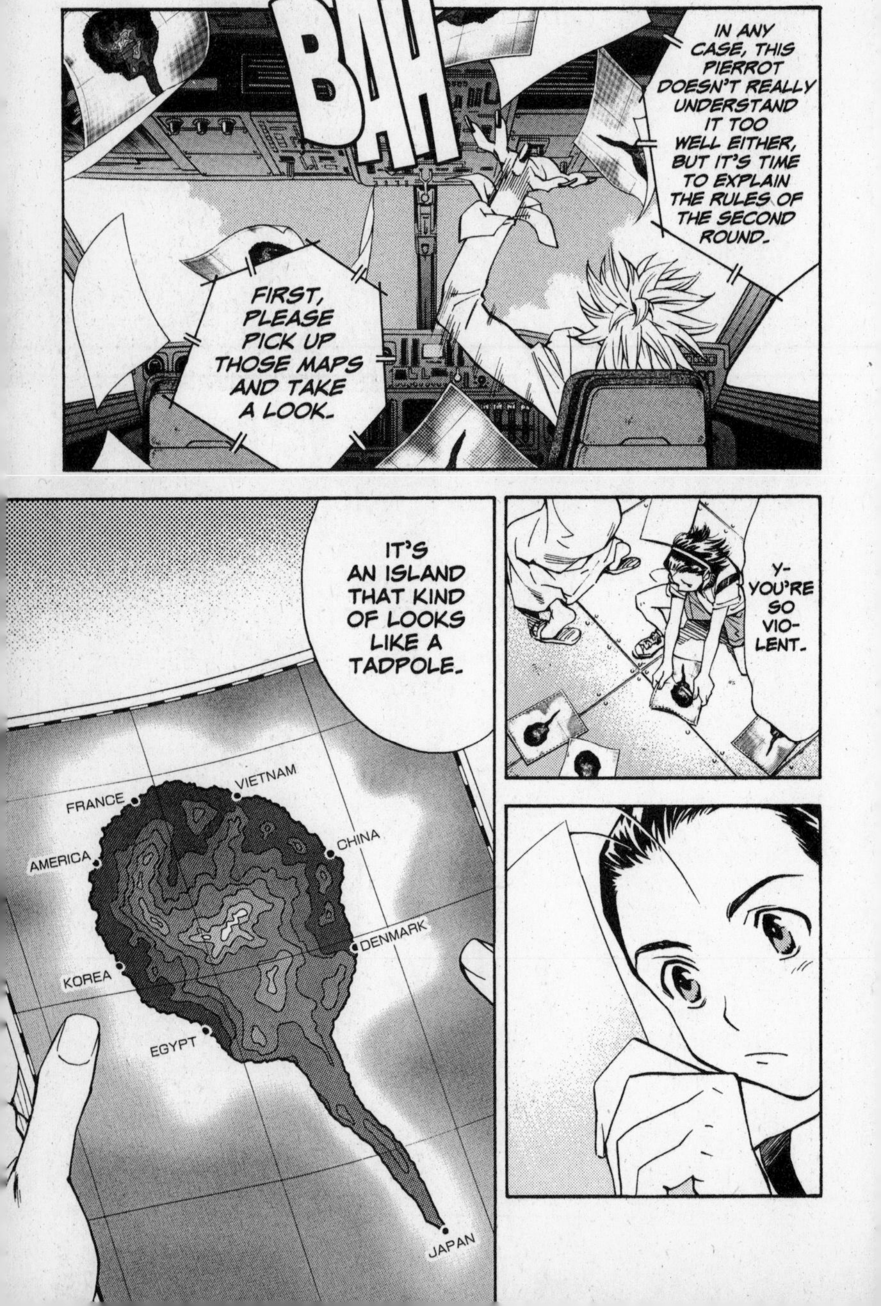
BAH
IN ANY CASE, THIS PIERROT DOESN'T REALLY UNDERSTAND IT TOO WELL EITHER, BUT IT'S TIME TO EXPLAIN THE RULES OF THE SECOND ROUND.
FIRST, PLEASE PICK UP THOSE MAPS AND TAKE A LOOK.
Y-YOU'RE SO VIO-LENT.
IT'S AN ISLAND THAT KIND OF LOOKS LIKE A TADPOLE.
VIETNAM
FRANCE
CHINA
AMERICA
DENMARK
KOREA
EGYPT
JAPAN

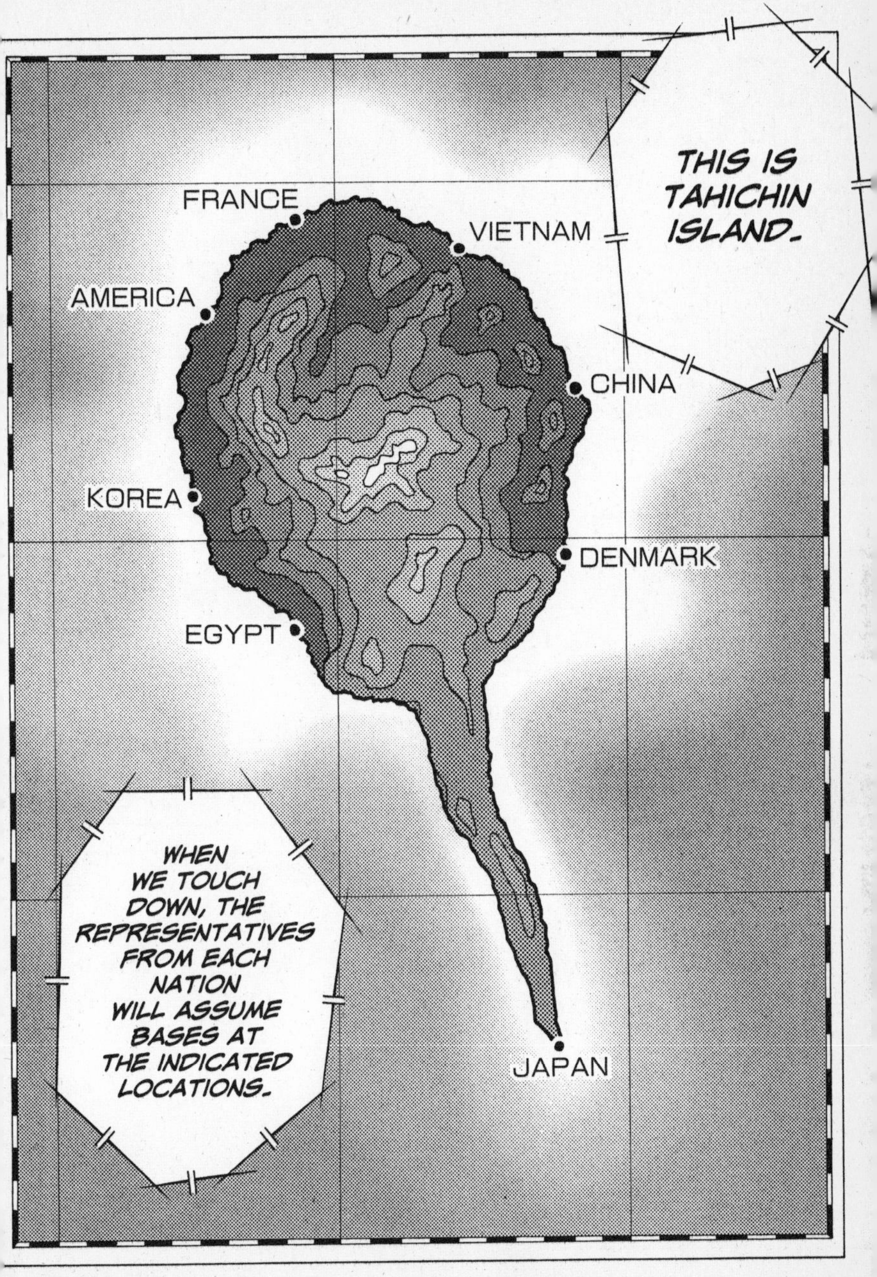
THIS IS TAHICHIN ISLAND.
FRANCE
VIETNAM
AMERICA
CHINA
KOREA
DENMARK
EGYPT
JAPAN
WHEN WE TOUCH DOWN, THE REPRESENTATIVES FROM EACH NATION WILL ASSUME BASES AT THE INDICATED LOCATIONS.

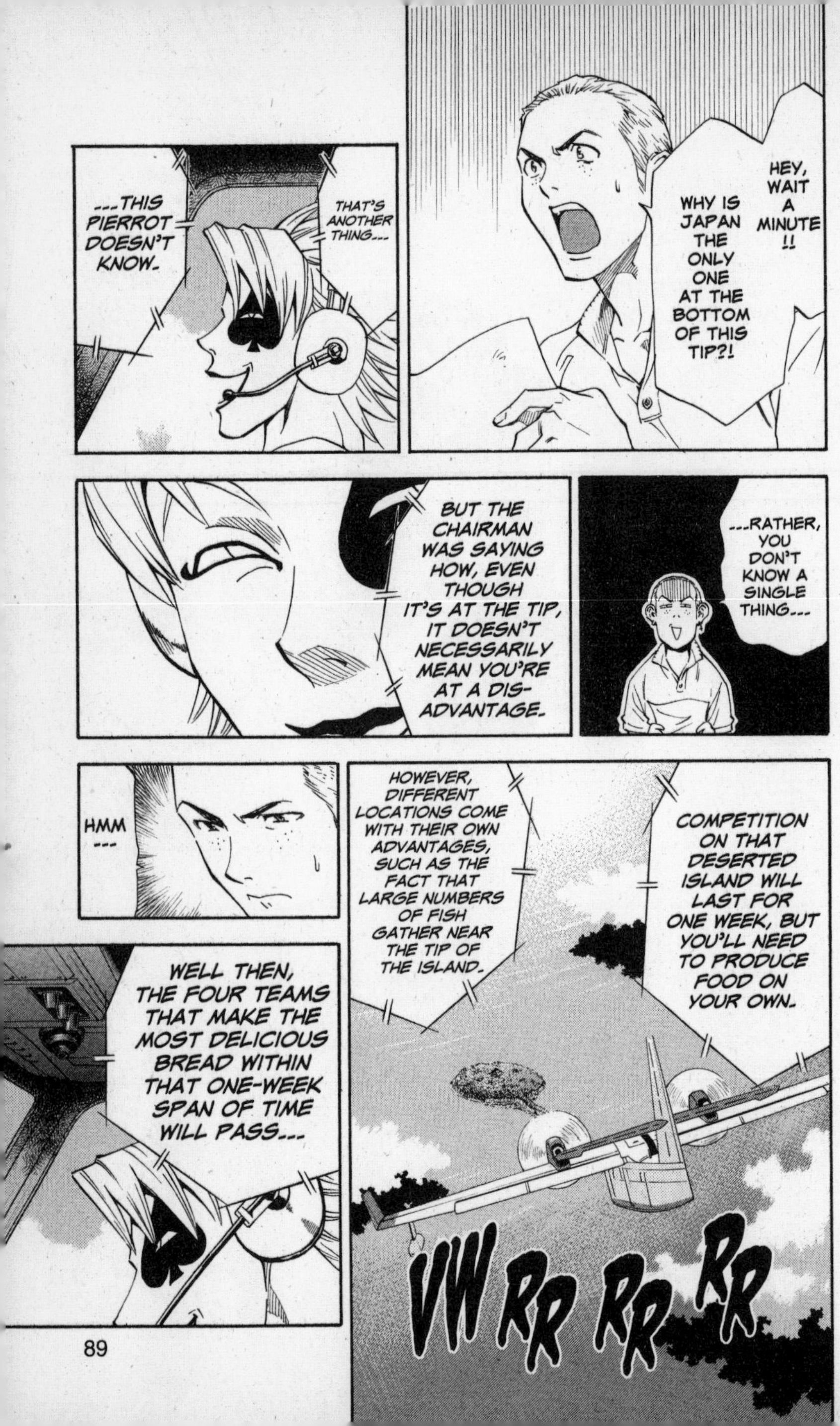
HEY, WAIT A MINUTE !!
WHY IS JAPAN THE ONLY ONE AT THE BOTTOM OF THIS TIP?!
THAT'S ANOTHER THING...
...THIS PIERROT DOESN'T KNOW.
...RATHER, YOU DON'T KNOW A SINGLE THING...
BUT THE CHAIRMAN WAS SAYING HOW, EVEN THOUGH IT'S AT THE TIP, IT DOESN'T NECESSARILY MEAN YOU'RE AT A DIS-ADVANTAGE.
COMPETITION ON THAT DESERTED ISLAND WILL LAST FOR ONE WEEK, BUT YOU'LL NEED TO PRODUCE FOOD ON YOUR OWN.
HOWEVER, DIFFERENT LOCATIONS COME WITH THEIR OWN ADVANTAGES, SUCH AS THE FACT THAT LARGE NUMBERS OF FISH GATHER NEAR THE TIP OF THE ISLAND.
VW RR RR RR
HMM ...
WELL THEN, THE FOUR TEAMS THAT MAKE THE MOST DELICIOUS BREAD WITHIN THAT ONE-WEEK SPAN OF TIME WILL PASS...

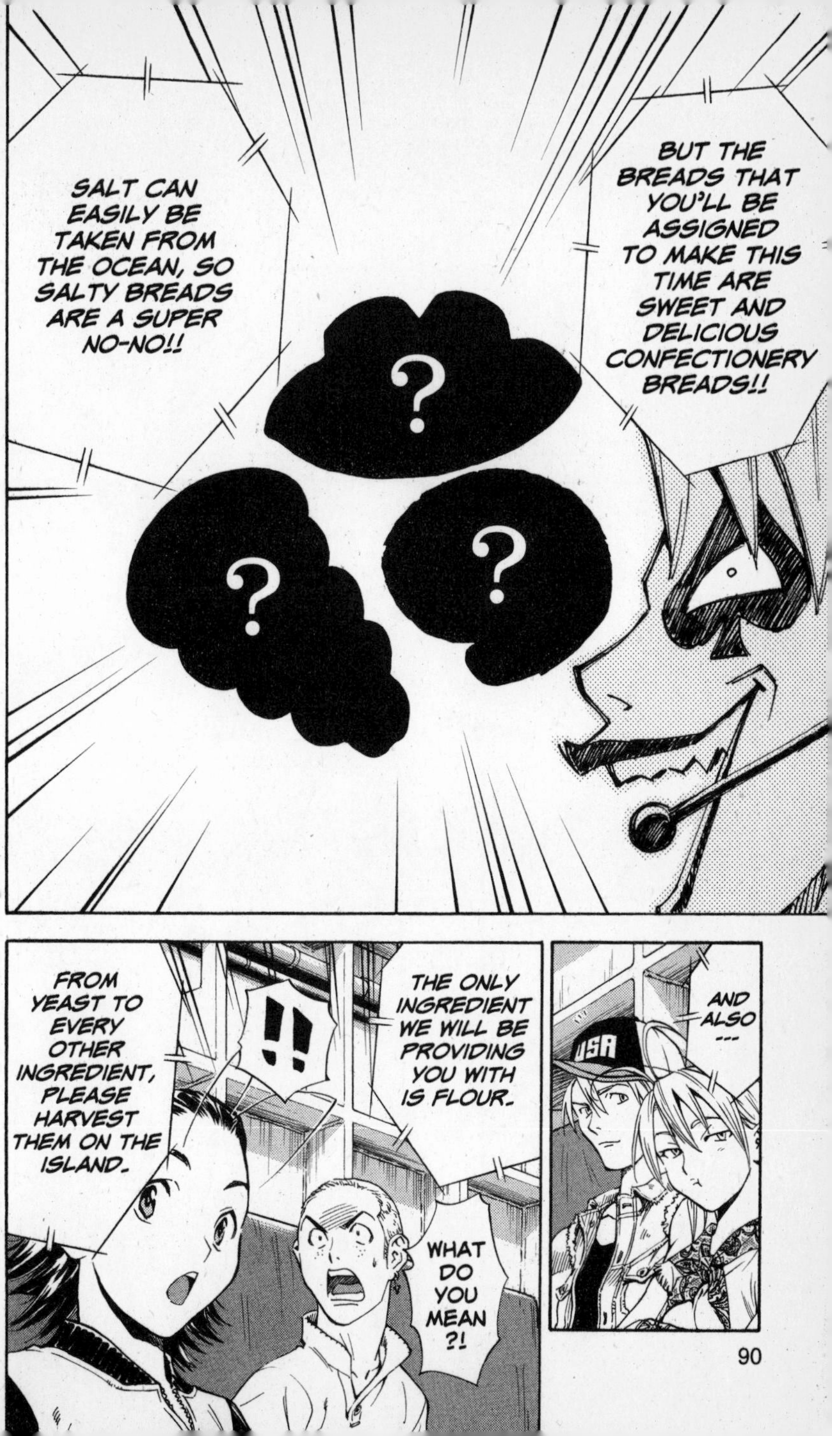
BUT THE BREADS THAT YOU'LL BE ASSIGNED TO MAKE THIS TIME ARE SWEET AND DELICIOUS CONFECTIONERY BREADS!!
SALT CAN EASILY BE TAKEN FROM THE OCEAN, SO SALTY BREADS ARE A SUPER NO-NO!!
?
?
?
AND ALSO ---
THE ONLY INGREDIENT WE WILL BE PROVIDING YOU WITH IS FLOUR.
!!
FROM YEAST TO EVERY OTHER INGREDIENT, PLEASE HARVEST THEM ON THE ISLAND.
WHAT DO YOU MEAN?!
USA

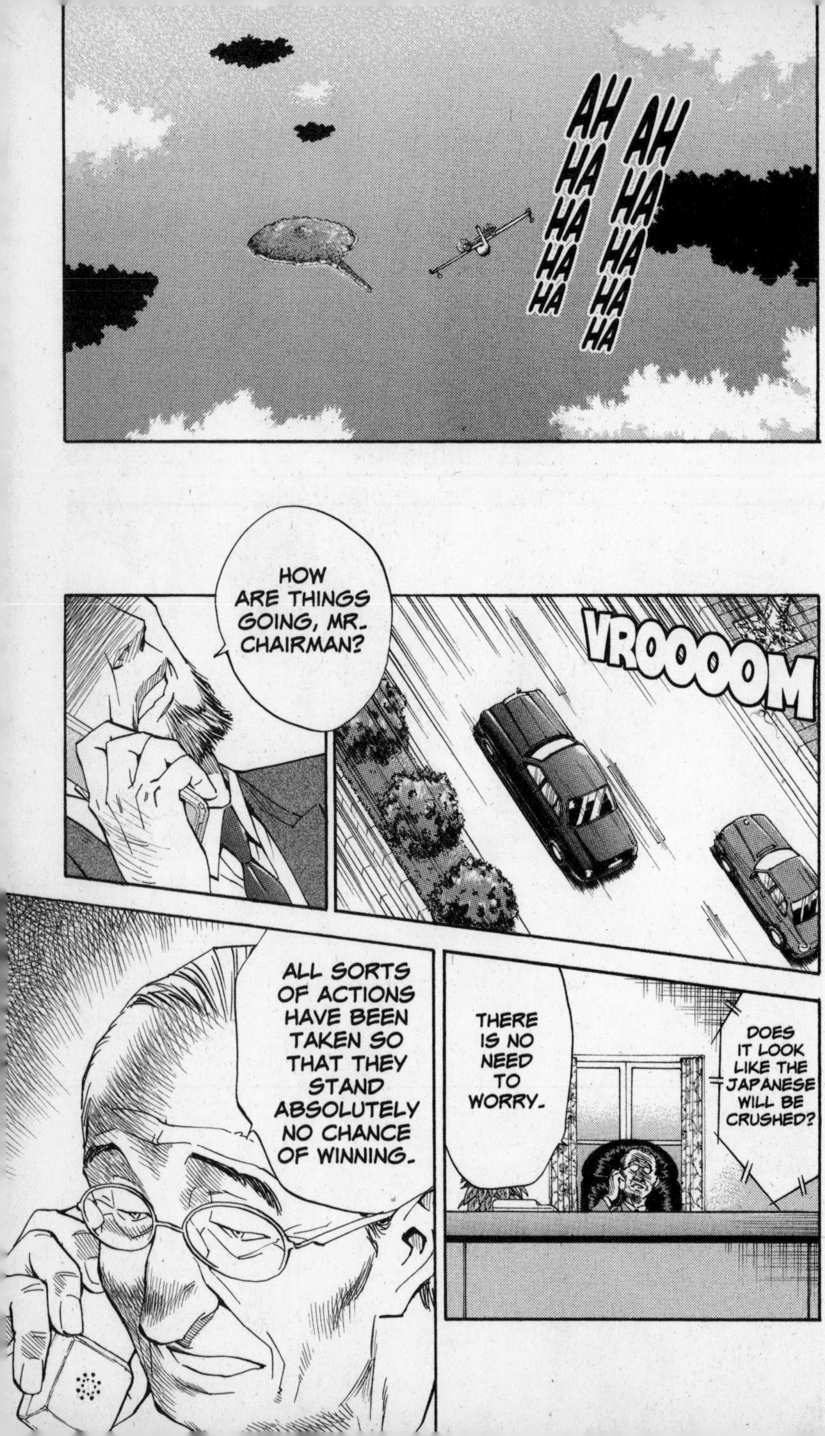
AH HA HA HA HA HA
AH HA HA HA HA HA
VROOOOM
HOW ARE THINGS GOING, MR. CHAIRMAN?
DOES IT LOOK LIKE THE JAPANESE WILL BE CRUSHED?
THERE IS NO NEED TO WORRY.
ALL SORTS OF ACTIONS HAVE BEEN TAKEN SO THAT THEY STAND ABSOLUTELY NO CHANCE OF WINNING.

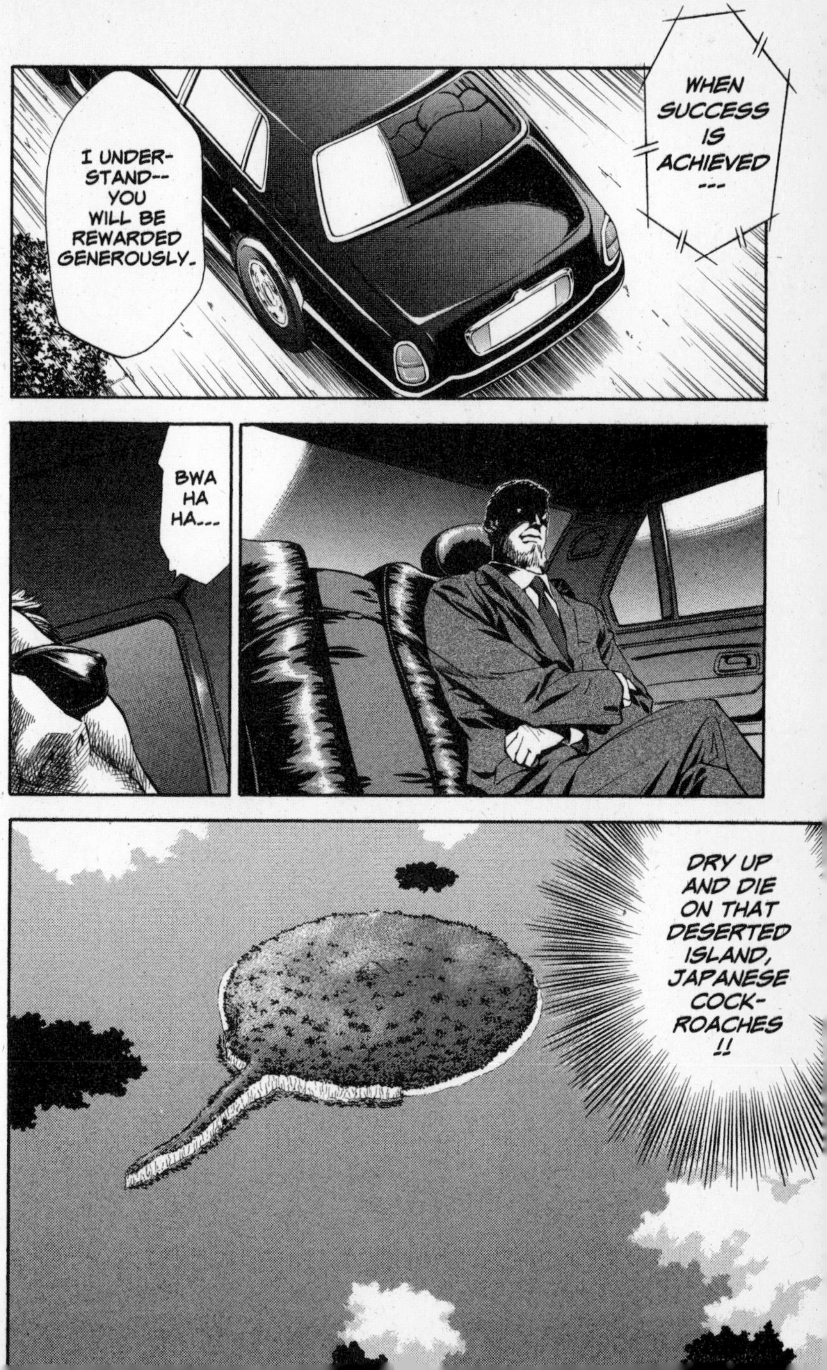
WHEN SUCCESS IS ACHIEVED---
I UNDER-STAND-- YOU WILL BE REWARDED GENEROUSLY.
BWA HA HA...
DRY UP AND DIE ON THAT DESERTED ISLAND, JAPANESE COCK-ROACHES!!

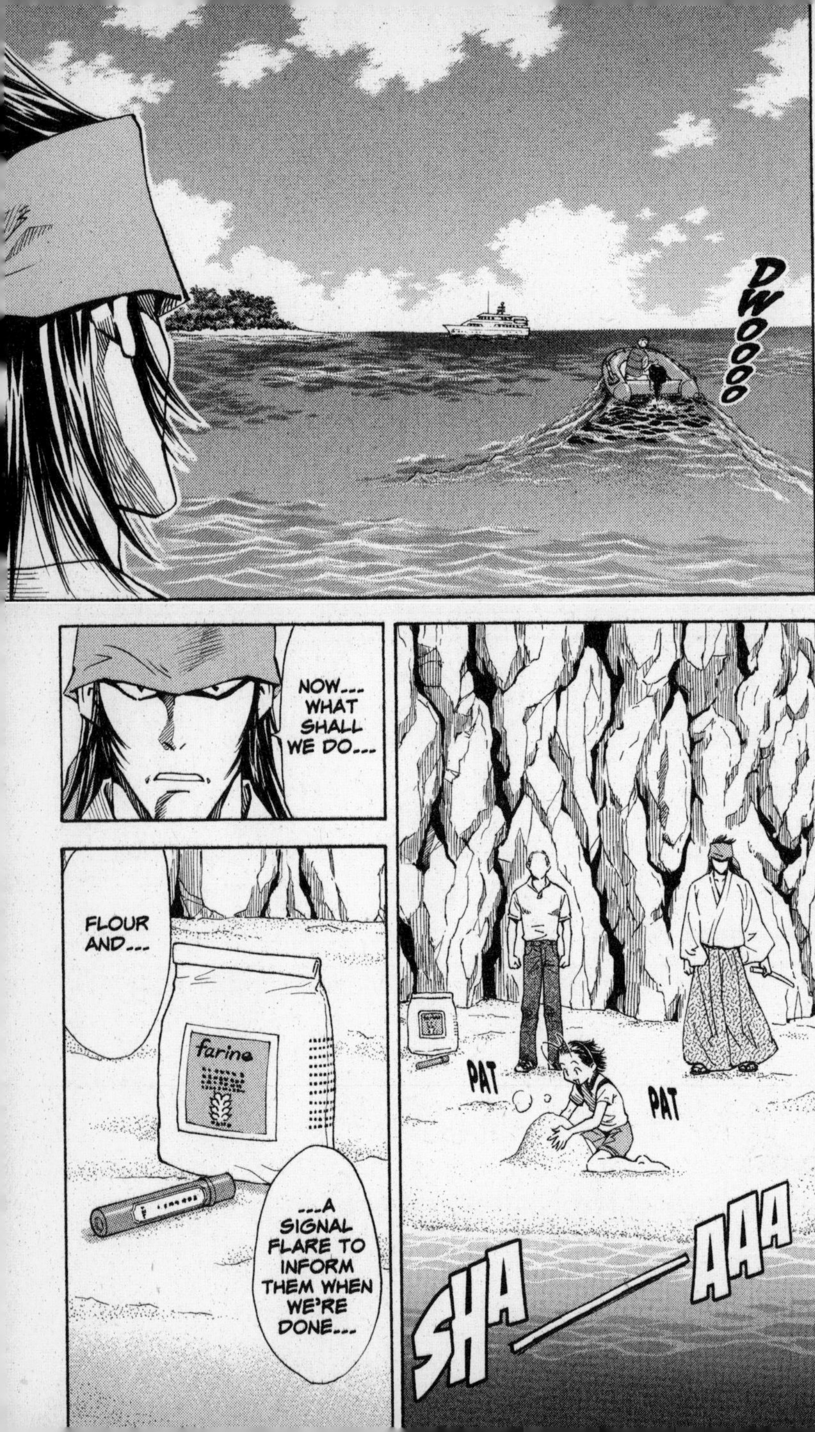
DWOOOOO
PAT
PAT
SHA—AAA
NOW... WHAT SHALL WE DO...
FLOUR AND...
farina
...A SIGNAL FLARE TO INFORM THEM WHEN WE'RE DONE...

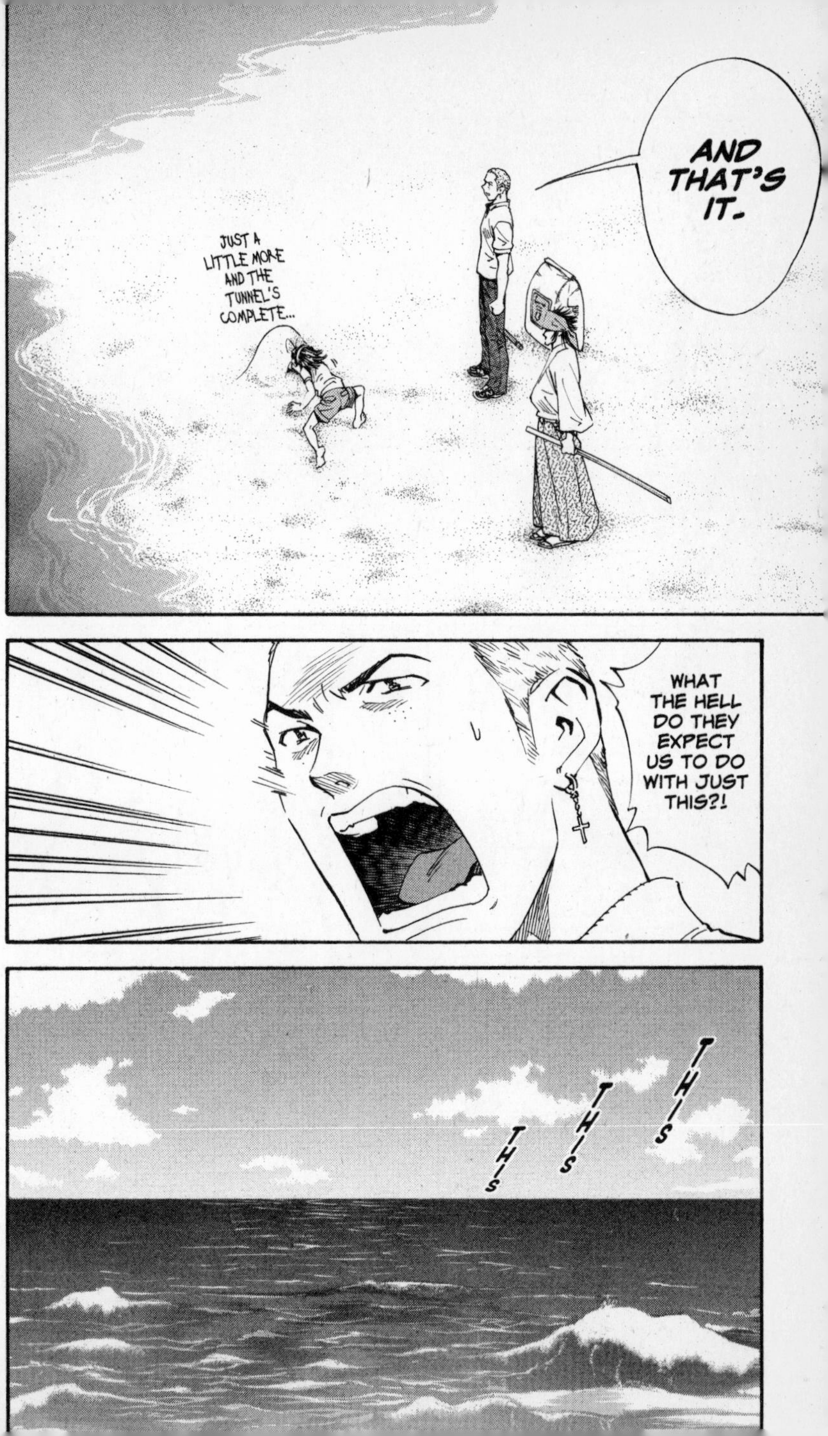
AND THAT'S IT.
JUST A LITTLE MORE AND THE TUNNEL'S COMPLETE...
WHAT THE HELL DO THEY EXPECT US TO DO WITH JUST THIS?!
THIS
THIS
THIS

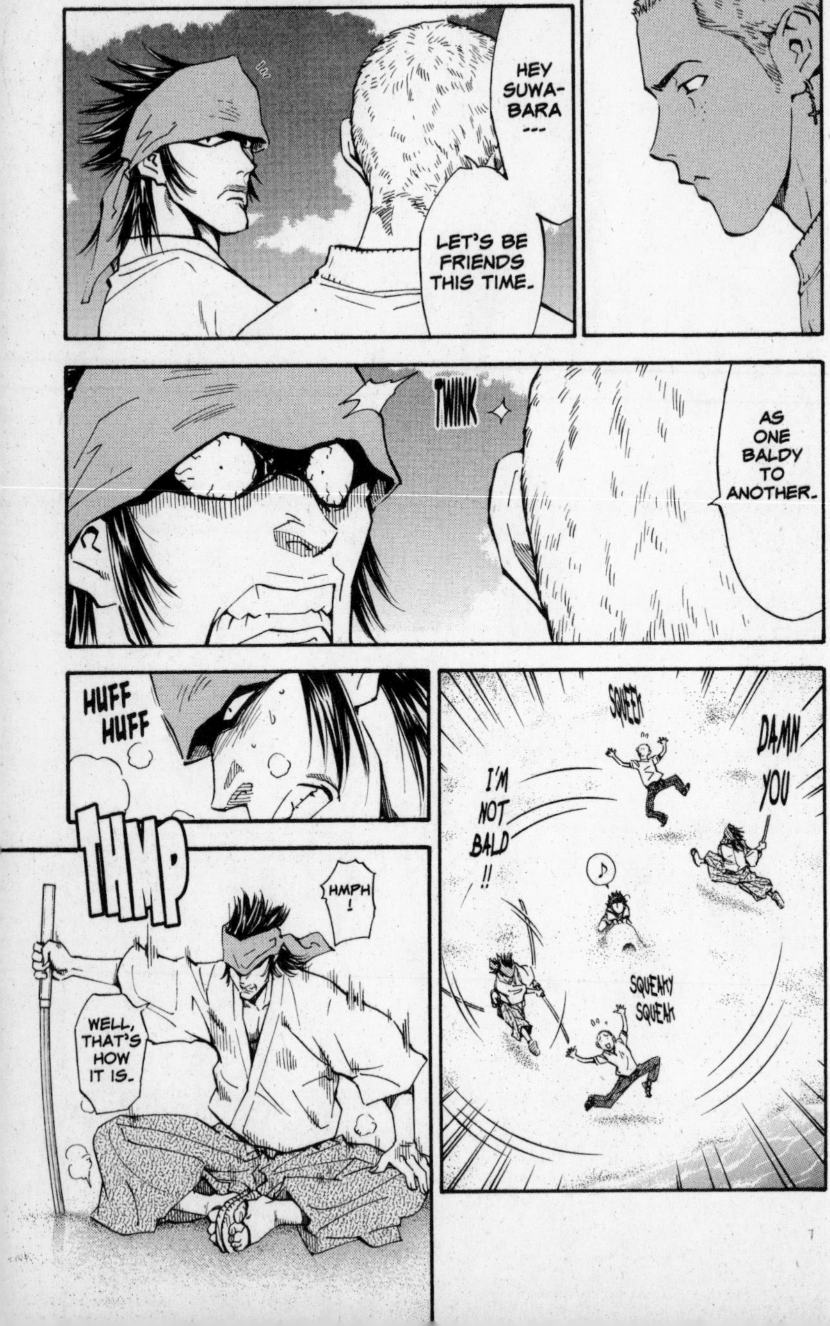
HEY SUWA-BARA ---
LET'S BE FRIENDS THIS TIME.
AS ONE BALDY TO ANOTHER.
TWINK
SQUEE!!
DAMN YOU
I'M NOT BALD!!
SQUEAKY SQUEAK
HUFF HUFF
THMP
HMPH!
WELL, THAT'S HOW IT IS.

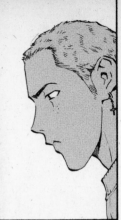

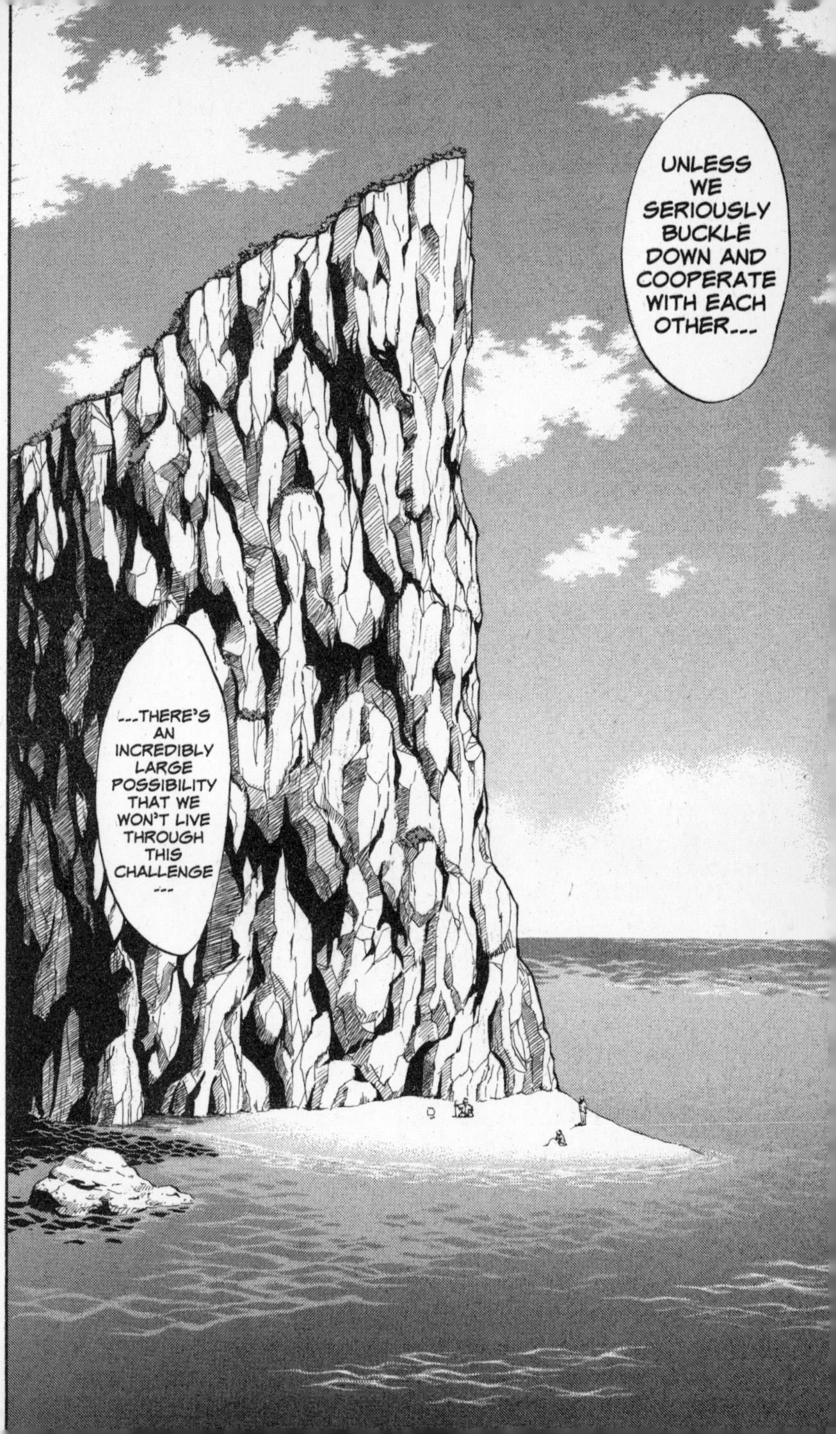
UNLESS WE SERIOUSLY BUCKLE DOWN AND COOPERATE WITH EACH OTHER...
...THERE'S AN INCREDIBLY LARGE POSSIBILITY THAT WE WON'T LIVE THROUGH THIS CHALLENGE...

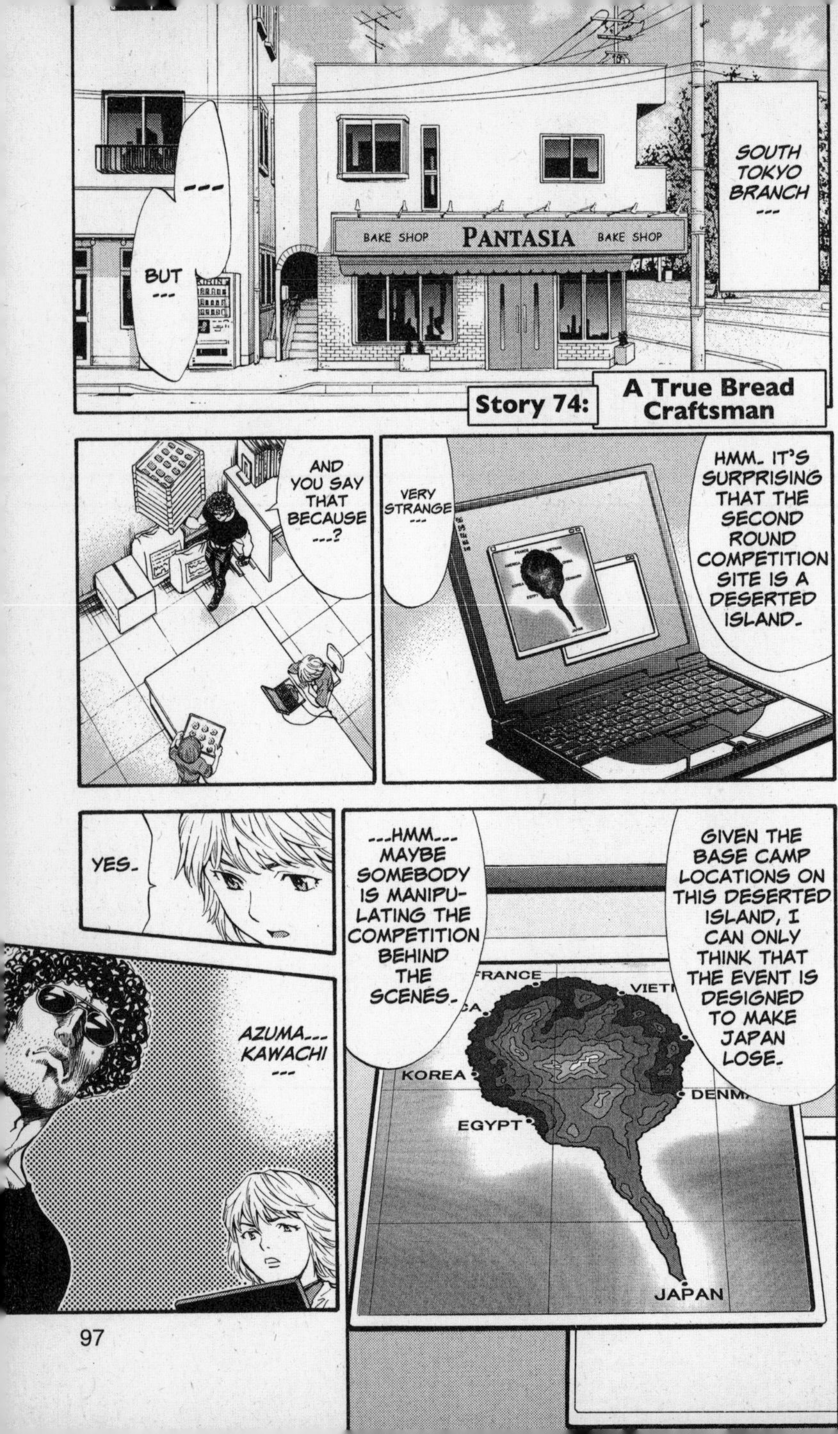
SOUTH TOKYO BRANCH ---
BAKE SHOP PANTASIA BAKE SHOP
---
BUT ---
Story 74: A True Bread Craftsman
HMM. IT'S SURPRISING THAT THE SECOND ROUND COMPETITION SITE IS A DESERTED ISLAND.
VERY STRANGE ---
AND YOU SAY THAT BECAUSE ---?
GIVEN THE BASE CAMP LOCATIONS ON THIS DESERTED ISLAND, I CAN ONLY THINK THAT THE EVENT IS DESIGNED TO MAKE JAPAN LOSE.
---HMM--- MAYBE SOMEBODY IS MANIPULATING THE COMPETITION BEHIND THE SCENES.
FRANCE
KOREA
EGYPT
JAPAN
YES.
AZUMA--- KAWACHI ---

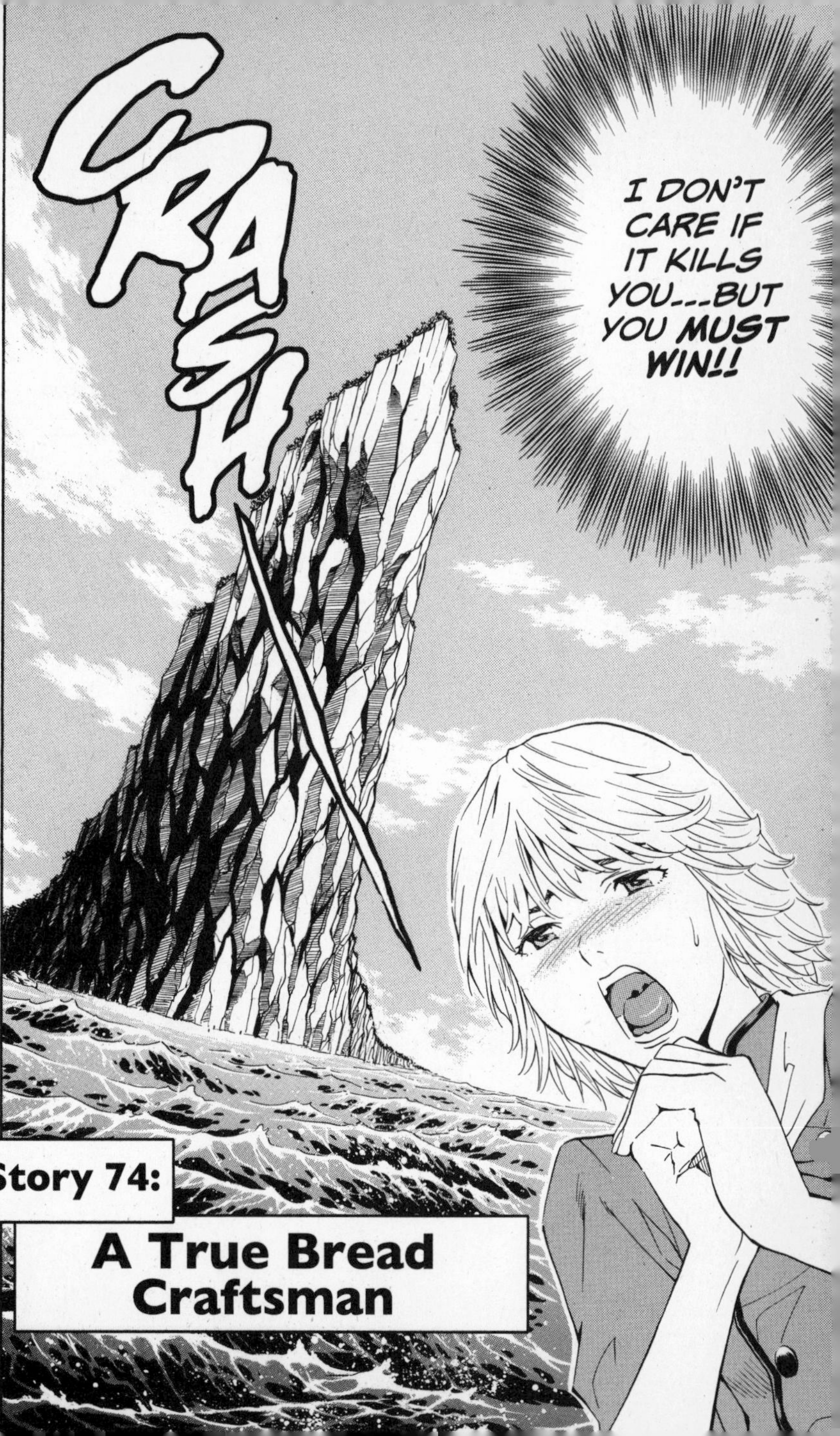
I DON'T CARE IF IT KILLS YOU...BUT YOU MUST WIN!!
CRASH
Story 74:
A True Bread Craftsman

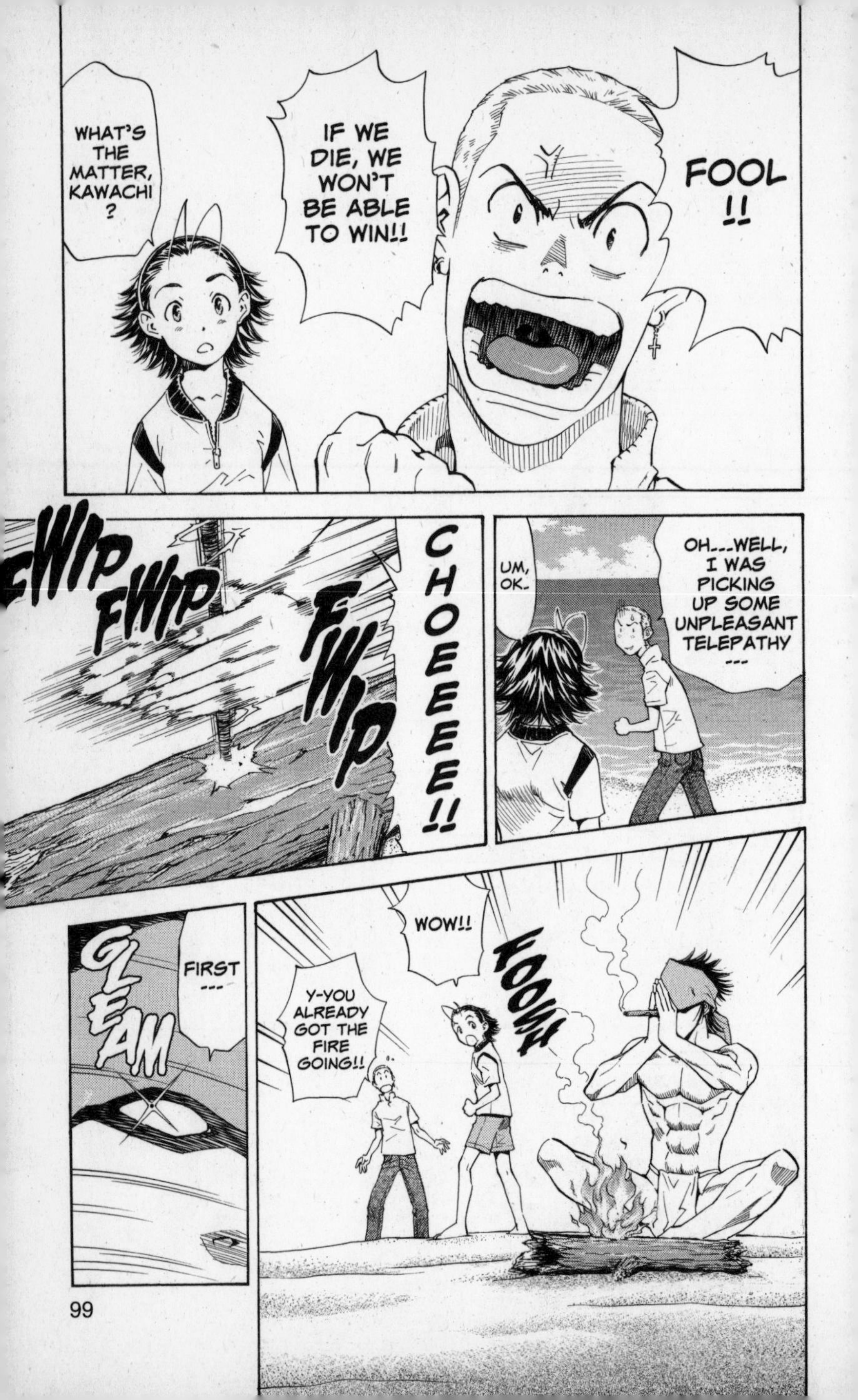
FOOL!!
IF WE DIE, WE WON'T BE ABLE TO WIN!!
WHAT'S THE MATTER, KAWACHI?
OH...WELL, I WAS PICKING UP SOME UNPLEASANT TELEPATHY...
UM, OK.
CHOEEEEE!!
FWIP
FWIP FWIP
FOOOM
WOW!!
Y-YOU ALREADY GOT THE FIRE GOING!!
FIRST...
GLEAM

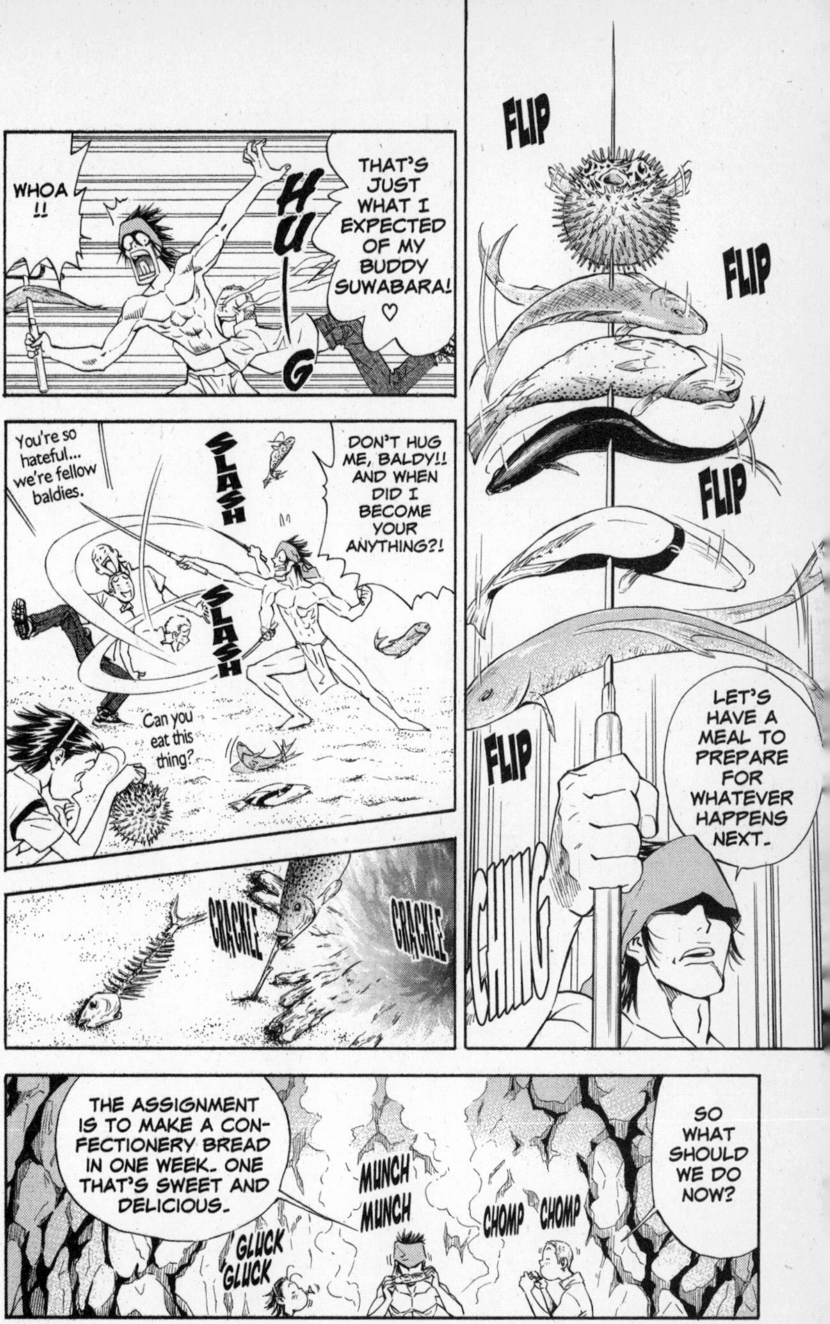
FLIP
FLIP
FLIP
FLIP
LET'S HAVE A MEAL TO PREPARE FOR WHATEVER HAPPENS NEXT.
CHING
THAT'S JUST WHAT I EXPECTED OF MY BUDDY SUWABARA! ♡
HUG
WHOA !!
DON'T HUG ME, BALDY!! AND WHEN DID I BECOME YOUR ANYTHING?!
SLASH
SLASH
You're so hateful... we're fellow baldies.
Can you eat this thing?
CRACKLE
CRACKLE
SO WHAT SHOULD WE DO NOW?
CHOMP CHOMP
MUNCH MUNCH
THE ASSIGNMENT IS TO MAKE A CONFECTIONERY BREAD IN ONE WEEK. ONE THAT'S SWEET AND DELICIOUS.
GLUCK GLUCK

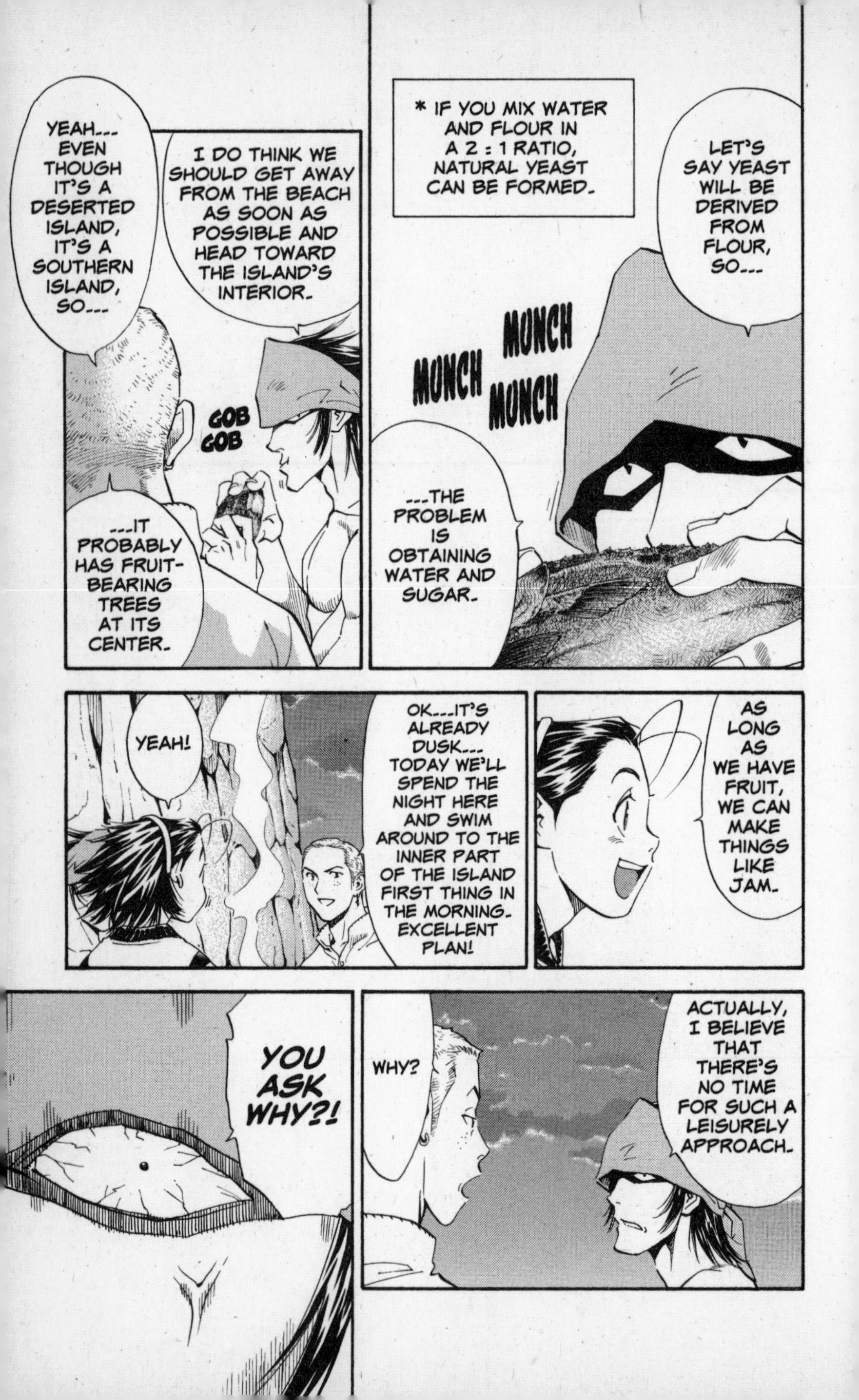
LET'S SAY YEAST WILL BE DERIVED FROM FLOUR, SO...
* IF YOU MIX WATER AND FLOUR IN A 2 : 1 RATIO, NATURAL YEAST CAN BE FORMED.
MUNCH
MUNCH
MUNCH
...THE PROBLEM IS OBTAINING WATER AND SUGAR.
I DO THINK WE SHOULD GET AWAY FROM THE BEACH AS SOON AS POSSIBLE AND HEAD TOWARD THE ISLAND'S INTERIOR.
YEAH... EVEN THOUGH IT'S A DESERTED ISLAND, IT'S A SOUTHERN ISLAND, SO...
GOB GOB
...IT PROBABLY HAS FRUIT-BEARING TREES AT ITS CENTER.
AS LONG AS WE HAVE FRUIT, WE CAN MAKE THINGS LIKE JAM.
OK...IT'S ALREADY DUSK... TODAY WE'LL SPEND THE NIGHT HERE AND SWIM AROUND TO THE INNER PART OF THE ISLAND FIRST THING IN THE MORNING. EXCELLENT PLAN!
YEAH!
ACTUALLY, I BELIEVE THAT THERE'S NO TIME FOR SUCH A LEISURELY APPROACH.
WHY?
YOU ASK WHY?!

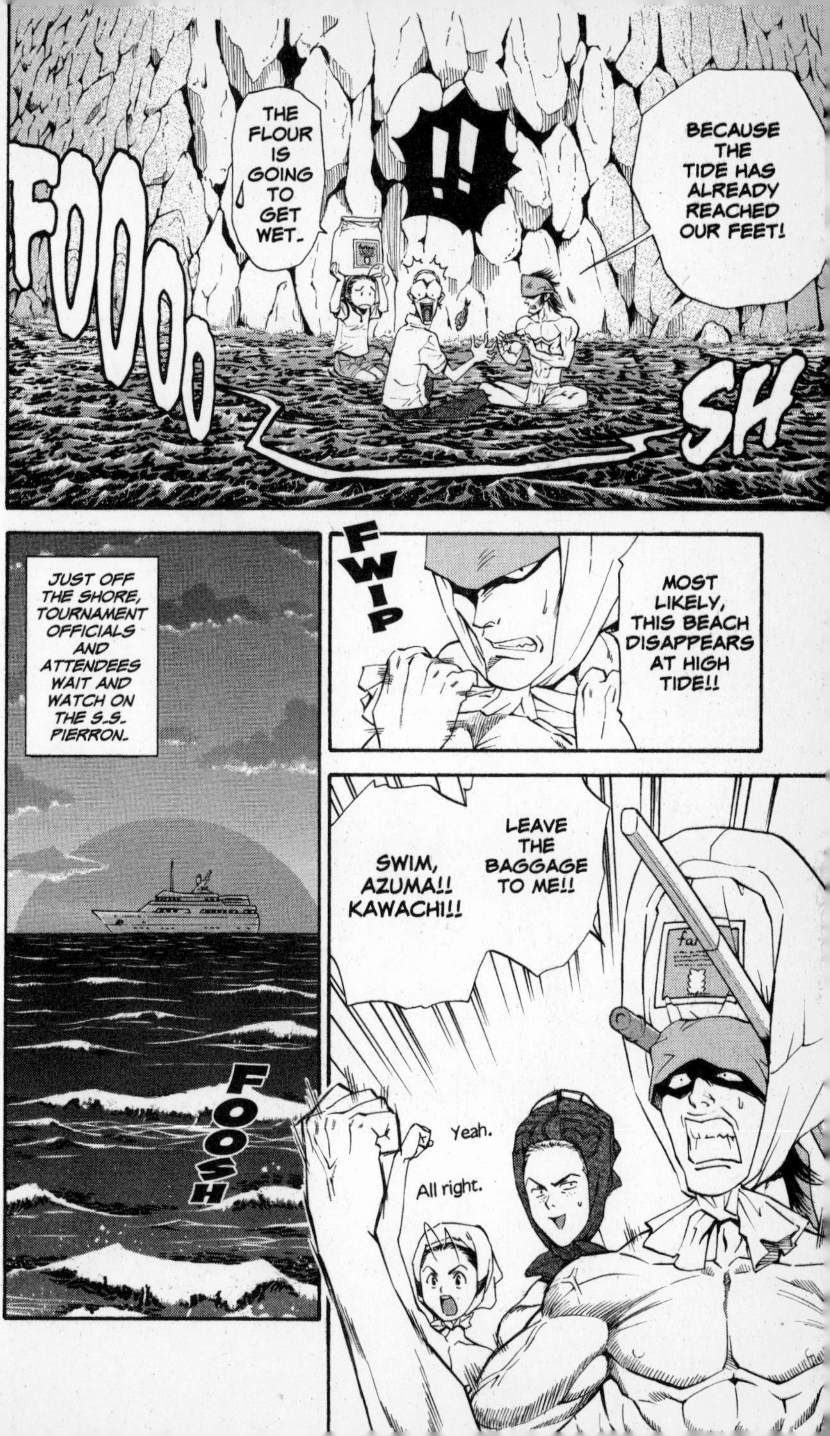
BECAUSE THE TIDE HAS ALREADY REACHED OUR FEET!
!!
THE FLOUR IS GOING TO GET WET.
FOOOOOSH
FWIP
MOST LIKELY, THIS BEACH DISAPPEARS AT HIGH TIDE!!
LEAVE THE BAGGAGE TO ME!!
SWIM, AZUMA!! KAWACHI!!
Yeah.
All right.
JUST OFF THE SHORE, TOURNAMENT OFFICIALS AND ATTENDEES WAIT AND WATCH ON THE S.S. PIERRON.
FOOSH

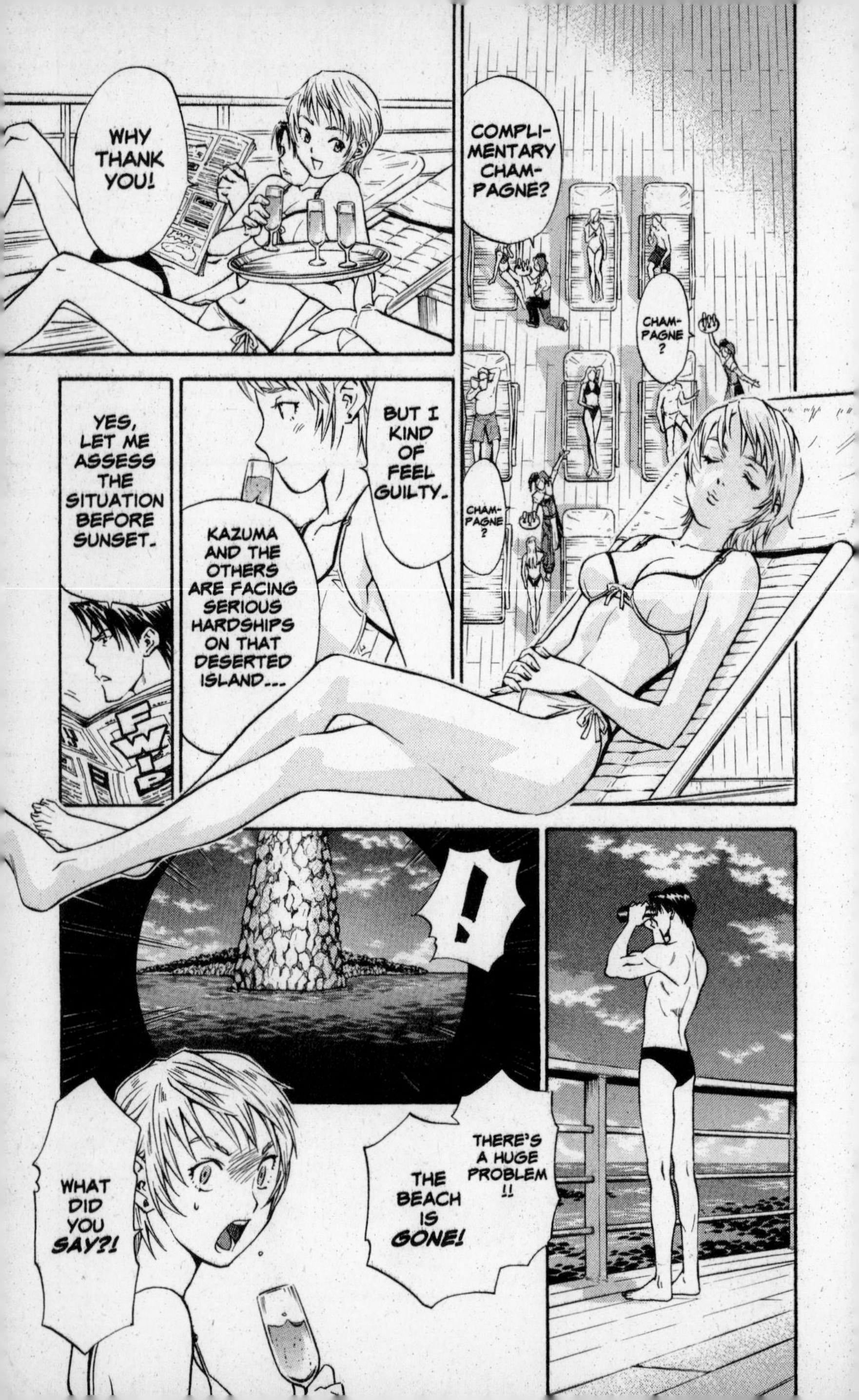
COMPLI-MENTARY CHAM-PAGNE?
CHAM-PAGNE?
CHAM-PAGNE?
WHY THANK YOU!
BUT I KIND OF FEEL GUILTY...
KAZUMA AND THE OTHERS ARE FACING SERIOUS HARDSHIPS ON THAT DESERTED ISLAND...
YES, LET ME ASSESS THE SITUATION BEFORE SUNSET...
FWIP
THERE'S A HUGE PROBLEM!!
THE BEACH IS GONE!
!
WHAT DID YOU SAY?!

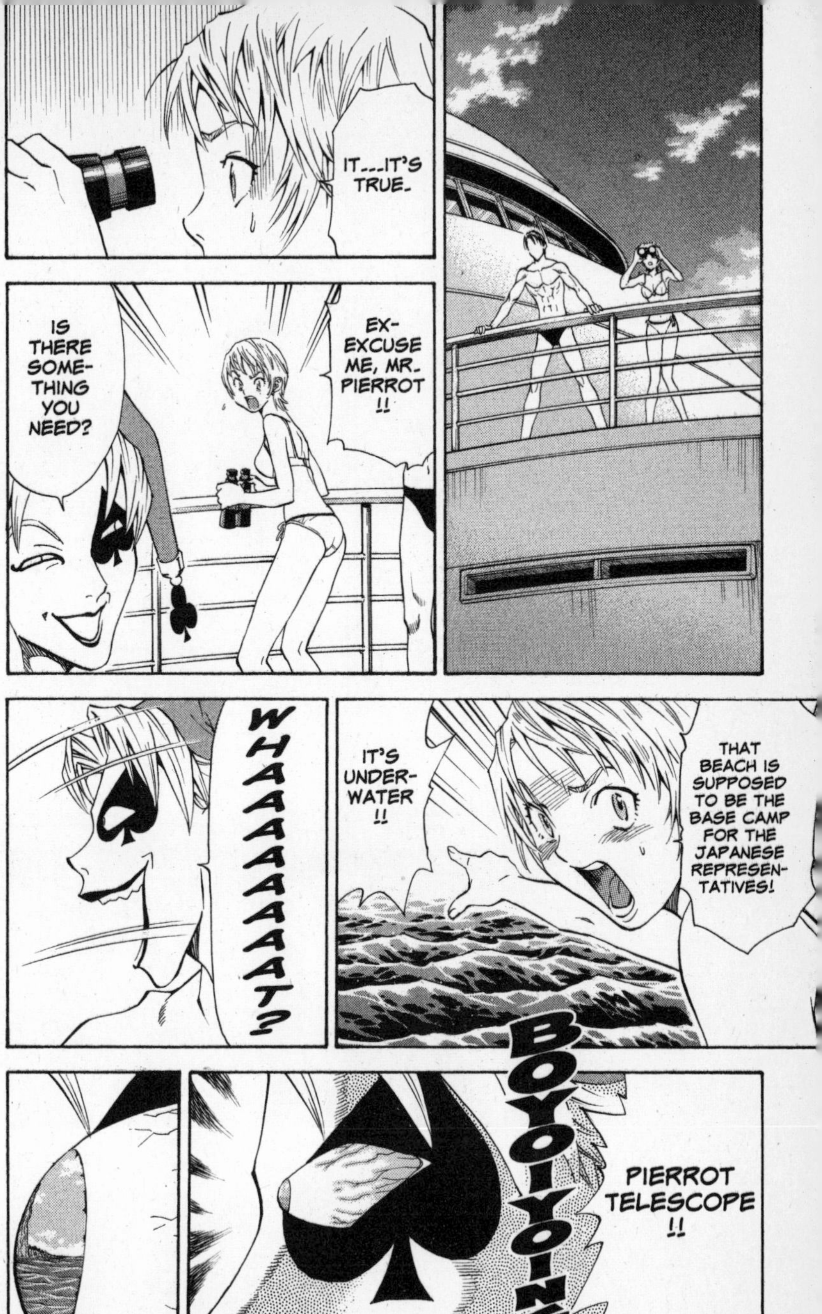
IT---IT'S TRUE.
EX-EXCUSE ME, MR. PIERROT!!
IS THERE SOMETHING YOU NEED?
THAT BEACH IS SUPPOSED TO BE THE BASE CAMP FOR THE JAPANESE REPRESENTATIVES!
IT'S UNDERWATER!!
WHAAAAAAAAT?
PIERROT TELESCOPE!!
BOYOYOING!!

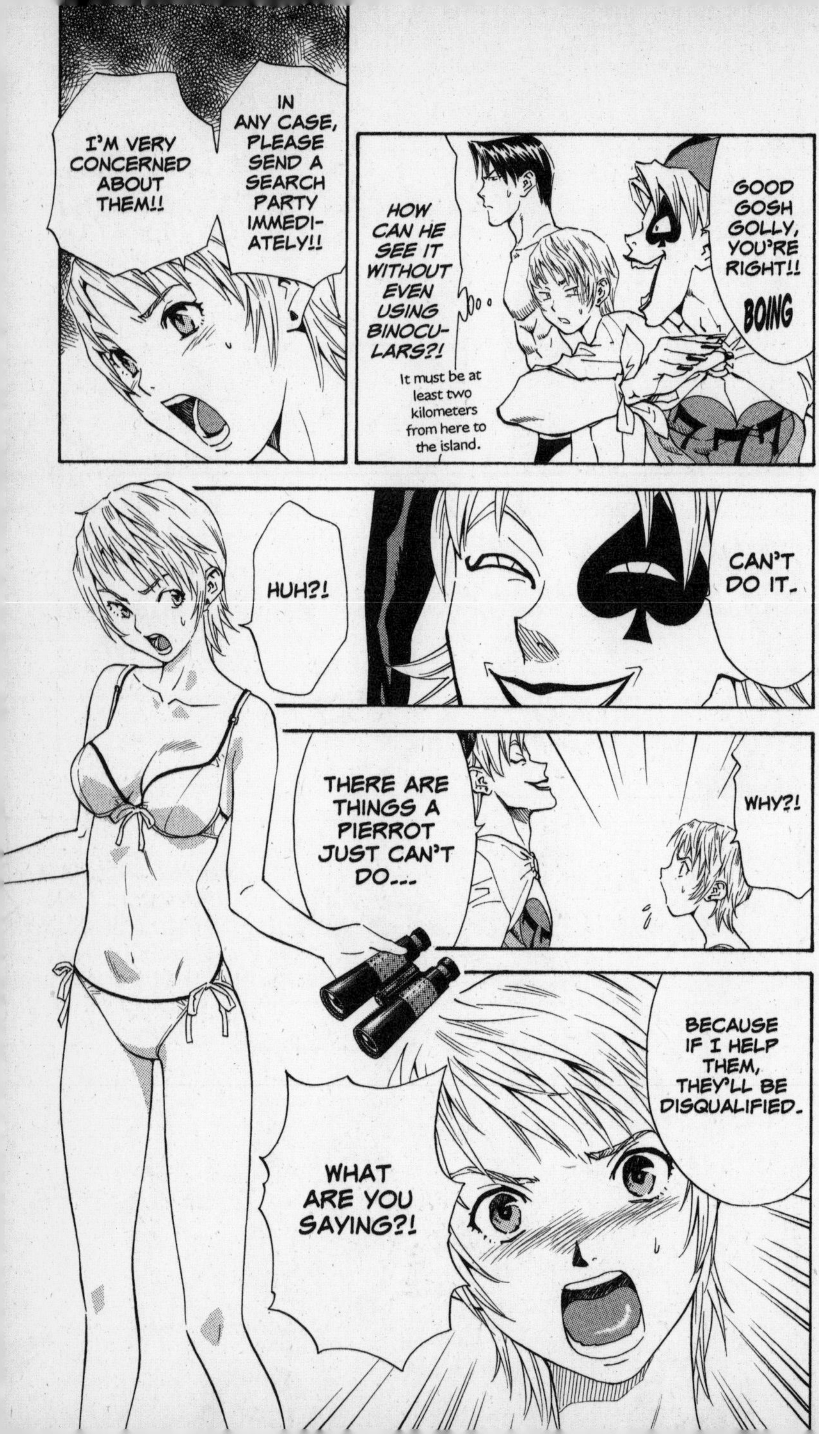
GOOD GOSH GOLLY, YOU'RE RIGHT!!
BOING
HOW CAN HE SEE IT WITHOUT EVEN USING BINOCULARS?!
It must be at least two kilometers from here to the island.
IN ANY CASE, PLEASE SEND A SEARCH PARTY IMMEDIATELY!!
I'M VERY CONCERNED ABOUT THEM!!
CAN'T DO IT.
HUH?!
WHY?!
THERE ARE THINGS A PIERROT JUST CAN'T DO...
BECAUSE IF I HELP THEM, THEY'LL BE DISQUALIFIED.
WHAT ARE YOU SAYING?!

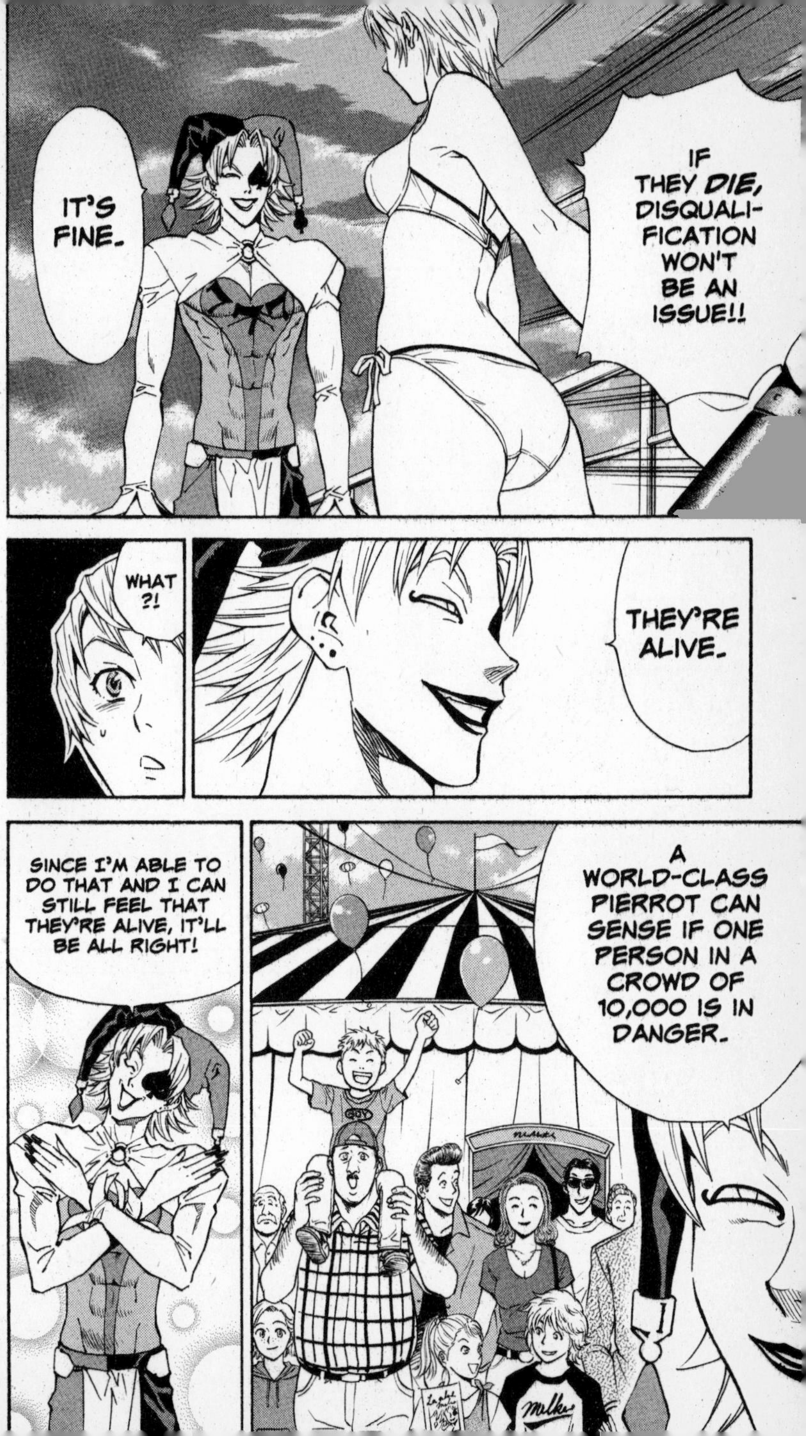
IF THEY *DIE*, DISQUALIFICATION WON'T BE AN ISSUE!!
IT'S FINE.
THEY'RE ALIVE.
WHAT ?!
A WORLD-CLASS PIERROT CAN SENSE IF ONE PERSON IN A CROWD OF 10,000 IS IN DANGER.
SINCE I'M ABLE TO DO THAT AND I CAN STILL FEEL THAT THEY'RE ALIVE, IT'LL BE ALL RIGHT!

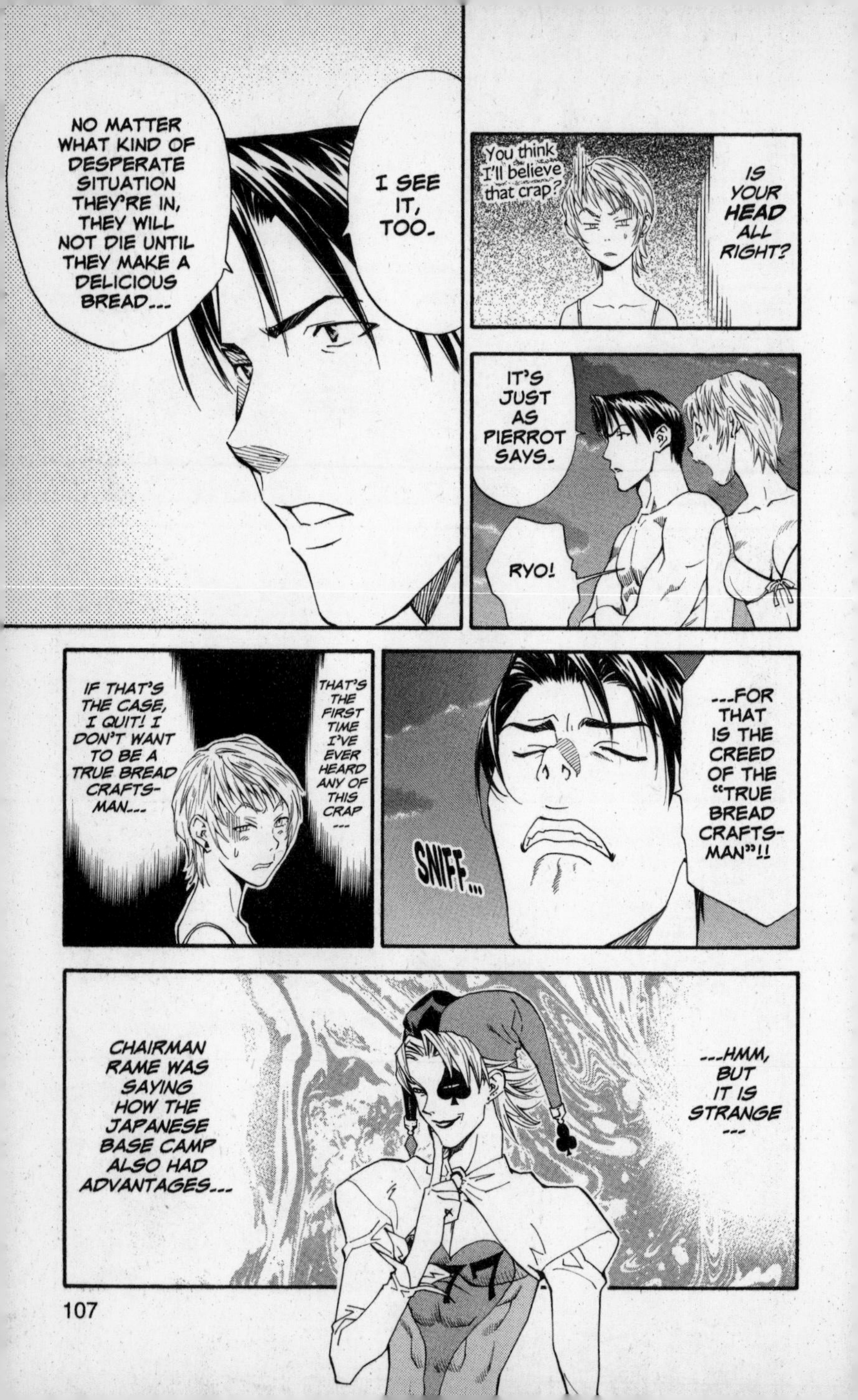
IS YOUR HEAD ALL RIGHT?
You think I'll believe that crap?
IT'S JUST AS PIERROT SAYS.
RYO!
I SEE IT, TOO.
NO MATTER WHAT KIND OF DESPERATE SITUATION THEY'RE IN, THEY WILL NOT DIE UNTIL THEY MAKE A DELICIOUS BREAD...
...FOR THAT IS THE CREED OF THE "TRUE BREAD CRAFTSMAN"!!
SNIFF...
THAT'S THE FIRST TIME I'VE EVER HEARD ANY OF THIS CRAP...
IF THAT'S THE CASE, I QUIT! I DON'T WANT TO BE A TRUE BREAD CRAFTSMAN...
...HMM, BUT IT IS STRANGE...
CHAIRMAN RAME WAS SAYING HOW THE JAPANESE BASE CAMP ALSO HAD ADVANTAGES...

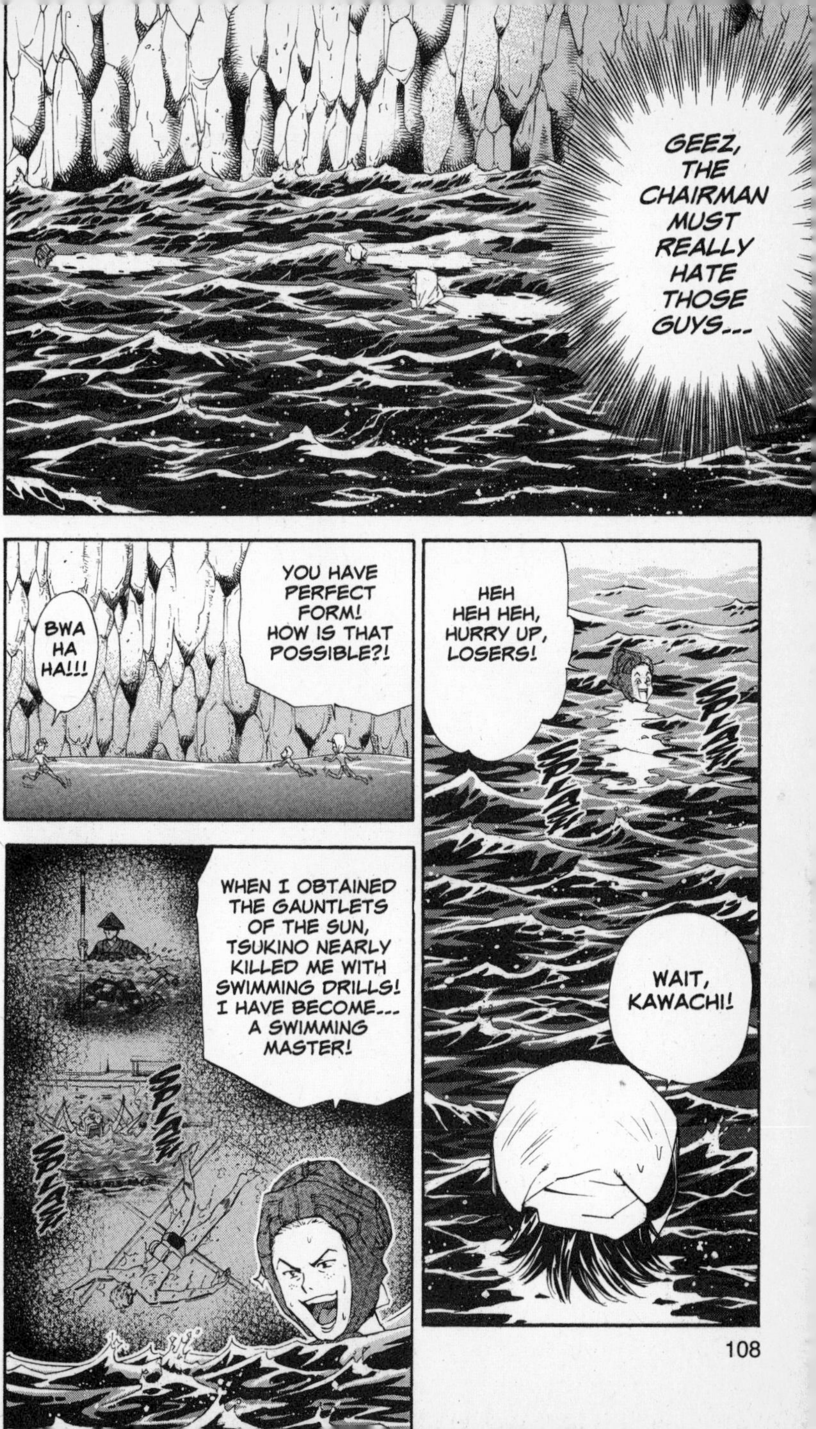
GEEZ, THE CHAIRMAN MUST REALLY HATE THOSE GUYS...
HEH HEH HEH, HURRY UP, LOSERS!
WAIT, KAWACHI!
YOU HAVE PERFECT FORM! HOW IS THAT POSSIBLE?!
BWA HA HA!!!
WHEN I OBTAINED THE GAUNTLETS OF THE SUN, TSUKINO NEARLY KILLED ME WITH SWIMMING DRILLS! I HAVE BECOME... A SWIMMING MASTER!

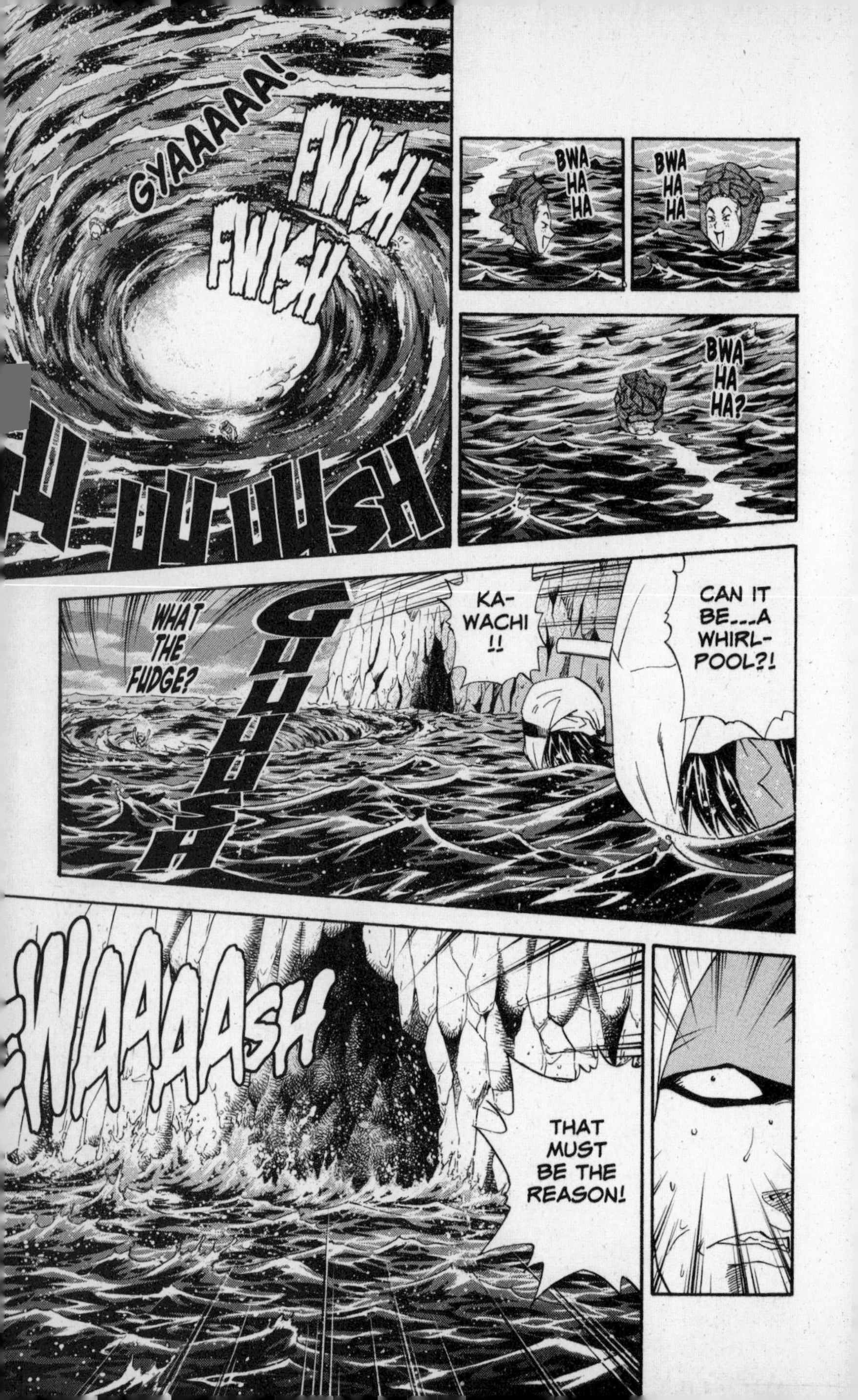
BWA HA HA
BWA HA HA
BWA HA HA?
GYAAAAA!
FWISH
FWISH
UUUUSH
CAN IT BE...A WHIRL-POOL?!
KA-WACHI !!
GUUUUSH
WHAT THE FUDGE?
THAT MUST BE THE REASON!
WAAAASH

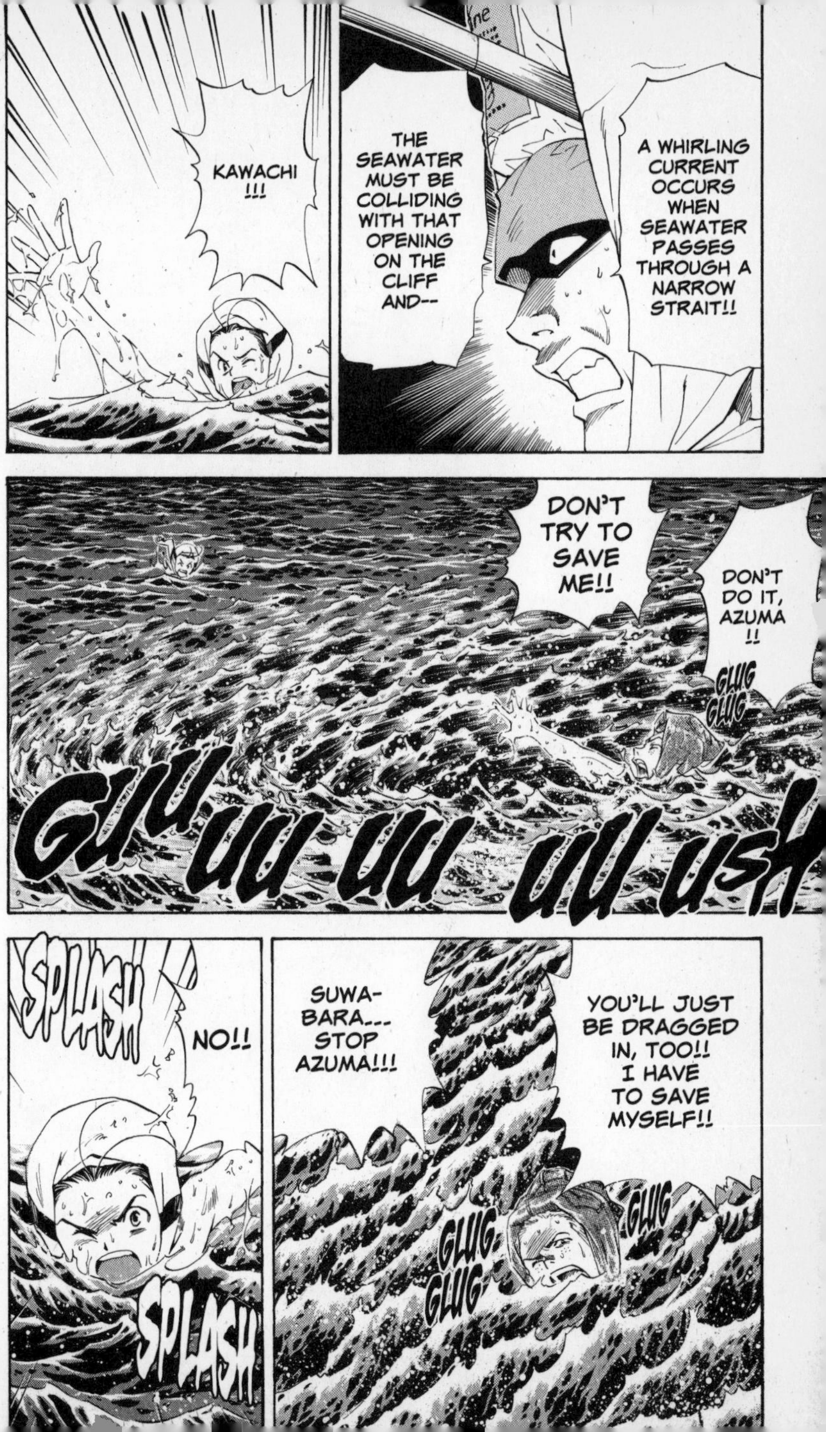
A WHIRLING CURRENT OCCURS WHEN SEAWATER PASSES THROUGH A NARROW STRAIT!!
THE SEAWATER MUST BE COLLIDING WITH THAT OPENING ON THE CLIFF AND--
KAWACHI!!!
DON'T TRY TO SAVE ME!!
DON'T DO IT, AZUMA!!
GLUG GLUG
GUUUUUUUUSH
YOU'LL JUST BE DRAGGED IN, TOO!! I HAVE TO SAVE MYSELF!!
SUWA-BARA... STOP AZUMA!!!
GLUG
GLUG GLUG
SPLASH
NO!!
SPLASH

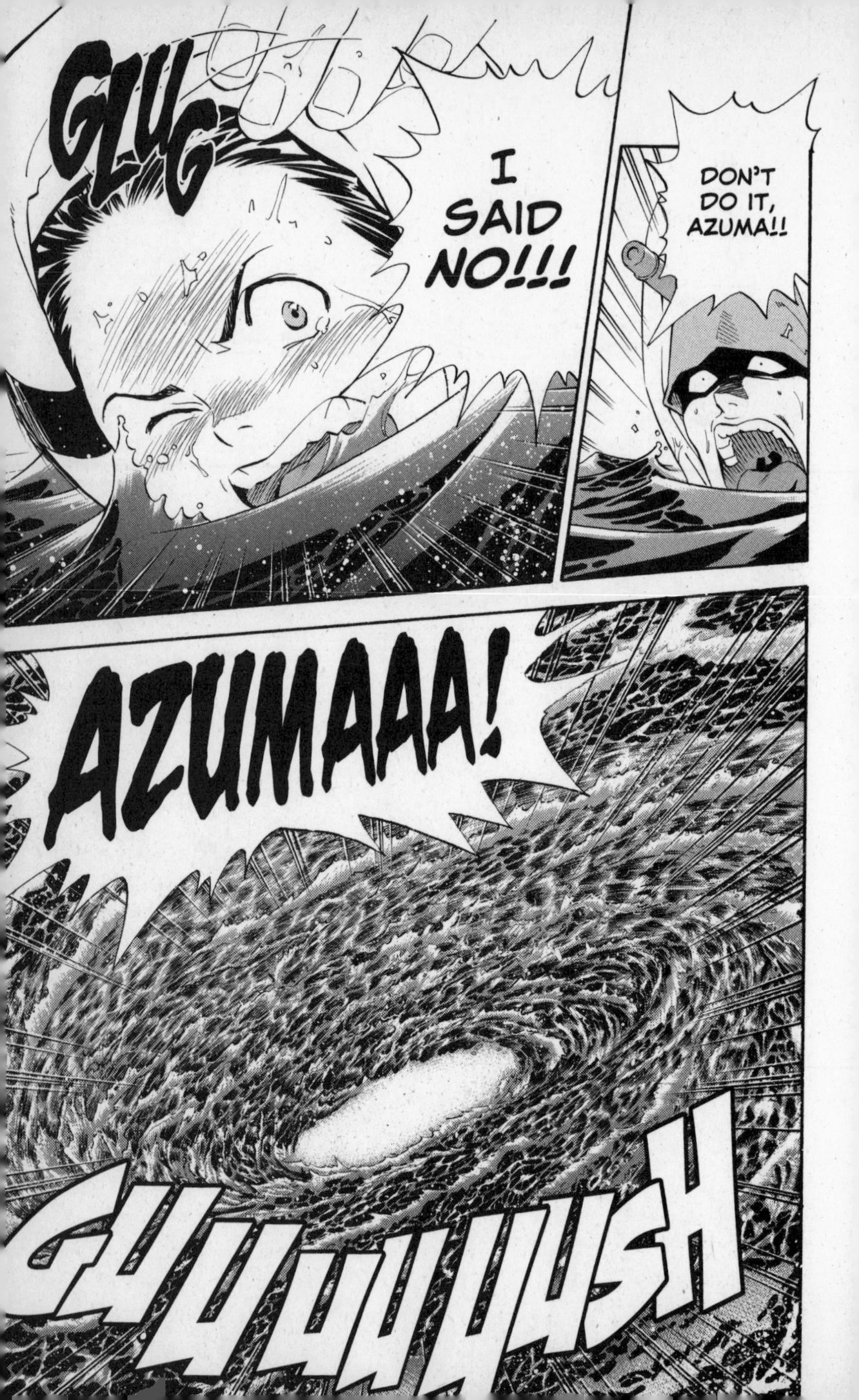
DON'T DO IT, AZUMA!!
GLUG
I SAID NO!!!
AZUMAAA!
GUUUUUSH

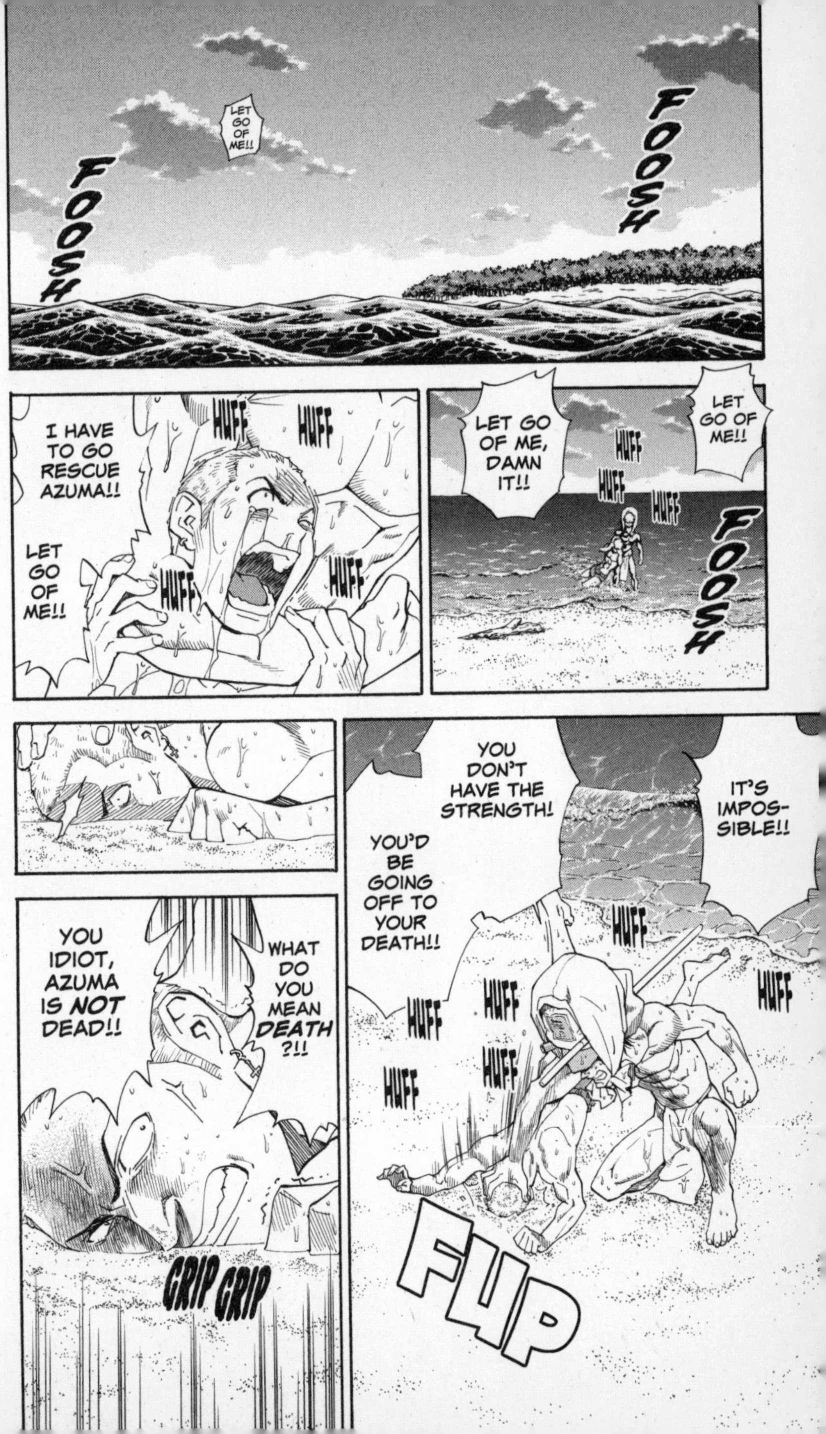
FOOSH
LET GO OF ME!!
FOOSH
LET GO OF ME!!
LET GO OF ME, DAMN IT!!
HUFF
HUFF
HUFF
FOOSH
HUFF
HUFF
I HAVE TO GO RESCUE AZUMA!!
HUFF
HUFF
LET GO OF ME!!
IT'S IMPOS-SIBLE!!
YOU DON'T HAVE THE STRENGTH!
YOU'D BE GOING OFF TO YOUR DEATH!!
HUFF
HUFF
HUFF
HUFF
HUFF
HUFF
FLIP
WHAT DO YOU MEAN *DEATH*?!!
YOU IDIOT, AZUMA IS *NOT* DEAD!!
GRIP GRIP

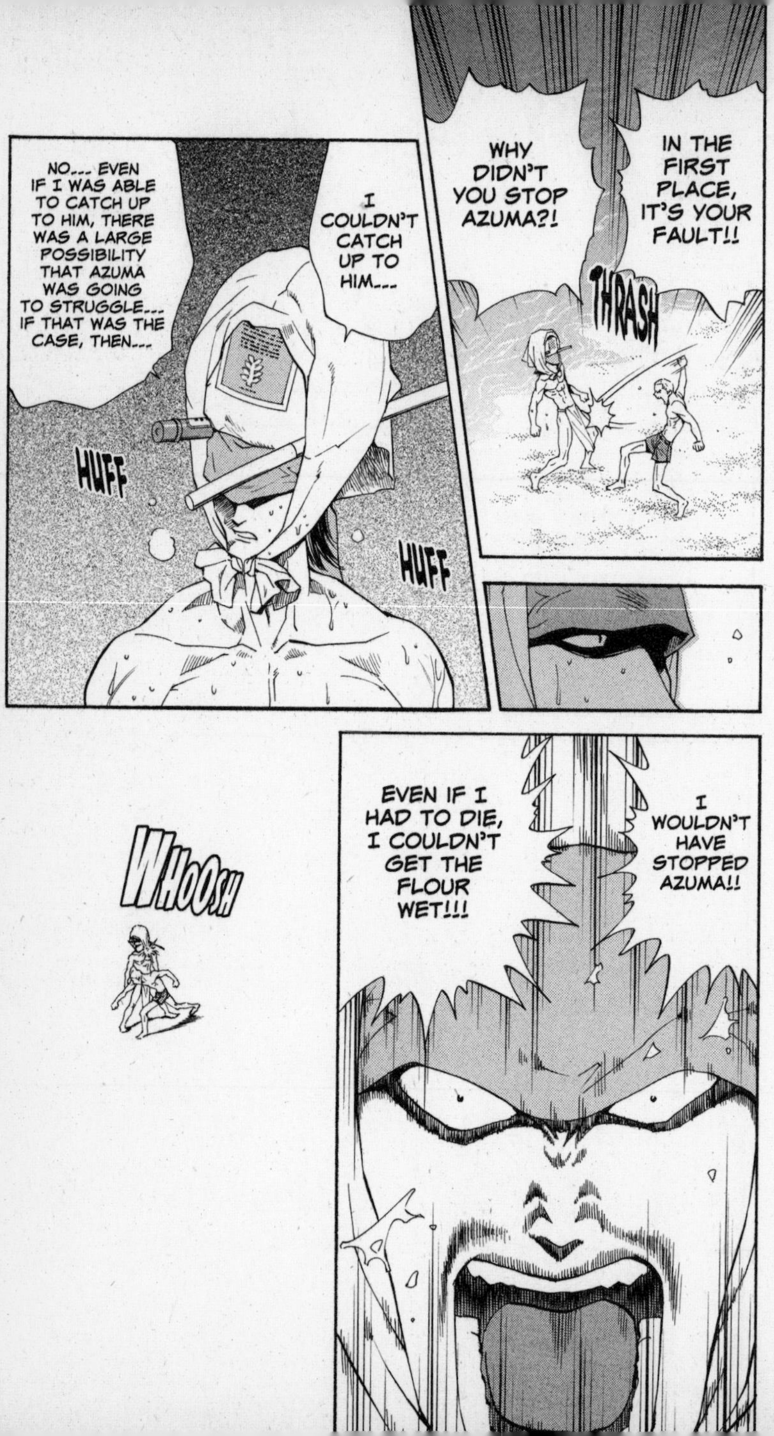
IN THE FIRST PLACE, IT'S YOUR FAULT!!
WHY DIDN'T YOU STOP AZUMA?!
THRASH
I COULDN'T CATCH UP TO HIM...
NO... EVEN IF I WAS ABLE TO CATCH UP TO HIM, THERE WAS A LARGE POSSIBILITY THAT AZUMA WAS GOING TO STRUGGLE... IF THAT WAS THE CASE, THEN...
HUFF
HUFF
I WOULDN'T HAVE STOPPED AZUMA!!
EVEN IF I HAD TO DIE, I COULDN'T GET THE FLOUR WET!!!
WHOOSH

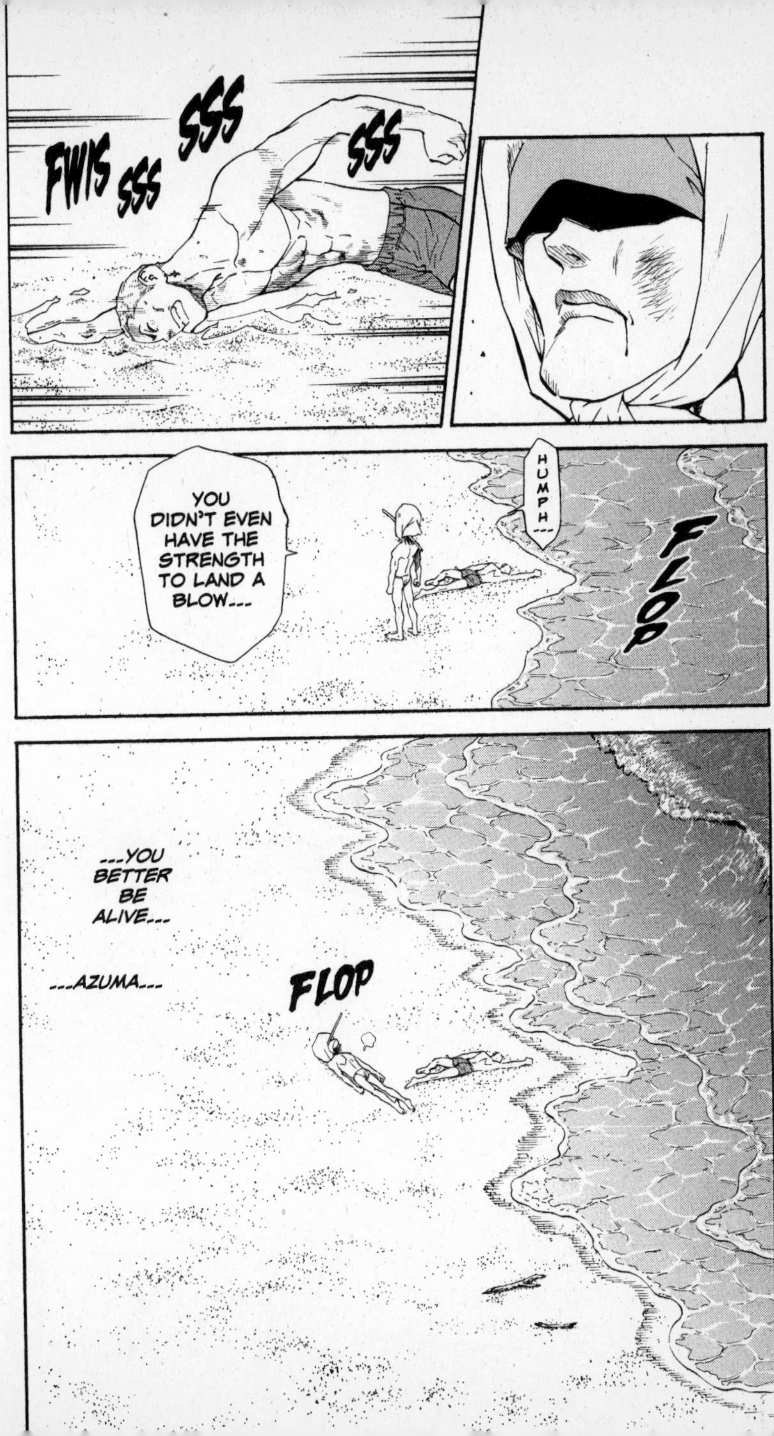
FWIS SSS SSS SSS
HUMPH---
YOU DIDN'T EVEN HAVE THE STRENGTH TO LAND A BLOW---
FLOP
---YOU BETTER BE ALIVE---
---AZUMA---
FLOP

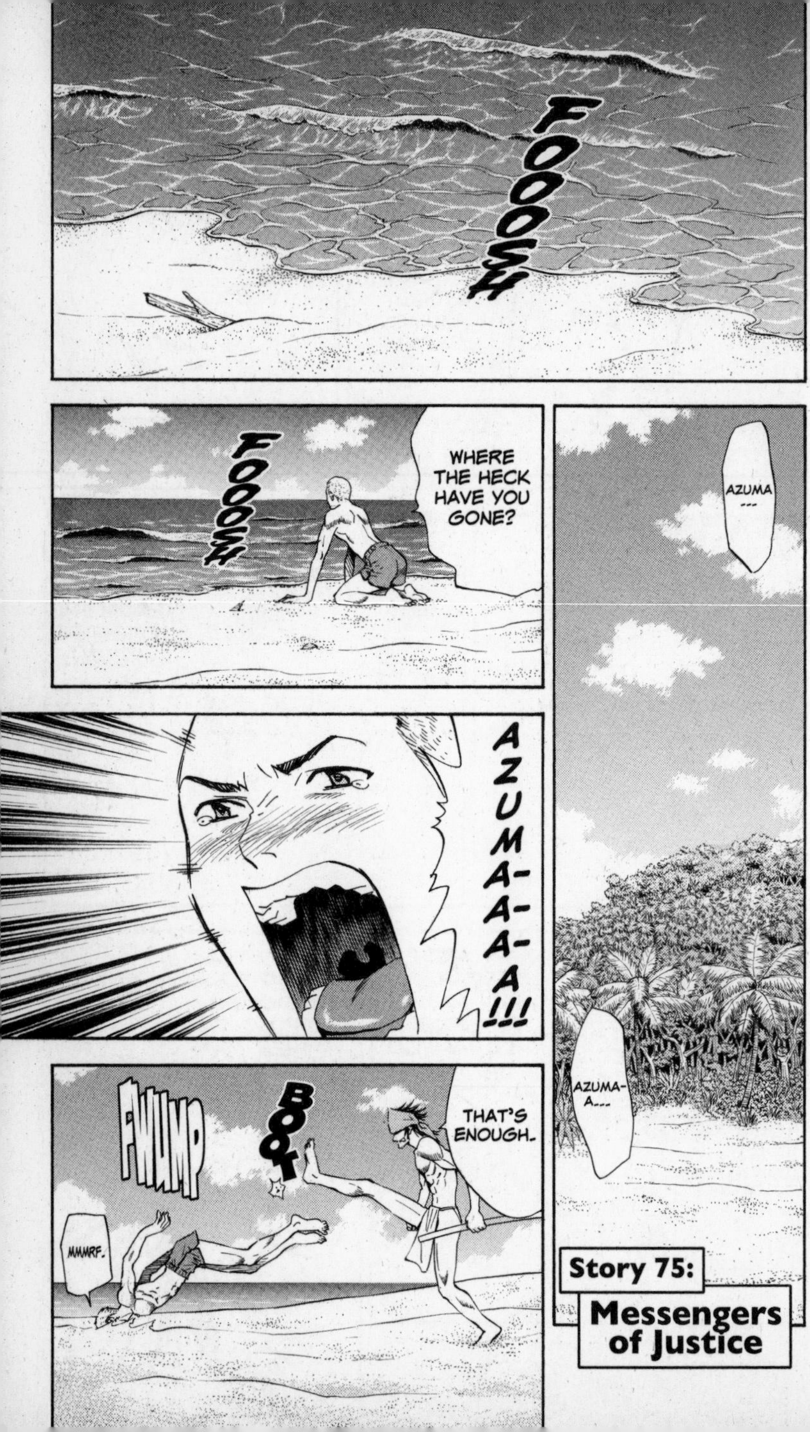
FOOOOSH
AZUMA...
AZUMA-A...
FOOOOSH
WHERE THE HECK HAVE YOU GONE?
AZUMAA-A-A-A!!!
THAT'S ENOUGH.
BOOT
FWUMP
MMMRF.

## Story 75: Messengers of Justice

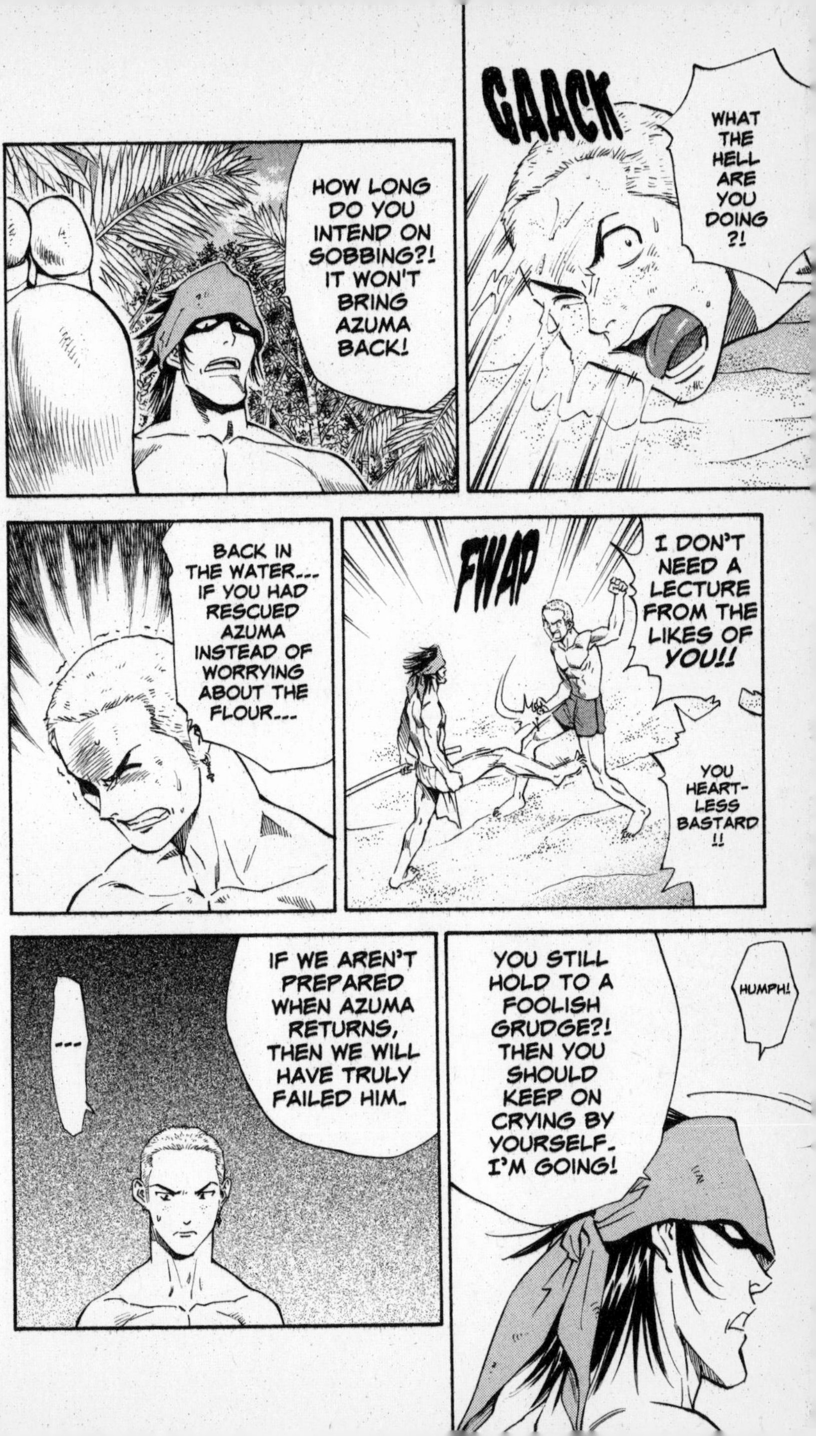
GAACK
WHAT THE HELL ARE YOU DOING?!
HOW LONG DO YOU INTEND ON SOBBING?! IT WON'T BRING AZUMA BACK!
FWAP
I DON'T NEED A LECTURE FROM THE LIKES OF YOU!!
YOU HEARTLESS BASTARD!!
BACK IN THE WATER... IF YOU HAD RESCUED AZUMA INSTEAD OF WORRYING ABOUT THE FLOUR...
YOU STILL HOLD TO A FOOLISH GRUDGE?! THEN YOU SHOULD KEEP ON CRYING BY YOURSELF. I'M GOING!
HUMPH!
IF WE AREN'T PREPARED WHEN AZUMA RETURNS, THEN WE WILL HAVE TRULY FAILED HIM.
...

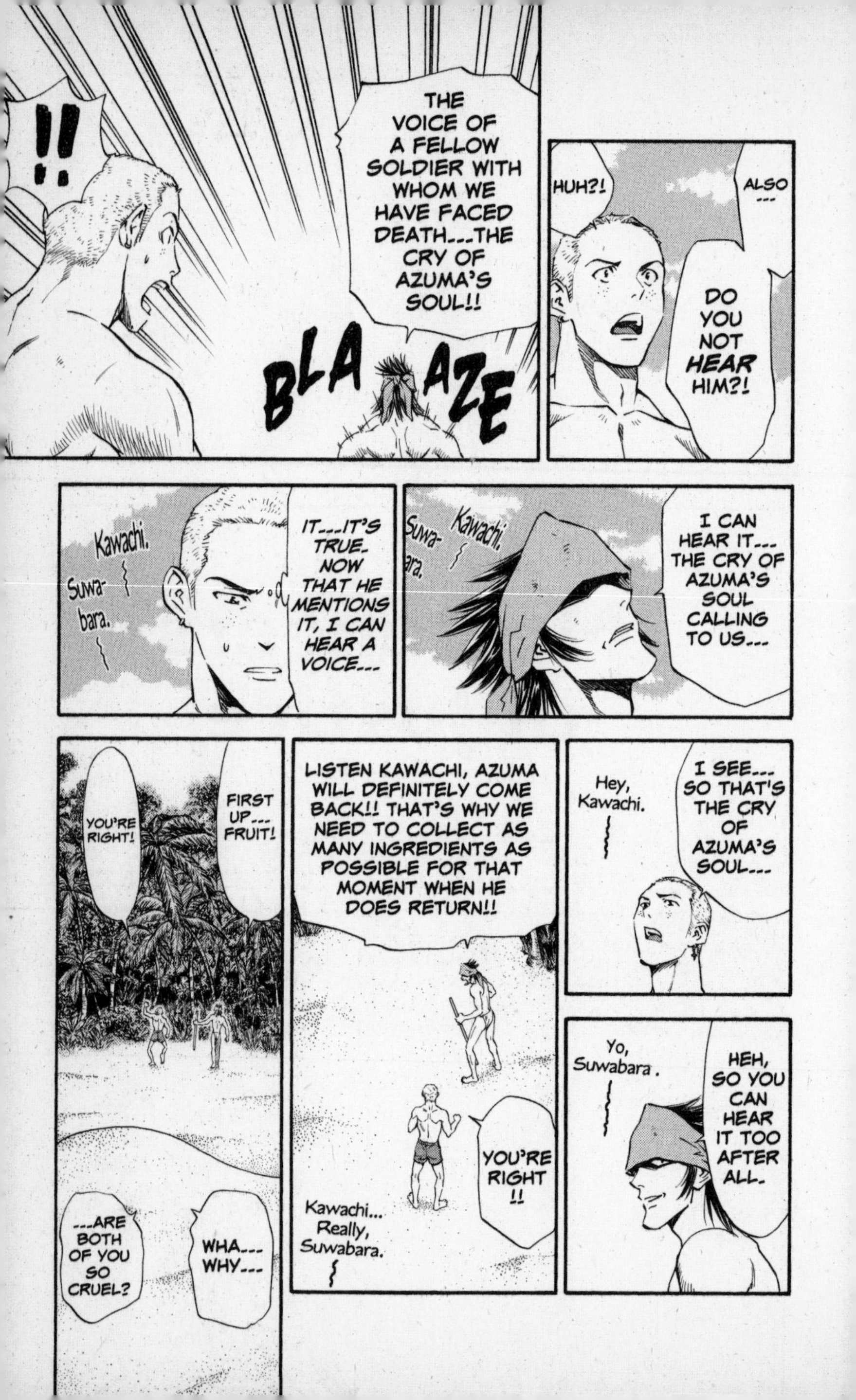
ALSO ---
HUH?!
DO YOU NOT HEAR HIM?!
THE VOICE OF A FELLOW SOLDIER WITH WHOM WE HAVE FACED DEATH---THE CRY OF AZUMA'S SOUL!!
!!
BLAAZE
I CAN HEAR IT--- THE CRY OF AZUMA'S SOUL CALLING TO US---
Kawachi.
Suwabara.
IT---IT'S TRUE. NOW THAT HE MENTIONS IT, I CAN HEAR A VOICE---
Kawachi.
Suwabara.
I SEE--- SO THAT'S THE CRY OF AZUMA'S SOUL---
Hey, Kawachi.
HEH, SO YOU CAN HEAR IT TOO AFTER ALL.
Yo, Suwabara.
LISTEN KAWACHI, AZUMA WILL DEFINITELY COME BACK!! THAT'S WHY WE NEED TO COLLECT AS MANY INGREDIENTS AS POSSIBLE FOR THAT MOMENT WHEN HE DOES RETURN!!
YOU'RE RIGHT!!
Kawachi... Really, Suwabara.
FIRST UP--- FRUIT!
YOU'RE RIGHT!
WHA--- WHY---
---ARE BOTH OF YOU SO CRUEL?

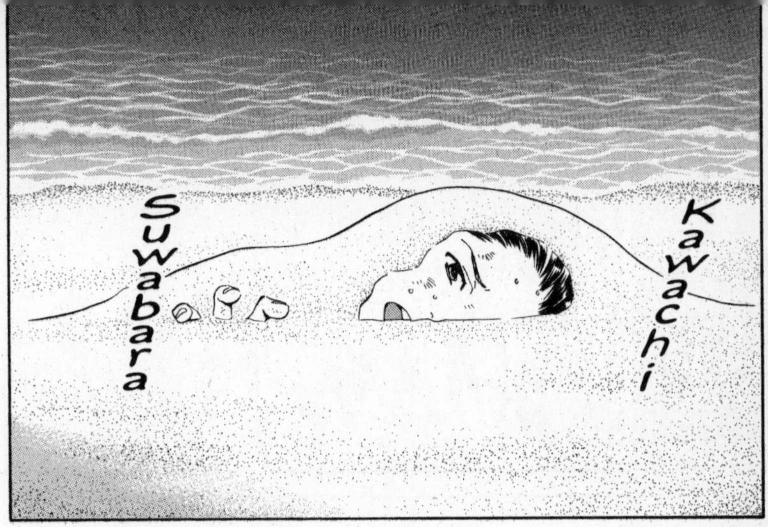
Kawachi
Suwabara

# Story 75: Messengers of Justice

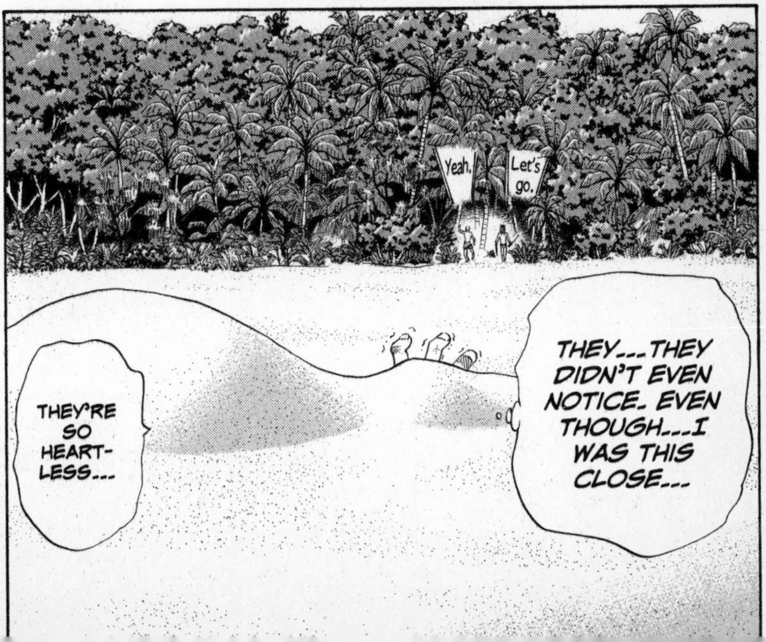
Let's go.
Yeah.
THEY...THEY DIDN'T EVEN NOTICE. EVEN THOUGH...I WAS THIS CLOSE...
THEY'RE SO HEART-LESS...

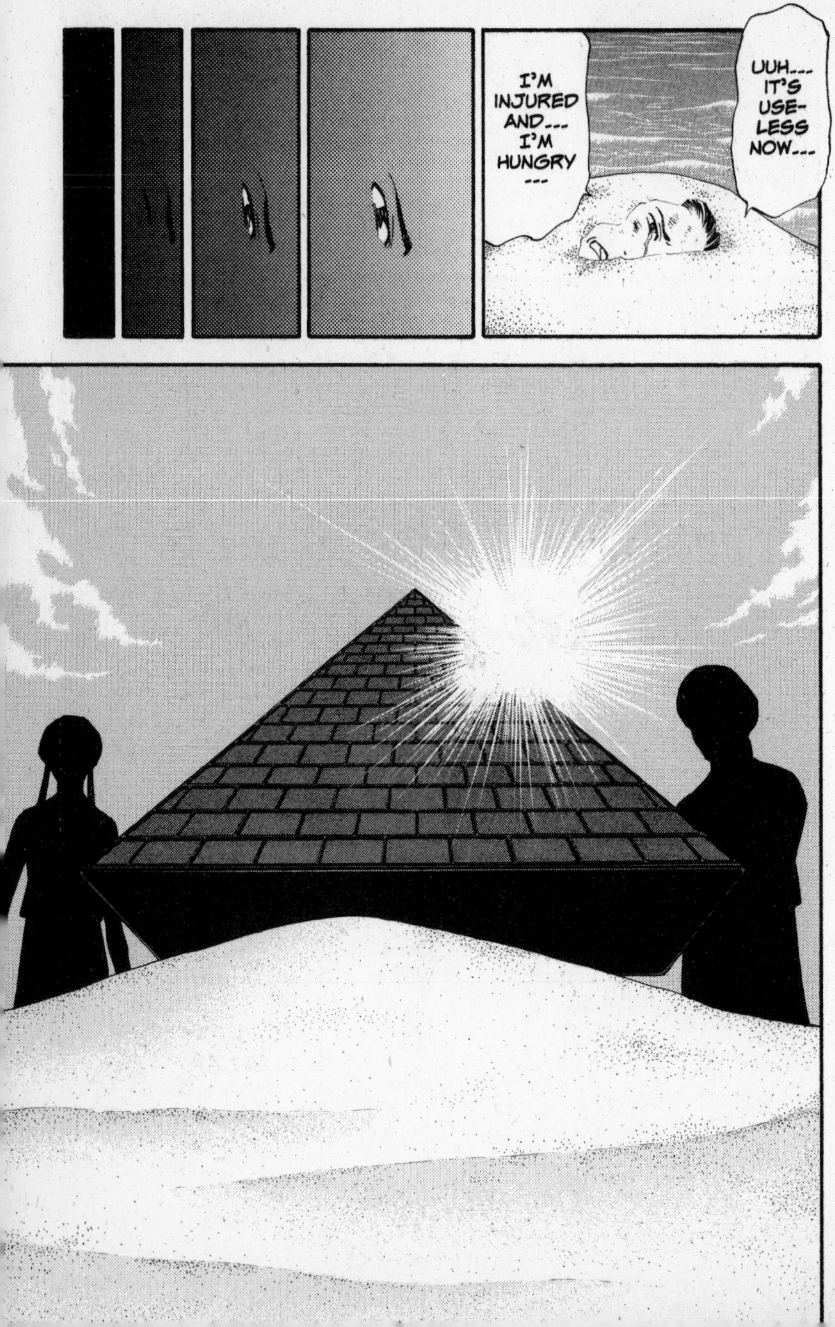
UUH... IT'S USE-LESS NOW...
I'M INJURED AND... I'M HUNGRY ...

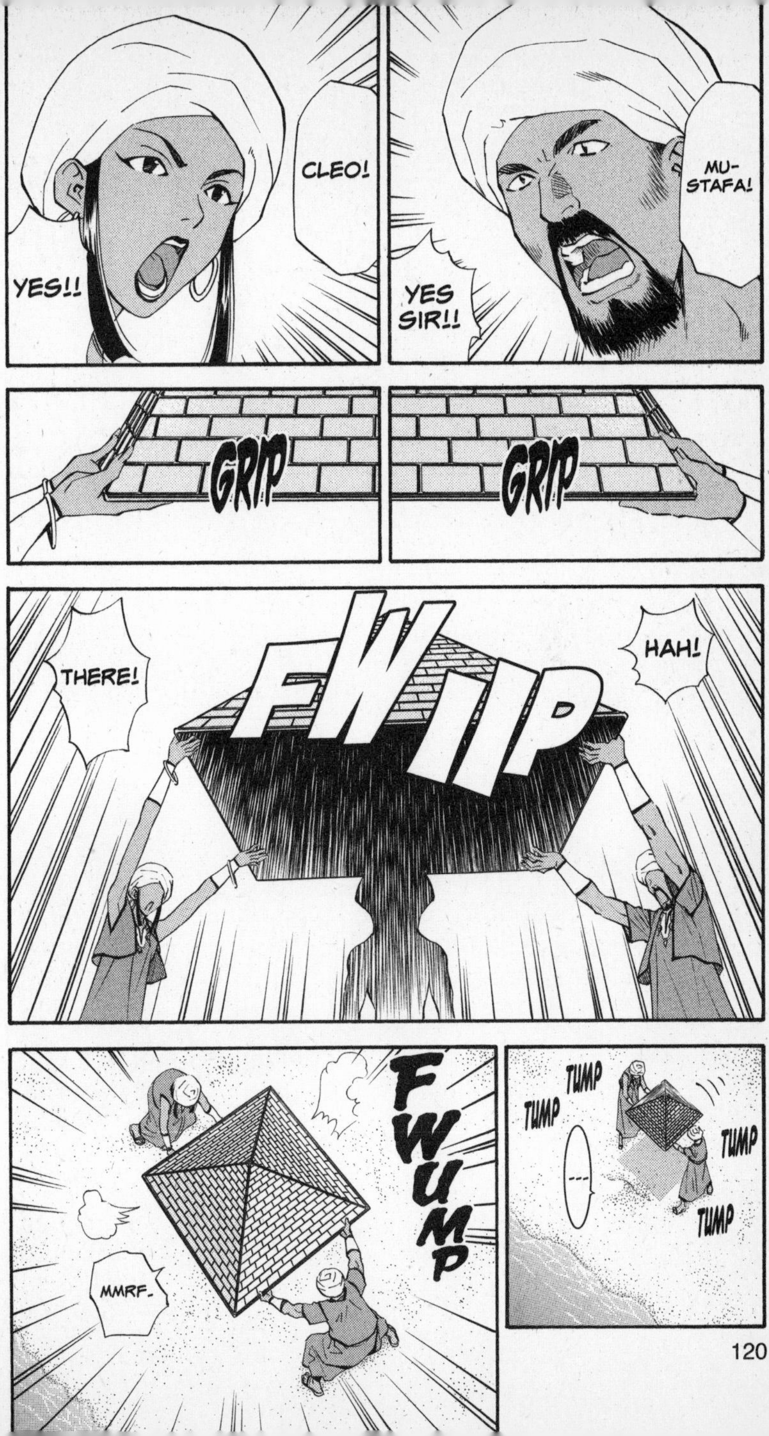
MU-
STAFA!
YES
SIR!!
CLEO!
YES!!
GRIP
GRIP
HAH!
FWIIP
THERE!
TUMP
TUMP
TUMP
TUMP
...
FWUMP
MMRF.

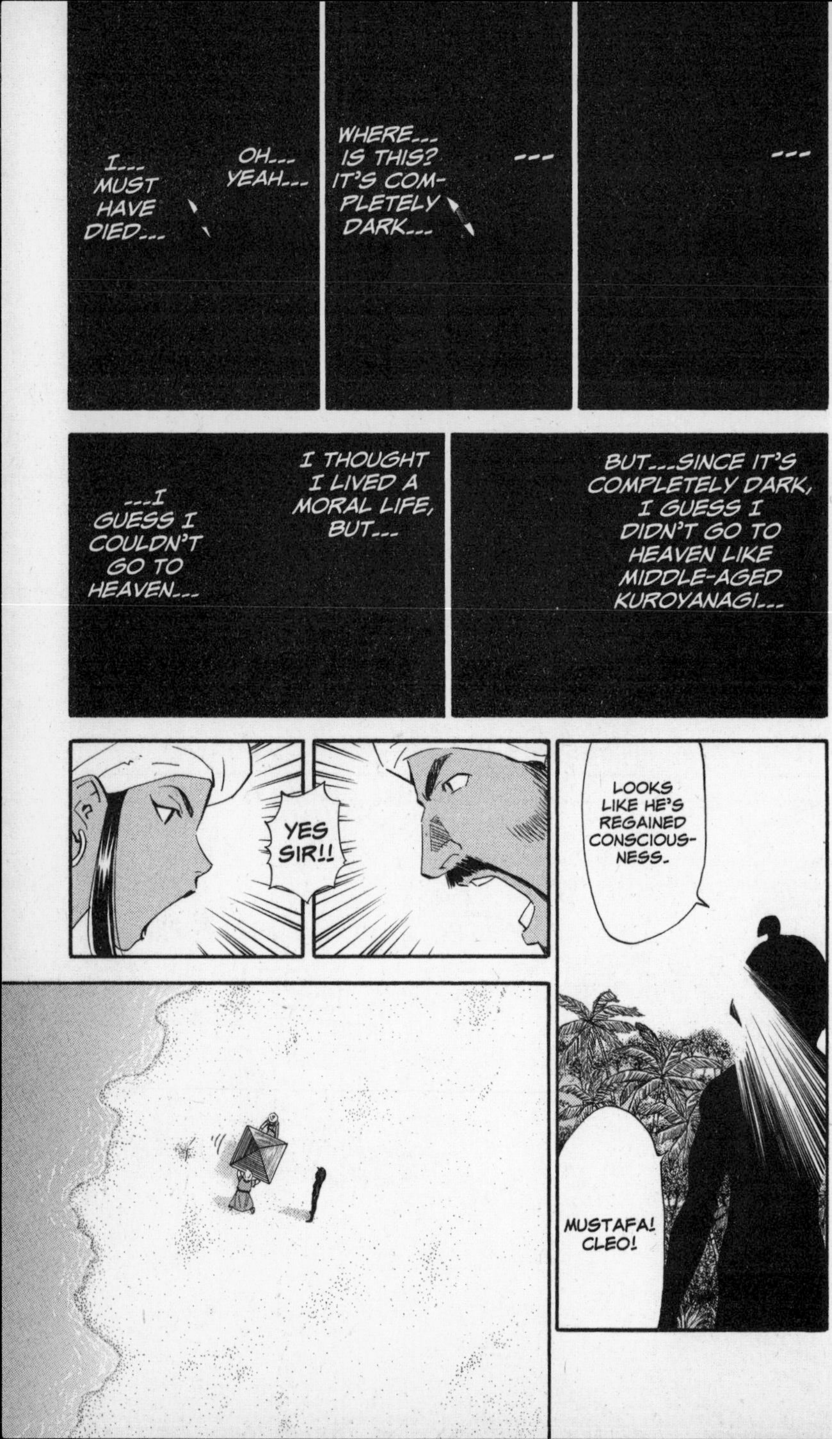
...
...
WHERE... IS THIS? IT'S COM-PLETELY DARK...
OH... YEAH...
I... MUST HAVE DIED...
BUT...SINCE IT'S COMPLETELY DARK, I GUESS I DIDN'T GO TO HEAVEN LIKE MIDDLE-AGED KUROYANAGI...
I THOUGHT I LIVED A MORAL LIFE, BUT...
...I GUESS I COULDN'T GO TO HEAVEN...
LOOKS LIKE HE'S REGAINED CONSCIOUS-NESS.
MUSTAFA! CLEO!
YES SIR!!

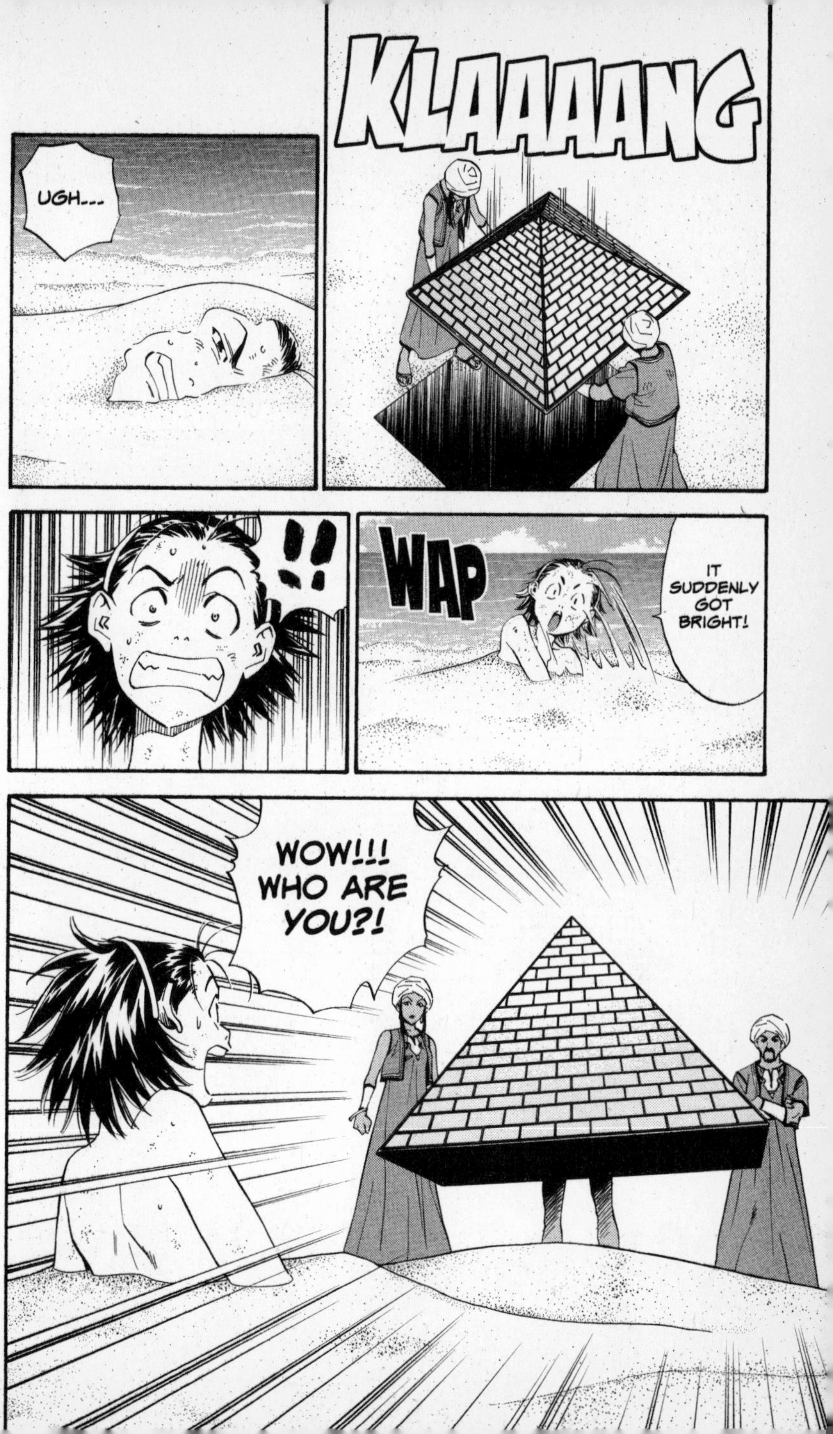
KLAAAANG
UGH...
WAP
IT SUDDENLY GOT BRIGHT!
!!
WOW!!! WHO ARE YOU?!

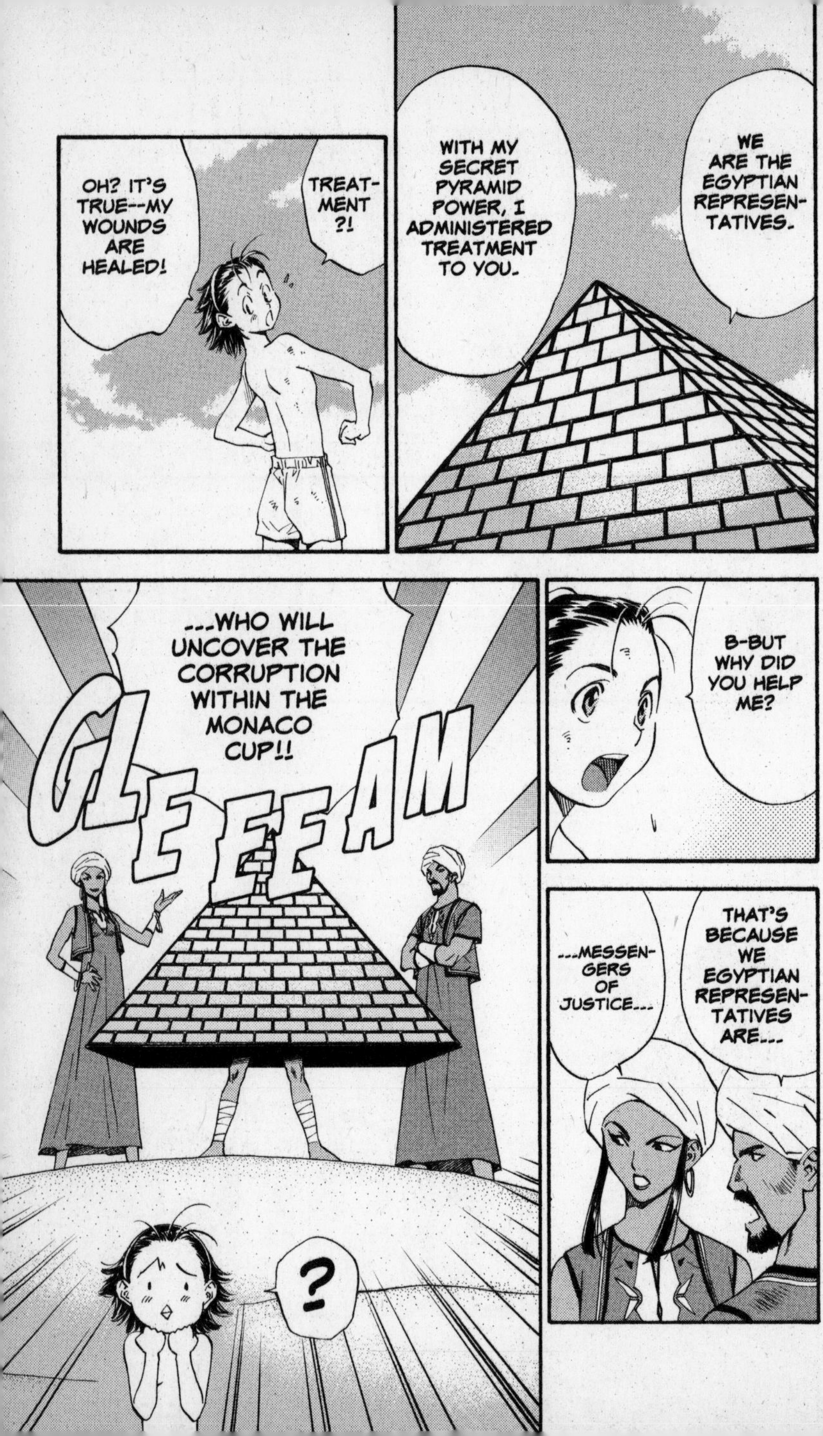
WE ARE THE EGYPTIAN REPRESENTATIVES.
WITH MY SECRET PYRAMID POWER, I ADMINISTERED TREATMENT TO YOU.
TREATMENT?!
OH? IT'S TRUE--MY WOUNDS ARE HEALED!
B-BUT WHY DID YOU HELP ME?
THAT'S BECAUSE WE EGYPTIAN REPRESENTATIVES ARE...
...MESSENGERS OF JUSTICE...
...WHO WILL UNCOVER THE CORRUPTION WITHIN THE MONACO CUP!!
GLEEEAM
?

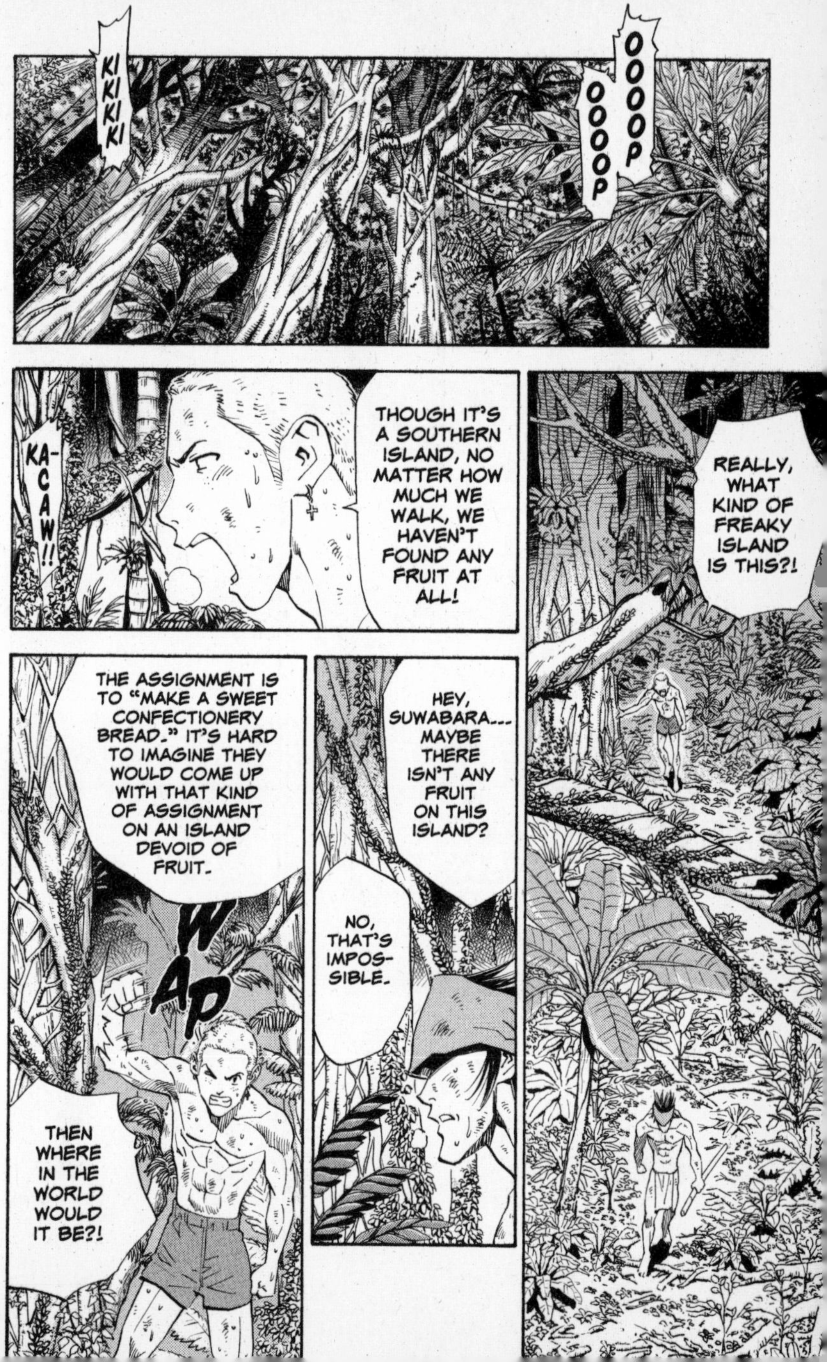
OOOOP
OOOOP
KIKIKIKI
REALLY, WHAT KIND OF FREAKY ISLAND IS THIS?!
THOUGH IT'S A SOUTHERN ISLAND, NO MATTER HOW MUCH WE WALK, WE HAVEN'T FOUND ANY FRUIT AT ALL!
KA-CAW!!
HEY, SUWABARA... MAYBE THERE ISN'T ANY FRUIT ON THIS ISLAND?
NO, THAT'S IMPOS-SIBLE.
THE ASSIGNMENT IS TO "MAKE A SWEET CONFECTIONERY BREAD." IT'S HARD TO IMAGINE THEY WOULD COME UP WITH THAT KIND OF ASSIGNMENT ON AN ISLAND DEVOID OF FRUIT.
WAP
THEN WHERE IN THE WORLD WOULD IT BE?!

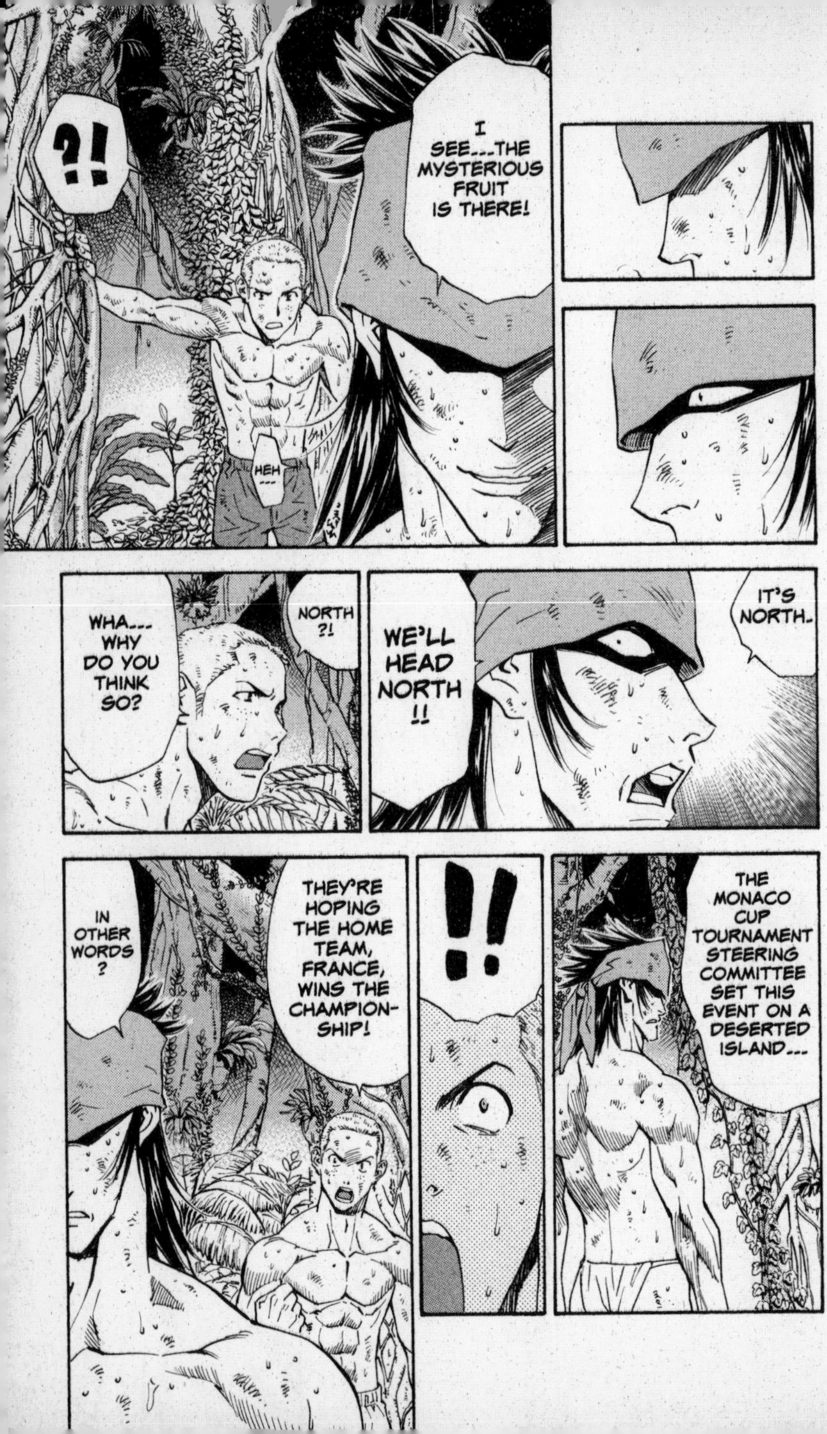
I SEE...THE MYSTERIOUS FRUIT IS THERE!
?!
HEH...
IT'S NORTH.
WE'LL HEAD NORTH!!
NORTH?!
WHA... WHY DO YOU THINK SO?
THE MONACO CUP TOURNAMENT STEERING COMMITTEE SET THIS EVENT ON A DESERTED ISLAND...
!!
IN OTHER WORDS?
THEY'RE HOPING THE HOME TEAM, FRANCE, WINS THE CHAMPIONSHIP!

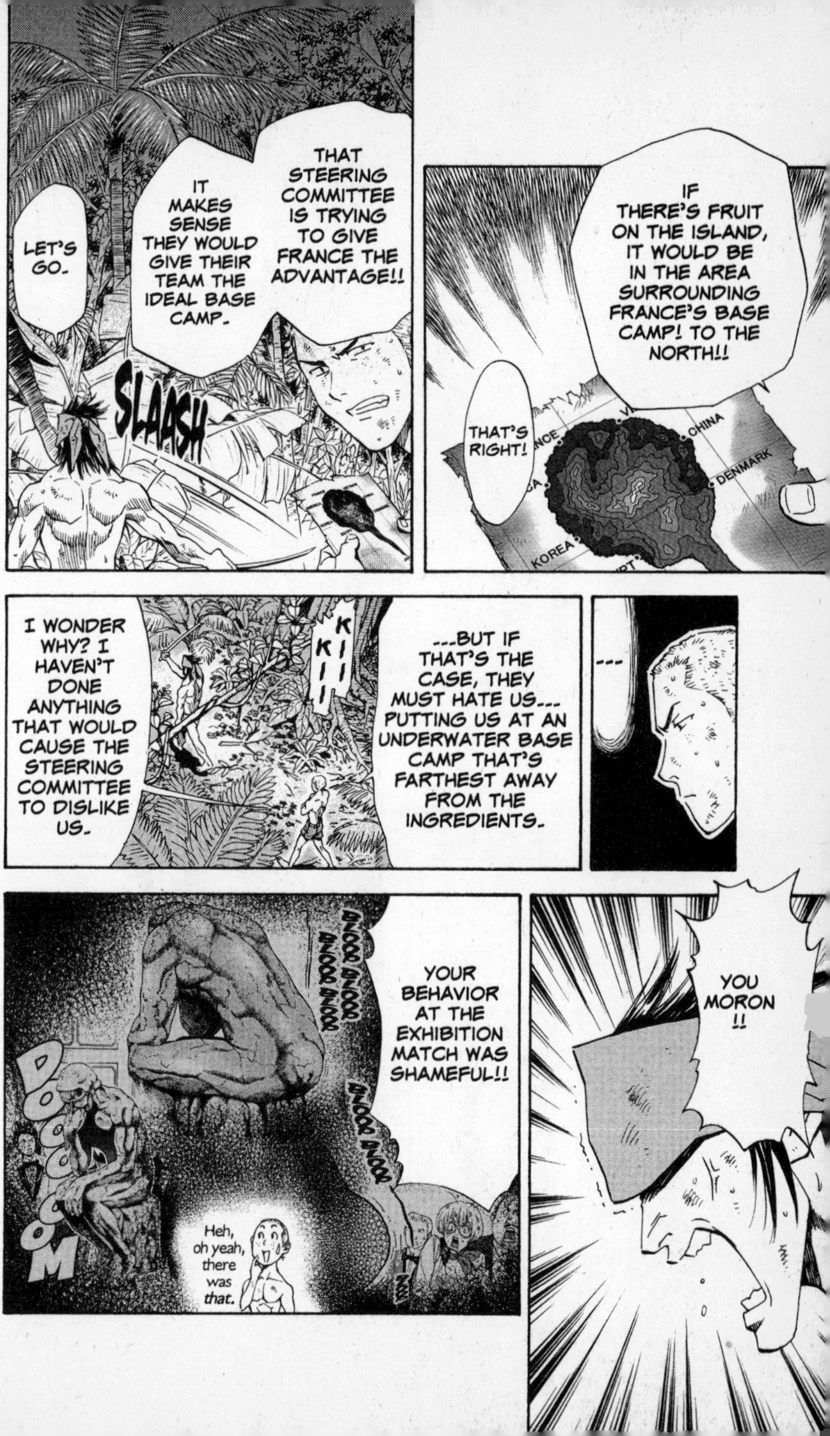
IF THERE'S FRUIT ON THE ISLAND, IT WOULD BE IN THE AREA SURROUNDING FRANCE'S BASE CAMP! TO THE NORTH!!
THAT'S RIGHT!
CHINA
DENMARK
KOREA
THAT STEERING COMMITTEE IS TRYING TO GIVE FRANCE THE ADVANTAGE!!
IT MAKES SENSE THEY WOULD GIVE THEIR TEAM THE IDEAL BASE CAMP.
SLAASH
LET'S GO.
...
...BUT IF THAT'S THE CASE, THEY MUST HATE US... PUTTING US AT AN UNDERWATER BASE CAMP THAT'S FARTHEST AWAY FROM THE INGREDIENTS.
KIII
KIII
I WONDER WHY? I HAVEN'T DONE ANYTHING THAT WOULD CAUSE THE STEERING COMMITTEE TO DISLIKE US.
YOU MORON !!
YOUR BEHAVIOR AT THE EXHIBITION MATCH WAS SHAMEFUL!!
DOOOOOM
Heh, oh yeah, there was *that*.

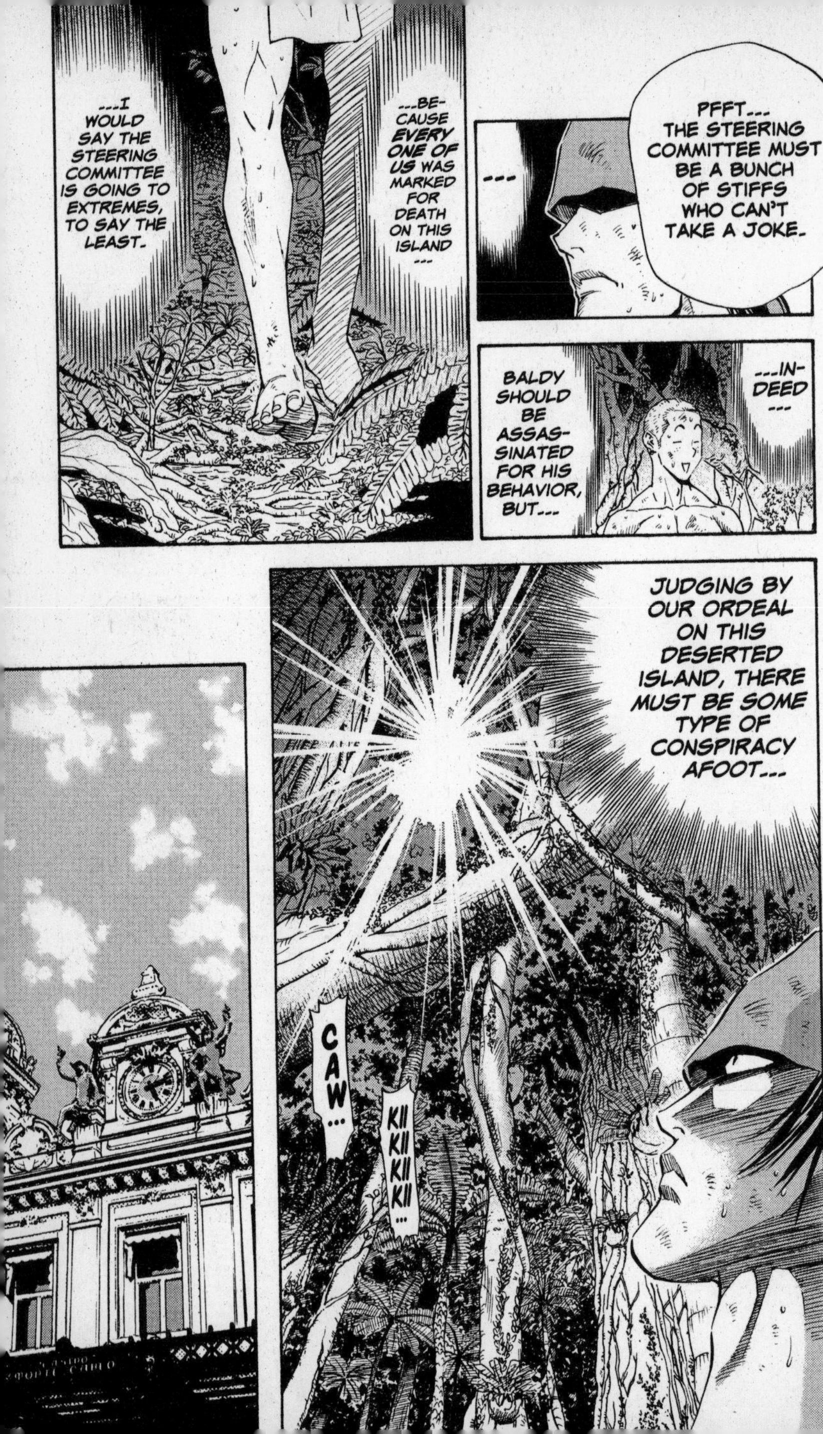
PFFT... THE STEERING COMMITTEE MUST BE A BUNCH OF STIFFS WHO CAN'T TAKE A JOKE.
...
...INDEED...
BALDY SHOULD BE ASSASSINATED FOR HIS BEHAVIOR, BUT...
...I WOULD SAY THE STEERING COMMITTEE IS GOING TO EXTREMES, TO SAY THE LEAST.
...BECAUSE EVERY ONE OF US WAS MARKED FOR DEATH ON THIS ISLAND...
JUDGING BY OUR ORDEAL ON THIS DESERTED ISLAND, THERE MUST BE SOME TYPE OF CONSPIRACY AFOOT...
CAW...
KII KII KII KII...

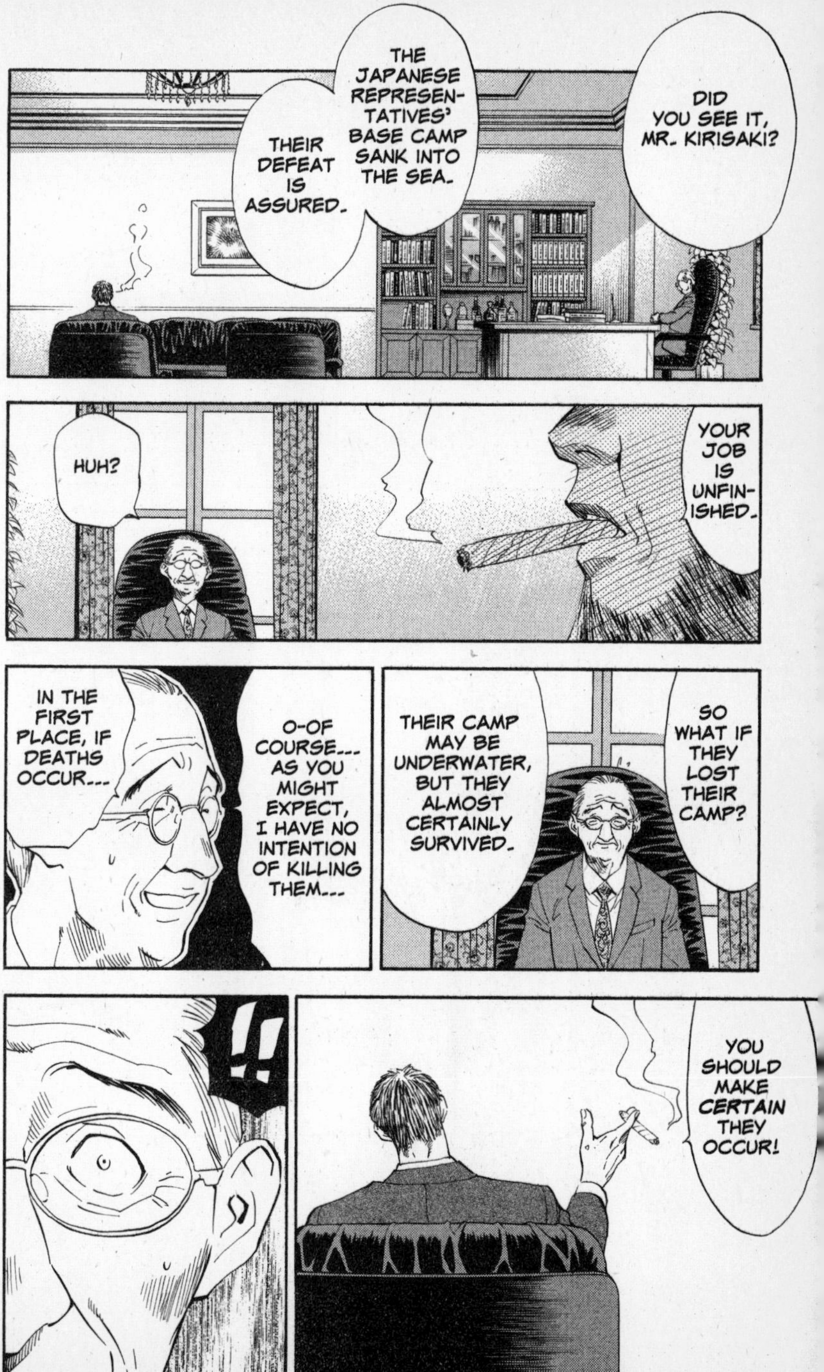
DID YOU SEE IT, MR. KIRISAKI?
THE JAPANESE REPRESENTATIVES' BASE CAMP SANK INTO THE SEA.
THEIR DEFEAT IS ASSURED.
YOUR JOB IS UNFINISHED.
HUH?
SO WHAT IF THEY LOST THEIR CAMP?
THEIR CAMP MAY BE UNDERWATER, BUT THEY ALMOST CERTAINLY SURVIVED.
O-OF COURSE... AS YOU MIGHT EXPECT, I HAVE NO INTENTION OF KILLING THEM...
IN THE FIRST PLACE, IF DEATHS OCCUR...
YOU SHOULD MAKE CERTAIN THEY OCCUR!
!!

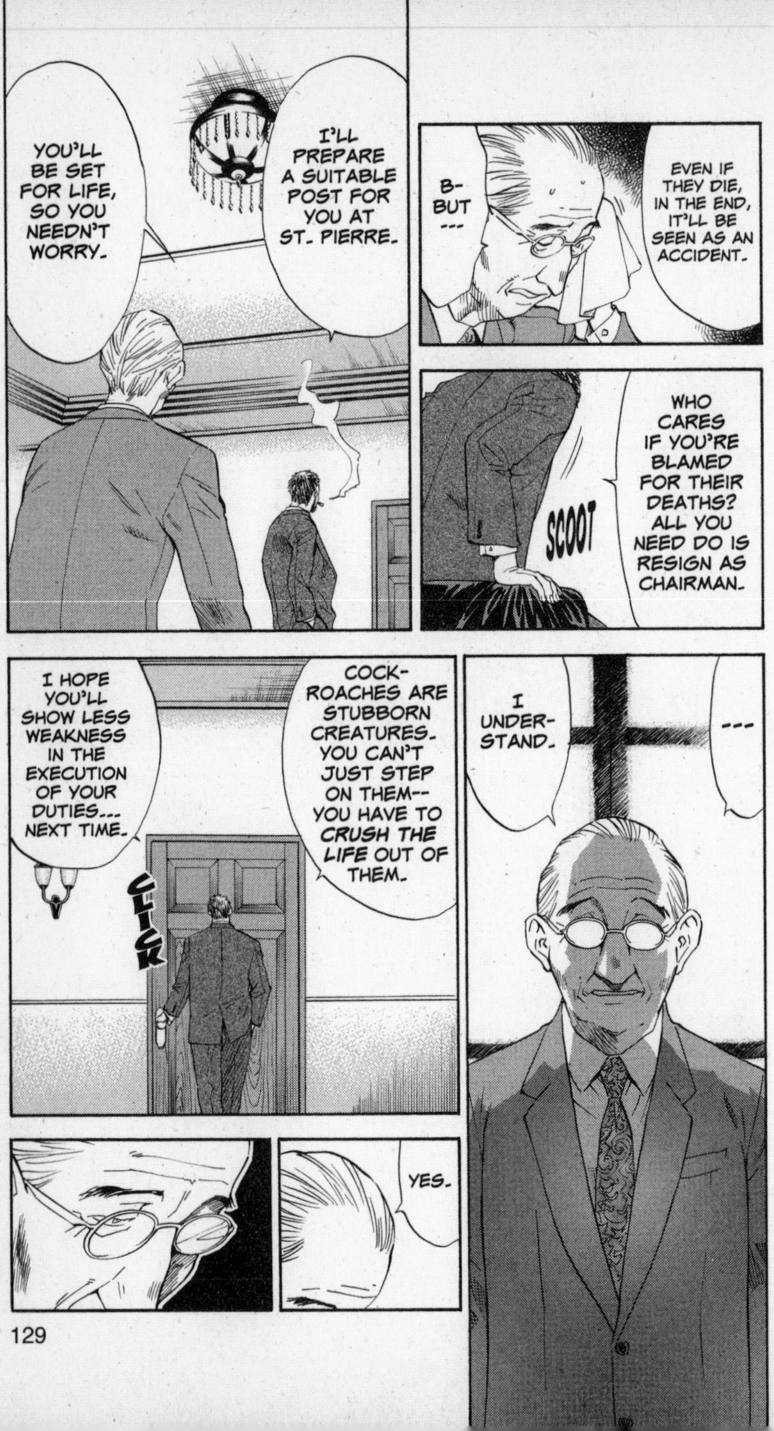
EVEN IF THEY DIE, IN THE END, IT'LL BE SEEN AS AN ACCIDENT.
B-BUT ...
WHO CARES IF YOU'RE BLAMED FOR THEIR DEATHS? ALL YOU NEED DO IS RESIGN AS CHAIRMAN.
SCOOT
I'LL PREPARE A SUITABLE POST FOR YOU AT ST. PIERRE.
YOU'LL BE SET FOR LIFE, SO YOU NEEDN'T WORRY.
...
I UNDERSTAND.
COCKROACHES ARE STUBBORN CREATURES. YOU CAN'T JUST STEP ON THEM-- YOU HAVE TO CRUSH THE LIFE OUT OF THEM.
I HOPE YOU'LL SHOW LESS WEAKNESS IN THE EXECUTION OF YOUR DUTIES... NEXT TIME.
CLICK
YES.

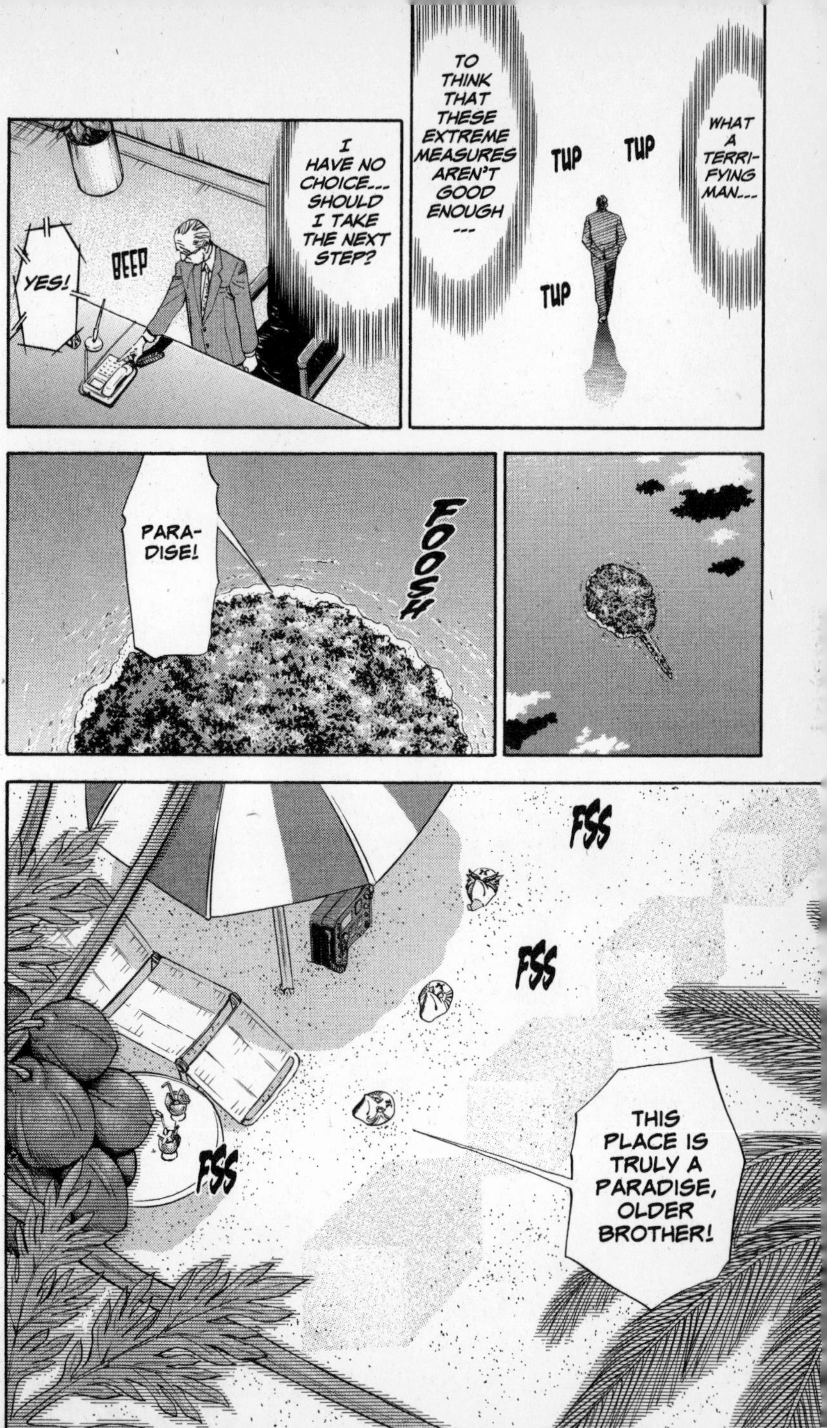
TO THINK THAT THESE EXTREME MEASURES AREN'T GOOD ENOUGH---
TUP
TUP
TUP
WHAT A TERRI-FYING MAN---
I HAVE NO CHOICE--- SHOULD I TAKE THE NEXT STEP?
BEEP
YES!
FOOSH
PARA-DISE!
FSS
FSS
FSS
THIS PLACE IS TRULY A PARADISE, OLDER BROTHER!

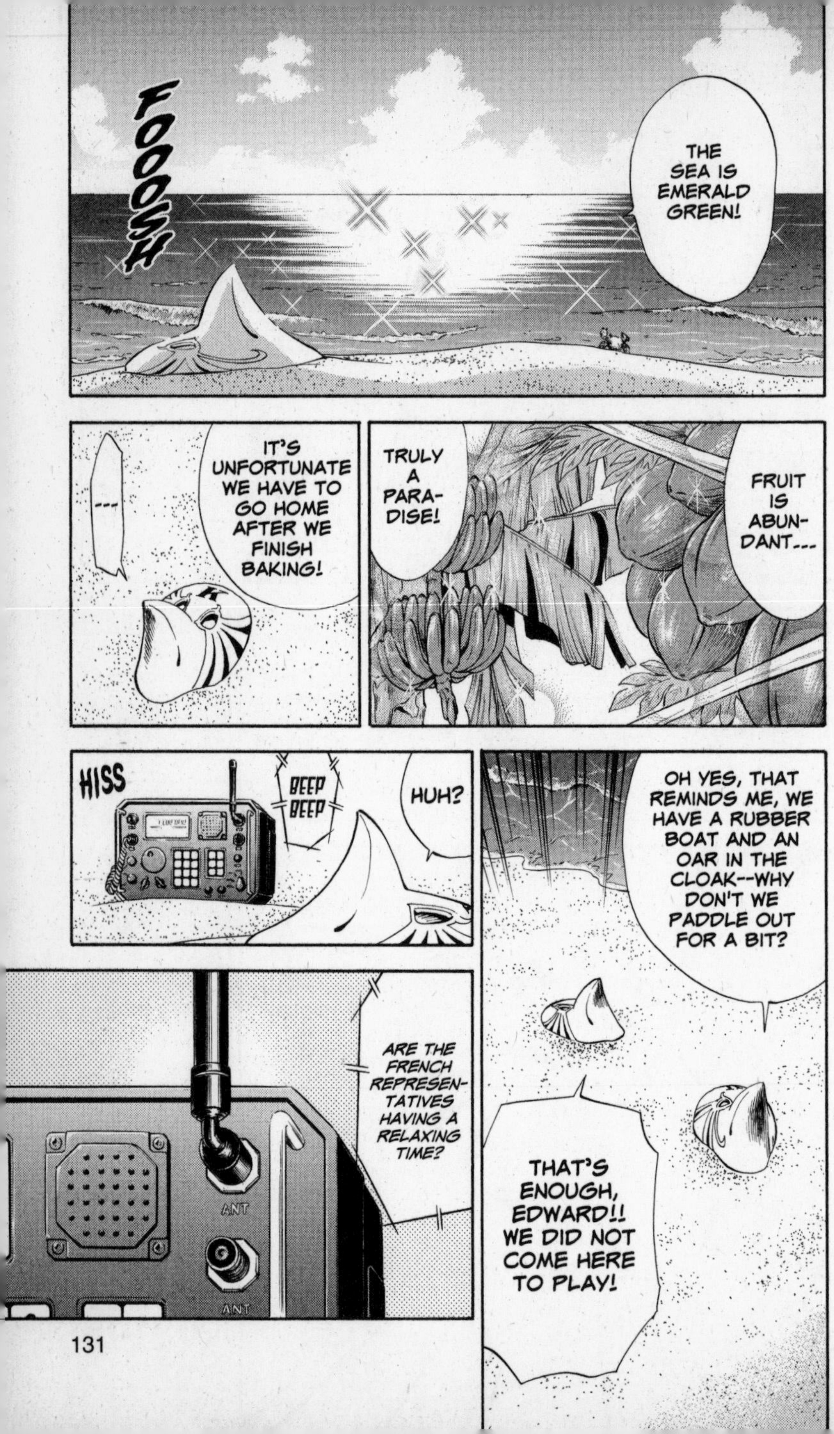
THE SEA IS EMERALD GREEN!
FOOOSH
FRUIT IS ABUN-DANT...
TRULY A PARA-DISE!
IT'S UNFORTUNATE WE HAVE TO GO HOME AFTER WE FINISH BAKING!
...
OH YES, THAT REMINDS ME, WE HAVE A RUBBER BOAT AND AN OAR IN THE CLOAK--WHY DON'T WE PADDLE OUT FOR A BIT?
THAT'S ENOUGH, EDWARD!! WE DID NOT COME HERE TO PLAY!
HUH?
BEEP BEEP
HISS
ARE THE FRENCH REPRESEN-TATIVES HAVING A RELAXING TIME?
ANT
ANT

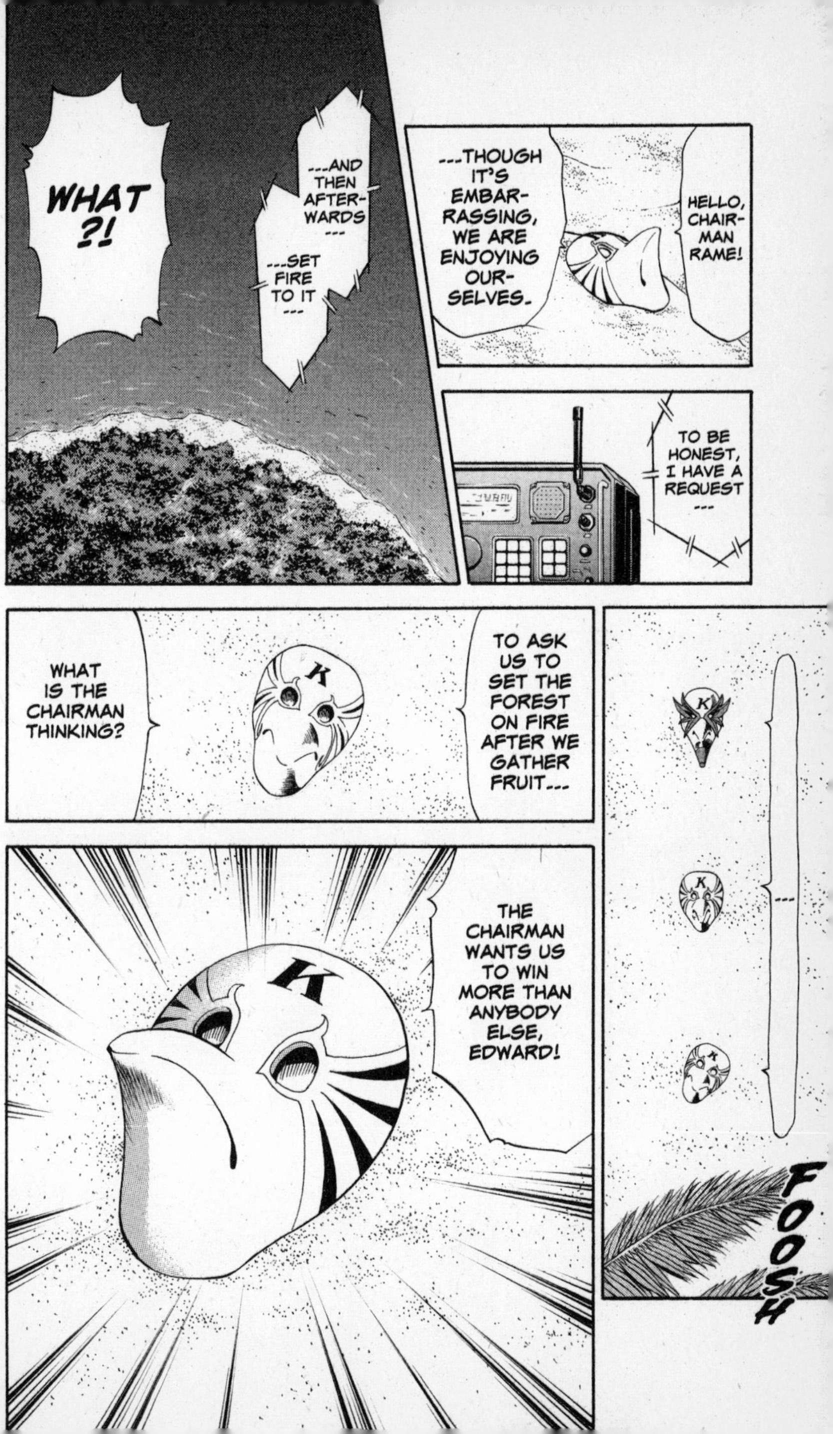
HELLO, CHAIR-MAN RAME!
...THOUGH IT'S EMBAR-RASSING, WE ARE ENJOYING OUR-SELVES.
TO BE HONEST, I HAVE A REQUEST...
...AND THEN AFTER-WARDS...
...SET FIRE TO IT...
WHAT ?!
...
FOOSH
TO ASK US TO SET THE FOREST ON FIRE AFTER WE GATHER FRUIT...
WHAT IS THE CHAIRMAN THINKING?
THE CHAIRMAN WANTS US TO WIN MORE THAN ANYBODY ELSE, EDWARD!

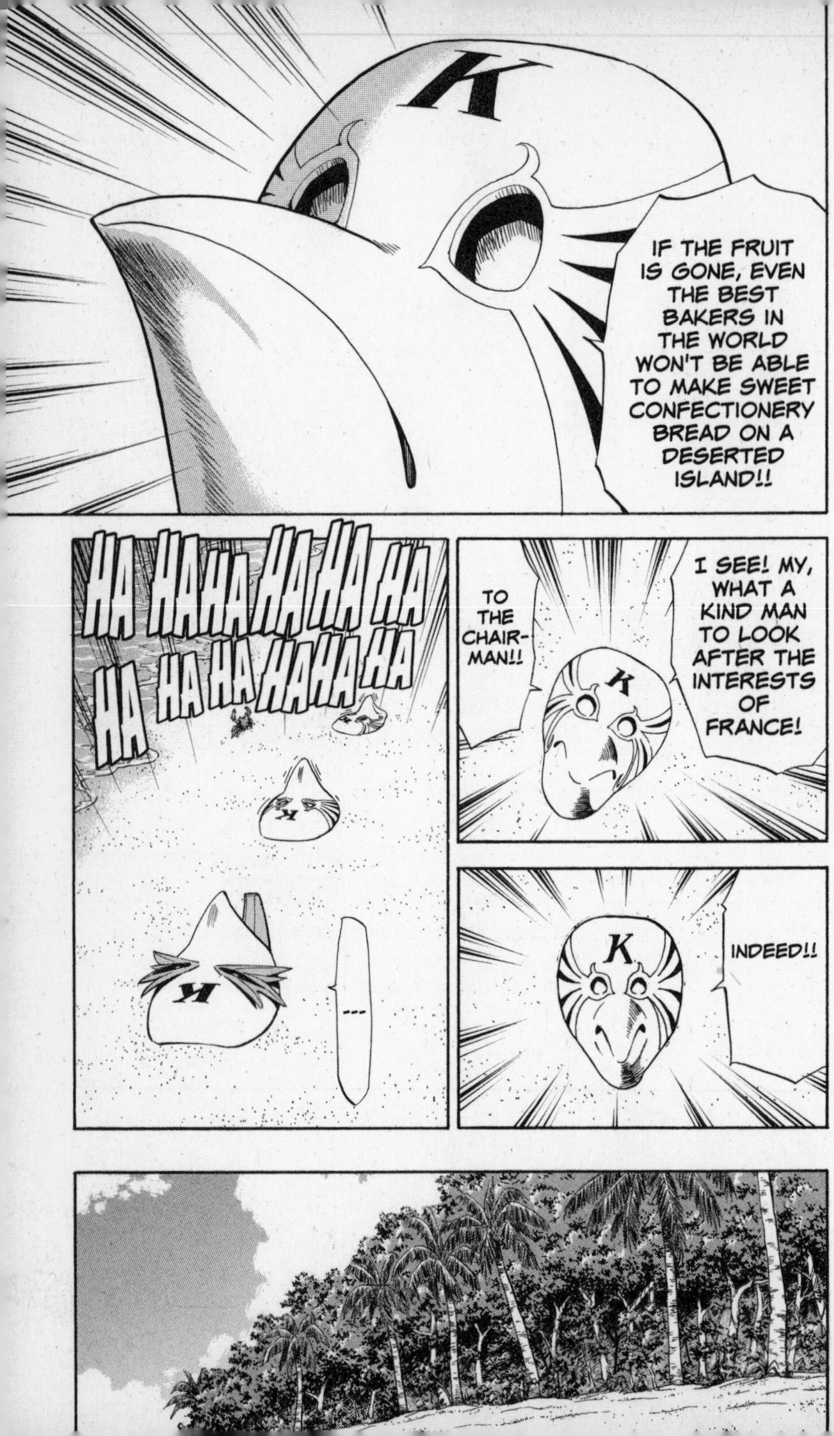
IF THE FRUIT IS GONE, EVEN THE BEST BAKERS IN THE WORLD WON'T BE ABLE TO MAKE SWEET CONFECTIONERY BREAD ON A DESERTED ISLAND!!
I SEE! MY, WHAT A KIND MAN TO LOOK AFTER THE INTERESTS OF FRANCE!
TO THE CHAIRMAN!!
INDEED!!
HA HAHA HAHA HA HA HA HAHA HA HA HA HA
...

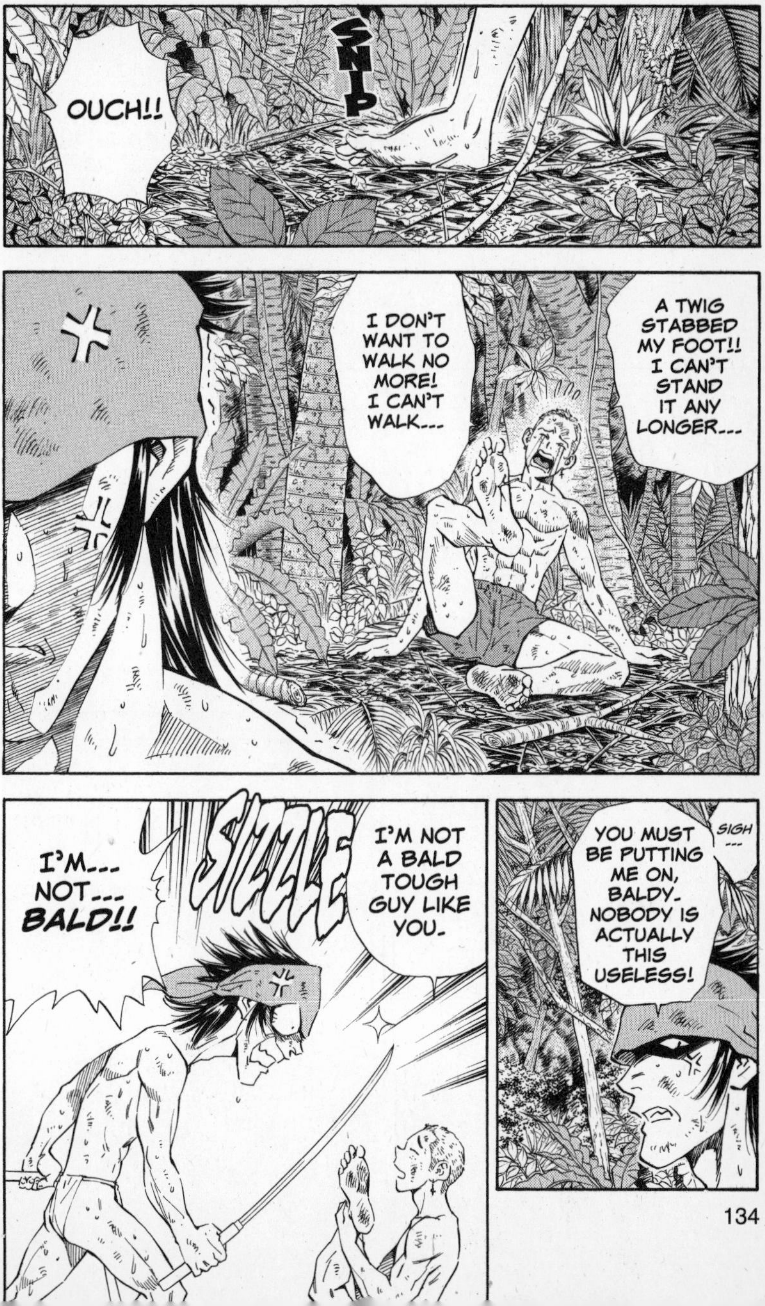
SNIP
OUCH!!
A TWIG STABBED MY FOOT!! I CAN'T STAND IT ANY LONGER...
I DON'T WANT TO WALK NO MORE! I CAN'T WALK...
SIGH...
YOU MUST BE PUTTING ME ON, BALDY. NOBODY IS ACTUALLY THIS USELESS!
I'M NOT A BALD TOUGH GUY LIKE YOU.
SIZZLE
I'M... NOT... BALD!!

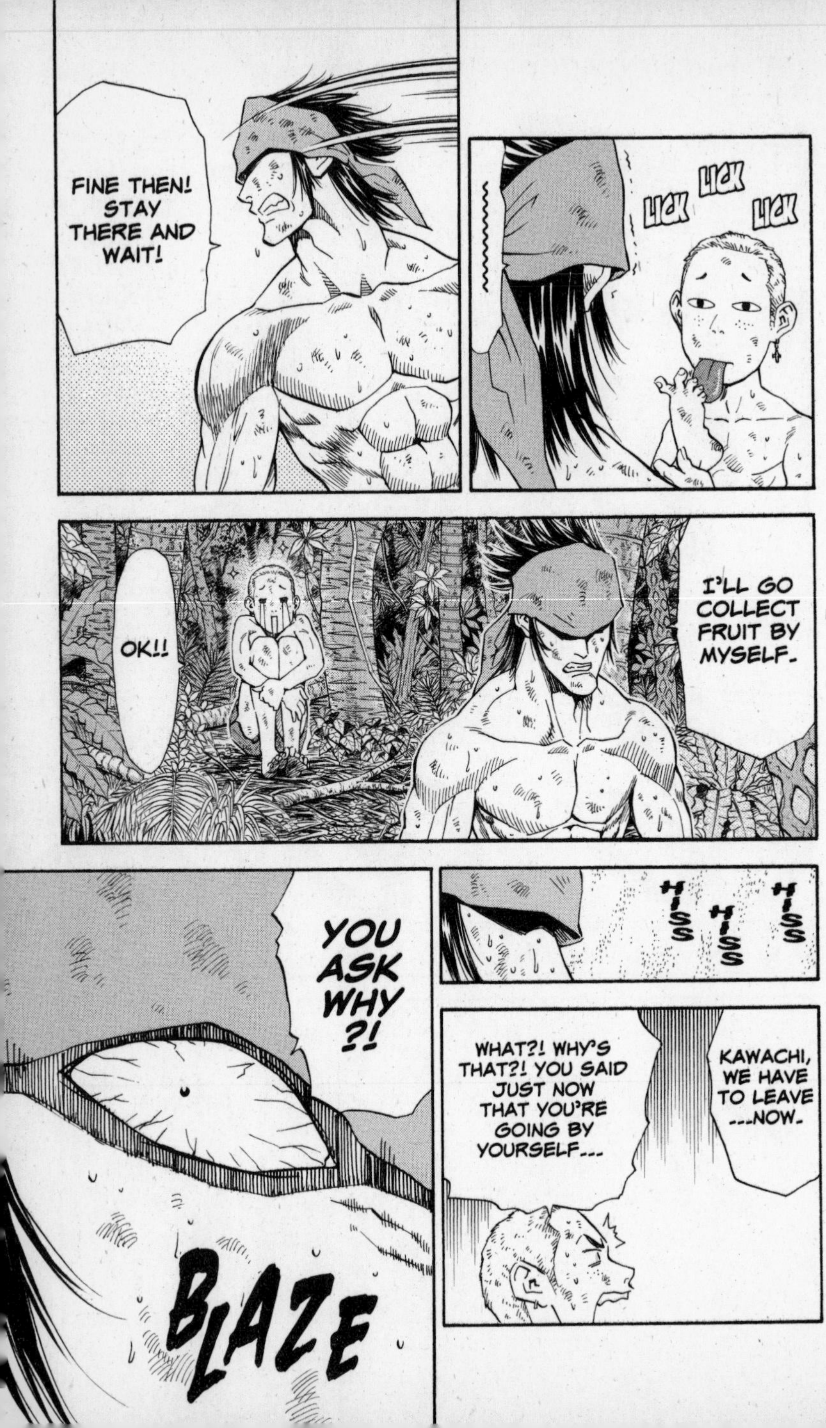
LICK LICK LICK
FINE THEN! STAY THERE AND WAIT!
I'LL GO COLLECT FRUIT BY MYSELF.
OK!!
HISS HISS HISS
KAWACHI, WE HAVE TO LEAVE ...NOW.
WHAT?! WHY'S THAT?! YOU SAID JUST NOW THAT YOU'RE GOING BY YOURSELF...
YOU ASK WHY?!
BLAZE

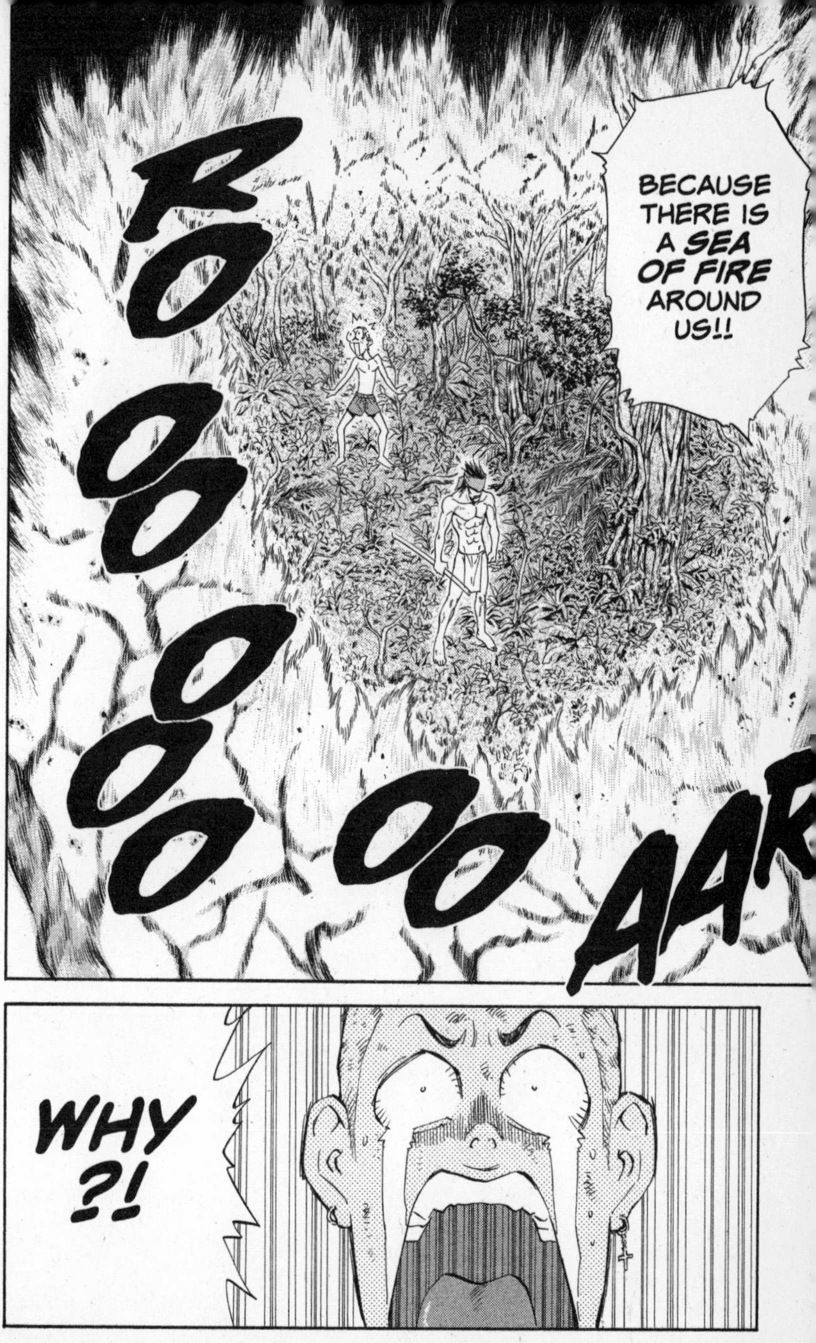
BECAUSE THERE IS A SEA OF FIRE AROUND US!!
ROOOOOOOOAAR
WHY ?!

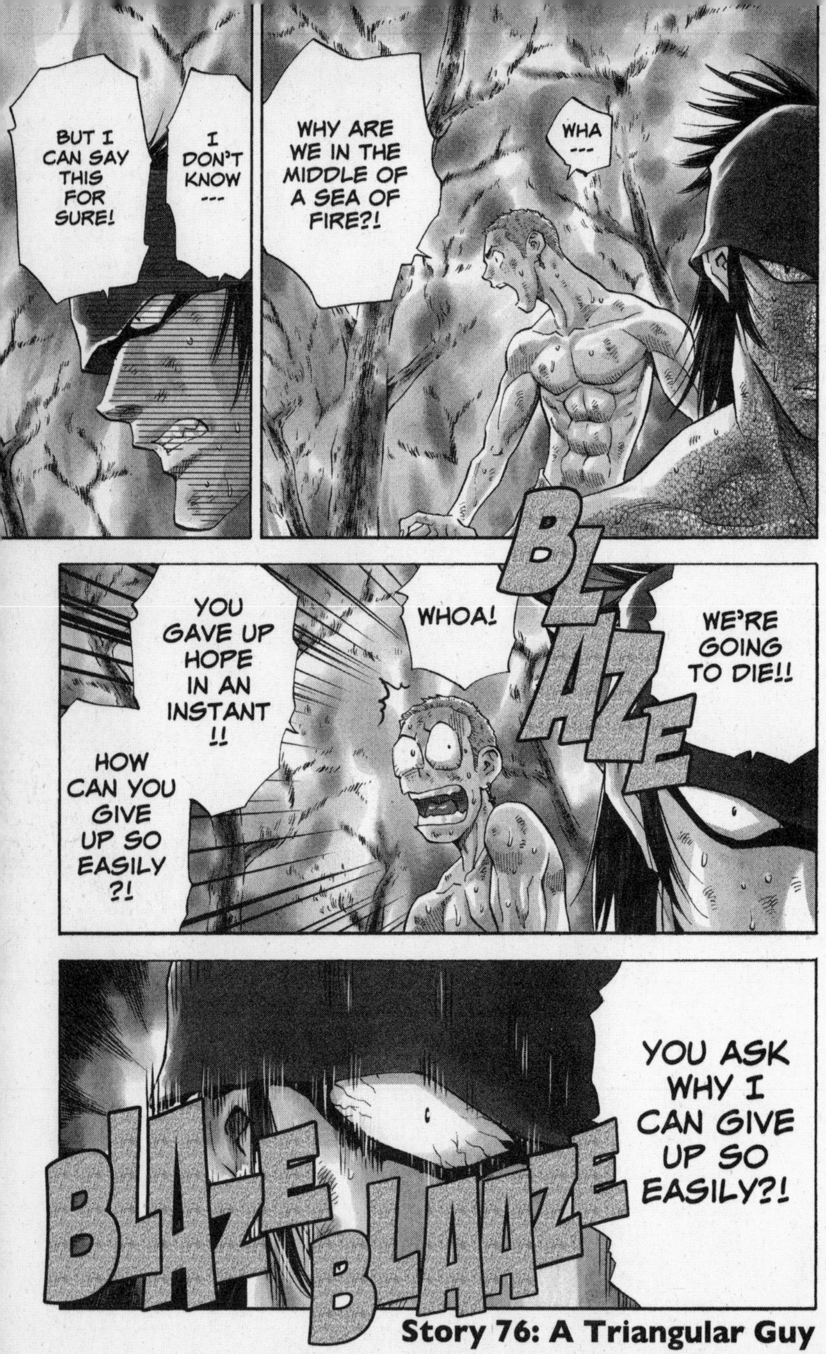
WHA---
WHY ARE WE IN THE MIDDLE OF A SEA OF FIRE?!
I DON'T KNOW---
BUT I CAN SAY THIS FOR SURE!
WE'RE GOING TO DIE!!
BLAZE
WHOA!
YOU GAVE UP HOPE IN AN INSTANT!!
HOW CAN YOU GIVE UP SO EASILY?!
YOU ASK WHY I CAN GIVE UP SO EASILY?!
BLAZE
BLAAZE

## Story 76: A Triangular Guy

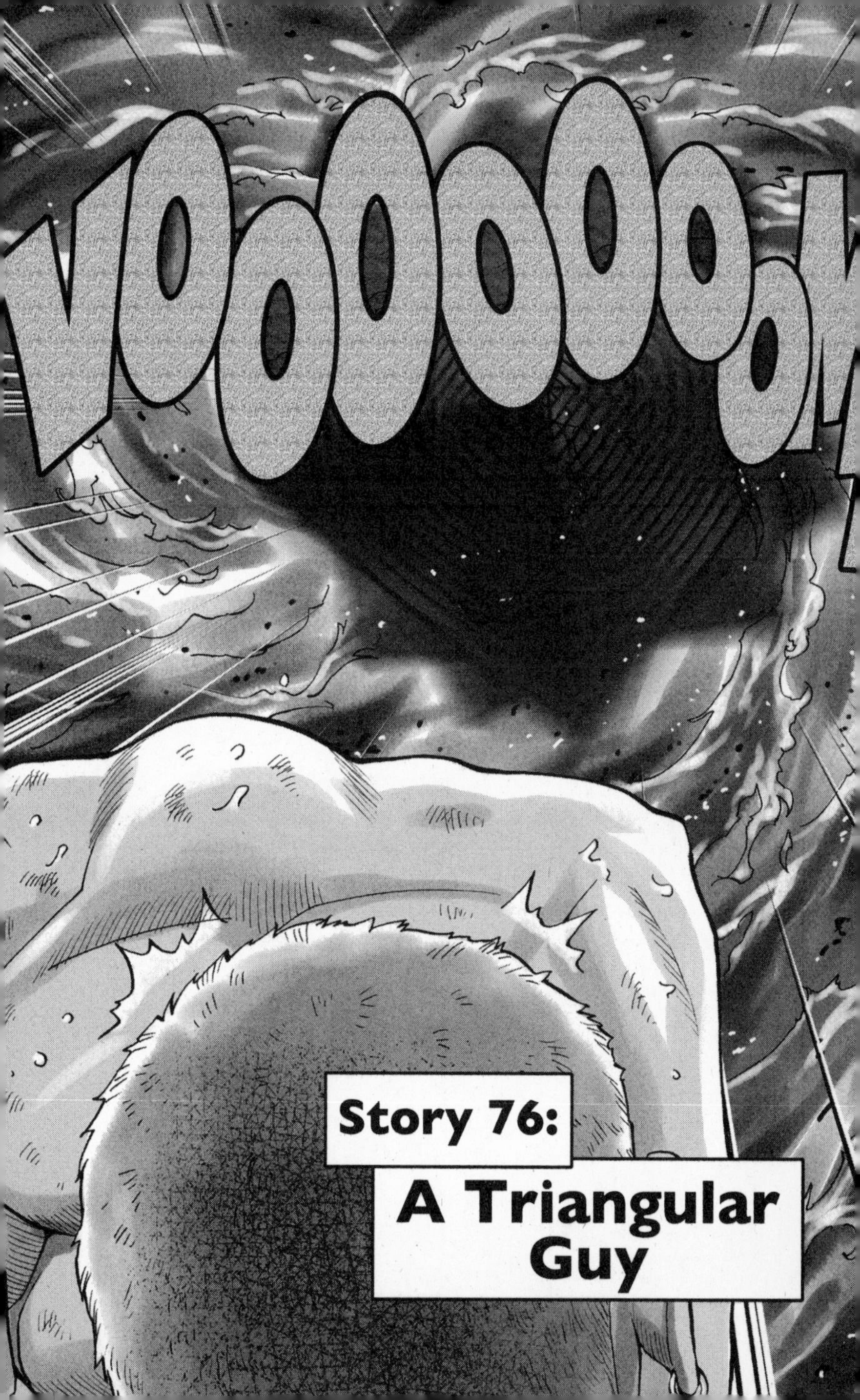
VOOOOOOM
Story 76:
A Triangular Guy

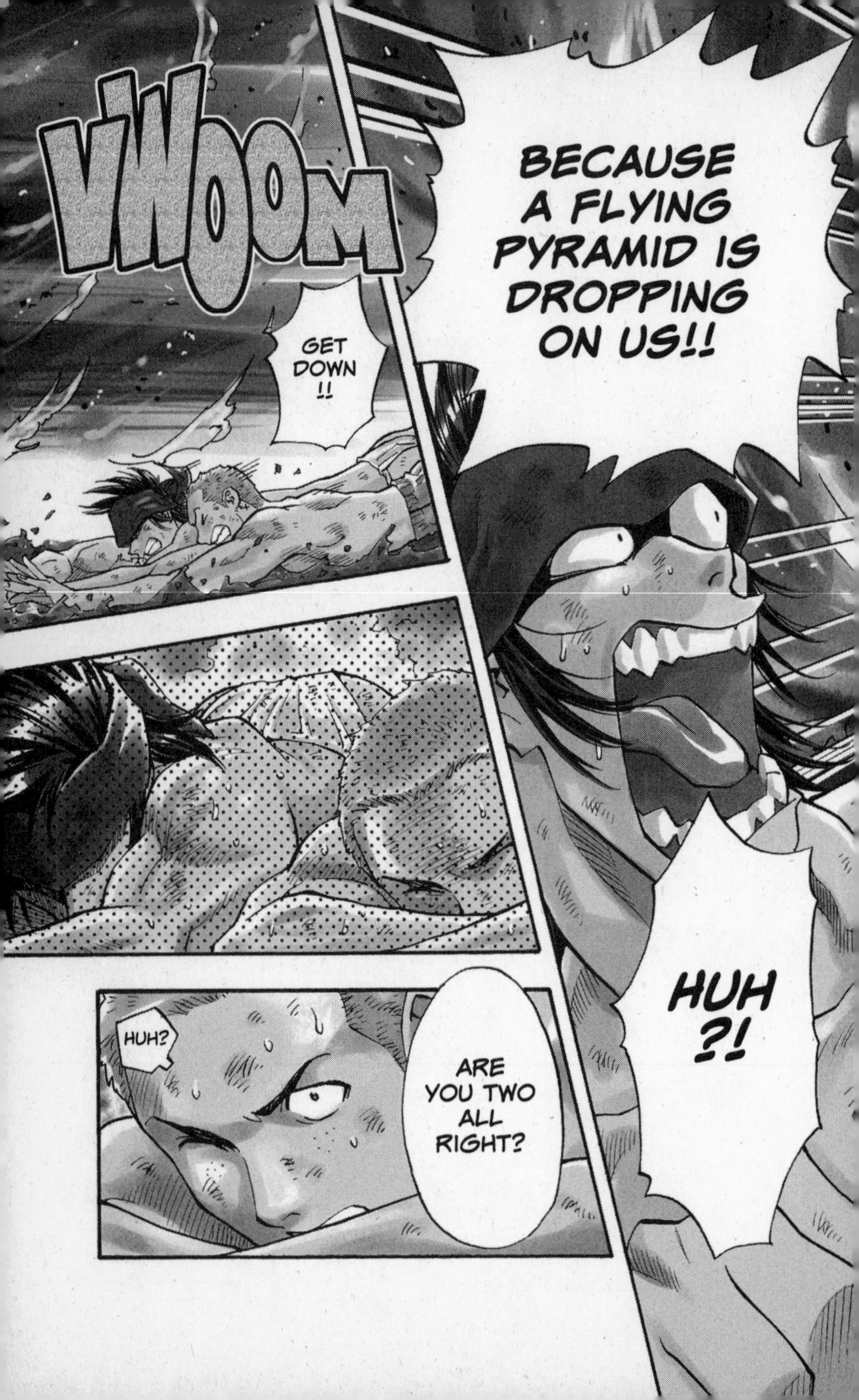
BECAUSE A FLYING PYRAMID IS DROPPING ON US!!
HUH ?!
VWOOM
GET DOWN !!
ARE YOU TWO ALL RIGHT?
HUH?

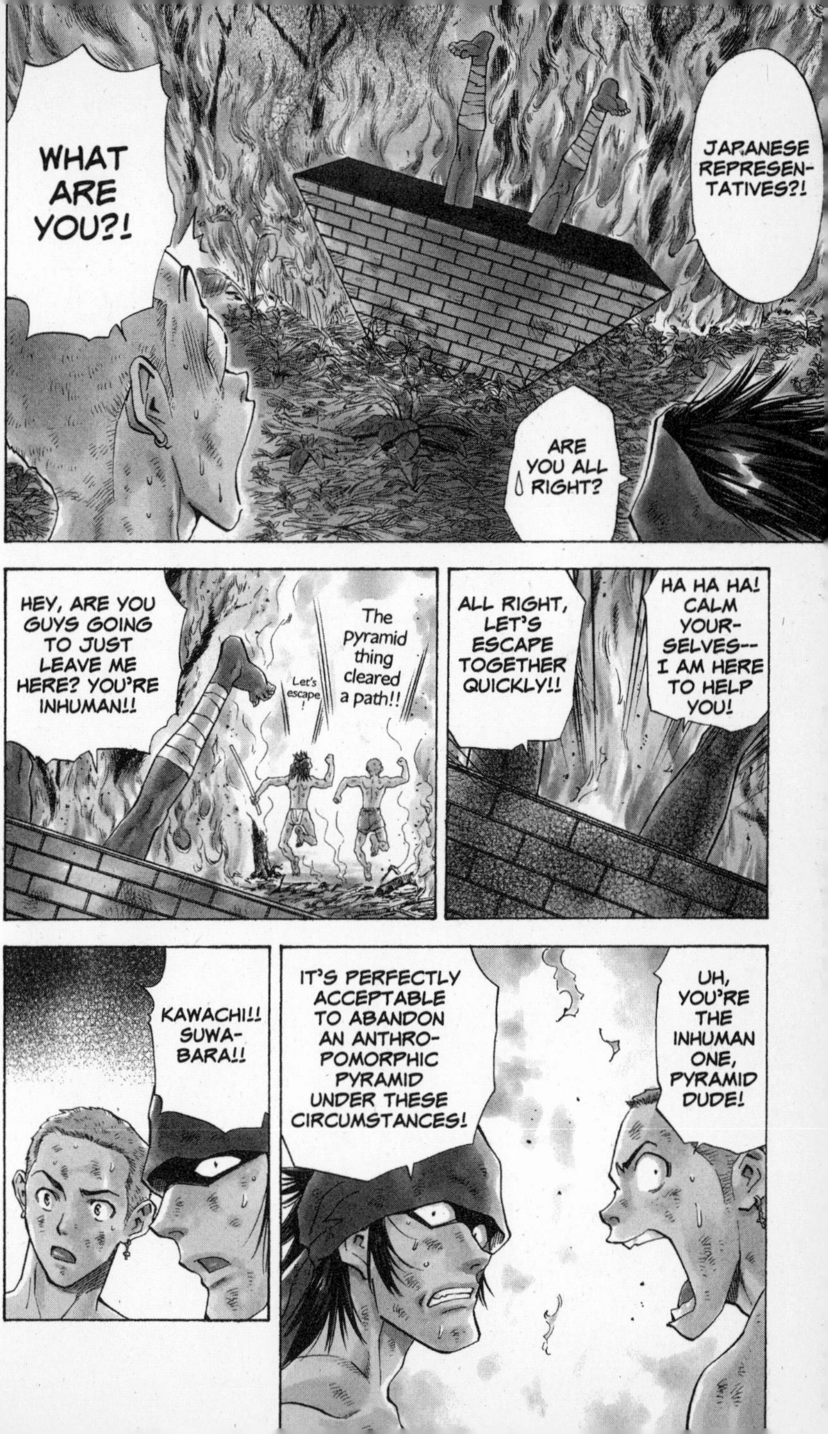
JAPANESE REPRESEN-TATIVES?!
ARE YOU ALL RIGHT?
WHAT ARE YOU?!
HA HA HA! CALM YOUR-SELVES-- I AM HERE TO HELP YOU!
ALL RIGHT, LET'S ESCAPE TOGETHER QUICKLY!!
The pyramid thing cleared a path!!
Let's escape!
HEY, ARE YOU GUYS GOING TO JUST LEAVE ME HERE? YOU'RE INHUMAN!!
UH, YOU'RE THE INHUMAN ONE, PYRAMID DUDE!
IT'S PERFECTLY ACCEPTABLE TO ABANDON AN ANTHRO-POMORPHIC PYRAMID UNDER THESE CIRCUMSTANCES!
KAWACHI!! SUWA-BARA!!

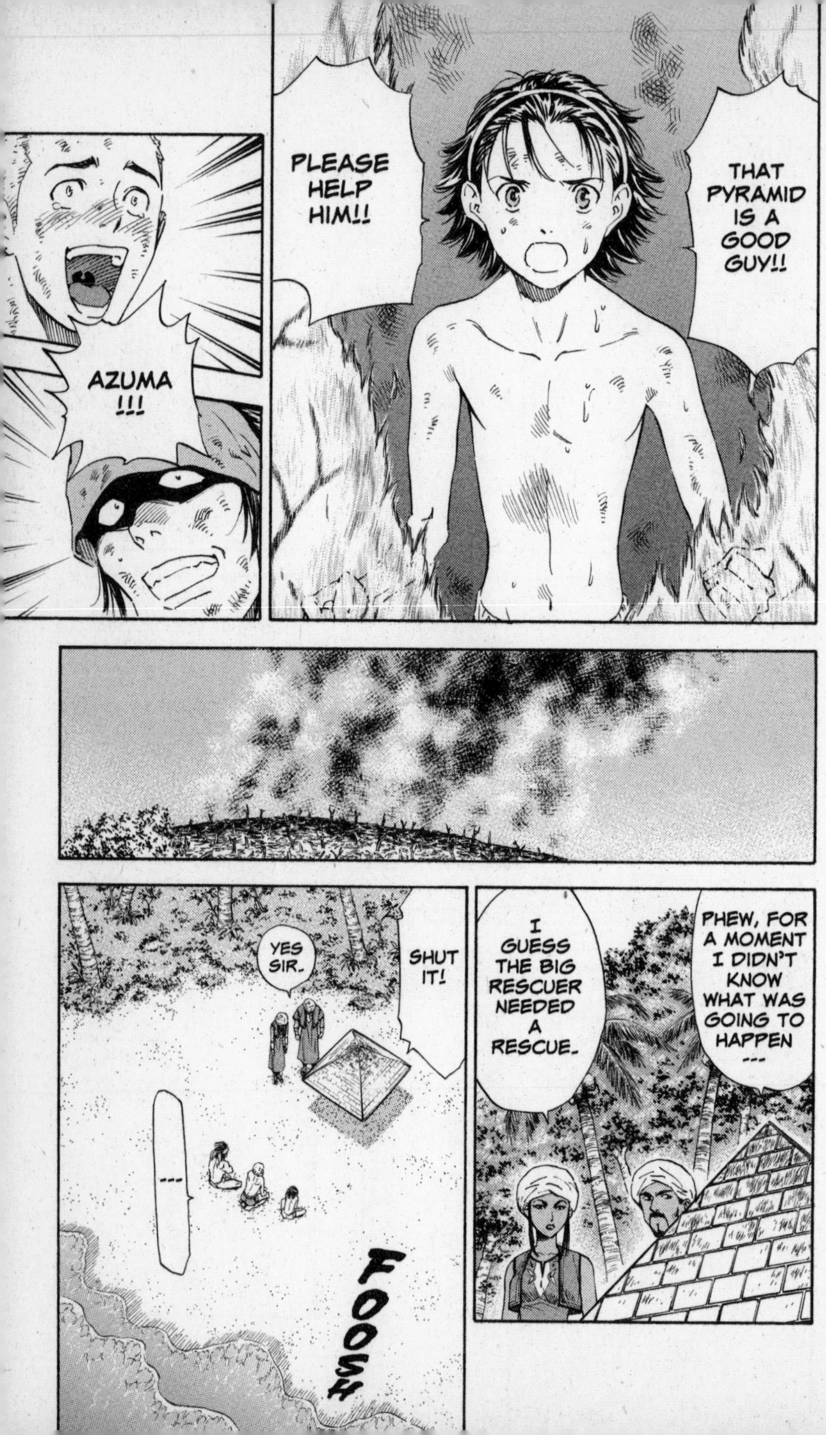

THAT PYRAMID IS A GOOD GUY!!
PLEASE HELP HIM!!
AZUMA !!!
PHEW, FOR A MOMENT I DIDN'T KNOW WHAT WAS GOING TO HAPPEN ---
I GUESS THE BIG RESCUER NEEDED A RESCUE.
SHUT IT!
YES SIR.
---
FOOSH

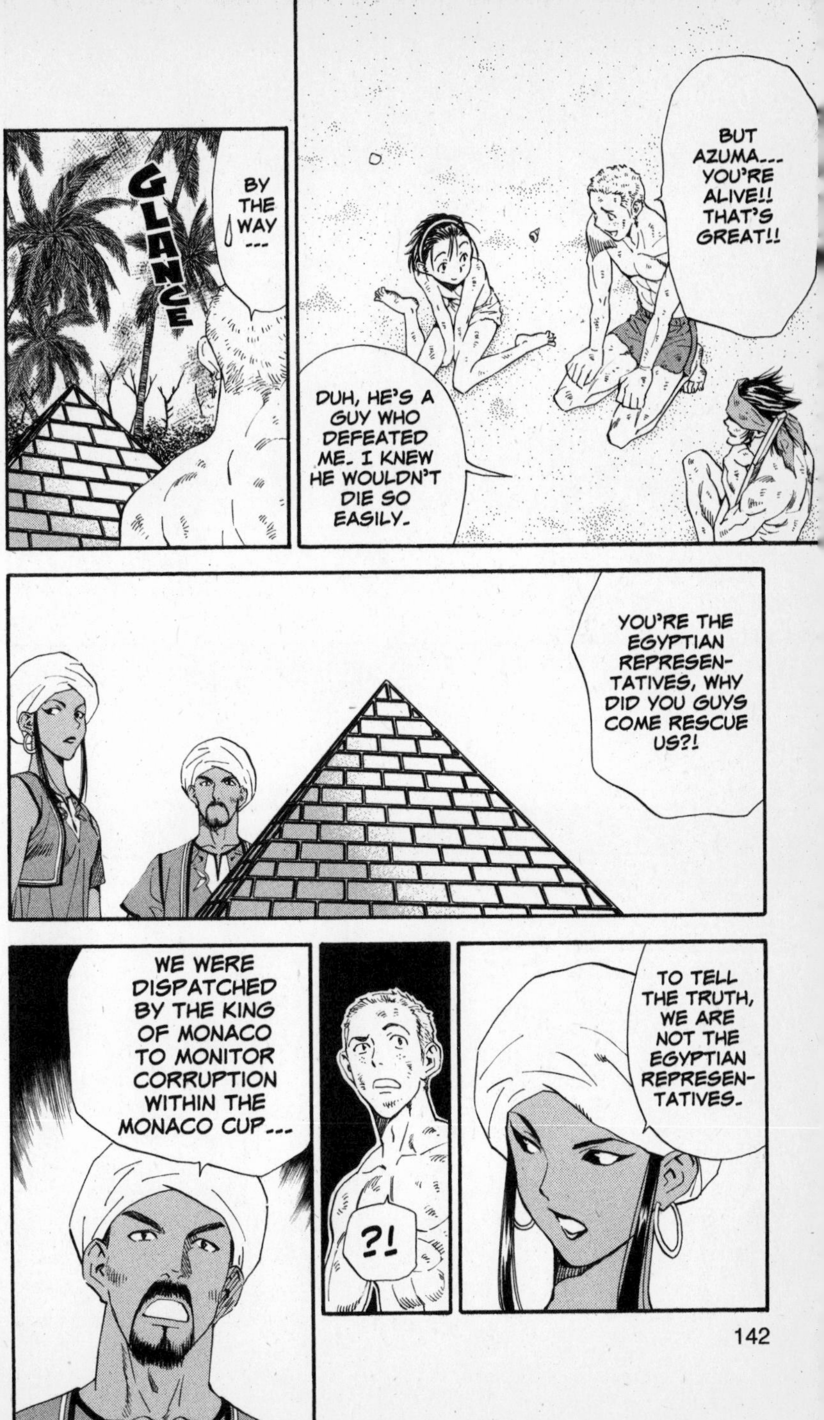
BUT AZUMA... YOU'RE ALIVE!! THAT'S GREAT!!
DUH, HE'S A GUY WHO DEFEATED ME. I KNEW HE WOULDN'T DIE SO EASILY.
BY THE WAY ---
GLANCE
YOU'RE THE EGYPTIAN REPRESEN-TATIVES, WHY DID YOU GUYS COME RESCUE US?!
TO TELL THE TRUTH, WE ARE NOT THE EGYPTIAN REPRESEN-TATIVES.
?!
WE WERE DISPATCHED BY THE KING OF MONACO TO MONITOR CORRUPTION WITHIN THE MONACO CUP...

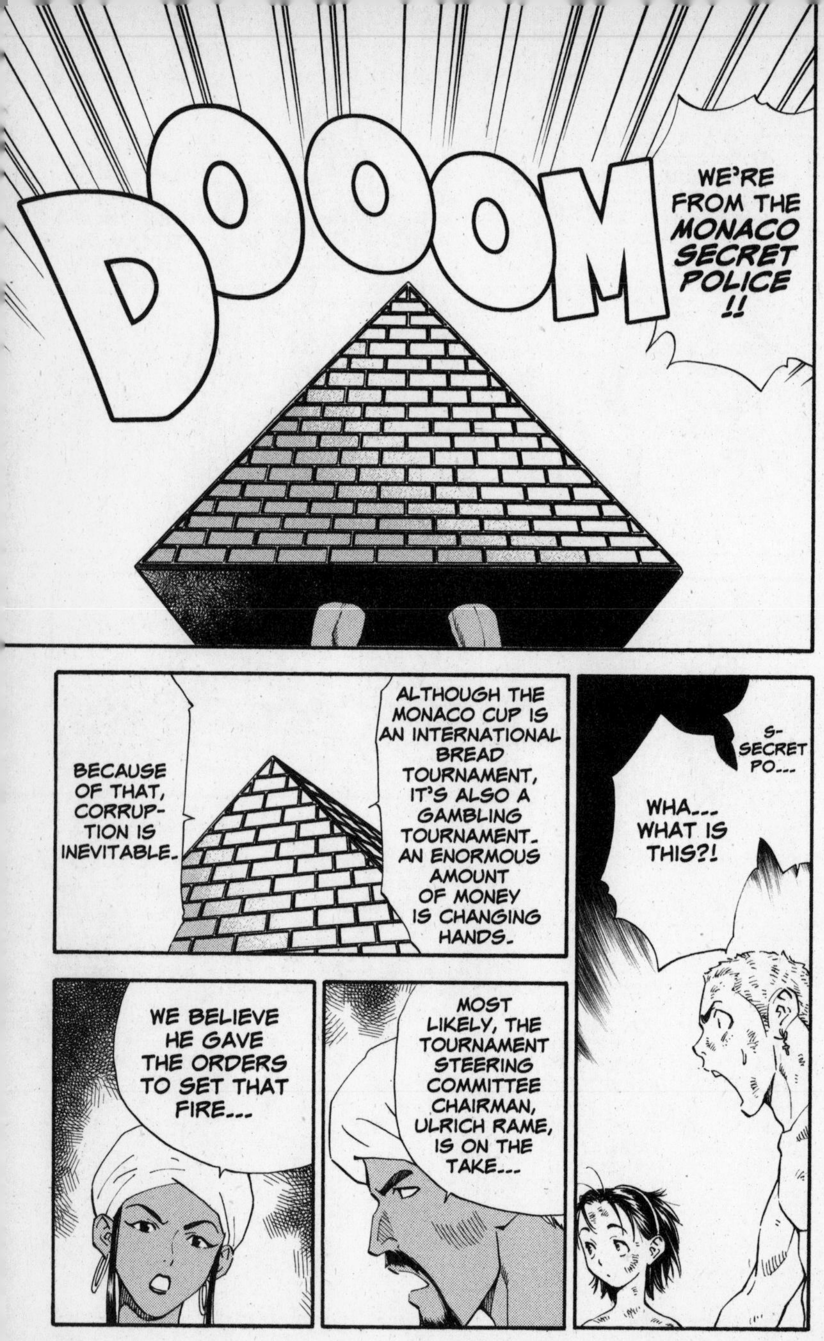
DOOOM
WE'RE FROM THE MONACO SECRET POLICE!!
S- SECRET PO...
WHA... WHAT IS THIS?!
ALTHOUGH THE MONACO CUP IS AN INTERNATIONAL BREAD TOURNAMENT, IT'S ALSO A GAMBLING TOURNAMENT. AN ENORMOUS AMOUNT OF MONEY IS CHANGING HANDS.
BECAUSE OF THAT, CORRUPTION IS INEVITABLE.
MOST LIKELY, THE TOURNAMENT STEERING COMMITTEE CHAIRMAN, ULRICH RAME, IS ON THE TAKE...
WE BELIEVE HE GAVE THE ORDERS TO SET THAT FIRE...

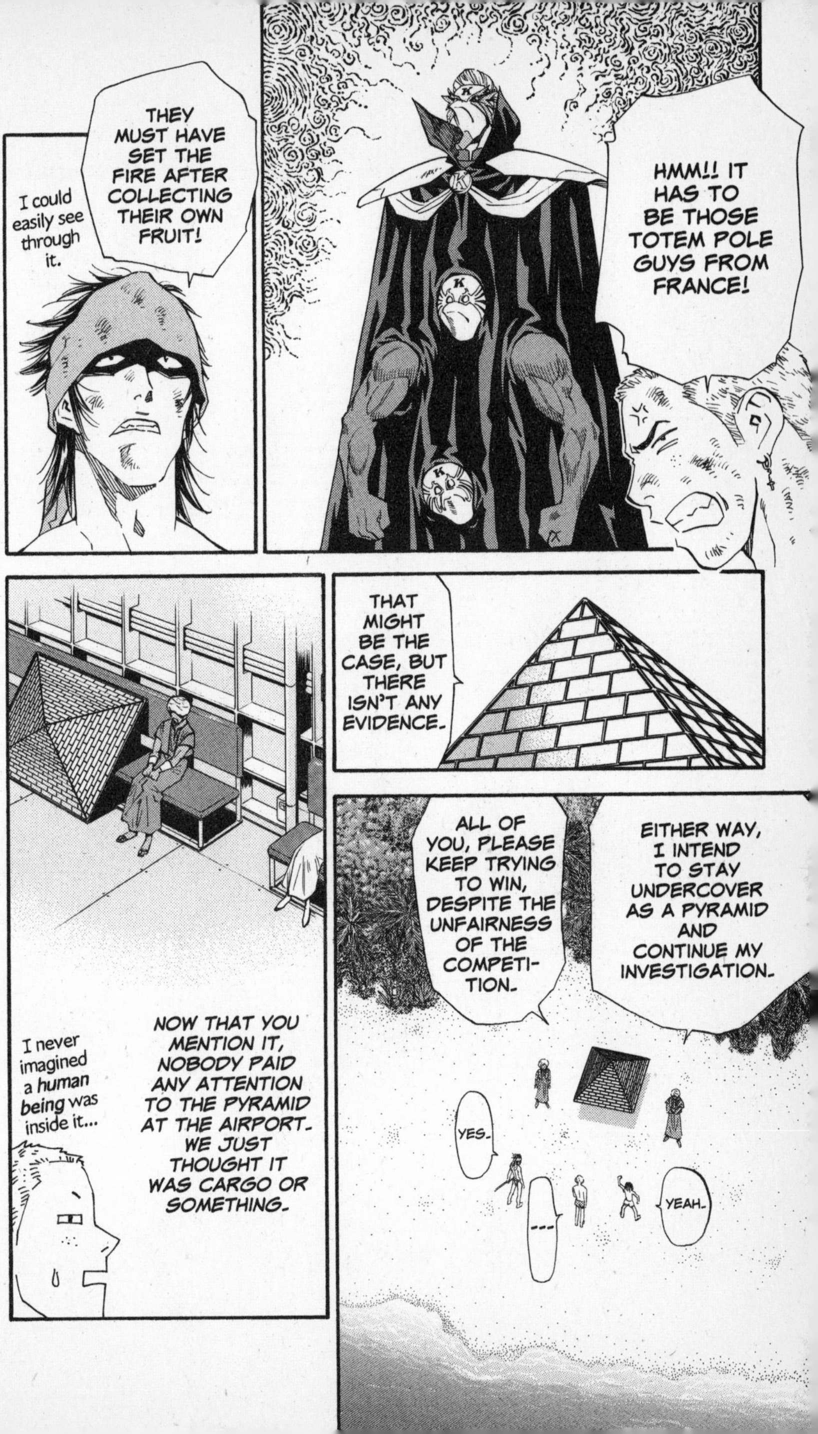
HMM!! IT HAS TO BE THOSE TOTEM POLE GUYS FROM FRANCE!
THEY MUST HAVE SET THE FIRE AFTER COLLECTING THEIR OWN FRUIT!
I could easily see through it.
THAT MIGHT BE THE CASE, BUT THERE ISN'T ANY EVIDENCE.
EITHER WAY, I INTEND TO STAY UNDERCOVER AS A PYRAMID AND CONTINUE MY INVESTIGATION.
ALL OF YOU, PLEASE KEEP TRYING TO WIN, DESPITE THE UNFAIRNESS OF THE COMPETI-TION.
YEAH.
...
YES.
NOW THAT YOU MENTION IT, NOBODY PAID ANY ATTENTION TO THE PYRAMID AT THE AIRPORT. WE JUST THOUGHT IT WAS CARGO OR SOMETHING.
I never imagined a human being was inside it...

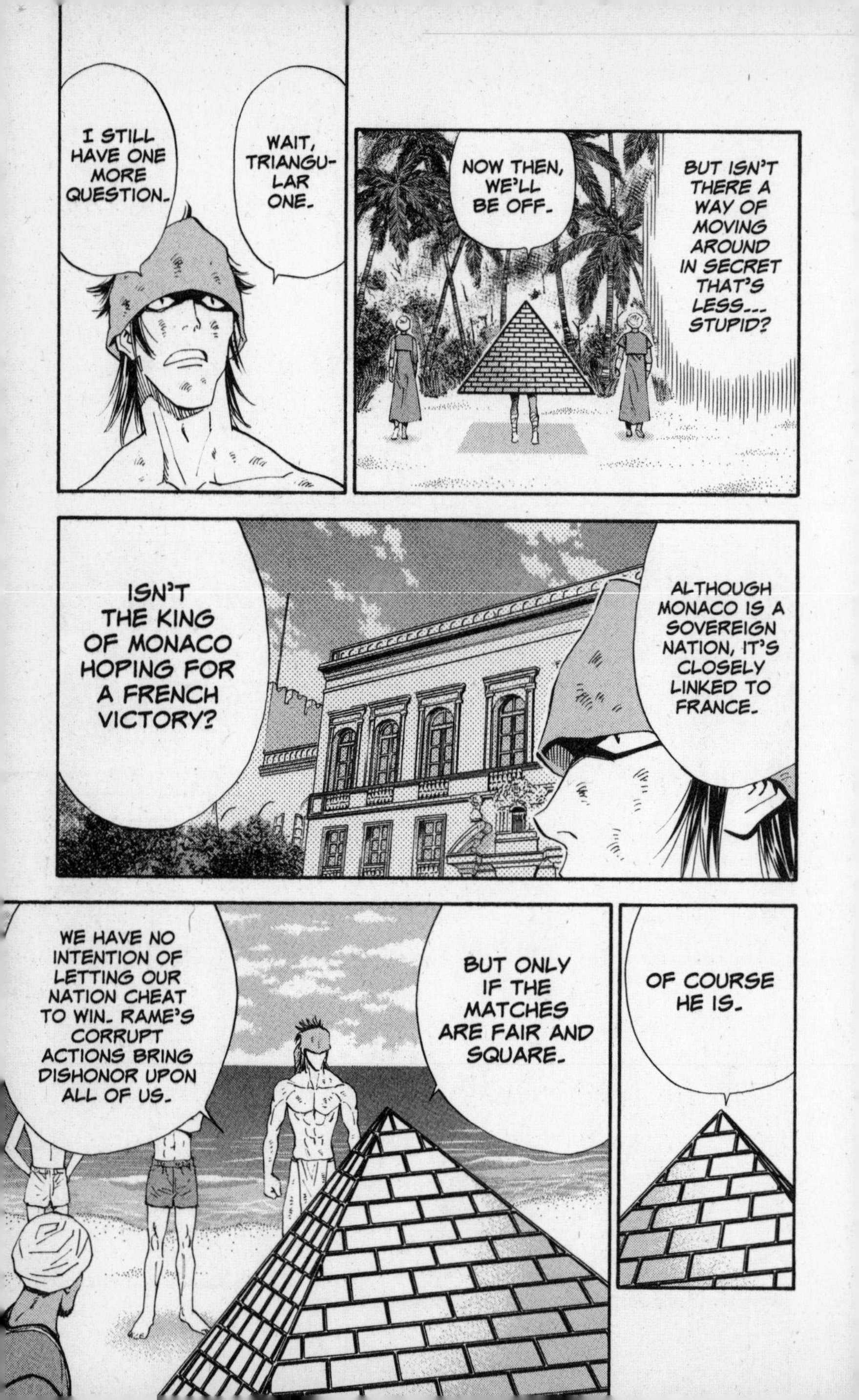
BUT ISN'T THERE A WAY OF MOVING AROUND IN SECRET THAT'S LESS... STUPID?
NOW THEN, WE'LL BE OFF.
WAIT, TRIANGU-LAR ONE.
I STILL HAVE ONE MORE QUESTION.
ALTHOUGH MONACO IS A SOVEREIGN NATION, IT'S CLOSELY LINKED TO FRANCE.
ISN'T THE KING OF MONACO HOPING FOR A FRENCH VICTORY?
OF COURSE HE IS.
BUT ONLY IF THE MATCHES ARE FAIR AND SQUARE.
WE HAVE NO INTENTION OF LETTING OUR NATION CHEAT TO WIN. RAME'S CORRUPT ACTIONS BRING DISHONOR UPON ALL OF US.

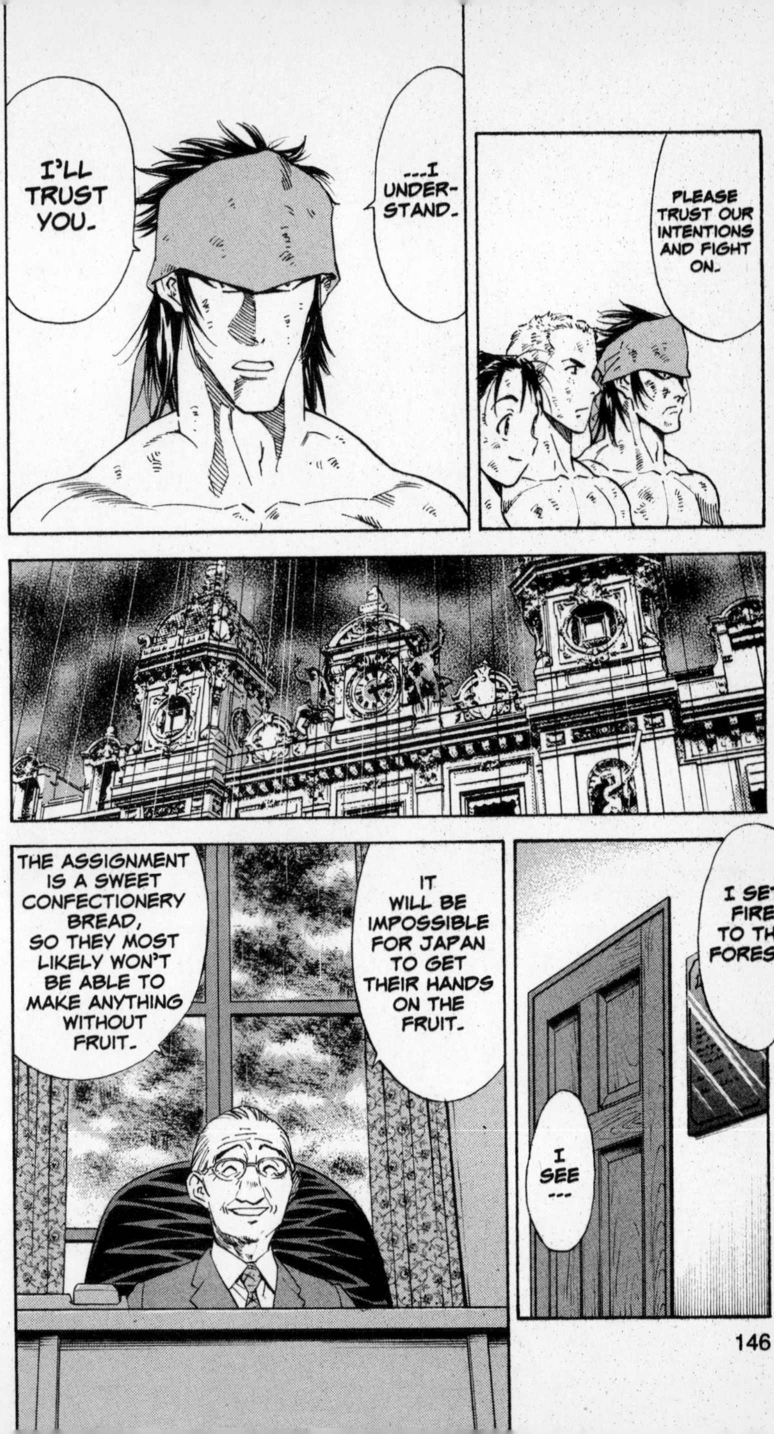
PLEASE TRUST OUR INTENTIONS AND FIGHT ON.
...I UNDER-STAND.
I'LL TRUST YOU.
I SET FIRE TO THE FOREST.
I SEE...
IT WILL BE IMPOSSIBLE FOR JAPAN TO GET THEIR HANDS ON THE FRUIT.
THE ASSIGNMENT IS A SWEET CONFECTIONERY BREAD, SO THEY MOST LIKELY WON'T BE ABLE TO MAKE ANYTHING WITHOUT FRUIT.

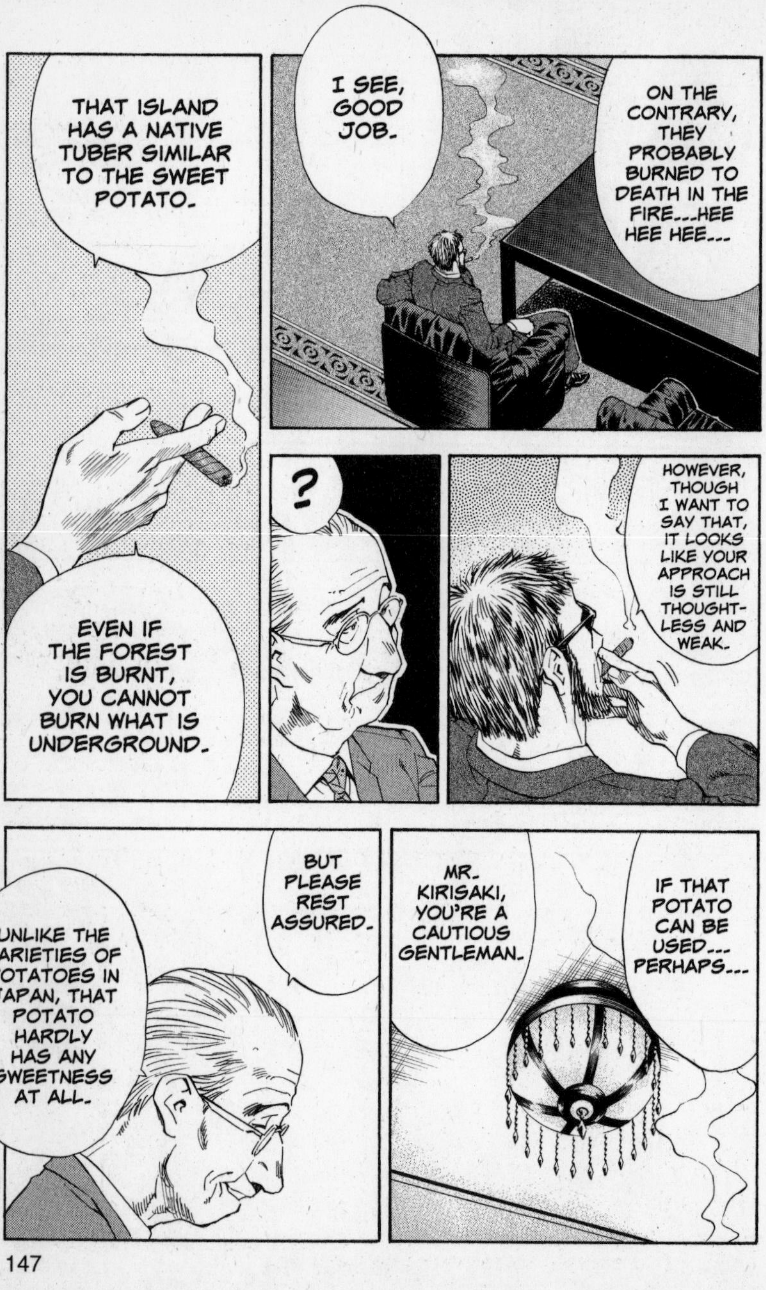
ON THE CONTRARY, THEY PROBABLY BURNED TO DEATH IN THE FIRE...HEE HEE HEE...
I SEE, GOOD JOB.
HOWEVER, THOUGH I WANT TO SAY THAT, IT LOOKS LIKE YOUR APPROACH IS STILL THOUGHTLESS AND WEAK.
?
THAT ISLAND HAS A NATIVE TUBER SIMILAR TO THE SWEET POTATO.
EVEN IF THE FOREST IS BURNT, YOU CANNOT BURN WHAT IS UNDERGROUND.
IF THAT POTATO CAN BE USED... PERHAPS...
MR. KIRISAKI, YOU'RE A CAUTIOUS GENTLEMAN.
BUT PLEASE REST ASSURED.
UNLIKE THE VARIETIES OF POTATOES IN JAPAN, THAT POTATO HARDLY HAS ANY SWEETNESS AT ALL.

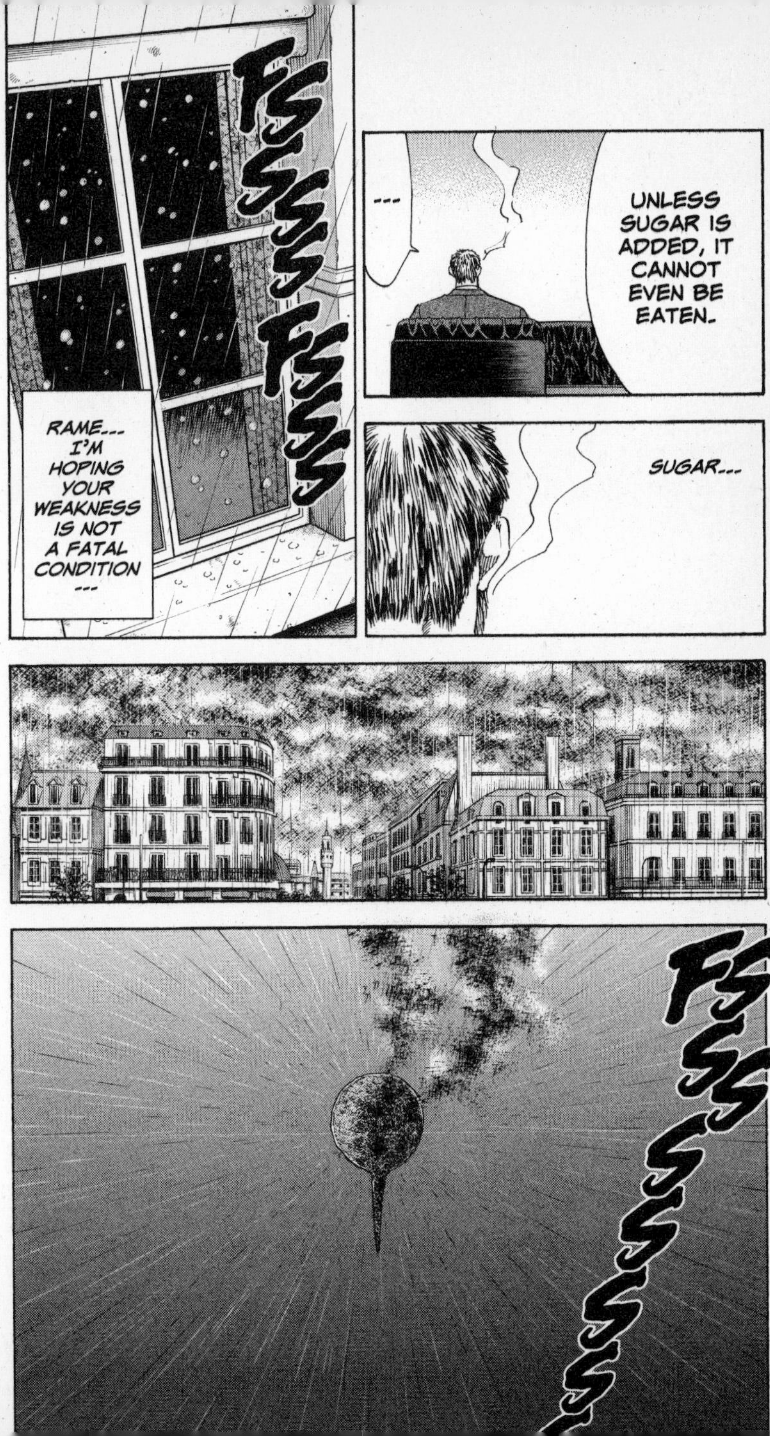
UNLESS SUGAR IS ADDED, IT CANNOT EVEN BE EATEN.
...
SUGAR...
FSSSS FSSSS
RAME... I'M HOPING YOUR WEAKNESS IS NOT A FATAL CONDITION ...
FSSSSSSSSS

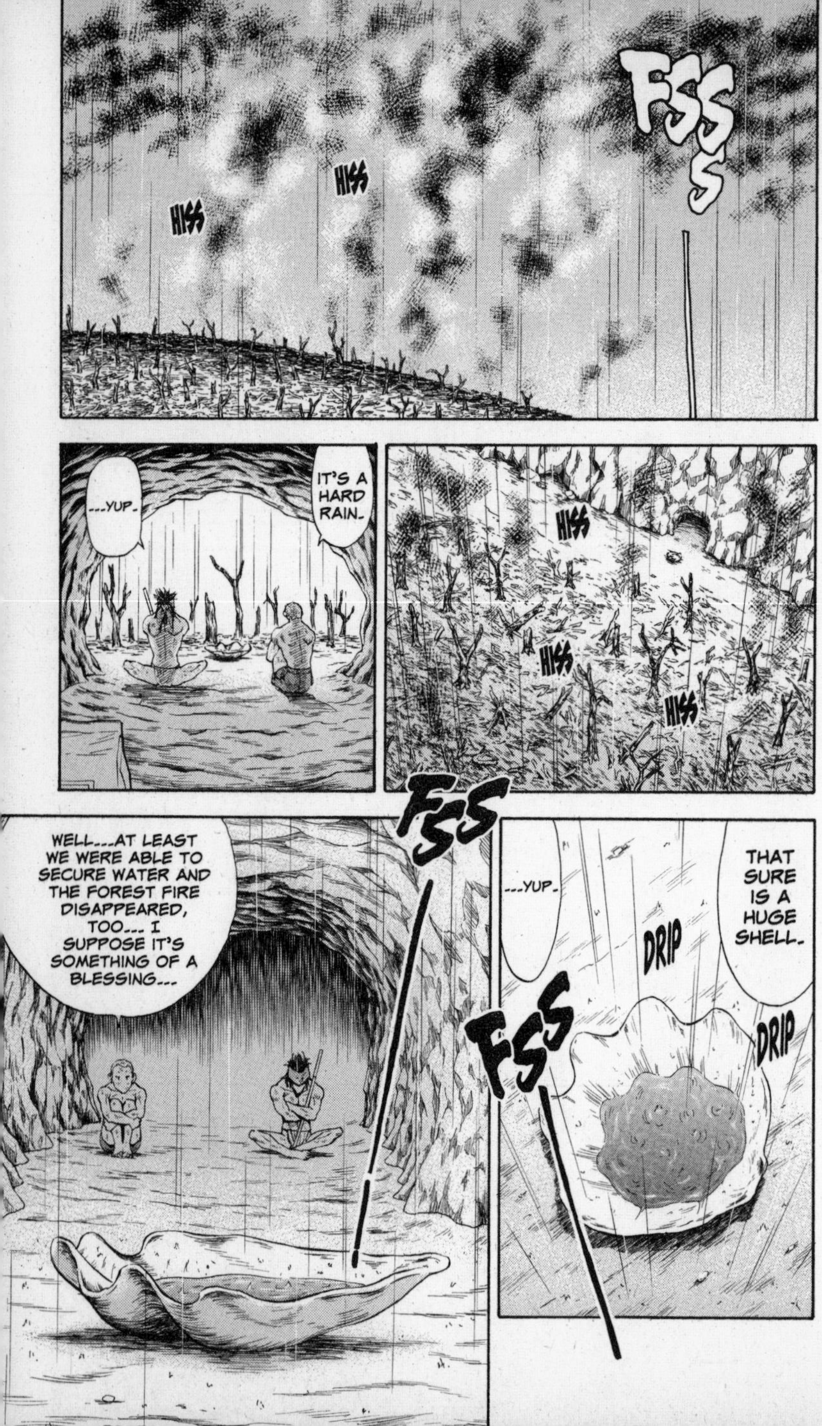
FSSS
HISS
HISS
HISS
HISS
HISS
IT'S A HARD RAIN.
...YUP.
THAT SURE IS A HUGE SHELL.
...YUP.
DRIP
DRIP
FSS
FSS
WELL...AT LEAST WE WERE ABLE TO SECURE WATER AND THE FOREST FIRE DISAPPEARED, TOO... I SUPPOSE IT'S SOMETHING OF A BLESSING...

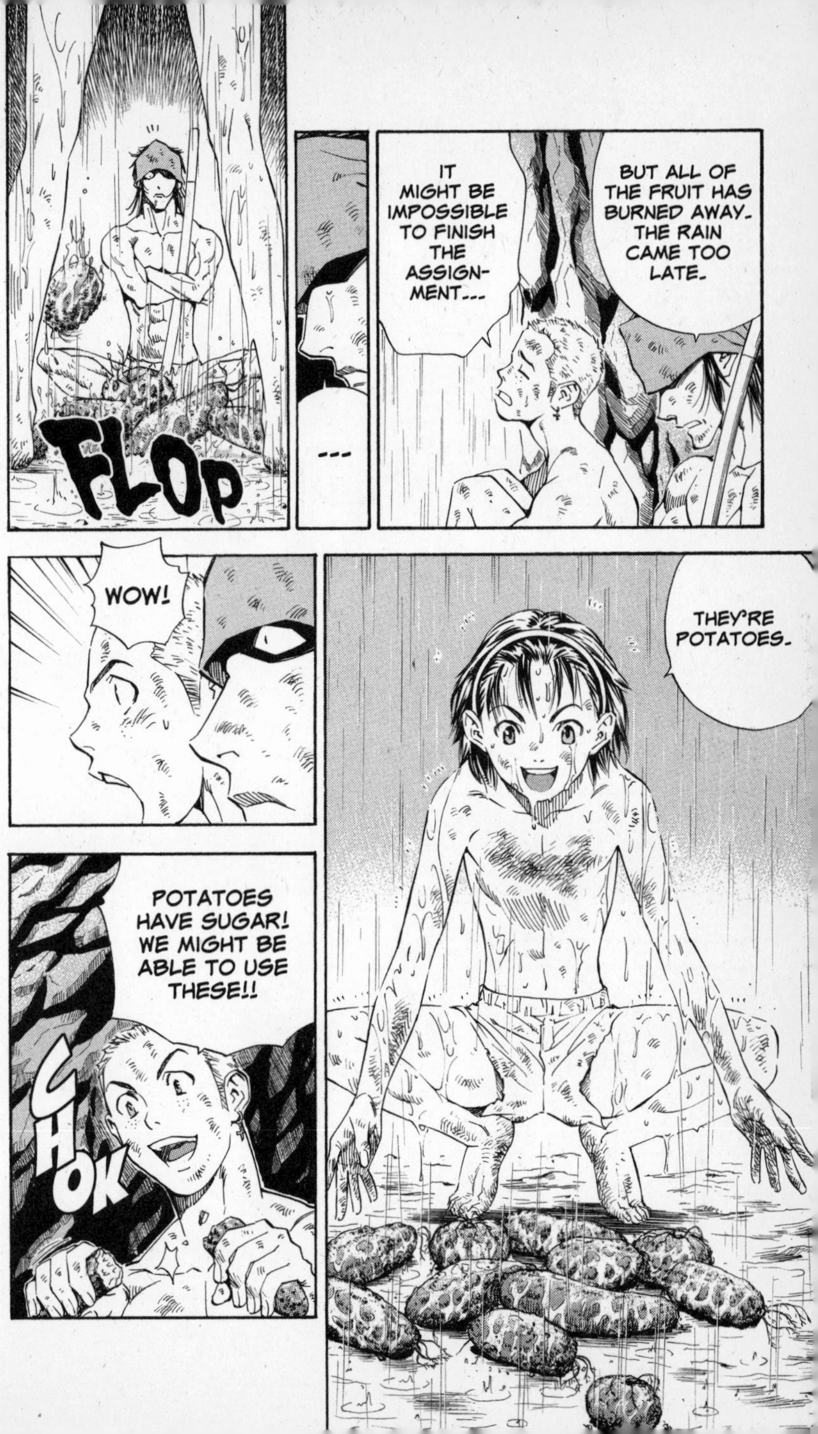
BUT ALL OF THE FRUIT HAS BURNED AWAY. THE RAIN CAME TOO LATE.
IT MIGHT BE IMPOSSIBLE TO FINISH THE ASSIGNMENT...
...
FLOP
THEY'RE POTATOES.
WOW!
POTATOES HAVE SUGAR! WE MIGHT BE ABLE TO USE THESE!!
CHOK

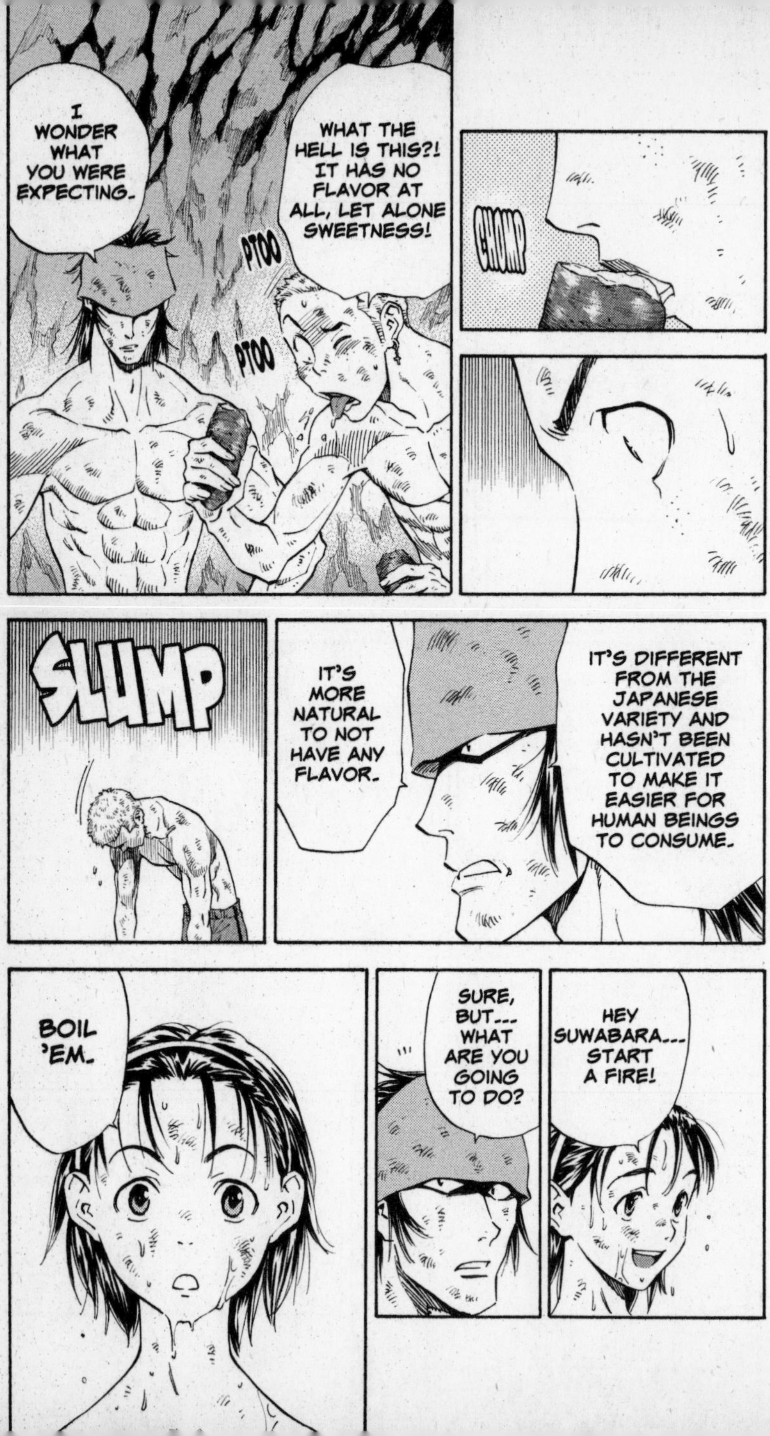
CHOMP
WHAT THE HELL IS THIS?! IT HAS NO FLAVOR AT ALL, LET ALONE SWEETNESS!
PTOO
PTOO
I WONDER WHAT YOU WERE EXPECTING.
IT'S DIFFERENT FROM THE JAPANESE VARIETY AND HASN'T BEEN CULTIVATED TO MAKE IT EASIER FOR HUMAN BEINGS TO CONSUME.
IT'S MORE NATURAL TO NOT HAVE ANY FLAVOR.
SLUMP
HEY SUWABARA... START A FIRE!
SURE, BUT... WHAT ARE YOU GOING TO DO?
BOIL 'EM.

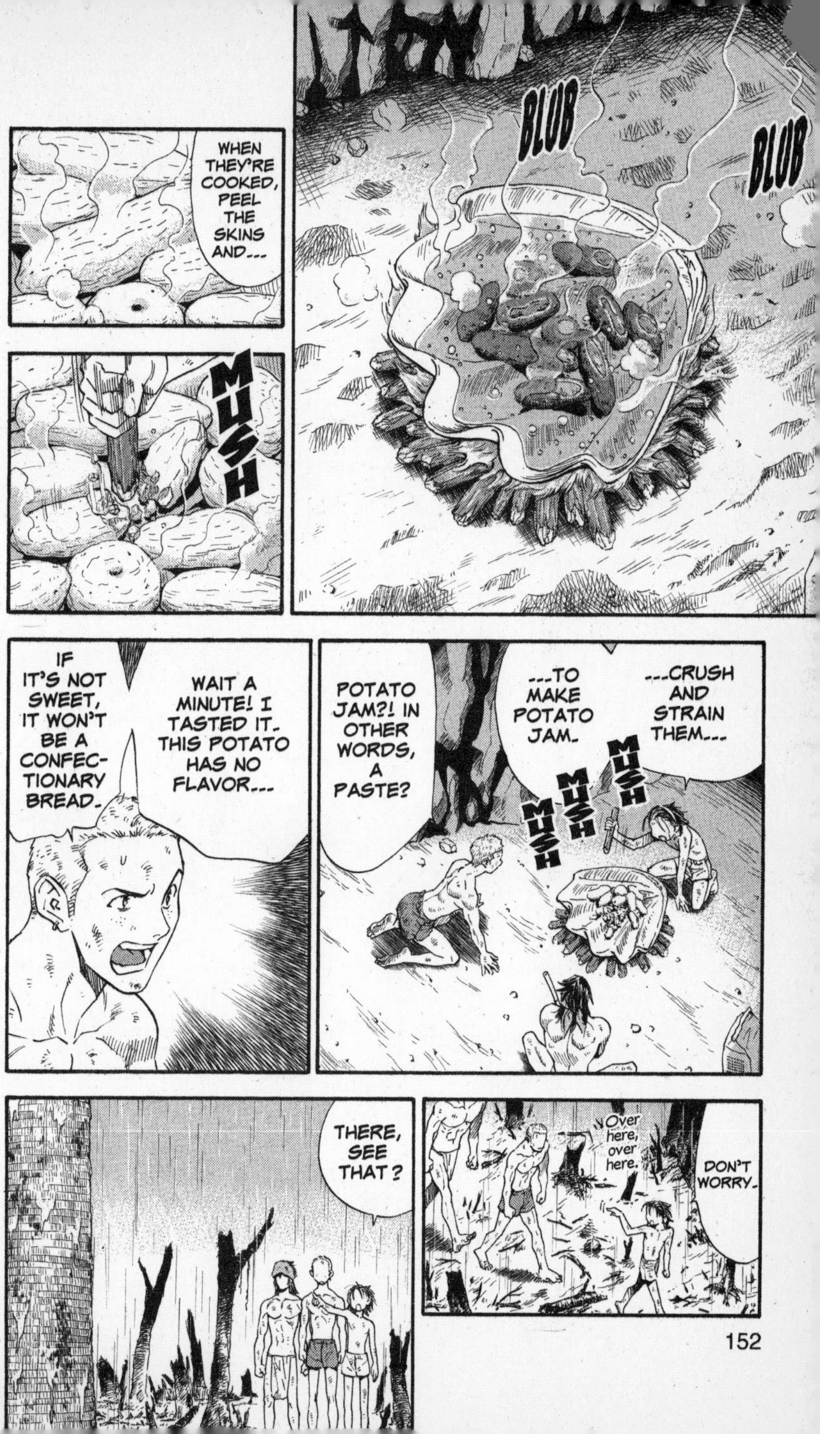
BLUB
BLUB
WHEN THEY'RE COOKED, PEEL THE SKINS AND...
MUSH
...CRUSH AND STRAIN THEM...
...TO MAKE POTATO JAM.
MUSH
MUSH
MUSH
POTATO JAM?! IN OTHER WORDS, A PASTE?
WAIT A MINUTE! I TASTED IT. THIS POTATO HAS NO FLAVOR...
IF IT'S NOT SWEET, IT WON'T BE A CONFECTIONARY BREAD.
DON'T WORRY.
Over here, over here.
THERE, SEE THAT?

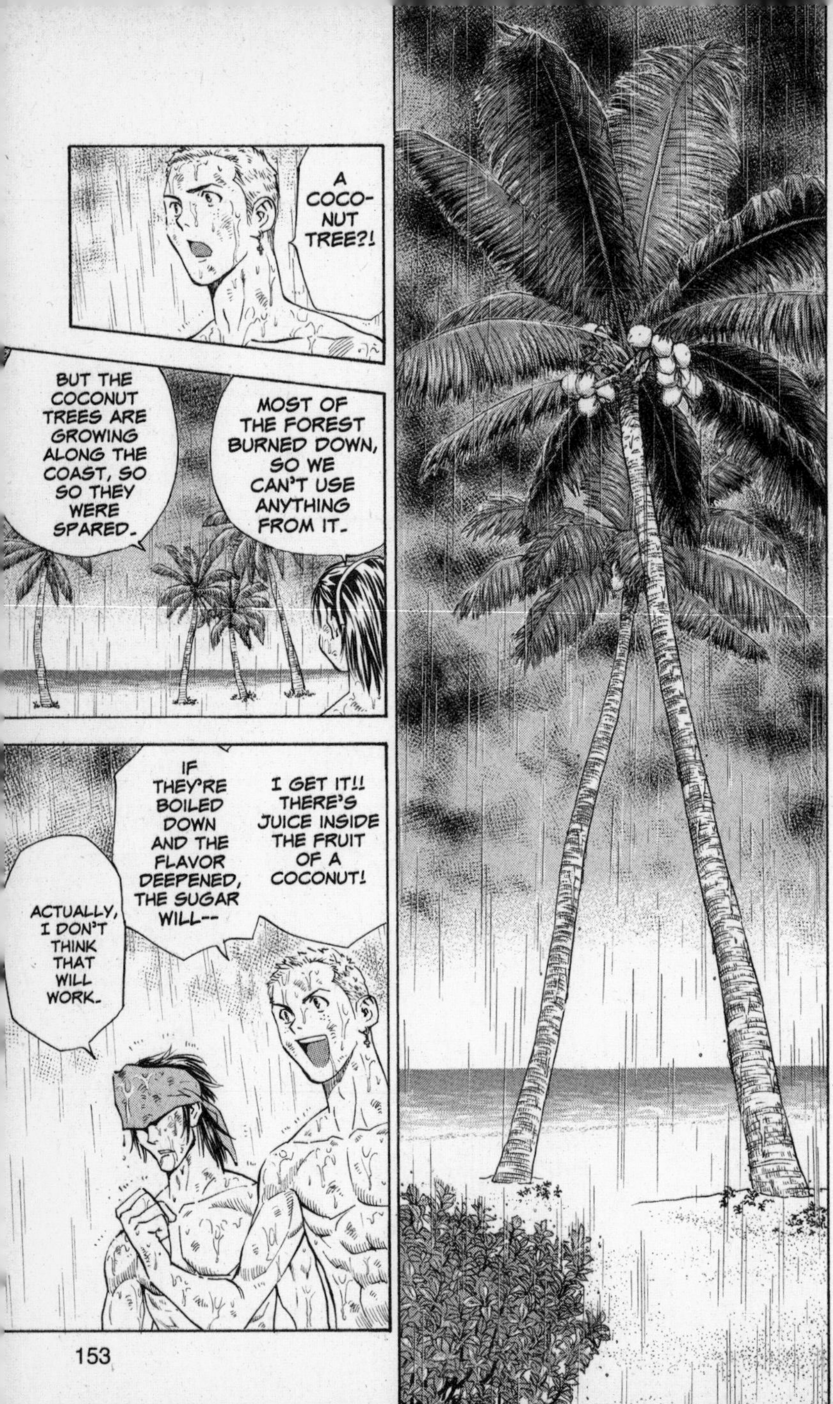
A COCO-NUT TREE?!
MOST OF THE FOREST BURNED DOWN, SO WE CAN'T USE ANYTHING FROM IT.
BUT THE COCONUT TREES ARE GROWING ALONG THE COAST, SO SO THEY WERE SPARED.
I GET IT!! THERE'S JUICE INSIDE THE FRUIT OF A COCONUT!
IF THEY'RE BOILED DOWN AND THE FLAVOR DEEPENED, THE SUGAR WILL--
ACTUALLY, I DON'T THINK THAT WILL WORK.

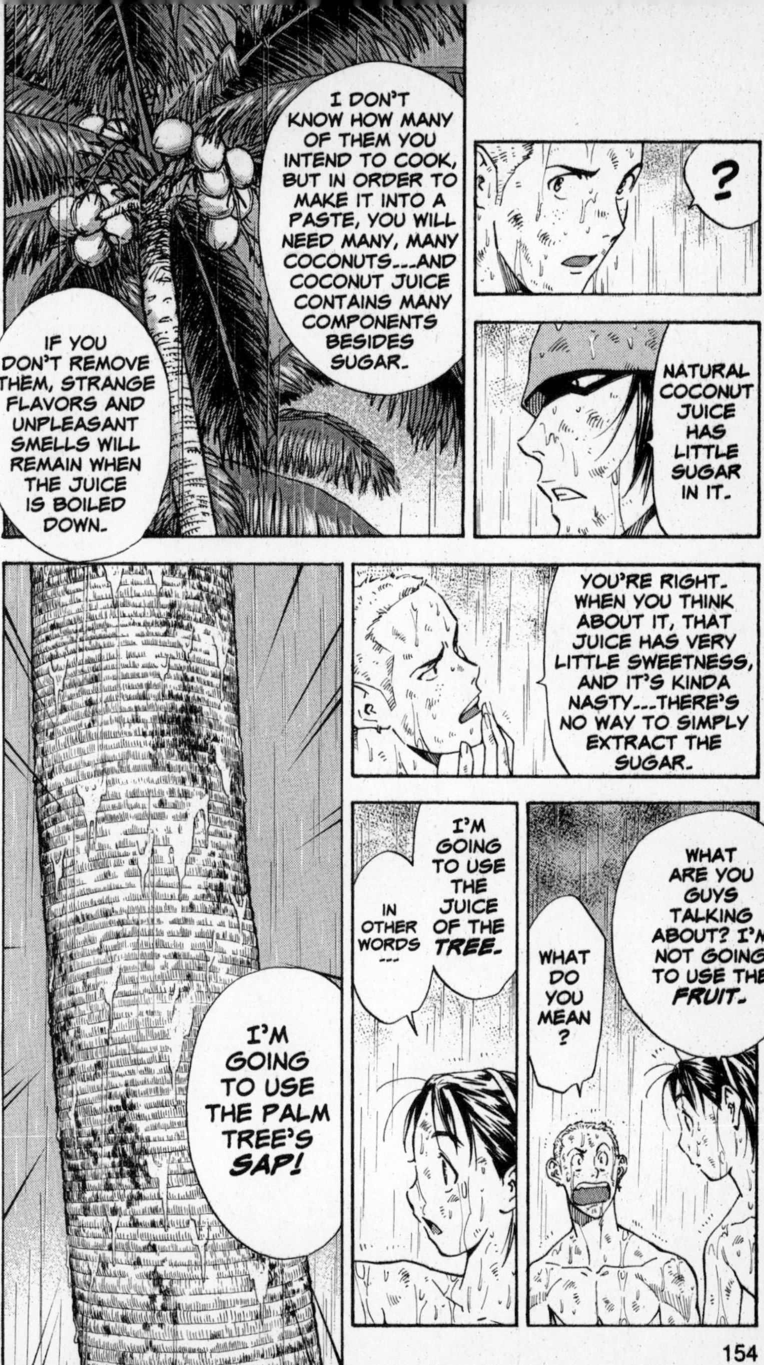
?
NATURAL COCONUT JUICE HAS LITTLE SUGAR IN IT.
I DON'T KNOW HOW MANY OF THEM YOU INTEND TO COOK, BUT IN ORDER TO MAKE IT INTO A PASTE, YOU WILL NEED MANY, MANY COCONUTS...AND COCONUT JUICE CONTAINS MANY COMPONENTS BESIDES SUGAR.
IF YOU DON'T REMOVE THEM, STRANGE FLAVORS AND UNPLEASANT SMELLS WILL REMAIN WHEN THE JUICE IS BOILED DOWN.
YOU'RE RIGHT. WHEN YOU THINK ABOUT IT, THAT JUICE HAS VERY LITTLE SWEETNESS, AND IT'S KINDA NASTY...THERE'S NO WAY TO SIMPLY EXTRACT THE SUGAR.
WHAT ARE YOU GUYS TALKING ABOUT? I'M NOT GOING TO USE THE *FRUIT*.
WHAT DO YOU MEAN?
I'M GOING TO USE THE JUICE OF THE *TREE*.
IN OTHER WORDS...
I'M GOING TO USE THE PALM TREE'S *SAP!*

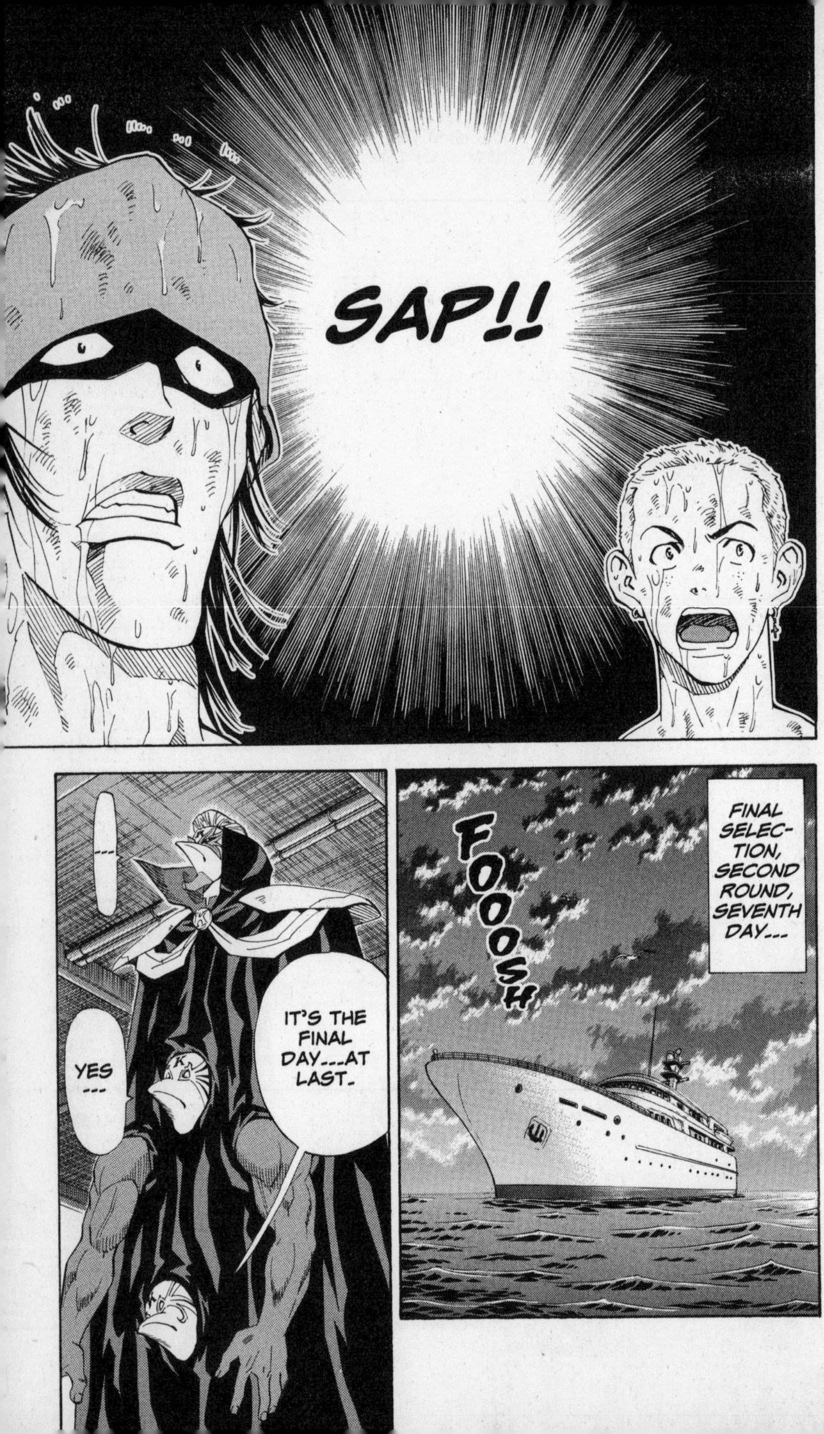
SAP!!
FINAL SELECTION, SECOND ROUND, SEVENTH DAY...
FOOOSH
...
IT'S THE FINAL DAY...AT LAST.
YES...

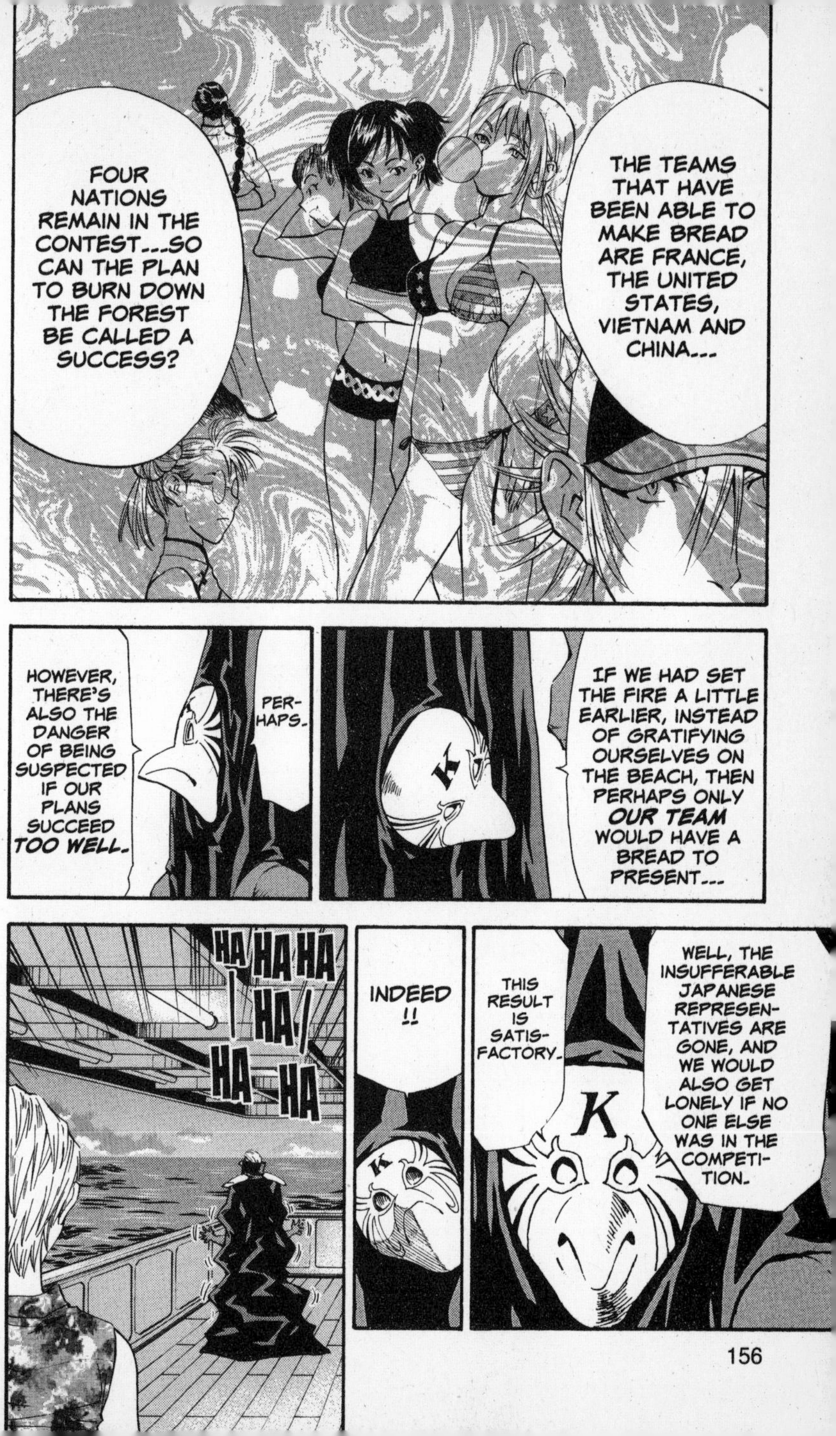
THE TEAMS THAT HAVE BEEN ABLE TO MAKE BREAD ARE FRANCE, THE UNITED STATES, VIETNAM AND CHINA...
FOUR NATIONS REMAIN IN THE CONTEST...SO CAN THE PLAN TO BURN DOWN THE FOREST BE CALLED A SUCCESS?
IF WE HAD SET THE FIRE A LITTLE EARLIER, INSTEAD OF GRATIFYING OURSELVES ON THE BEACH, THEN PERHAPS ONLY *OUR TEAM* WOULD HAVE A BREAD TO PRESENT...
PER-HAPS.
HOWEVER, THERE'S ALSO THE DANGER OF BEING SUSPECTED IF OUR PLANS SUCCEED *TOO WELL.*
WELL, THE INSUFFERABLE JAPANESE REPRESEN-TATIVES ARE GONE, AND WE WOULD ALSO GET LONELY IF NO ONE ELSE WAS IN THE COMPETI-TION.
THIS RESULT IS SATIS-FACTORY.
INDEED!!
HA HA HA HA! HA! HA HA

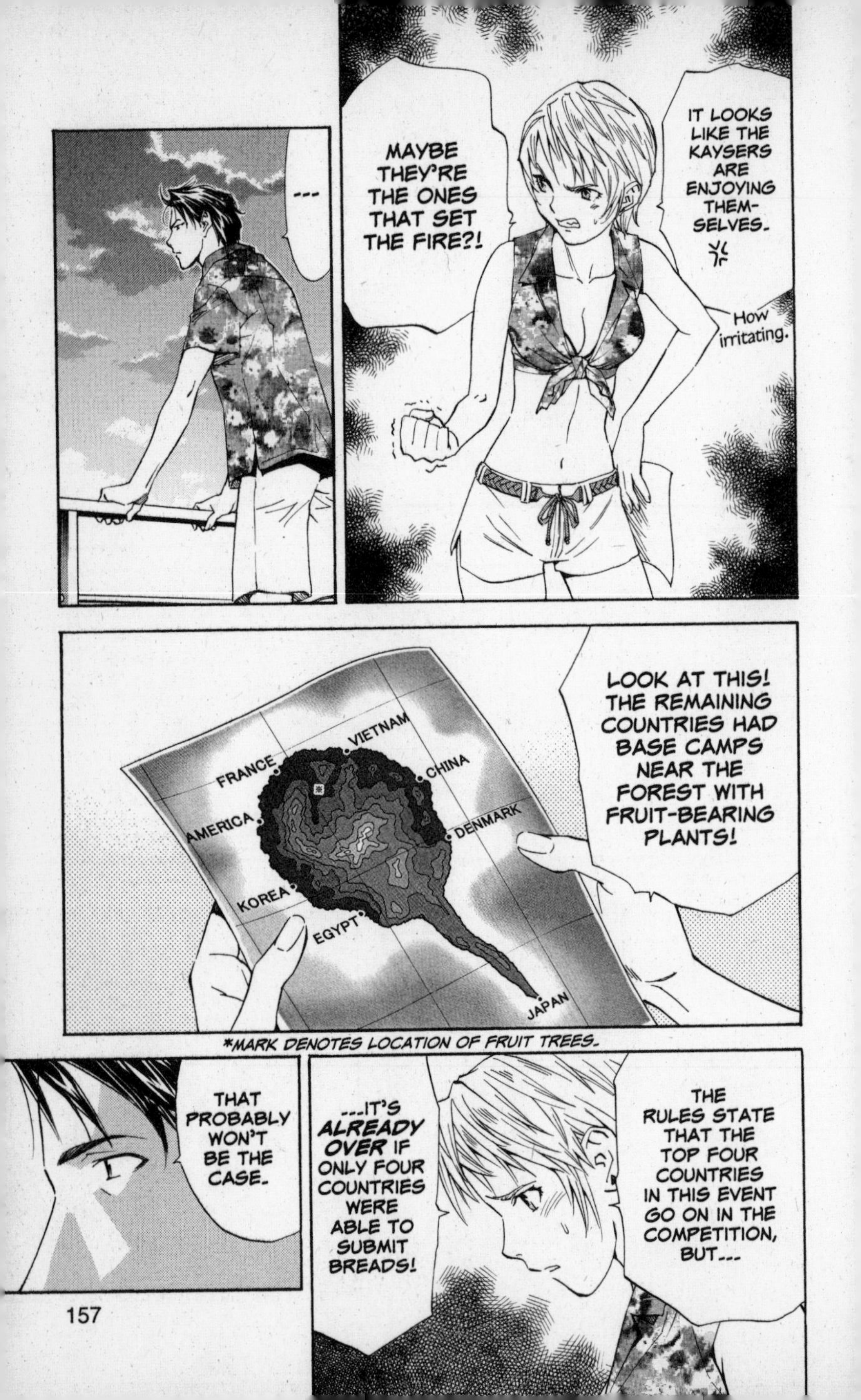
IT LOOKS LIKE THE KAYSERS ARE ENJOYING THEMSELVES.
How irritating.
MAYBE THEY'RE THE ONES THAT SET THE FIRE?!
...
LOOK AT THIS! THE REMAINING COUNTRIES HAD BASE CAMPS NEAR THE FOREST WITH FRUIT-BEARING PLANTS!
VIETNAM
FRANCE
CHINA
AMERICA
DENMARK
KOREA
EGYPT
JAPAN
*MARK DENOTES LOCATION OF FRUIT TREES.
THE RULES STATE THAT THE TOP FOUR COUNTRIES IN THIS EVENT GO ON IN THE COMPETITION, BUT...
...IT'S ALREADY OVER IF ONLY FOUR COUNTRIES WERE ABLE TO SUBMIT BREADS!
THAT PROBABLY WON'T BE THE CASE.

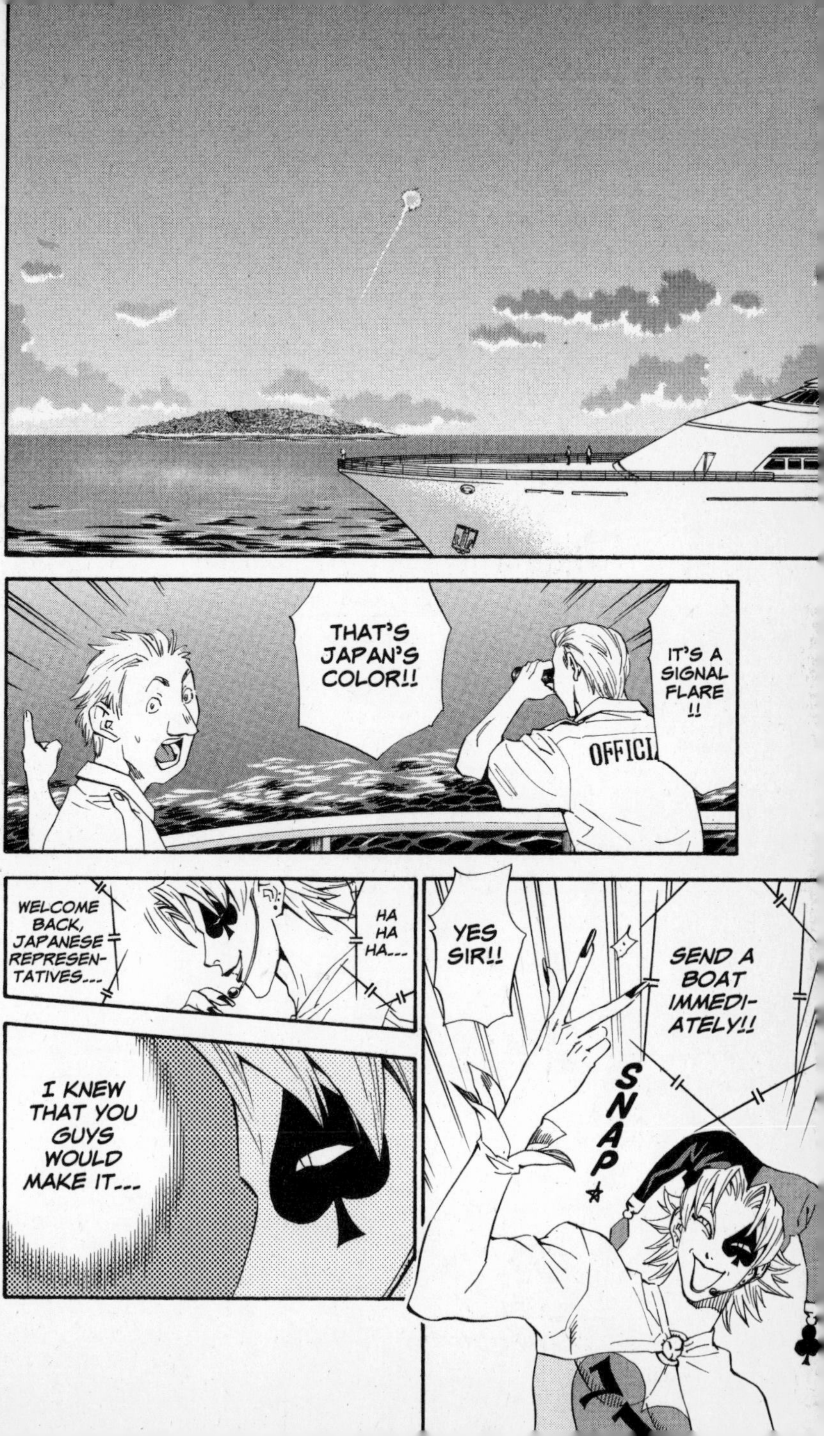
IT'S A SIGNAL FLARE!!
OFFICI
THAT'S JAPAN'S COLOR!!
SEND A BOAT IMMEDIATELY!!
YES SIR!!
SNAP
HA HA HA...
WELCOME BACK, JAPANESE REPRESENTATIVES...
I KNEW THAT YOU GUYS WOULD MAKE IT...

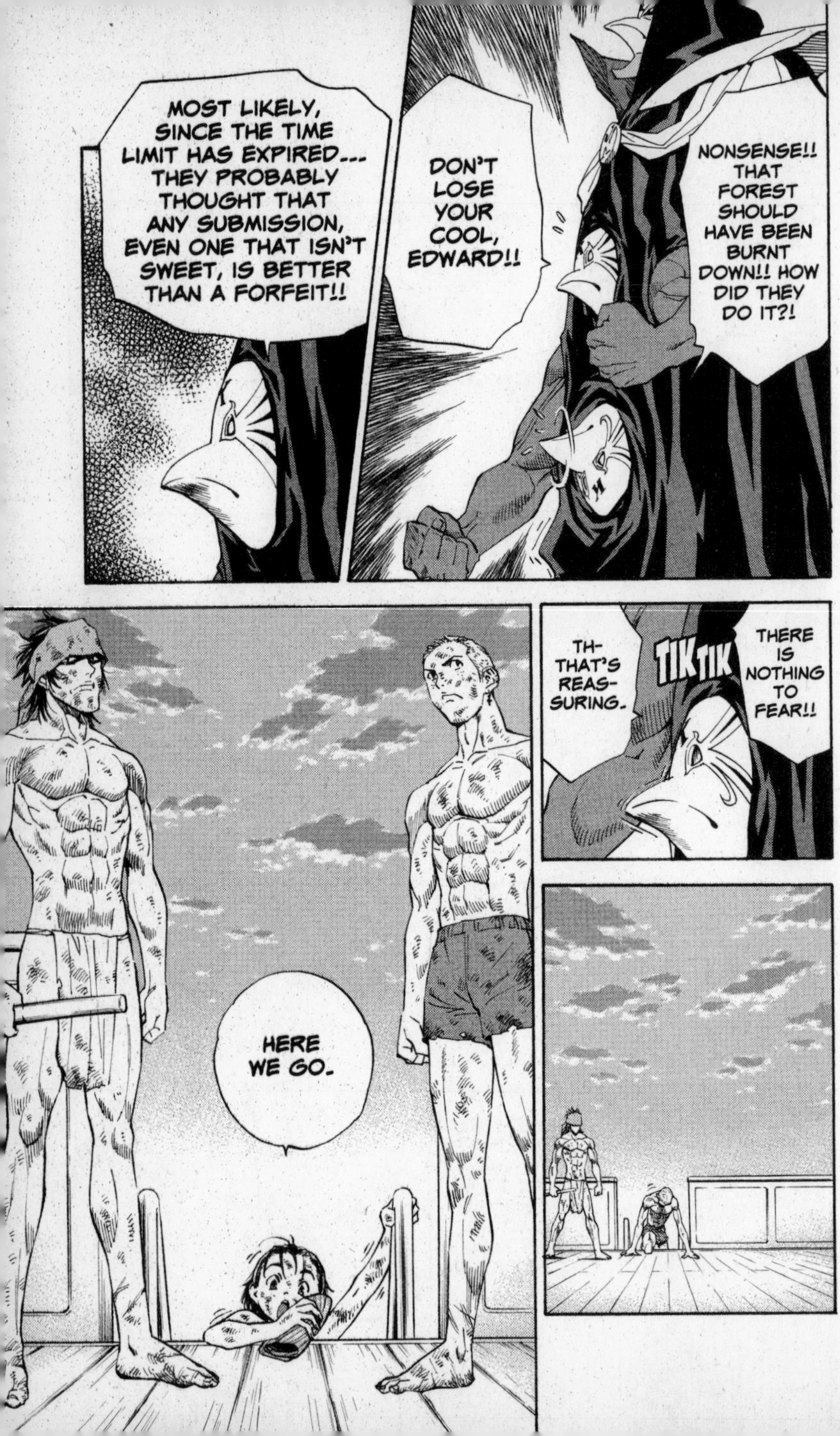
NONSENSE!! THAT FOREST SHOULD HAVE BEEN BURNT DOWN!! HOW DID THEY DO IT?!
DON'T LOSE YOUR COOL, EDWARD!!
MOST LIKELY, SINCE THE TIME LIMIT HAS EXPIRED... THEY PROBABLY THOUGHT THAT ANY SUBMISSION, EVEN ONE THAT ISN'T SWEET, IS BETTER THAN A FORFEIT!!
THERE IS NOTHING TO FEAR!!
TIK TIK
TH-THAT'S REAS-SURING.
HERE WE GO.

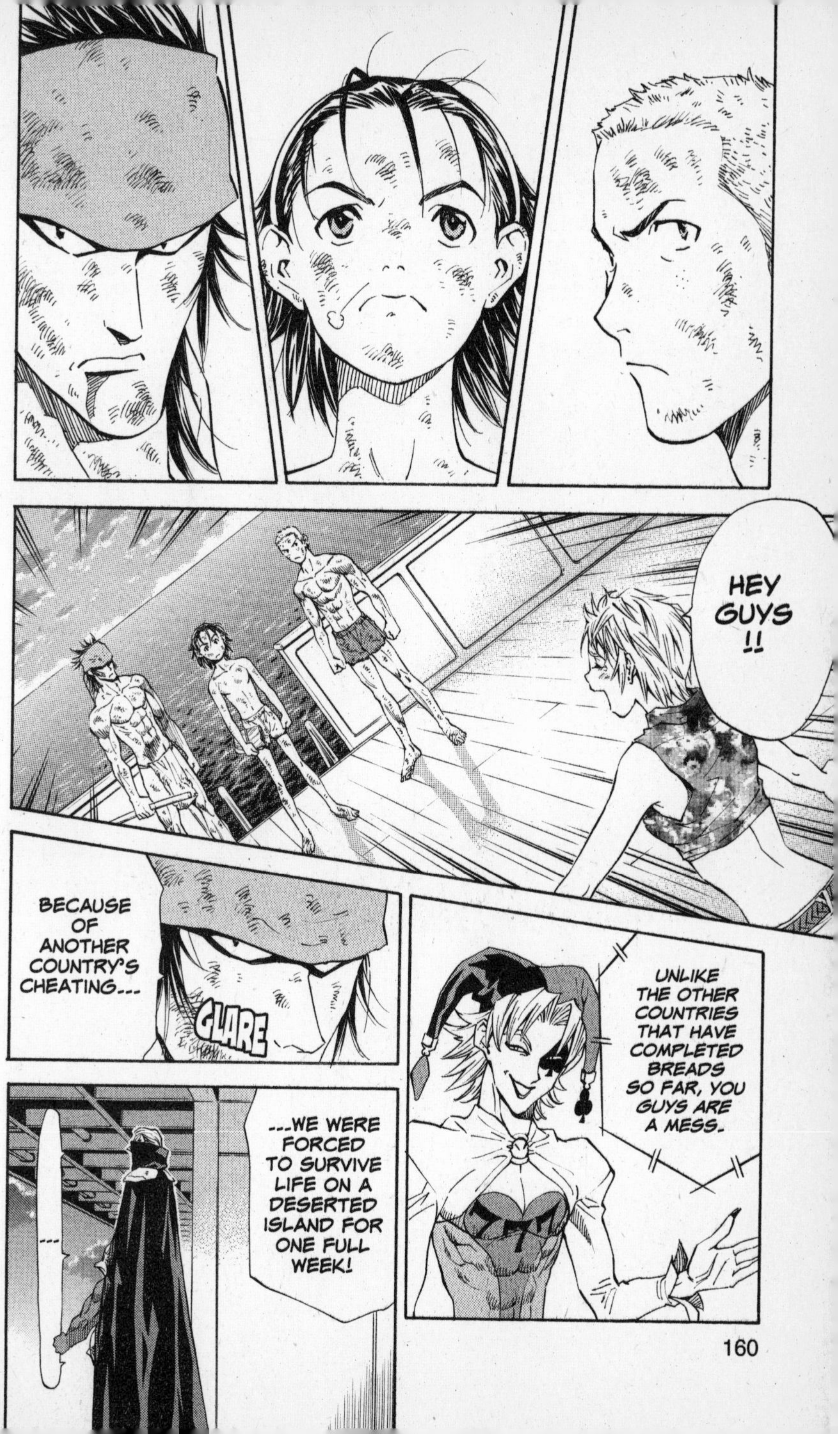
HEY GUYS !!
UNLIKE THE OTHER COUNTRIES THAT HAVE COMPLETED BREADS SO FAR, YOU GUYS ARE A MESS.
BECAUSE OF ANOTHER COUNTRY'S CHEATING...
GLARE
...WE WERE FORCED TO SURVIVE LIFE ON A DESERTED ISLAND FOR ONE FULL WEEK!
...

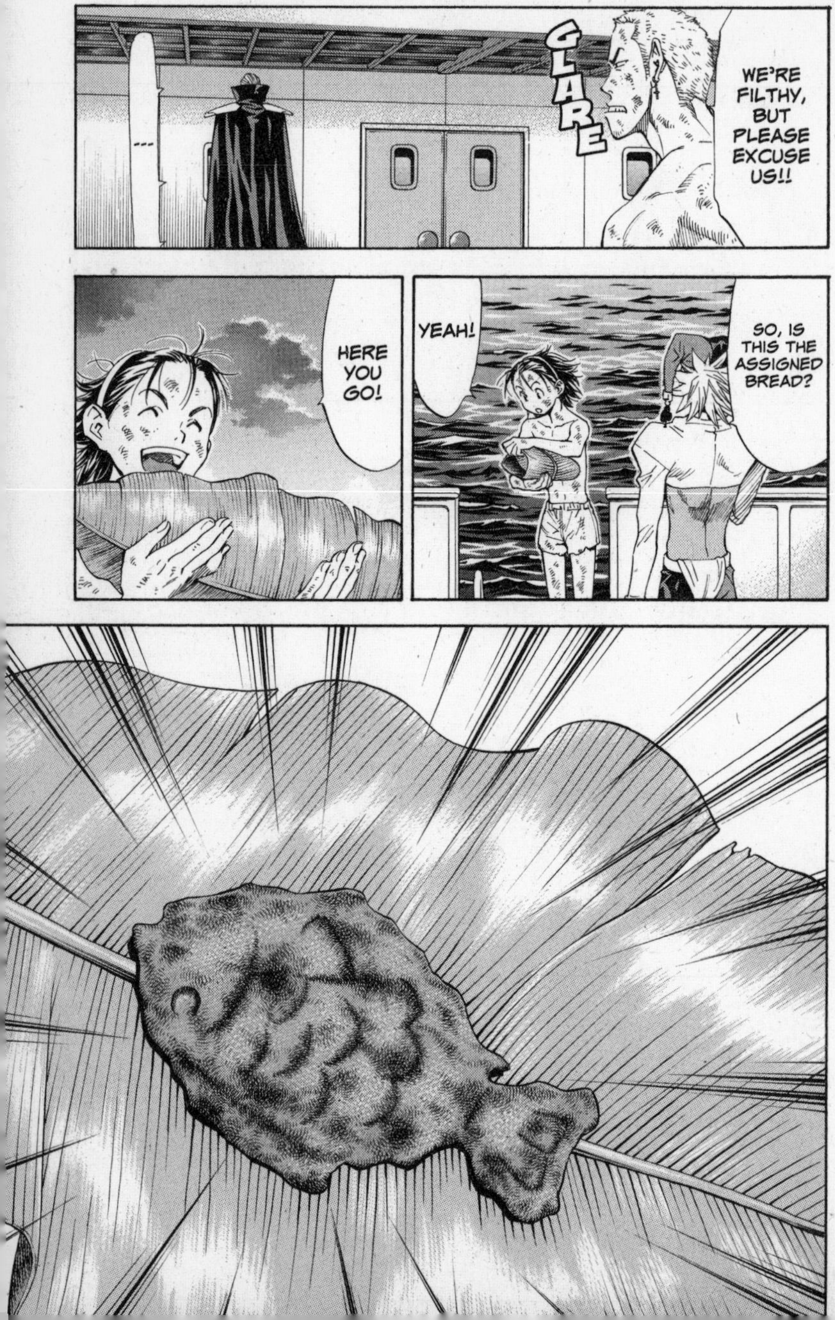
WE'RE FILTHY, BUT PLEASE EXCUSE US!!
GLARE
...
SO, IS THIS THE ASSIGNED BREAD?
YEAH!
HERE YOU GO!

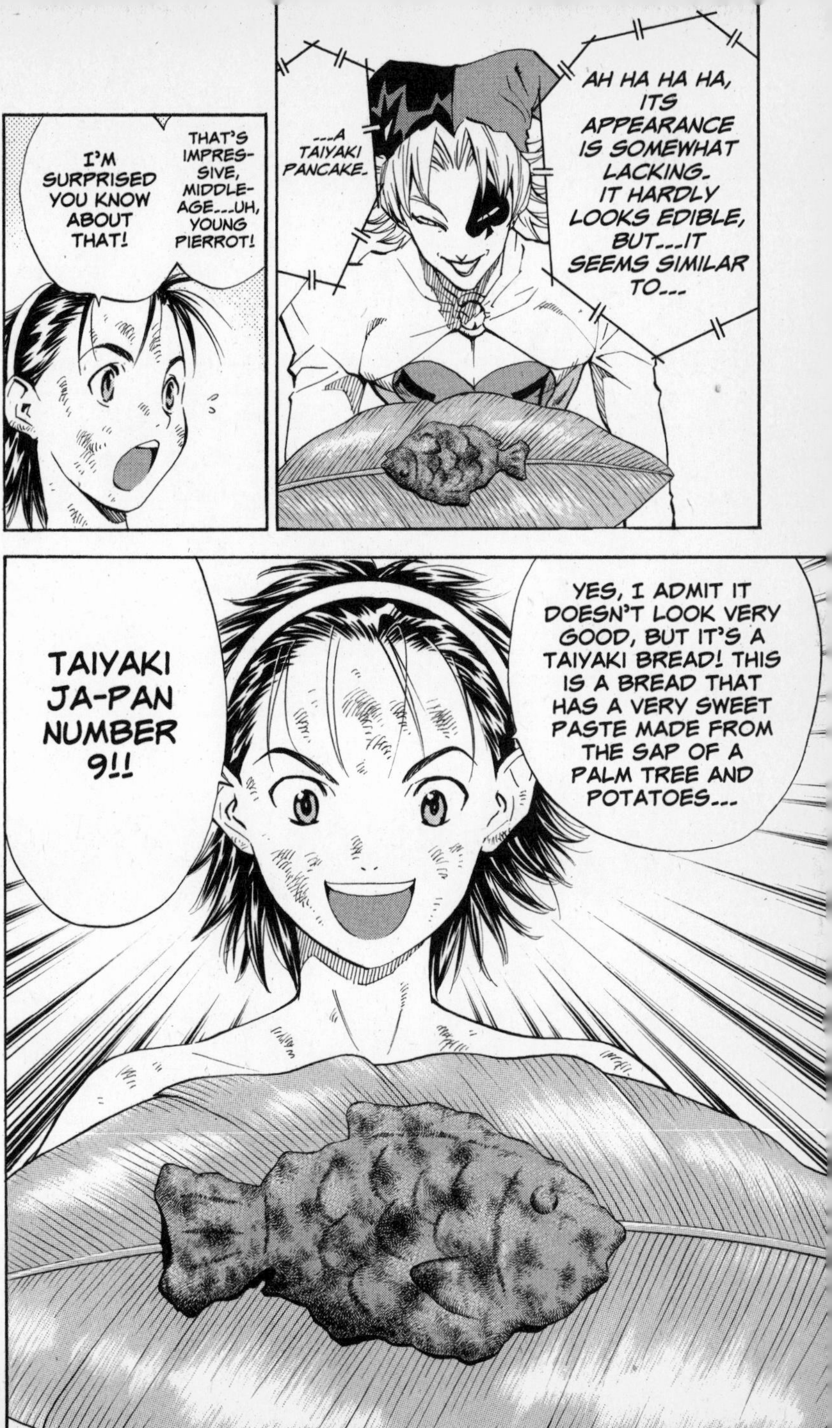
AH HA HA HA, ITS APPEARANCE IS SOMEWHAT LACKING. IT HARDLY LOOKS EDIBLE, BUT...IT SEEMS SIMILAR TO...
...A TAIYAKI PANCAKE.
THAT'S IMPRESSIVE, MIDDLE-AGE...UH, YOUNG PIERROT!
I'M SURPRISED YOU KNOW ABOUT THAT!
YES, I ADMIT IT DOESN'T LOOK VERY GOOD, BUT IT'S A TAIYAKI BREAD! THIS IS A BREAD THAT HAS A VERY SWEET PASTE MADE FROM THE SAP OF A PALM TREE AND POTATOES...
TAIYAKI JA-PAN NUMBER 9!!

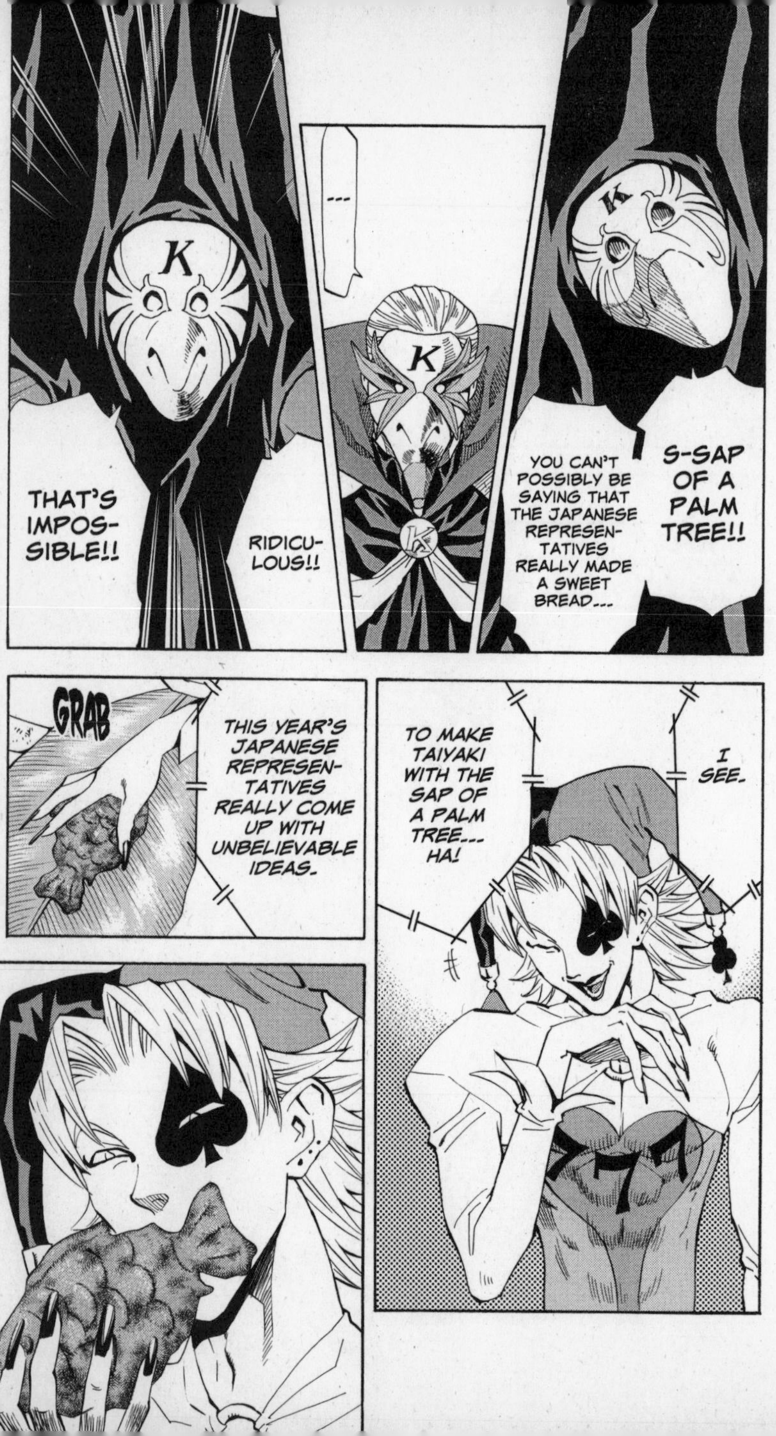
S-SAP OF A PALM TREE!!
YOU CAN'T POSSIBLY BE SAYING THAT THE JAPANESE REPRESEN-TATIVES REALLY MADE A SWEET BREAD...
...
RIDICU-LOUS!!
THAT'S IMPOS-SIBLE!!
I SEE.
TO MAKE TAIYAKI WITH THE SAP OF A PALM TREE... HA!
THIS YEAR'S JAPANESE REPRESEN-TATIVES REALLY COME UP WITH UNBELIEVABLE IDEAS.
GRAB

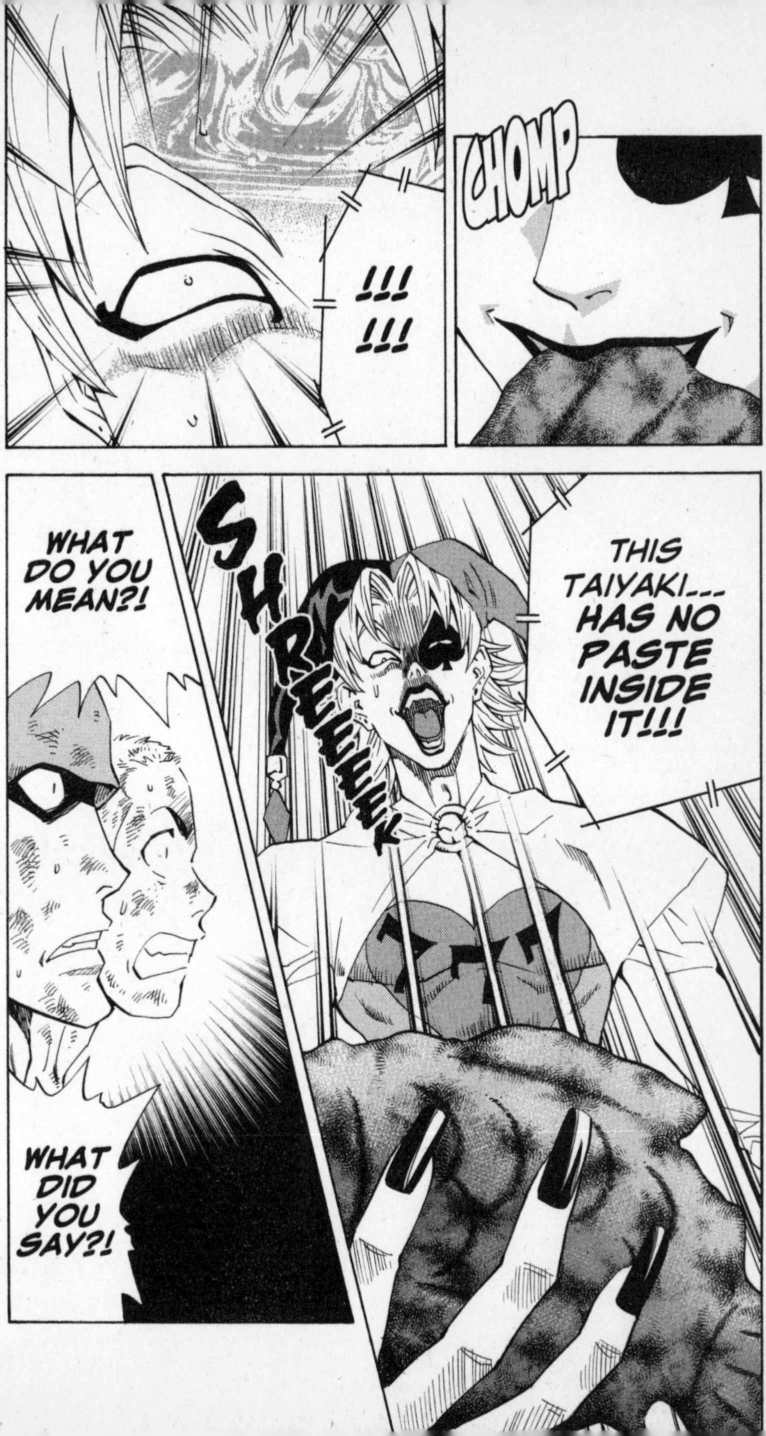
CHOMP
!!!
!!!
SHREEEEEK
THIS TAIYAKI... HAS NO PASTE INSIDE IT!!!
WHAT DO YOU MEAN?!
WHAT DID YOU SAY?!

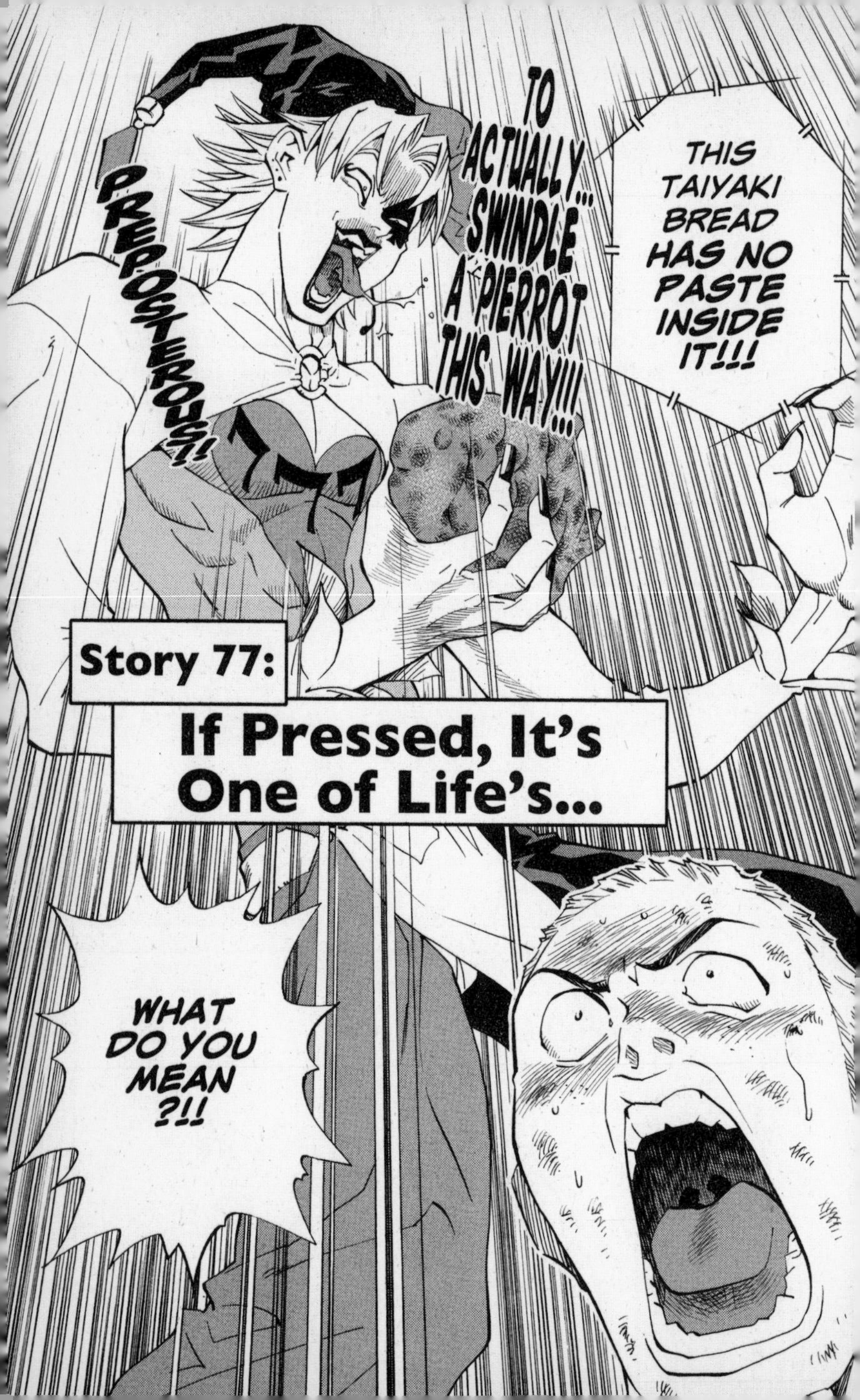
THIS TAIYAKI BREAD HAS NO PASTE INSIDE IT!!!
TO ACTUALLY... SWINDLE A PIERROT THIS WAY!!!
PREPOSTEROUS?!!
Story 77:
If Pressed, It's One of Life's...
WHAT DO YOU MEAN ?!!

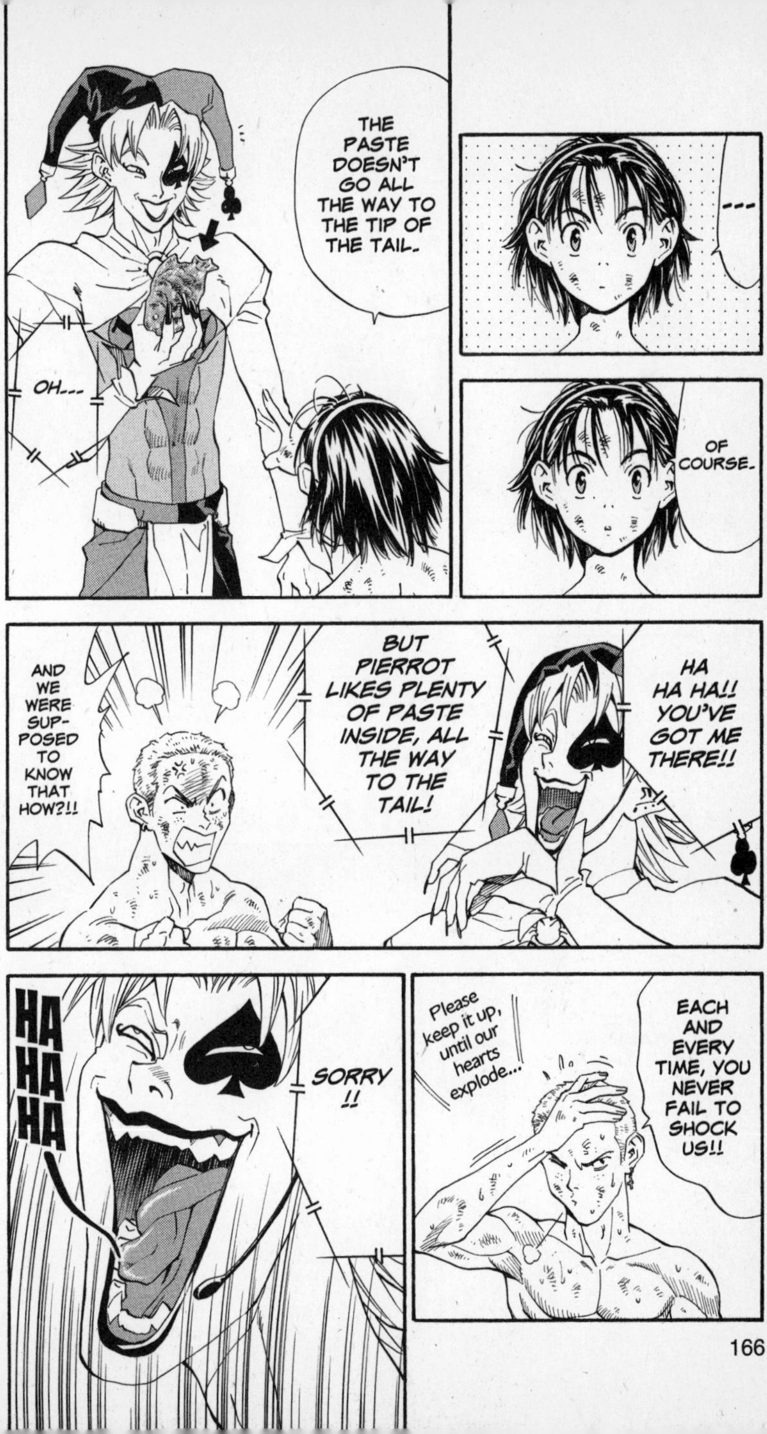
...
OF COURSE.
THE PASTE DOESN'T GO ALL THE WAY TO THE TIP OF THE TAIL.
OH...
HA HA HA!! YOU'VE GOT ME THERE!!
BUT PIERROT LIKES PLENTY OF PASTE INSIDE, ALL THE WAY TO THE TAIL!
AND WE WERE SUPPOSED TO KNOW THAT HOW?!!
EACH AND EVERY TIME, YOU NEVER FAIL TO SHOCK US!!
Please keep it up, until our hearts explode...
SORRY!!
HA HA HA

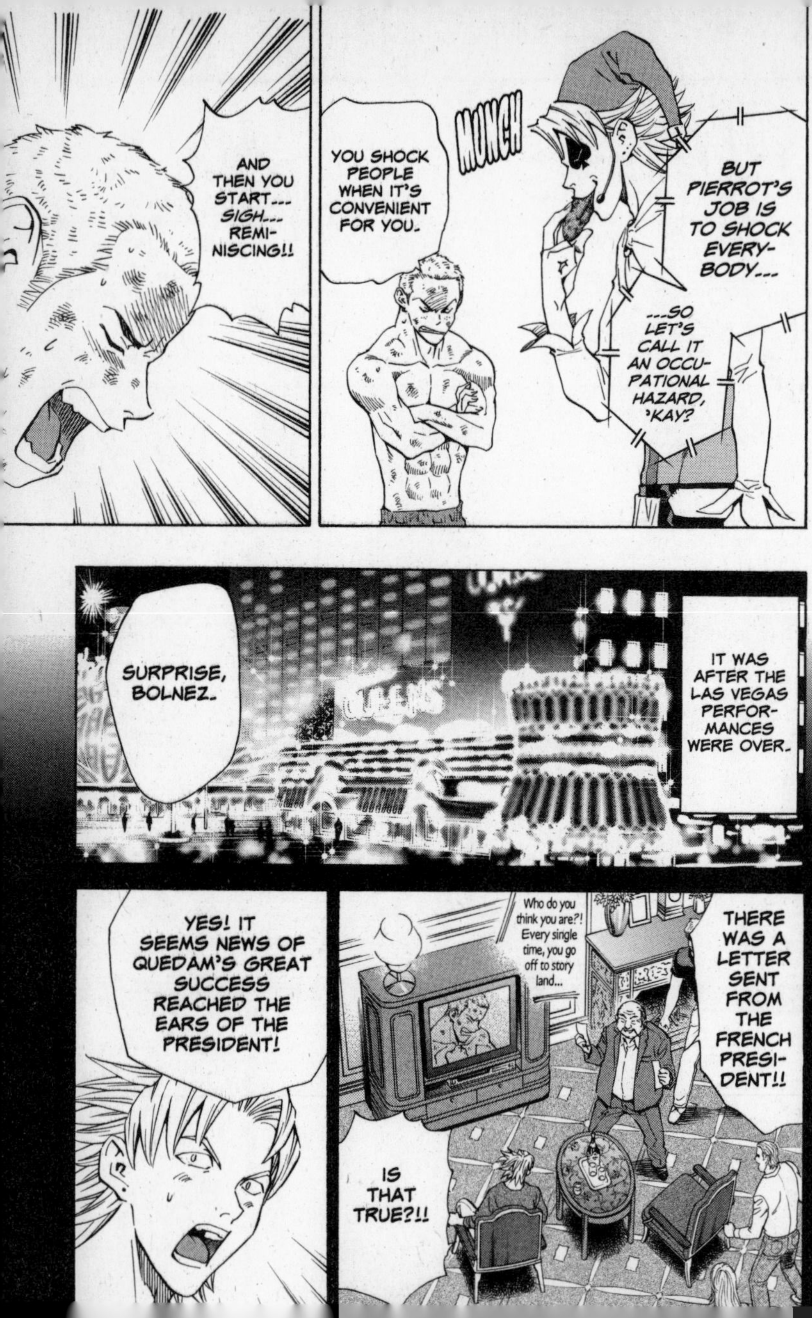
BUT PIERROT'S JOB IS TO SHOCK EVERYBODY...
...SO LET'S CALL IT AN OCCUPATIONAL HAZARD, 'KAY?
MUNCH
YOU SHOCK PEOPLE WHEN IT'S CONVENIENT FOR YOU.
AND THEN YOU START... SIGH... REMINISCING!!
IT WAS AFTER THE LAS VEGAS PERFORMANCES WERE OVER.
SURPRISE, BOLNEZ.
THERE WAS A LETTER SENT FROM THE FRENCH PRESIDENT!!
Who do you think you are?! Every single time, you go off to story land...
IS THAT TRUE?!!
YES! IT SEEMS NEWS OF QUEDAM'S GREAT SUCCESS REACHED THE EARS OF THE PRESIDENT!

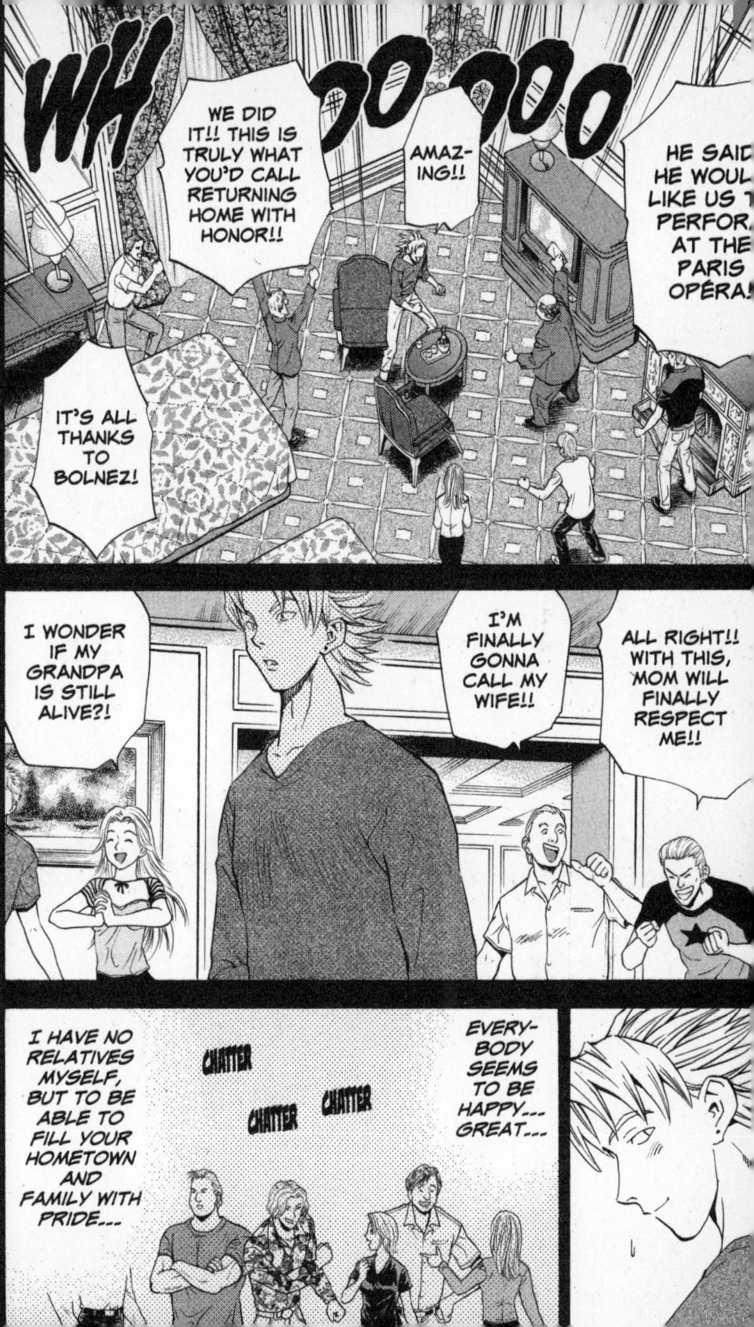
WHOOOOOO
HE SAID HE WOUL LIKE US T PERFOR AT THE PARIS OPÉRA!
AMAZ-ING!!
WE DID IT!! THIS IS TRULY WHAT YOU'D CALL RETURNING HOME WITH HONOR!!
IT'S ALL THANKS TO BOLNEZ!
ALL RIGHT!! WITH THIS, MOM WILL FINALLY RESPECT ME!!
I'M FINALLY GONNA CALL MY WIFE!!
I WONDER IF MY GRANDPA IS STILL ALIVE?!
EVERY-BODY SEEMS TO BE HAPPY... GREAT...
CHATTER
CHATTER
CHATTER
I HAVE NO RELATIVES MYSELF, BUT TO BE ABLE TO FILL YOUR HOMETOWN AND FAMILY WITH PRIDE...

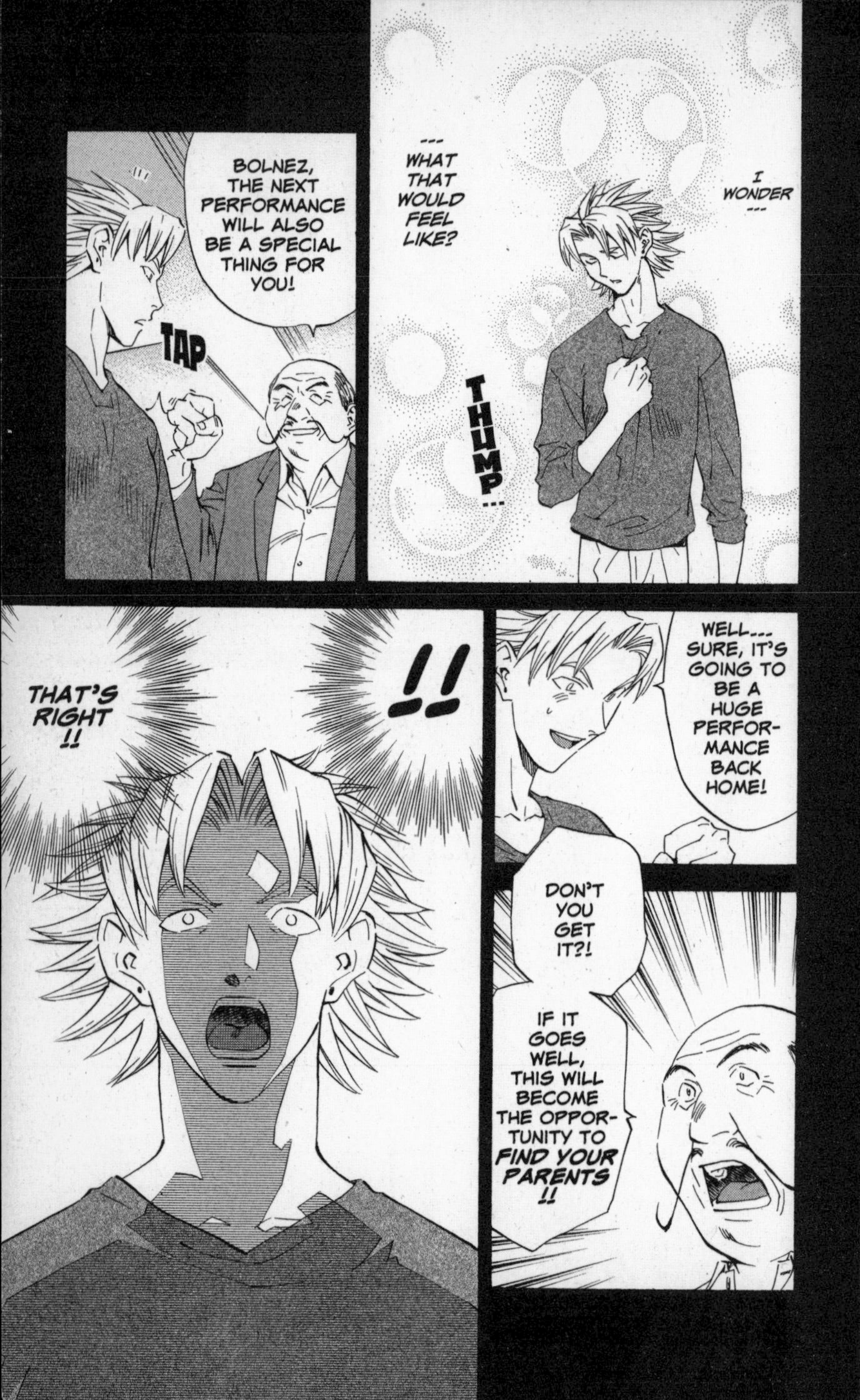
I WONDER ---
--- WHAT THAT WOULD FEEL LIKE?
THUMP...
BOLNEZ, THE NEXT PERFORMANCE WILL ALSO BE A SPECIAL THING FOR YOU!
TAP
WELL... SURE, IT'S GOING TO BE A HUGE PERFOR-MANCE BACK HOME!
DON'T YOU GET IT?!
IF IT GOES WELL, THIS WILL BECOME THE OPPOR-TUNITY TO *FIND YOUR PARENTS* !!
!!
*THAT'S RIGHT* !!

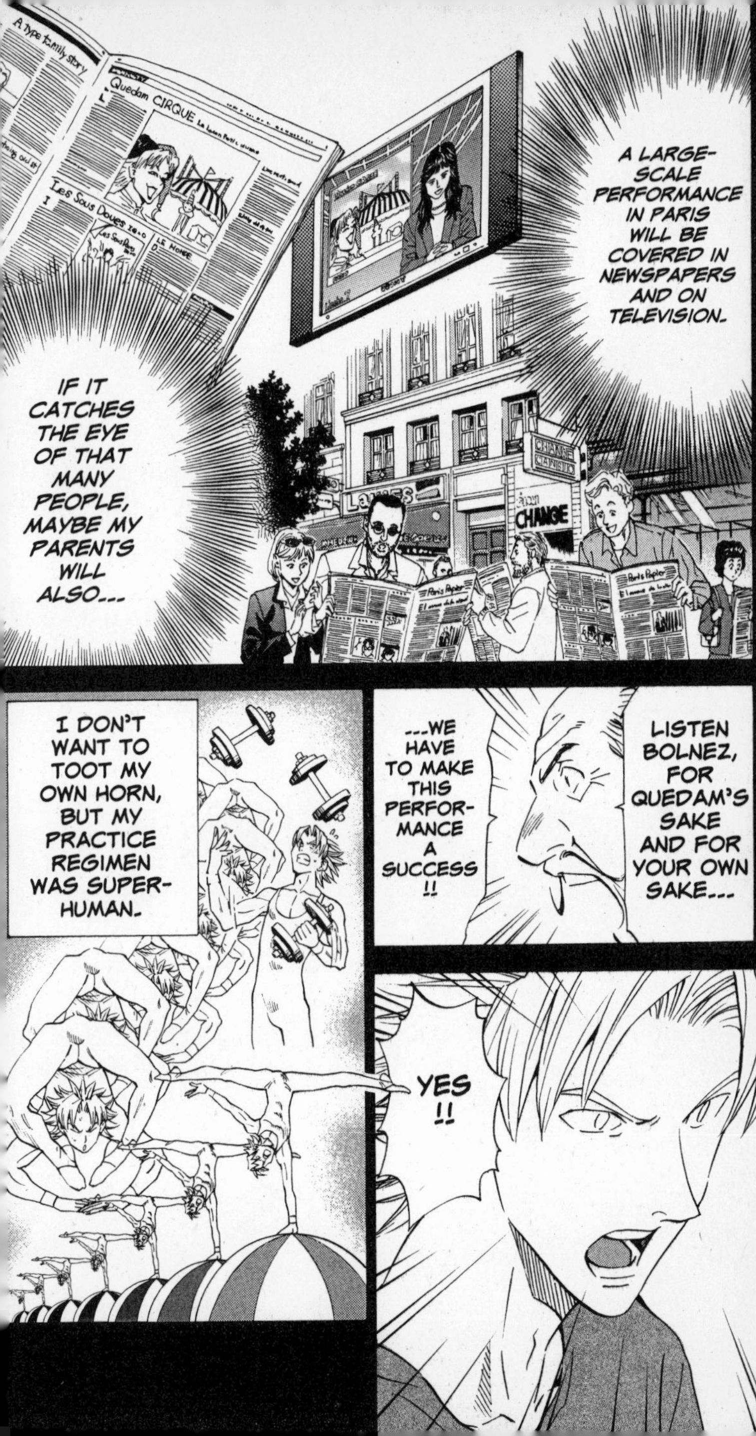
A LARGE-SCALE PERFORMANCE IN PARIS WILL BE COVERED IN NEWSPAPERS AND ON TELEVISION.
IF IT CATCHES THE EYE OF THAT MANY PEOPLE, MAYBE MY PARENTS WILL ALSO...
LISTEN BOLNEZ, FOR QUEDAM'S SAKE AND FOR YOUR OWN SAKE...
...WE HAVE TO MAKE THIS PERFORMANCE A SUCCESS!!
YES!!
I DON'T WANT TO TOOT MY OWN HORN, BUT MY PRACTICE REGIMEN WAS SUPERHUMAN.

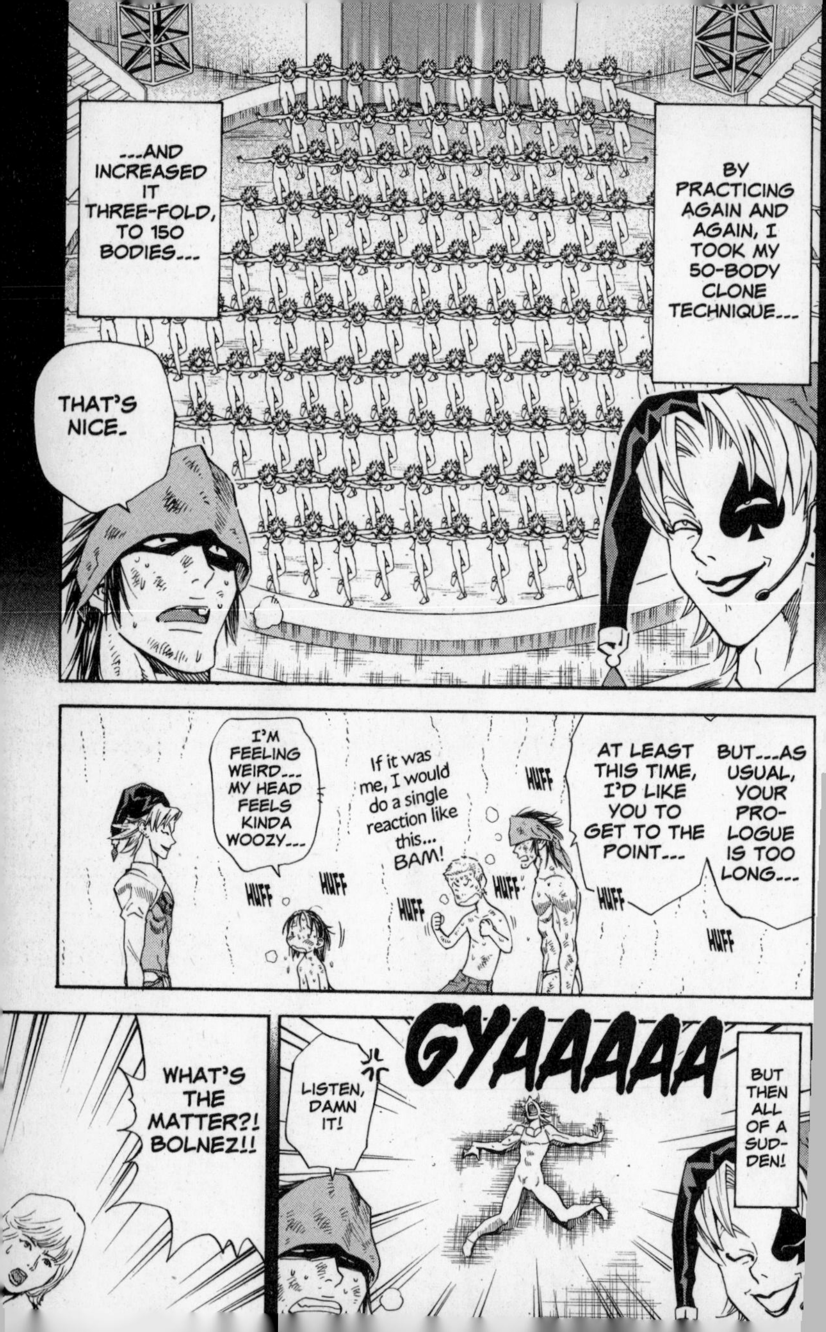
BY PRACTICING AGAIN AND AGAIN, I TOOK MY 50-BODY CLONE TECHNIQUE...
...AND INCREASED IT THREE-FOLD, TO 150 BODIES...
THAT'S NICE.
BUT...AS USUAL, YOUR PROLOGUE IS TOO LONG...
AT LEAST THIS TIME, I'D LIKE YOU TO GET TO THE POINT...
HUFF
HUFF
HUFF
HUFF
If it was me, I would do a single reaction like this... BAM!
HUFF
HUFF
I'M FEELING WEIRD... MY HEAD FEELS KINDA WOOZY...
BUT THEN ALL OF A SUDDEN!
GYAAAAAA
LISTEN, DAMN IT!
WHAT'S THE MATTER?! BOLNEZ!!

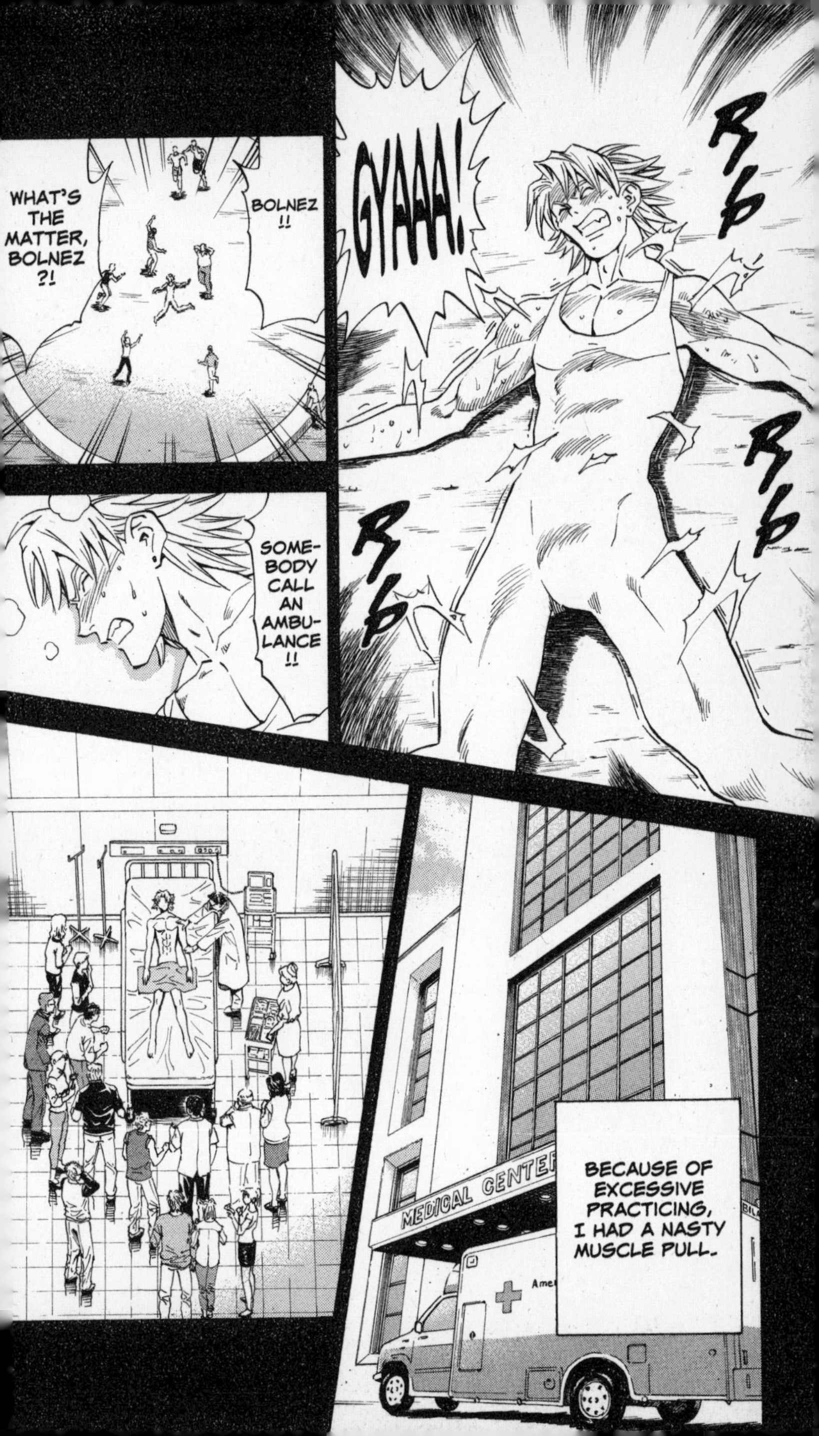
GYAAA!
BOLNEZ!!
WHAT'S THE MATTER, BOLNEZ?!
SOME-BODY CALL AN AMBU-LANCE!!
BECAUSE OF EXCESSIVE PRACTICING, I HAD A NASTY MUSCLE PULL.

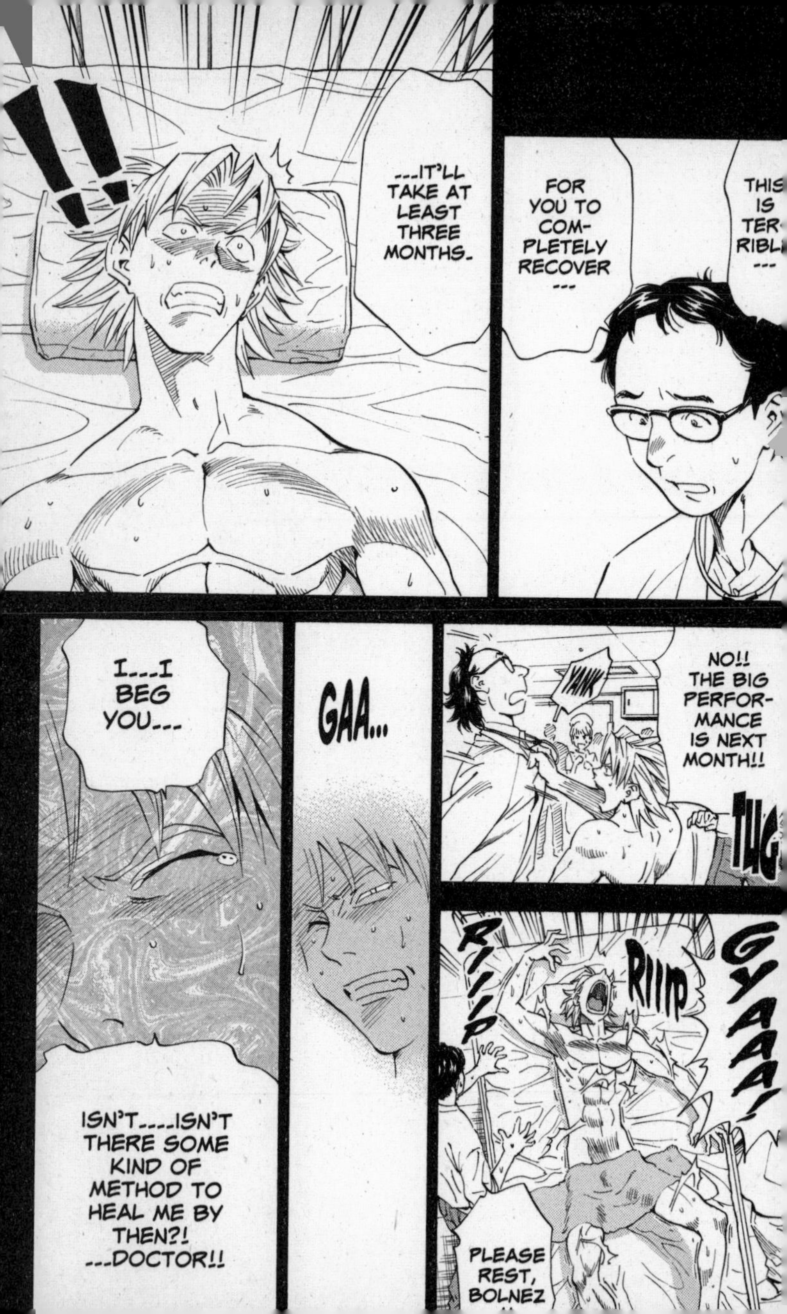
THIS IS TER- RIBL---
FOR YOU TO COM- PLETELY RECOVER ---
---IT'LL TAKE AT LEAST THREE MONTHS.
!!
NO!! THE BIG PERFOR- MANCE IS NEXT MONTH!!
YANK
TUG
GYAAA!
RIIIP
RIIIP
PLEASE REST, BOLNEZ
GAA...
I---I BEG YOU---
ISN'T----ISN'T THERE SOME KIND OF METHOD TO HEAL ME BY THEN?! ---DOCTOR!!

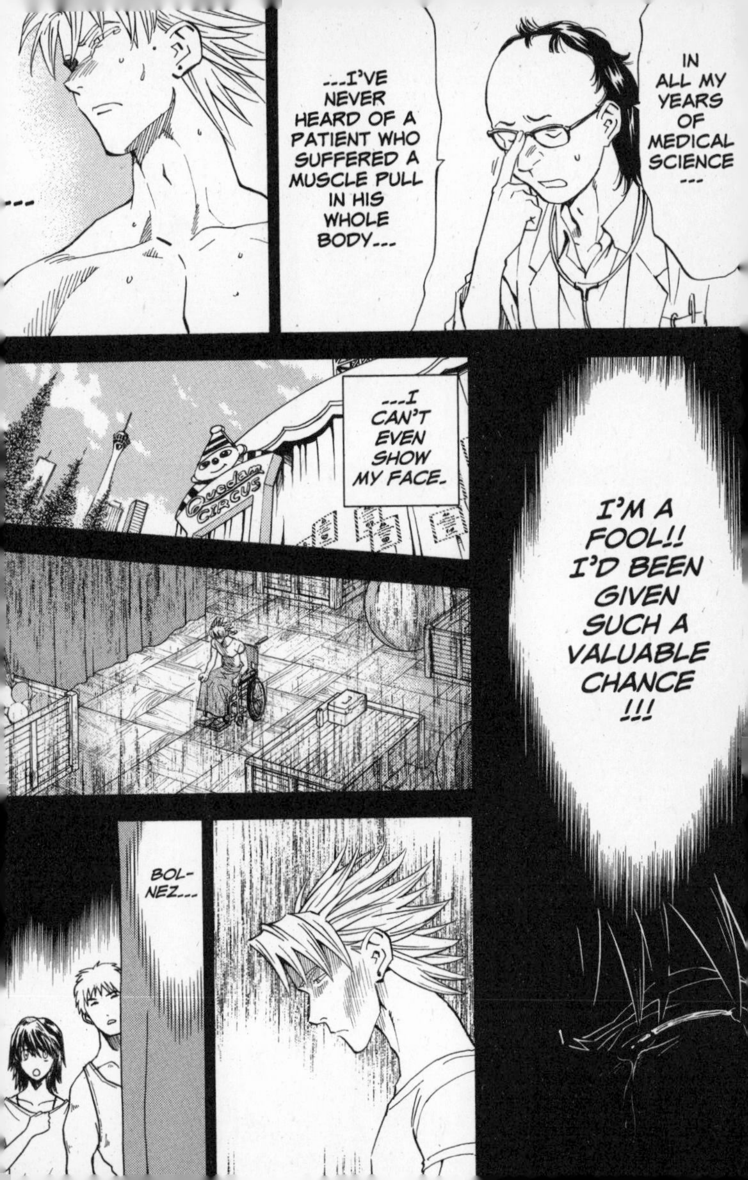
IN ALL MY YEARS OF MEDICAL SCIENCE ---
---I'VE NEVER HEARD OF A PATIENT WHO SUFFERED A MUSCLE PULL IN HIS WHOLE BODY---
---
I'M A FOOL!! I'D BEEN GIVEN SUCH A VALUABLE CHANCE !!!
---I CAN'T EVEN SHOW MY FACE.
Quedam CIRCUS
BOL-NEZ---

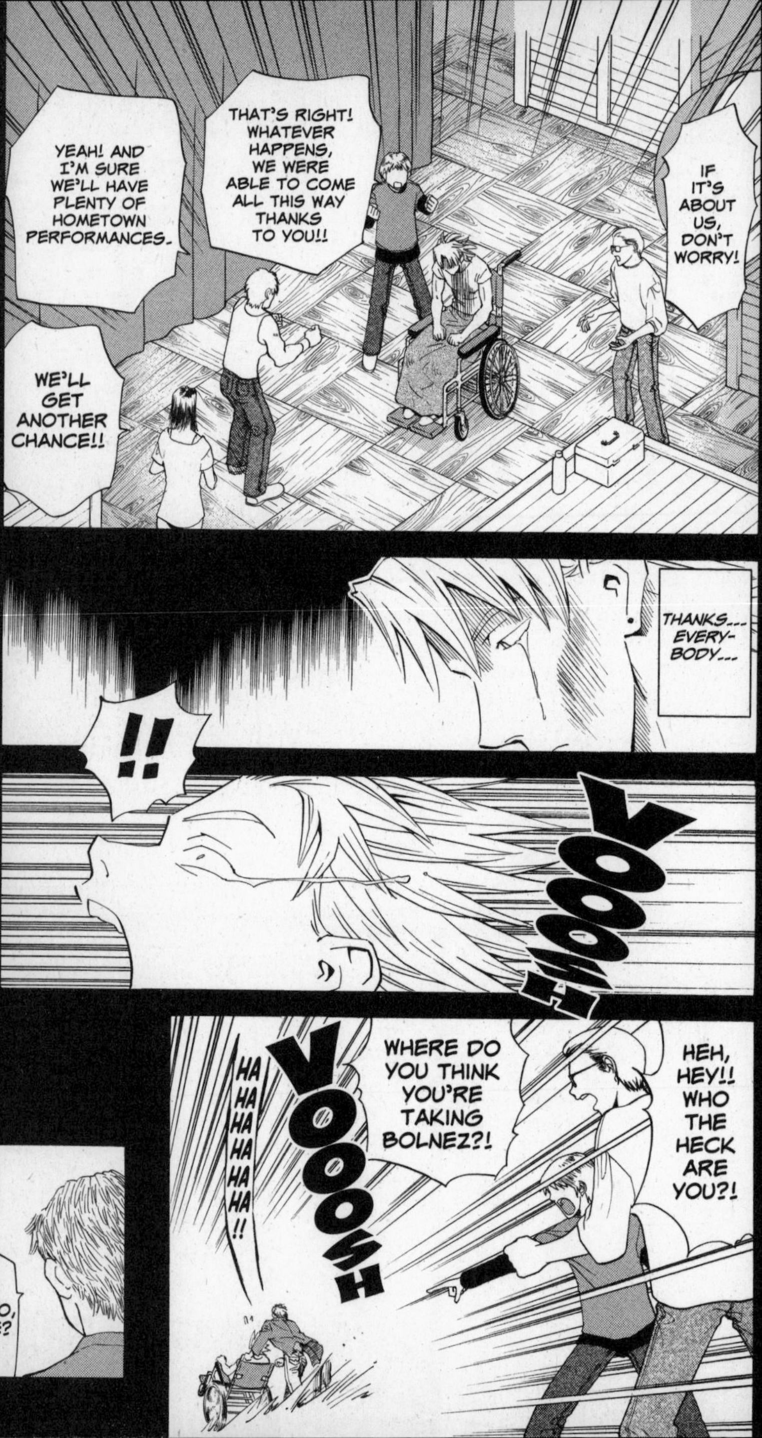
IF IT'S ABOUT US, DON'T WORRY!
THAT'S RIGHT! WHATEVER HAPPENS, WE WERE ABLE TO COME ALL THIS WAY THANKS TO YOU!!
YEAH! AND I'M SURE WE'LL HAVE PLENTY OF HOMETOWN PERFORMANCES.
WE'LL GET ANOTHER CHANCE!!
THANKS... EVERY-BODY...
VOOOOSH
!!
HEH, HEY!! WHO THE HECK ARE YOU?!
WHERE DO YOU THINK YOU'RE TAKING BOLNEZ?!
VOOOOSH
HA HA HA HA HA HA HA!!
WHO, ME?

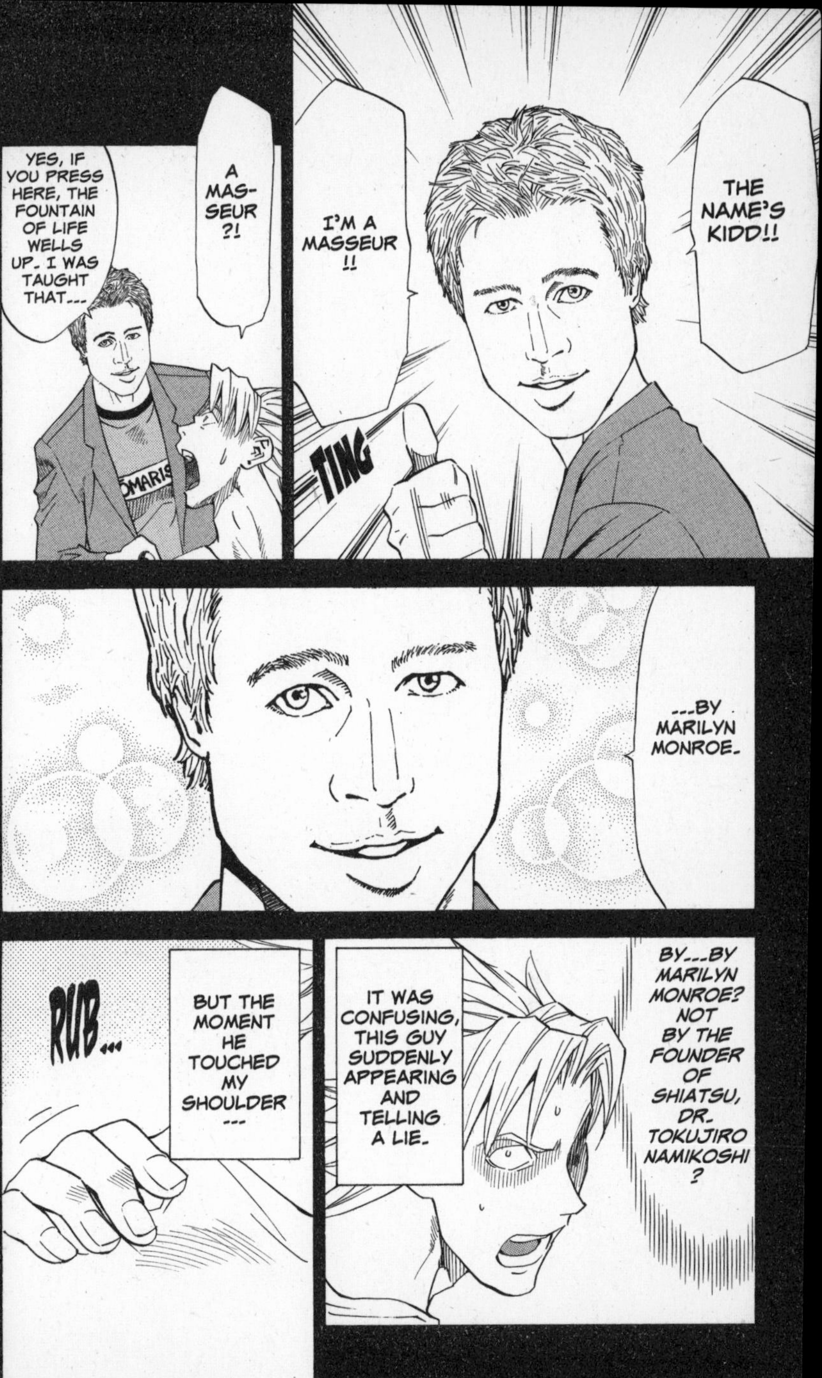
THE NAME'S KIDD!!
I'M A MASSEUR!!
TING
A MAS-SEUR?!
YES, IF YOU PRESS HERE, THE FOUNTAIN OF LIFE WELLS UP. I WAS TAUGHT THAT...
...BY MARILYN MONROE.
BY...BY MARILYN MONROE? NOT BY THE FOUNDER OF SHIATSU, DR. TOKUJIRO NAMIKOSHI?
IT WAS CONFUSING, THIS GUY SUDDENLY APPEARING AND TELLING A LIE.
BUT THE MOMENT HE TOUCHED MY SHOULDER...
RUB...

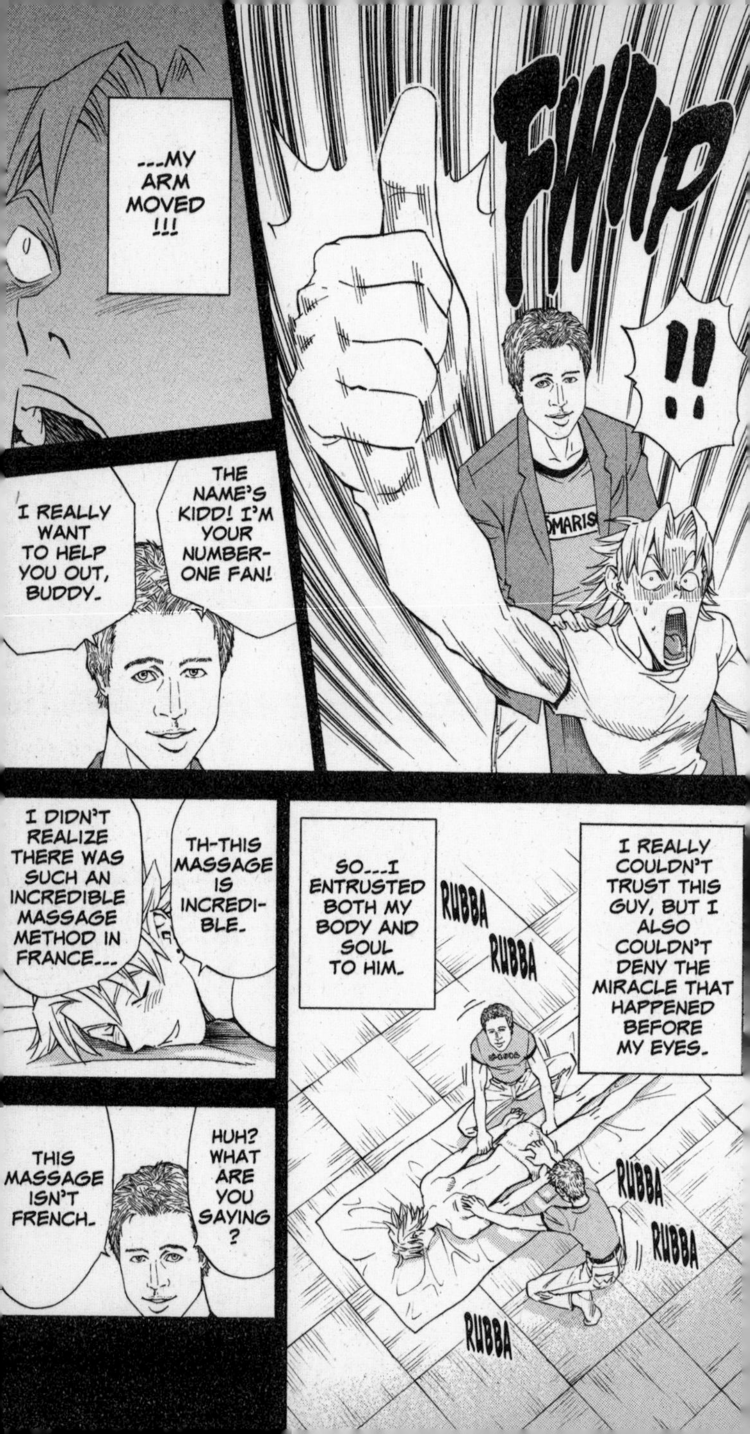
FWIP
!!
...MY ARM MOVED!!!
THE NAME'S KIDD! I'M YOUR NUMBER-ONE FAN!
I REALLY WANT TO HELP YOU OUT, BUDDY.
I REALLY COULDN'T TRUST THIS GUY, BUT I ALSO COULDN'T DENY THE MIRACLE THAT HAPPENED BEFORE MY EYES.
SO...I ENTRUSTED BOTH MY BODY AND SOUL TO HIM.
RUBBA RUBBA
RUBBA RUBBA
RUBBA
TH-THIS MASSAGE IS INCREDIBLE.
I DIDN'T REALIZE THERE WAS SUCH AN INCREDIBLE MASSAGE METHOD IN FRANCE...
HUH? WHAT ARE YOU SAYING?
THIS MASSAGE ISN'T FRENCH.

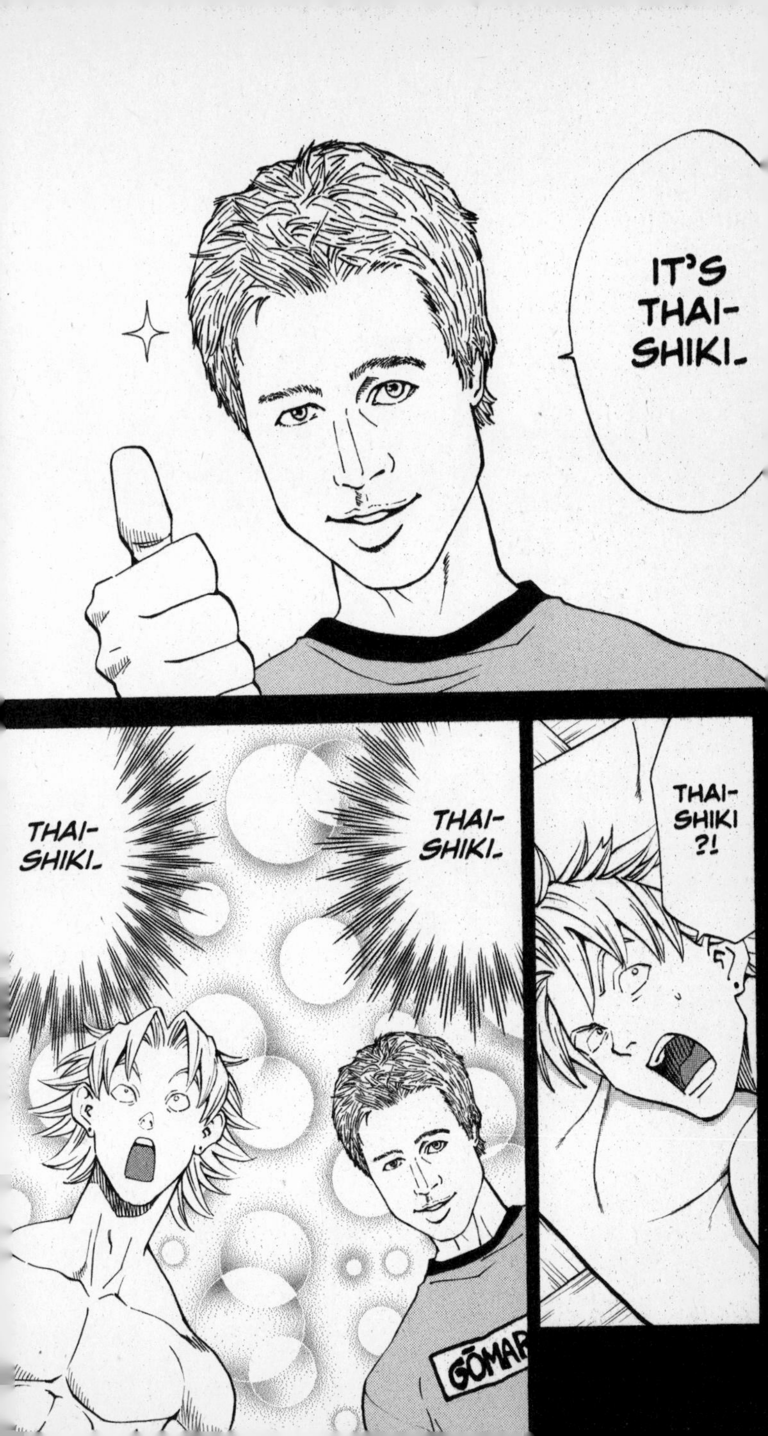
IT'S THAI-SHIKI…
THAI-SHIKI ?!
THAI-SHIKI…
THAI-SHIKI…
GŌMAR

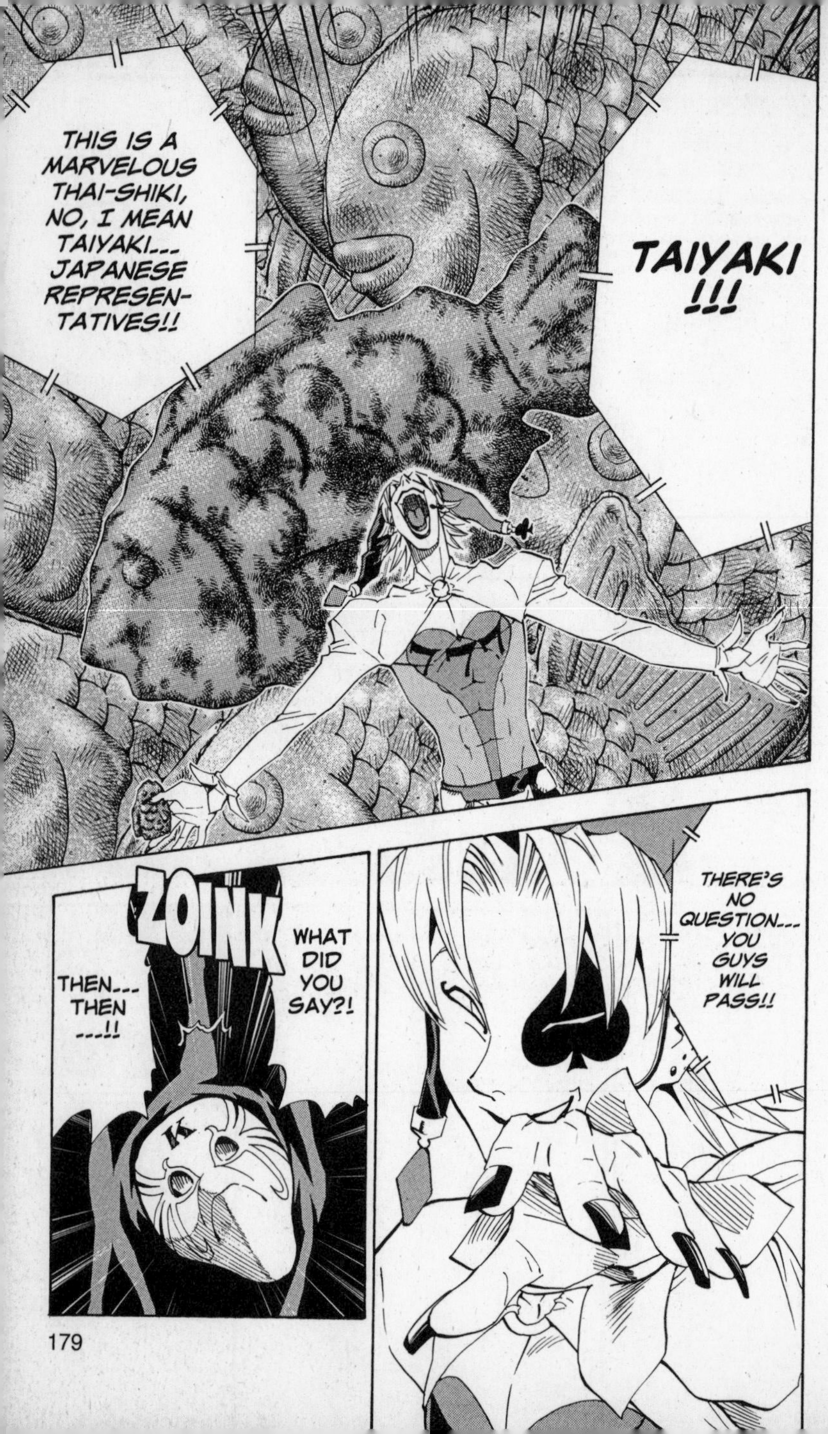
TAIYAKI!!!
THIS IS A MARVELOUS THAI-SHIKI, NO, I MEAN TAIYAKI... JAPANESE REPRESEN-TATIVES!!
THERE'S NO QUESTION... YOU GUYS WILL PASS!!
ZOINK
WHAT DID YOU SAY?!
THEN... THEN ...!!

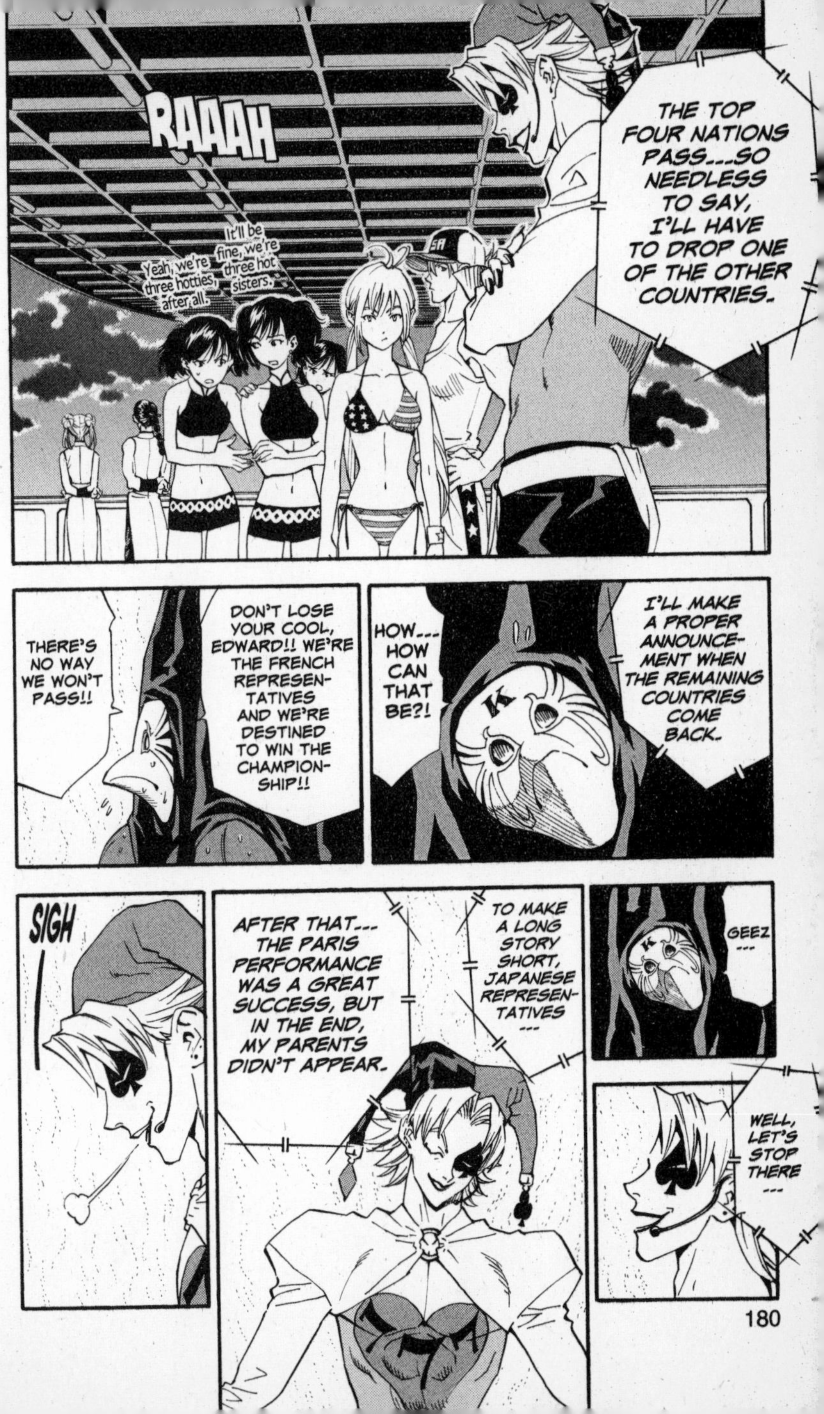
RAAAH
THE TOP FOUR NATIONS PASS... SO NEEDLESS TO SAY, I'LL HAVE TO DROP ONE OF THE OTHER COUNTRIES.
It'll be fine, we're three hot sisters.
Yeah, we're three hotties, after all.
I'LL MAKE A PROPER ANNOUNCEMENT WHEN THE REMAINING COUNTRIES COME BACK.
HOW... HOW CAN THAT BE?!
DON'T LOSE YOUR COOL, EDWARD!! WE'RE THE FRENCH REPRESENTATIVES AND WE'RE DESTINED TO WIN THE CHAMPIONSHIP!!
THERE'S NO WAY WE WON'T PASS!!
GEEZ...
WELL, LET'S STOP THERE...
TO MAKE A LONG STORY SHORT, JAPANESE REPRESENTATIVES...
AFTER THAT... THE PARIS PERFORMANCE WAS A GREAT SUCCESS, BUT IN THE END, MY PARENTS DIDN'T APPEAR.
SIGH

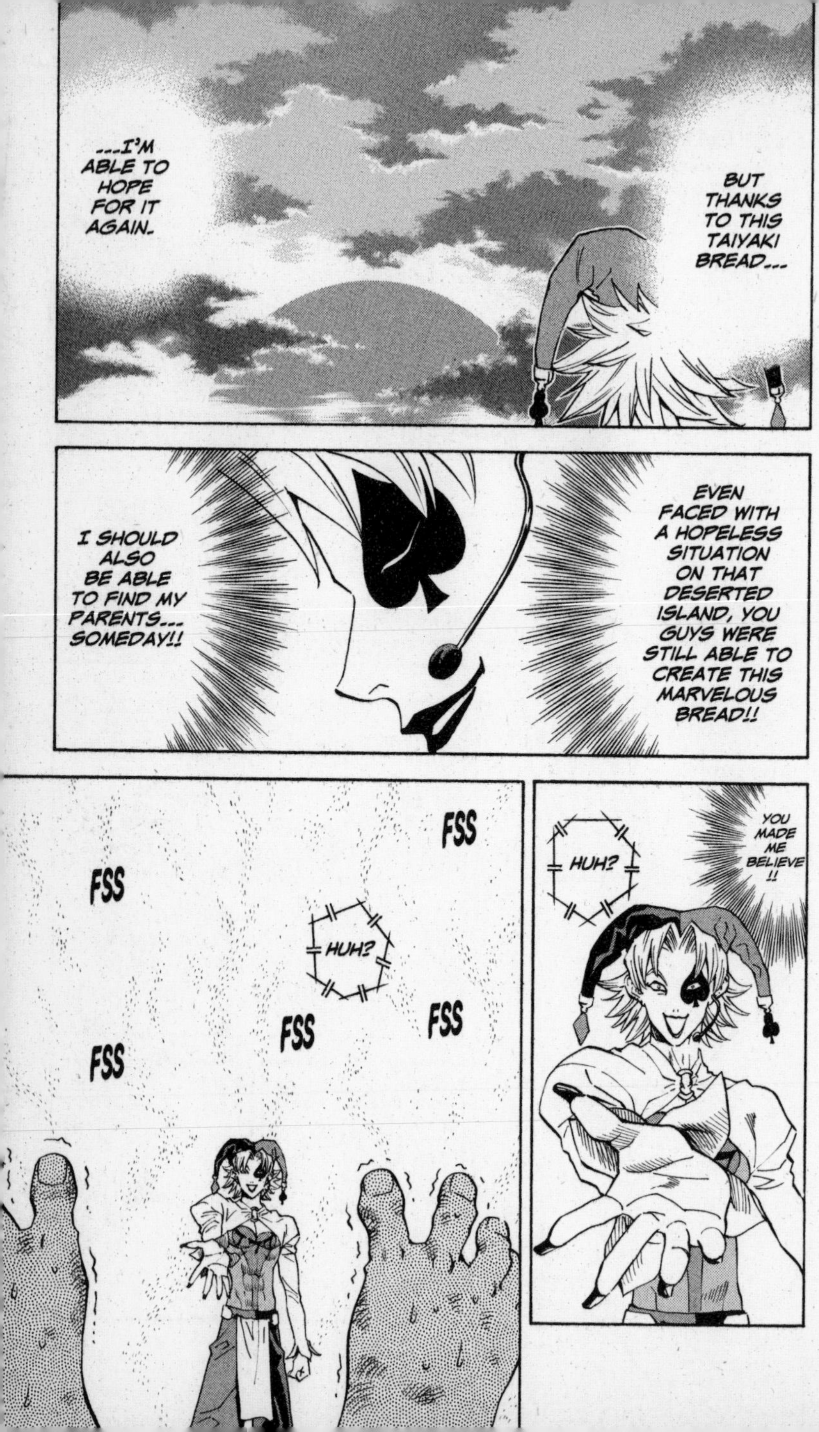
BUT THANKS TO THIS TAIYAKI BREAD...
...I'M ABLE TO HOPE FOR IT AGAIN.
EVEN FACED WITH A HOPELESS SITUATION ON THAT DESERTED ISLAND, YOU GUYS WERE STILL ABLE TO CREATE THIS MARVELOUS BREAD!!
I SHOULD ALSO BE ABLE TO FIND MY PARENTS... SOMEDAY!!
YOU MADE ME BELIEVE!!
HUH?
FSS
FSS
HUH?
FSS
FSS
FSS

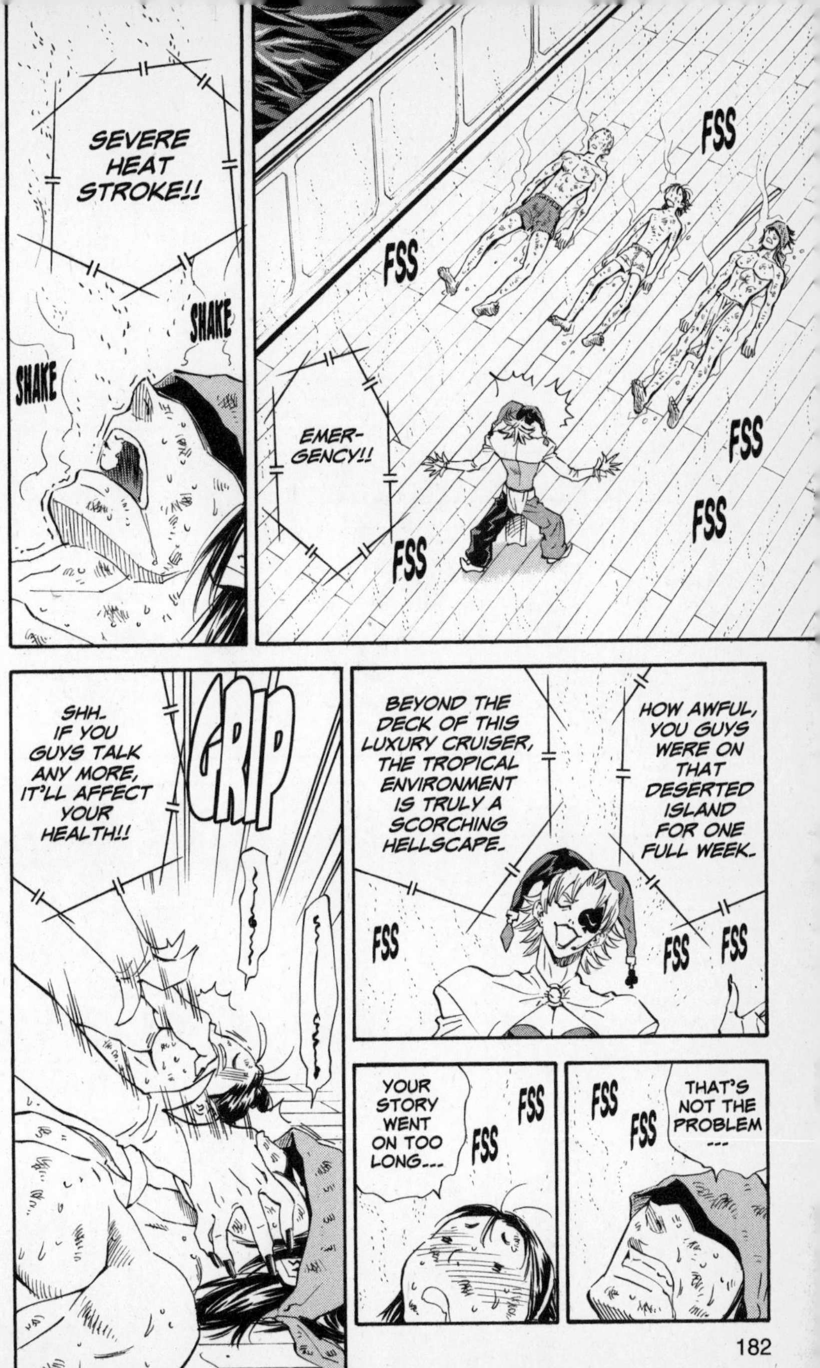
FSS
FSS
FSS
FSS
EMER-GENCY!!
FSS
SEVERE HEAT STROKE!!
SHAKE
SHAKE
HOW AWFUL, YOU GUYS WERE ON THAT DESERTED ISLAND FOR ONE FULL WEEK.
BEYOND THE DECK OF THIS LUXURY CRUISER, THE TROPICAL ENVIRONMENT IS TRULY A SCORCHING HELLSCAPE.
FSS
FSS
FSS
THAT'S NOT THE PROBLEM...
FSS
FSS
YOUR STORY WENT ON TOO LONG...
FSS
FSS
GRIP
SHH. IF YOU GUYS TALK ANY MORE, IT'LL AFFECT YOUR HEALTH!!

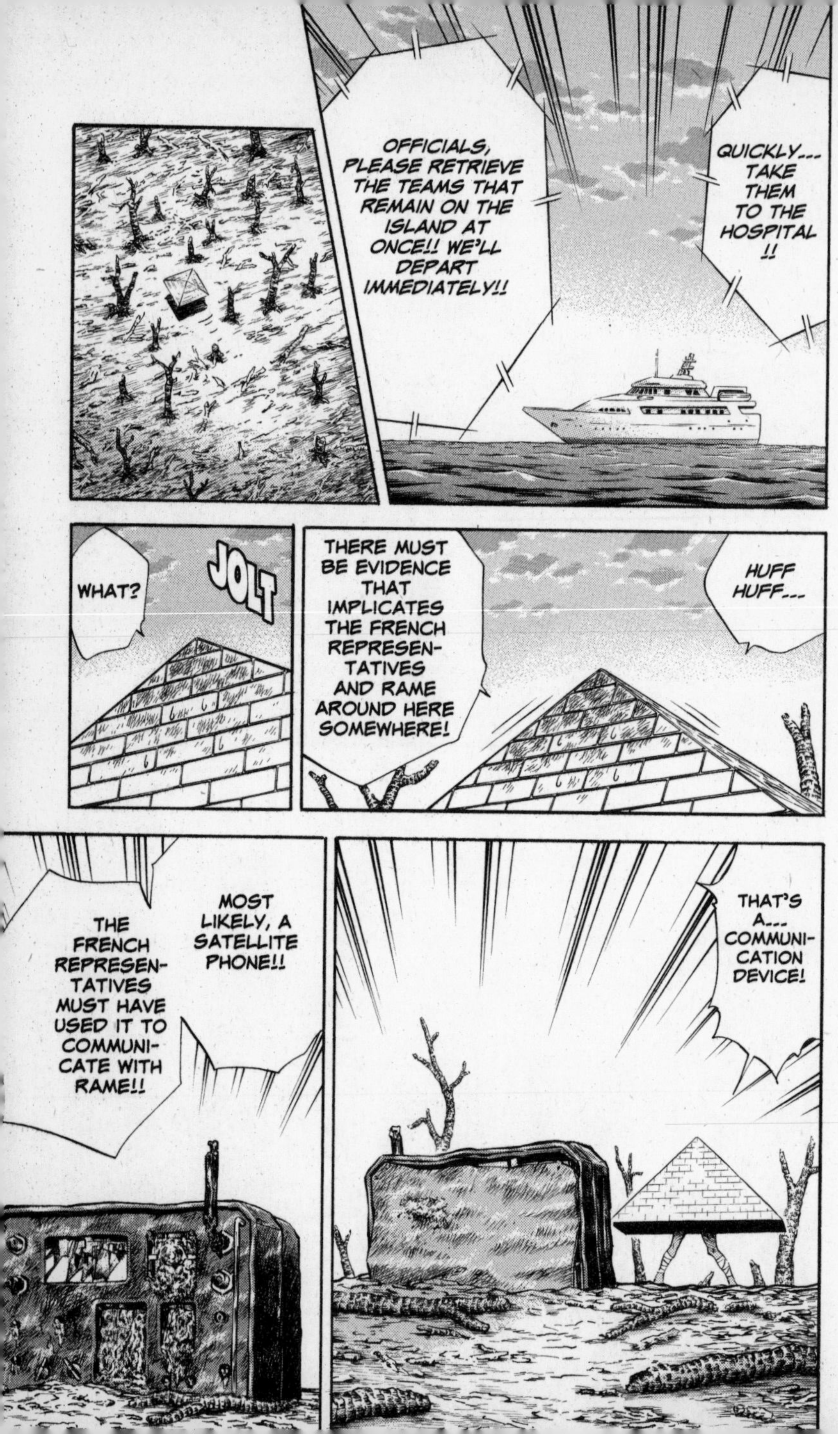
QUICKLY... TAKE THEM TO THE HOSPITAL !!
OFFICIALS, PLEASE RETRIEVE THE TEAMS THAT REMAIN ON THE ISLAND AT ONCE!! WE'LL DEPART IMMEDIATELY!!
HUFF HUFF...
THERE MUST BE EVIDENCE THAT IMPLICATES THE FRENCH REPRESEN-TATIVES AND RAME AROUND HERE SOMEWHERE!
JOLT
WHAT?
THAT'S A... COMMUNI-CATION DEVICE!
MOST LIKELY, A SATELLITE PHONE!!
THE FRENCH REPRESEN-TATIVES MUST HAVE USED IT TO COMMUNI-CATE WITH RAME!!

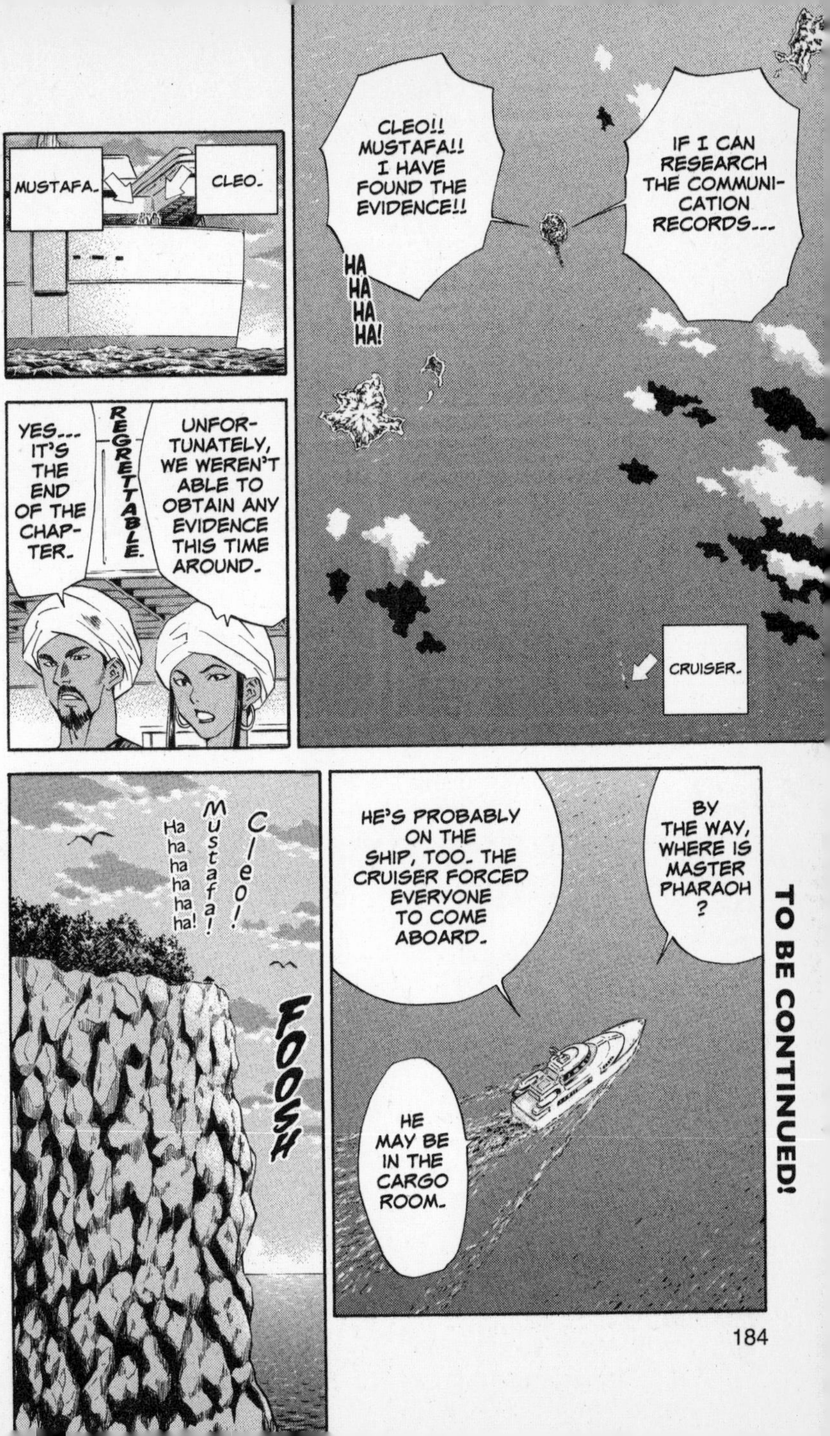
IF I CAN RESEARCH THE COMMUNICATION RECORDS...
CLEO!! MUSTAFA!! I HAVE FOUND THE EVIDENCE!!
HA HA HA HA!
CRUISER.
CLEO.
MUSTAFA.
UNFORTUNATELY, WE WEREN'T ABLE TO OBTAIN ANY EVIDENCE THIS TIME AROUND.
REGRETTABLE.
YES... IT'S THE END OF THE CHAPTER.
BY THE WAY, WHERE IS MASTER PHARAOH?
HE'S PROBABLY ON THE SHIP, TOO. THE CRUISER FORCED EVERYONE TO COME ABOARD.
HE MAY BE IN THE CARGO ROOM.
Cleo!
Mustafa!
Ha ha ha ha ha ha!
FOOOSH
TO BE CONTINUED!

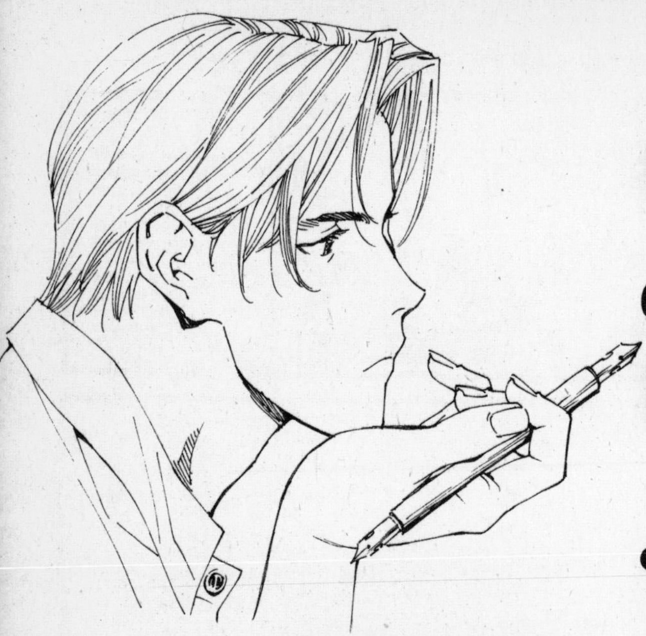

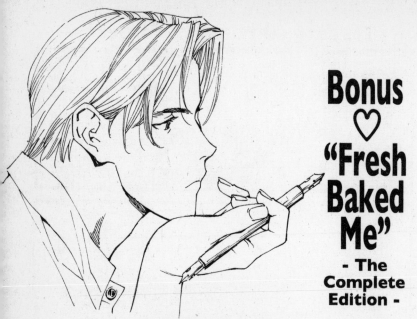

# Bonus ♡ "Fresh Baked Me"

**- The Complete Edition -**

## In the future...

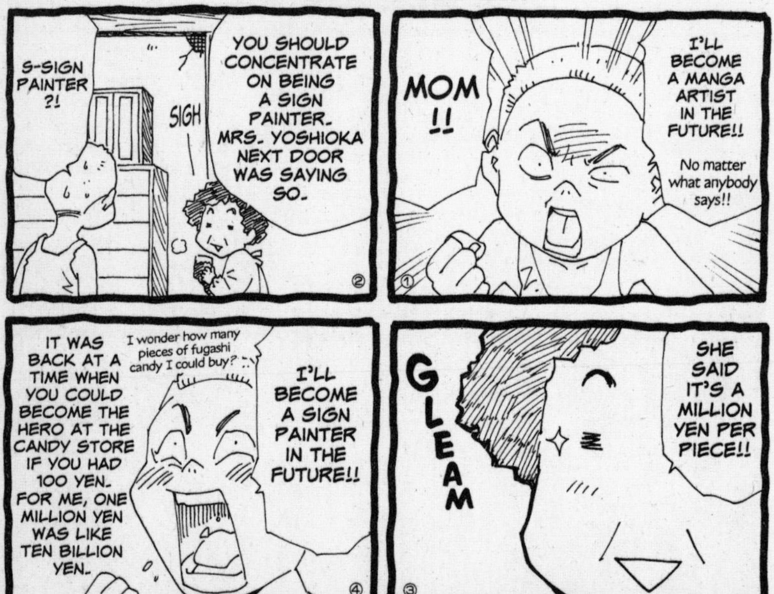

MOM!!
I'LL BECOME A MANGA ARTIST IN THE FUTURE!!
No matter what anybody says!!
S-SIGN PAINTER?!
SIGH
YOU SHOULD CONCENTRATE ON BEING A SIGN PAINTER. MRS. YOSHIOKA NEXT DOOR WAS SAYING SO.
SHE SAID IT'S A MILLION YEN PER PIECE!!
GLEAM
I'LL BECOME A SIGN PAINTER IN THE FUTURE!!
I wonder how many pieces of fugashi candy I could buy?
IT WAS BACK AT A TIME WHEN YOU COULD BECOME THE HERO AT THE CANDY STORE IF YOU HAD 100 YEN. FOR ME, ONE MILLION YEN WAS LIKE TEN BILLION YEN.


**The super bonus that depicts the youthful days of Hashiguchi sensei!**

# Staying Abreast of Puberty

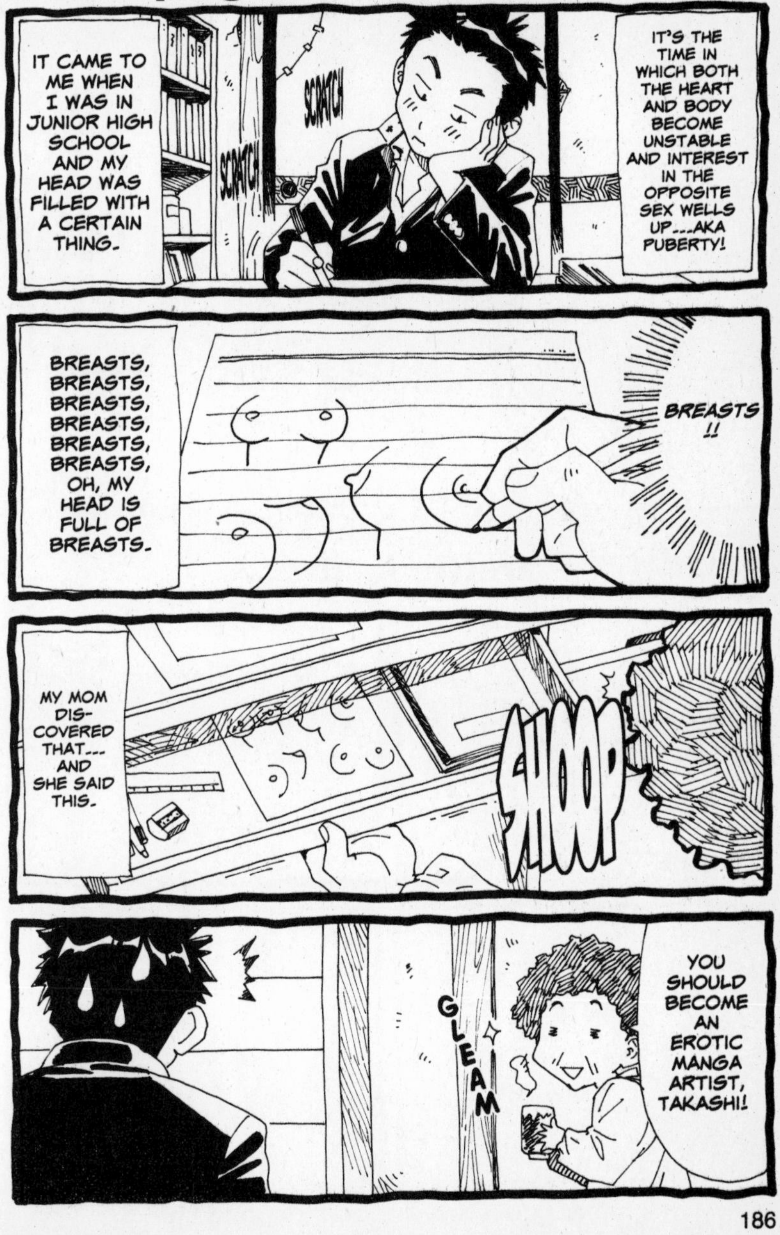
IT'S THE TIME IN WHICH BOTH THE HEART AND BODY BECOME UNSTABLE AND INTEREST IN THE OPPOSITE SEX WELLS UP...AKA PUBERTY!
SCRATCH
SCRATCH
IT CAME TO ME WHEN I WAS IN JUNIOR HIGH SCHOOL AND MY HEAD WAS FILLED WITH A CERTAIN THING.
BREASTS !!
BREASTS, BREASTS, BREASTS, BREASTS, BREASTS, BREASTS, OH, MY HEAD IS FULL OF BREASTS.
SHOOP
MY MOM DIS-COVERED THAT... AND SHE SAID THIS.
YOU SHOULD BECOME AN EROTIC MANGA ARTIST, TAKASHI!
GLEAM

# Selected for First Prize

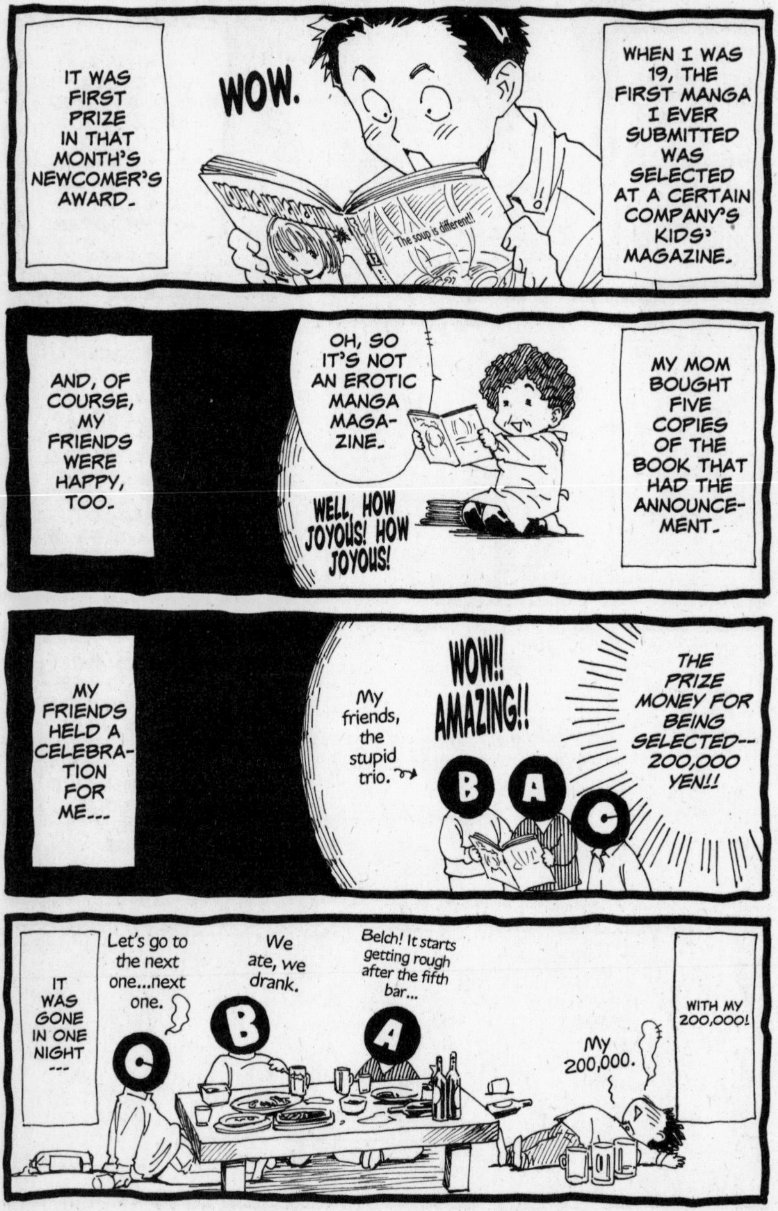

WHEN I WAS 19, THE FIRST MANGA I EVER SUBMITTED WAS SELECTED AT A CERTAIN COMPANY'S KIDS' MAGAZINE.
WOW.
The soup is different!!
IT WAS FIRST PRIZE IN THAT MONTH'S NEWCOMER'S AWARD.
MY MOM BOUGHT FIVE COPIES OF THE BOOK THAT HAD THE ANNOUNCEMENT.
OH, SO IT'S NOT AN EROTIC MANGA MAGAZINE.
WELL, HOW JOYOUS! HOW JOYOUS!
AND, OF COURSE, MY FRIENDS WERE HAPPY, TOO.
THE PRIZE MONEY FOR BEING SELECTED--200,000 YEN!!
WOW!! AMAZING!!
My friends, the stupid trio.
MY FRIENDS HELD A CELEBRATION FOR ME...
WITH MY 200,000!
My 200,000.
Belch! It starts getting rough after the fifth bar...
We ate, we drank.
Let's go to the next one...next one.
IT WAS GONE IN ONE NIGHT...

# Comedy

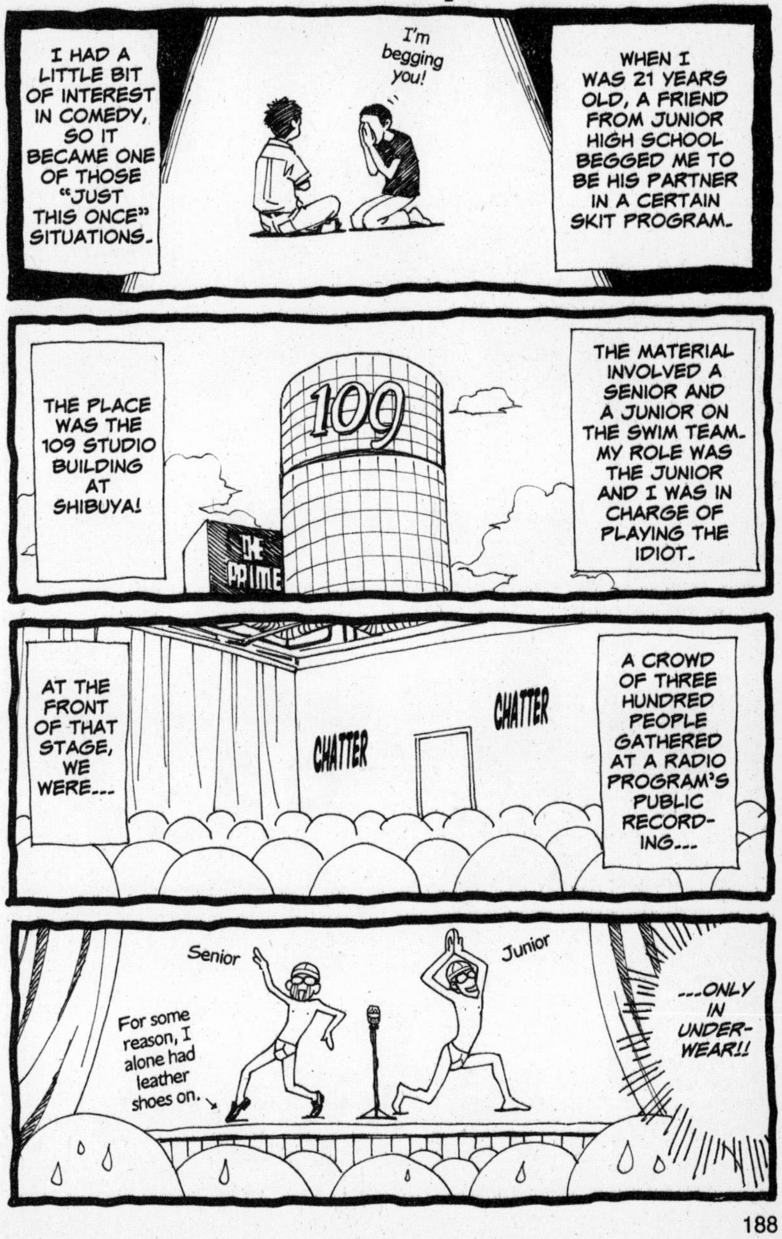
WHEN I WAS 21 YEARS OLD, A FRIEND FROM JUNIOR HIGH SCHOOL BEGGED ME TO BE HIS PARTNER IN A CERTAIN SKIT PROGRAM.
I'm begging you!
I HAD A LITTLE BIT OF INTEREST IN COMEDY, SO IT BECAME ONE OF THOSE "JUST THIS ONCE" SITUATIONS.
THE MATERIAL INVOLVED A SENIOR AND A JUNIOR ON THE SWIM TEAM. MY ROLE WAS THE JUNIOR AND I WAS IN CHARGE OF PLAYING THE IDIOT.
109
THE PRIME
THE PLACE WAS THE 109 STUDIO BUILDING AT SHIBUYA!
A CROWD OF THREE HUNDRED PEOPLE GATHERED AT A RADIO PROGRAM'S PUBLIC RECORDING...
CHATTER
CHATTER
AT THE FRONT OF THAT STAGE, WE WERE...
...ONLY IN UNDERWEAR!!
Junior
Senior
For some reason, I alone had leather shoes on.

# Forgetting the Manuscript

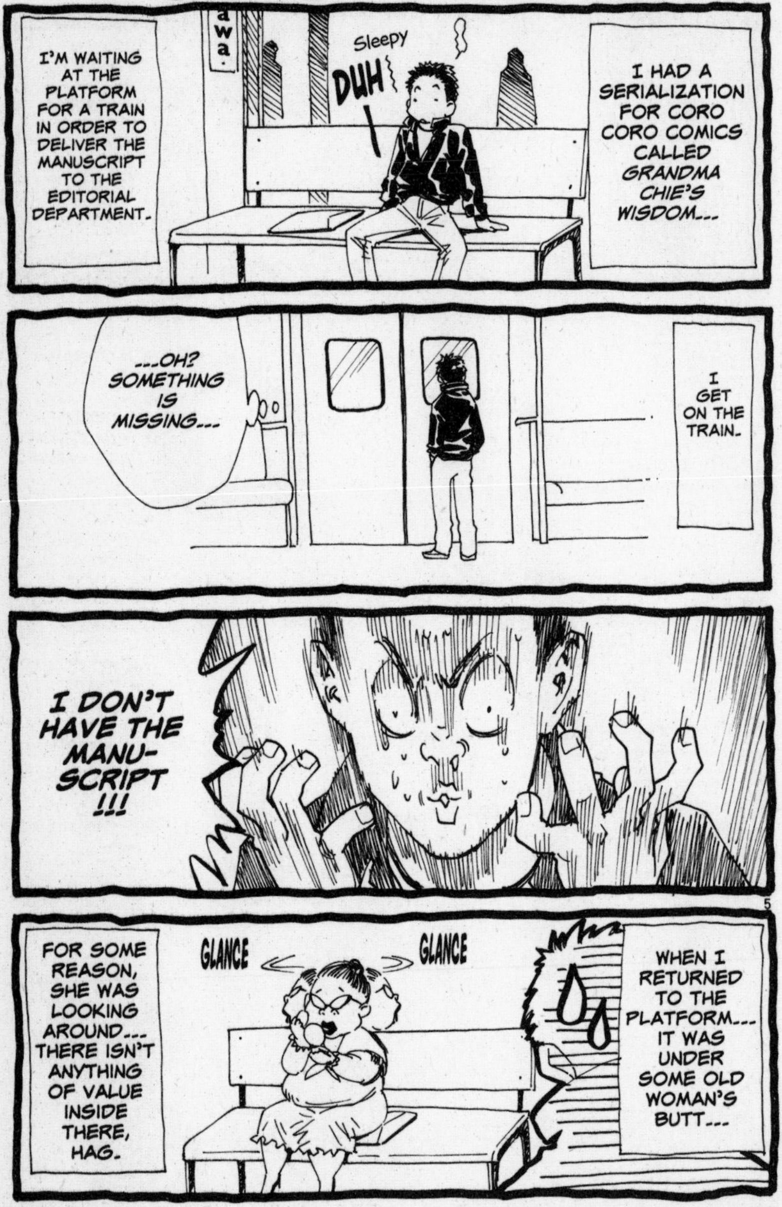
I HAD A SERIALIZATION FOR CORO CORO COMICS CALLED GRANDMA CHIE'S WISDOM...
Sleepy
DUH
I'M WAITING AT THE PLATFORM FOR A TRAIN IN ORDER TO DELIVER THE MANUSCRIPT TO THE EDITORIAL DEPARTMENT.
I GET ON THE TRAIN.
...OH? SOMETHING IS MISSING...
I DON'T HAVE THE MANU-SCRIPT !!!
WHEN I RETURNED TO THE PLATFORM... IT WAS UNDER SOME OLD WOMAN'S BUTT...
GLANCE
GLANCE
FOR SOME REASON, SHE WAS LOOKING AROUND... THERE ISN'T ANYTHING OF VALUE INSIDE THERE, HAG.

# Editor F and Me

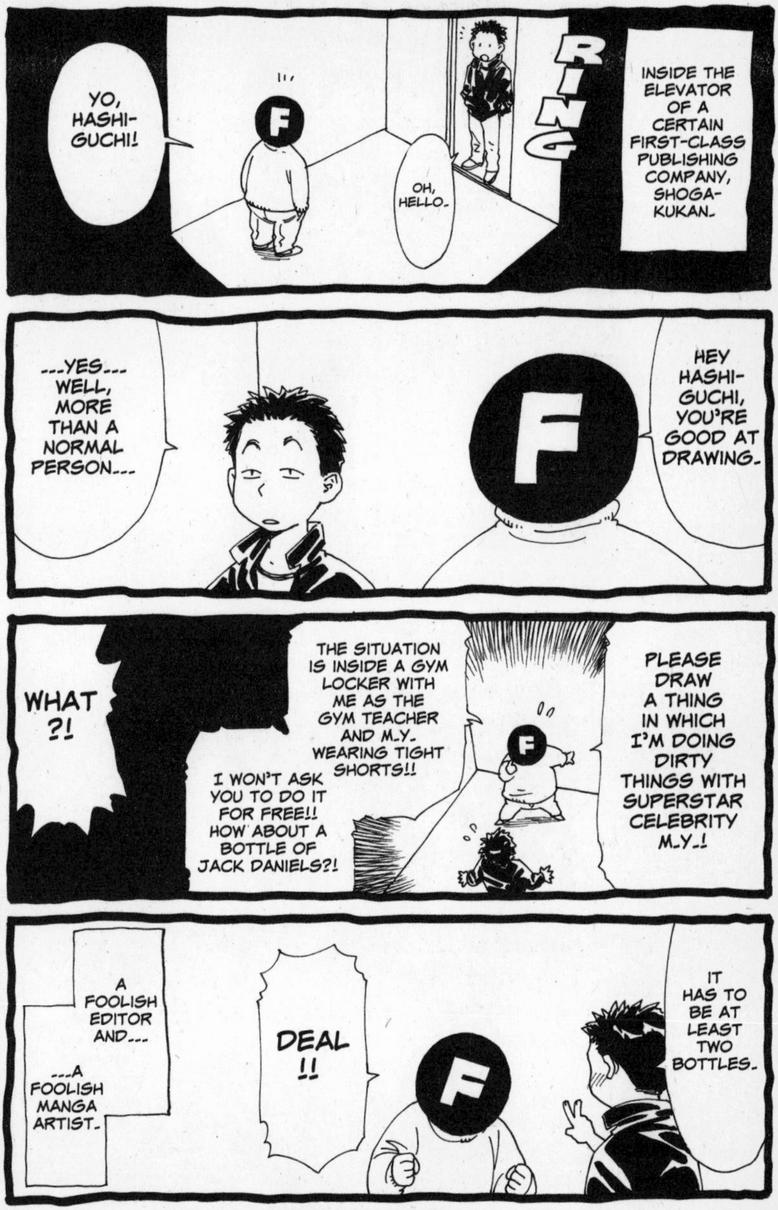
INSIDE THE ELEVATOR OF A CERTAIN FIRST-CLASS PUBLISHING COMPANY, SHOGAKUKAN.
RING
OH, HELLO.
YO, HASHI-GUCHI!
HEY HASHI-GUCHI, YOU'RE GOOD AT DRAWING.
...YES... WELL, MORE THAN A NORMAL PERSON...
PLEASE DRAW A THING IN WHICH I'M DOING DIRTY THINGS WITH SUPERSTAR CELEBRITY M.Y.!
THE SITUATION IS INSIDE A GYM LOCKER WITH ME AS THE GYM TEACHER AND M.Y. WEARING TIGHT SHORTS!!
I WON'T ASK YOU TO DO IT FOR FREE!! HOW ABOUT A BOTTLE OF JACK DANIELS?!
WHAT ?!
IT HAS TO BE AT LEAST TWO BOTTLES.
DEAL !!
A FOOLISH EDITOR AND...
...A FOOLISH MANGA ARTIST.

*THIS BONUS IS A "FRESH BAKED ME," WHICH WAS PUBLISHED IN *SUNDAY SPECIAL EXTRA ISSUE R*, REVISED WITH THREE ADDITIONAL PAGES.

**The end ♡**

# Freshly Baked!! Mini Information

## Microwave Bread

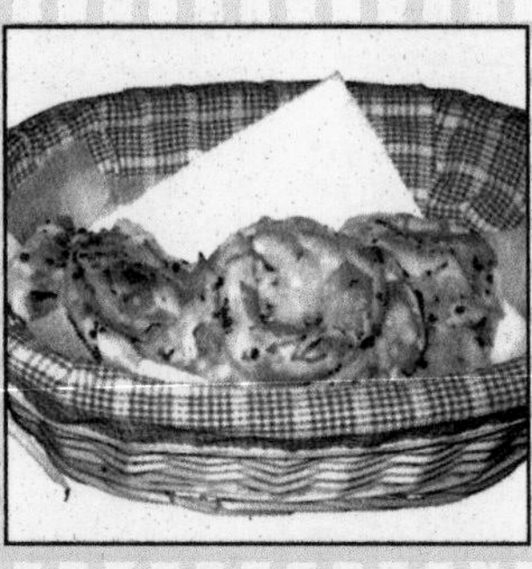

Ja-pan Number 3 isn't the only bread that can be made in a microwave oven.With a little creative thinking, a wide variety of bread, from melon bread to curry bread, can be made in a microwave. The flavor of any bread that you make on your own is exceptional. The method for making the bread dough is the same no matter what the ultimate outcome, so everybody should give it a whirl at least once.

Incidentally, the bread in the photograph is one that a member of the editorial staff made in a microwave. Doesn't it look super delicious?

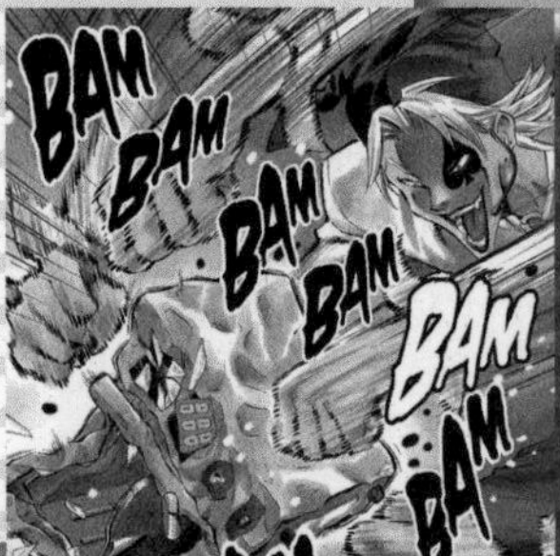
BAM
BAM
BAM
BAM
BAM
BAM
BAM
BAM
AM
BAM
BAM

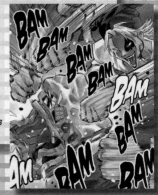

Source book: *Sachiko Murakami's Homemade Microwave Bread in 40 Minutes* – Bookman-Sha

# YAKITATE!! JAPAN
## VOL. 9

STORY AND ART BY
**TAKASHI HASHIGUCHI**

English Adaptation/Drew Williams
Translation/Noritaka Minami
Touch-up Art & Lettering/Steve Dutro
Cover Design/Yukiko Whitley
Editor/Kit Fox

Editor in Chief, Books/Alvin Lu
Editor in Chief, Magazines/Marc Weidenbaum
VP of Publishing Licensing/Rika Inouye
VP of Sales/Gonzalo Ferreyra
Sr. VP of Marketing/Liza Coppola
Publisher/Hyoe Narita



Printed in the U.S.A.

Published by VIZ Media, LLC
P.O. Box 77010
San Francisco, CA 94107

10 9 8 7 6 5 4 3 2 1
First printing, January 2008



viz media
www.viz.com

PARENTAL ADVISORY
YAKITATE!! JAPAN is rated T+ for Older Teen and is recommended for ages 16 and up. This volume contains alcohol and tobacco use, crude humor and mature situations.
ratings.viz.com